Magic Lands

Magic Lands

Western Cityscapes
and American Culture
After 1940

John M. Findlay

UNIVERSITY OF CALIFORNIA PRESS

Berkeley / Los Angeles / London

University of California Press
Berkeley and Los Angeles, California

University of California Press, Ltd.
London, England

First Paperback Printing 1993

Library of Congress Cataloging-in-Publication Data

Findlay, John M., 1955–
    Magic lands : western cityscapes and American culture after 1940 /
John M. Findlay.
        p.   cm.
    Includes bibliographical references (p.   ) and index.
    ISBN 0-520-08435-7
    1. Urbanization—West (U.S.)   2. Metropolitan areas—West
(U.S.)   3. City planning—West (U.S.)   I. Title.
HT384.U52A174   1992   91-34779
307.76'0978'09045—dc20   CIP

Printed in the United States of America
9 8 7 6 5 4 3 2

The paper used in this publication meets the minimum requirements
of American National Standard for Information Sciences—
Permanence of Paper for Printed Library Materials, ANSI Z39.48-
1984.∞

Contents

Illustrations

Acknowledgments

This book grew out of research on the history of gambling in successive American Wests. Writing about the development of mid-twentieth-century Las Vegas led me to think that a cultural history of the modern West could be written in large part around case studies of selected urban landscapes. However, like Las Vegas, and like so much of the recent urban West, the four places chosen for this project—Disneyland, Stanford Industrial Park, Sun City, and the 1962 Seattle World's Fair—had until recently received very little scholarly attention from historians. Furthermore, the records required for this study are widely dispersed throughout the region, and are not always readily accessible to researchers. To the extent that I have been able to write about western cityscapes and American culture since 1940, I am indebted to many individuals who helped by teaching me what I wished to know, and to many institutions which provided the resources that enabled me to teach myself.

This study was both begun and, after an interval, finished at the University of Washington. A visiting appointment to the department of history in 1983–84 gave me a first glimpse of the Seattle World's Fair as a research topic, and a chance to teach summer school in 1985, generously offered by Wilton Fowler, then chair of the department, helped me find my way back to the West Coast and its archival collections. Since returning to the University of Washington in 1987, I have received much encouragement for my research. The department of history, through the kind offices of Jere Bacharach, chair, has provided research assistants, computer support, secretarial aid, and, through its Howard and Frances Keller Endowed Fund in History, money for travel to out-of-state collections. A 1988 summer grant from the University of Washington Graduate School Research Fund facilitated completion of Chapter 4.

From 1984 to 1987 I had the good fortune to teach at The Pennsylvania State University, an eastern school that strongly supported my studies in western history. Penn State's Institute for the Arts and Humanistic Studies provided a Faculty Research Fellowship that enabled me to initiate research in southern California during the summer of 1985. In 1986, the Kent Forster Memorial Junior Faculty Development Award from the department of history and a Research Initiation Grant from the Graduate School permitted me to spend a semester at collections in California, Arizona, and Texas.

In June of 1988 an external award from the Sourisseau Academy, administered through the department of history, San Jose State University, helped to fund travel to collections in Santa Clara County.

My travels back and forth across the country took me to research collections that were inevitably staffed by kind and helpful people. At the University of Washington, I relied particularly upon the Architecture–Urban Planning Branch Library, as well as the manuscript and university archives division, map collection, microforms-newspapers section, and special collections division of Suzzallo Library. Within the walls of Suzzallo, Karyl Winn, Carla Rickerson, and Richard Engeman took a special interest in my work. I also profited from visits to the Seattle Public Library, from the assistance of Rick Caldwell at Seattle's Museum of History and Industry, and from the help of Jim Moore at the Washington State Archives Regional Center, Western Washington University, Bellingham. At Penn State I spent many productive hours in Pattee Library, where I received particularly efficient service from the interlibrary loan office.

The staffs at several collections in the San Francisco Bay Area made my visits productive ones. On the Berkeley campus of the University of California, The Bancroft Library; the map room, periodicals, and main stacks of Doe Library; the Environmental Design Branch Library; and the Institute of Governmental Studies Branch Library proved particularly rewarding. In Green Library at Stanford University, Mark Dimunation, Margaret J. Kimball, Henry Lowood, and Roxanne L. Nilan introduced me to the special collections and Stanford University archives. Bob Beyers and the staff at the Stanford News and Publications Service opened their files to me. Lenny Siegel guided me through the abundant holdings of the Pacific Studies Center in Mountain View; Jonathan B. Gifford and the late Birge M. Clark made available historical materials from CSS Associates, Architects, in Palo Alto; Vernon Andrews and Carol Parcels offered photographs from the files of the Hewlett-Packard Company, Palo Alto; Cheriel Moench Jensen provided access to historical materials at the Santa Clara County Department of Planning and Development, San Jose; and Jan Crane helped me find photographs at Pacific Aerial Surveys, Oakland.

In southern California I began my research in style at The Huntington Library, San Marino, where Martin Ridge pointed me to the papers of John Anson Ford and Fletcher Bowron, and where Britta Mack, among others, directed me to additional materials. David R. Smith and his staff introduced me to the remarkable holdings of the Walt Disney Archives, Burbank, and Margaret Adamic at Walt Disney Publications secured the historical photographs I wanted. First Opal Kissinger and then Mary Lou Begert helped me at the Anaheim History Room, Anaheim Public Library. At the University Library of California State University, Long Beach, Ed Whittington steered me through the photos of the Los Angeles area that he and his father had taken over several decades. The department of special collections, University Research Library, UCLA, also provided assistance.

In Arizona I benefited from the help of the staffs of the Arizona Collection and Arizona Historical Foundation, Hayden Library, Arizona State University, Tempe; the Arizona Room of the Phoenix Public Library; and the Sun City Library. Don Tuffs provided materials from the files of Del Webb Communities, Inc. In 1986 Jane Freeman welcomed me into her home, which at the time housed the collection of the Sun Cities Area Historical Society, and she has continued to assist me in using the society's holdings. My work profited as well from a trip to Texas. Although I ultimately dropped the Houston Astrodome from this project, research in the files of the Houston Sports Association, courtesy of Molly Glentzer, and in the Texas and Local History Room, Houston Public Library, added perspective to the study.

A number of knowledgeable individuals took the time to speak and correspond with me about the places I was studying, and I gained a great deal from their insights. Van Arsdale France, creator of the University of Disneyland, helped me to understand the theme park and let me use his unpublished memoir of a career with the Disney organization. David R. Smith eliminated several "Disney errors" from a draft of Chapter 2. Bob Beyers helped me to see Silicon Valley more clearly; Lenny Siegel and Birge M. Clark commented on a draft of Chapter 3; Henry Lowood generously shared the results of his own research on Stanford Industrial Park; and Alf Brandin and Edward L. Ginzton kindly consented to be interviewed about Stanford Industrial Park.

Jane Freeman, in addition to telling me a great deal herself about Sun City, reviewing a draft of Chapter 4, and arranging for reprints of historical photos, directed me to others who proved quite informative. Conversations with Doug Morris, Art West, and Murray Karsten of Sun City sharpened my understanding of the retirement community. At Arizona State University, Patricia Gober of the geography department shared two of her publications on Sun City, and Brad Luckingham of the history department directed me to several sources on the development of Phoenix. Don Tuffs and John Meeker agreed to be interviewed about the development of the retirement community, and Don Tuffs later critiqued a draft of Chapter 4. In Seattle, Ewen C. Dingwall let me interview him about the world's fair, and later reviewed a draft of Chapter 5.

Over the last few years I have presented portions of this work as talks, papers, or articles, and the resulting feedback from colleagues has been quite helpful. A portion of Chapter 5 was published in a somewhat different form as "The Off-Center Seattle Center: Downtown Seattle and the 1962 World's Fair" in *Pacific Northwest Quarterly* 80 (Jan. 1989): 2–11. I am grateful to *PNQ* for its editors' and reviewers' comments and for permission to take up the same themes here. Fragments of Chapters 2, 3, 4, and 6 appeared as "Far Western Cityscapes and American Culture Since 1940" in *Western Historical Quarterly* 22 (Feb. 1991): 19–43; once again, editors' and reviewers' advice helped to sharpen the focus of my work, and *WHQ* granted permission to rework the article in this book. A paper on Sun City at the 1989 Western History Association meeting in Tacoma elicited helpful remarks from Martin Melosi and Gene Moehring. Members of the History Research Group in the department of history, University of Washington, devoted three sessions over three years to fragments of this work, and I have benefited amply from their ample comments.

Brian Snure, Matt Redinger, and Robert Self served me capably as research assistants. Gary Cross, Paul Harvey, Tom Pressly, Bob Skotheim, and Carol Thomas saw a chapter or two of the work in draft form, and I am grateful for their comments and encouragement. Carl

Abbott, David Hodge, Gene Moehring, Anne Mosher, and Bill Rorabaugh responded to most or all of a draft of the book with useful and detailed suggestions as well as positive reinforcement. Wilbur Zelinsky kindly turned his perceptive eye to the manuscript at an important juncture, adding to the enormous amount that I have learned about cultural landscapes and other spatial matters from him and his colleagues in the geography department at The Pennsylvania State University. Melody Tannam drew the map for the book.

Several individuals not only gave particularly close readings to the manuscript but offered much else in the way of assistance. Dick Kirkendall was the first to wade through most of the manuscript and offer his thoughts. His enthusiastic support of my work has made a big difference to me, and I count myself fortunate that he is my colleague. Otis Pease, after a characteristically thorough and thoughtful reading of the manuscript, made a key suggestion for reorganizing it so that the chapters worked together more satisfactorily. He also offered recollections and papers from his own days at Stanford in the late 1950s and early 1960s. Gunther Barth has been scrutinizing my writing for more than a dozen years, and I have gained immeasurably from his gentle and telling remarks on this and other efforts. I have also relied on the example set by his own scholarship in cultural, urban, and western history.

While conducting research for this book, I never tired of looking at cultural landscapes or at sources of information about them. However, I generally tired very quickly of the traveling that all the looking required. At times I came to identify strongly with Macon Leary, the desperate and comic protagonist in Anne Tyler's novel *The Accidental Tourist*. (Macon summarizes travel as "just red tape, mostly," and he writes guidebooks for other reluctant travelers whose "concern was how to pretend they had never left home." One of his articles bears the subtitle "I Feel So Break-Up, I Want to Go Home.") Fortunately for me, friends and family have helped to mitigate what Macon Leary identified as "the lost feeling" my research trips often engendered. In the San Francisco Bay Area I have been fortunate to enjoy the hospitality of Colin Busby and Melody Tannam and of Lauren Lassleben. Jane Freeman made me feel less like a stranger in Phoenix. My parents and siblings have made southern California the easiest place to visit and work, and I am grateful for the many forms of support they have offered.

Taking my own family with me, or returning home to it, has always been the best part of any research trip. Linda, Geoffrey, and Gregory are the reasons I feel reluctant to travel in the first place. And I have no doubt that they are also the ones who taught me how to find the magic in what appears to be chaos.

Introduction

Perhaps the most distinguishing social feature of the American Far West during the twentieth century has been the nature of its population growth. In 1900 the region had barely 5 percent of the nation's population; by 1970 it had almost 17 percent. In every decade the percentage growth in the West far exceeded both the national average and the percentage increase of every other region. Furthermore, this population was increasingly headed toward metropolitan areas, again at a pace that no other section of the country could match.

Cities had been important to the Far West since the first onrush of Anglo-Americans during the mid-nineteenth century, yet its proportion of urbanites as late as 1920 remained near the national average. After 1930, however, while urban growth in other regions slackened, in the Far West it maintained its rapid pace. By the time of the 1970 census the West had become the most highly urbanized of the four American sections, with 83 percent of its population dwelling in urban areas. Ten years later, when the figure for the West reached 84 percent, its closest competitor, the Northeast, was at only 74 percent.

Paradoxically, as the population of the West grew larger and became more concentrated, historians supposed that the region's impact upon the rest of the country had diminished, though few of them doubted that the relatively lightly settled and largely rural West had been a crucial factor in the development of the nineteenth-century United States. Perhaps they believed that demographic and urban growth, along with other changes, had made the modern region too much like the rest of the country to be able to affect American culture in any significant way.

This book takes a different view. It argues that the ability of the West to influence the nation grew with its population and its urbanization. The West during the twentieth century remained a distinctive part of the United States, and it continued to exert a regional effect on American civilization. In fact, a primary source of its separate identity and influence was its expanding cities. The Far West stood apart from other sections not only because it had a higher percentage of urbanites, but also because its cities assumed a clearly regional form and then transmitted that form to the rest of the country.

Despite their obvious significance, cities have seldom been viewed as integral to the meaning of the West. Leading historians of the region, beginning with Frederick Jackson Turner, have emphasized wide open spaces, and especially their potential as farmland, as the key to the identity of the West. In 1950 Henry Nash Smith summarized this enduring sense of the region in the phrase "virgin land." This notion was primarily a product of the imagination, Smith explained, but the myths and symbols that defined the West as virgin land nonetheless exerted "a decided influence on practical affairs."[1]

By the mid-twentieth century, if not sooner, virgin cities had begun to replace virgin land in the minds of many Westerners as the key image in defining the region. People imagined that the urban West (that is, the western metropolis with its central city, suburbs, and nearby countryside) offered Americans a unique opportunity to live according to their preferences. In contrast to other sections of the country, the region seemed less troubled by urban problems and more open to improvements in metropolitan design, social relations, and styles of living.

The urban West, of course, was by no means virgin in fact. If its cities seemed newer, purer, or more malleable than other towns, they nonetheless had their own share of social and environmental problems, all of which were exacerbated by rapid growth after 1940. Yet their virgin image exerted a powerful influence on practical affairs, especially among Westerners who were seeking to fulfill hopes for a better life in the region and at the same time to protect the freshness of western cities.

These goals helped Westerners to create carefully planned metropolitan districts that attempted to preserve the promise the urban region had held after World War II. Virgin cities on a reduced scale, these urban landscapes represented a physical manifestation of the ideas and opportunities associated with the Far West after 1940. Perhaps because Americans continued to identify the West with wide open spaces rather than with a distinctive urban experience, the significance of virgin cities in the mind and on the ground emerged only slowly. However, historical perspective identifies the years 1953–55 as the time when these new landscapes began to emerge in metropolitan areas of the Pacific slope.

In 1953 Walt Disney commissioned a study to find a suitable site in southern California for a new kind of amusement park. The study recommended the town of Anaheim in Orange County as a good place to build, and in 1954 the Disney Company began construction there. The subsequent opening of Disneyland on July 17, 1955, marked a new era of western land development that affected the culture of the entire nation. The world's first theme park applied Hollywood's movie-making techniques to a three-dimensional setting for fun-seekers in the Los Angeles area. Its impact, however, traveled far beyond the world of entertainment, and far beyond southern California, to influence urban design and architecture across the United States.

It has been said that Walt Disney did not want "to change people's lives . . . only the environment in which they lived."[2] In fact, by attempting the latter he accomplished the former. One basis for Disneyland's impact resided in the absolute control its designers had over the grounds, which permitted them to organize the environs around a few selected themes. Disney and his associates laid out the park so that the whole and its constituent parts—Adventureland, Fantasyland, Frontierland, Tomorrowland, and Main Street U.S.A.—conveyed carefully selected messages. Success inside Disneyland's walls encouraged imitation outside. Both in the immediate vicinity of Orange County and in urban areas across the country, the theme park exerted a powerful influence on urban form.

The creators of Stanford Industrial Park in Palo Alto, California, arrived more hesitantly than Walt Disney at the notion of an environment organized conceptually. The land development began in 1951 as an undistinguished district intended to increase Stanford University's income through leases to light-industrial tenants. In 1954 and 1955, the park's purpose changed. Frederick E. Terman, Stanford's dean of engineering, incorporated the park into his program to transform Stanford into a great research university by creating a "community of technical scholars."[3] The university began to restrict tenancy in the industrial park to research-based companies that would benefit Stanford academically as well as financially.

The university orientation of the industrial park gave it a high-technology theme as well as an innovative appearance that merged the images of campus and suburb into a new setting for industry. By the 1960s, Stanford Industrial Park had become both the nation's prototypical research park and the intellectual downtown for that high-technology landscape that came to be known as Silicon Valley. Like Disneyland, Stanford Industrial Park not only set an example for other American landscapes but also had a considerable impact on its own metropolitan area.

While Stanford Industrial Park was becoming known as an exclusive setting for research-oriented manufacturing, another type of exclusive community appeared in the desert on the outskirts of Phoenix. In 1954 a realtor named Ben Schleifer laid out the village of Youngtown as a place where the elderly could retire. Youngtown never really prospered, but it did inspire the Del E. Webb Corporation of Phoenix to build another, much more successful retirement community right next door. Del Webb's Sun City, opening on January 1, 1960, became the largest and most influential retirement community in the United States.

Sun City was carefully tailored to senior citizens' tastes and needs, as identified by market research. Capitalizing on the growing financial independence and lengthening lifespan of the elderly, Sun City evolved from a population of strangers with relatively modest means into a cohesive community of self-selected migrants from among the more affluent retirees in American society. In the process Sun City became typical of much urbanization in greater Phoenix. Throughout its growth, the new town for old folks retained its identity as a retirement resort, contributing not only to the region's reputation for amenities and leisure, but also to new ways of thinking about the elderly.

As private developers laid out carefully planned enclaves in suburban Anaheim, Palo Alto, and Youngtown in 1955, businessmen conceived of a public project in downtown Seattle which would produce another innovative western cityscape. Their proposal to host a world's fair ultimately led to the Century 21 Exposition of 1962. Their chief motive was to stimulate growth and renewal in the city's central business district in order to help it compete against expanding suburbs. And, indeed, the 1962 fairgrounds exerted lasting influence after the exposition by becoming the Seattle Center, perhaps the most successful civic complex of its kind in the country.[4] Contrary to the expectations of its planners, however, the Seattle Center contributed less to renewing downtown than to dramatizing the increasing impact of suburban patterns on central cities.

As the nation's first major international exposition since 1940, Century 21 helped to redefine American world's fairs. More than earlier expositions, it was modeled on such suburban forms as theme parks and shopping malls, and it attracted a crowd that was rather suburban in outlook and orientation. The cold war encouraged Century 21 to emphasize those economic and technological forces responsible for the prosperous and futuristic character of Seattle and other western metropolitan areas after World War II.

Disneyland, Stanford Industrial Park, Sun City, and the Seattle World's Fair, like their respective urban areas, differed from one another in significant ways. Yet, from the perspectives of local, regional, and national history, the four places shared many features that permit them to be grouped together conceptually. At the level of local, urban history, each was conceived and built as an enclave within a metropolis, between 1951 and 1962, and each incorporated relatively careful and high-quality design. Each enclave was organized according to a conceptual theme of particular relevance to its designers and users. The four cityscapes were by no means typical American metropolitan districts, yet they constituted influential landmarks that acted both as exemplars of the idea of virgin cities and as antidotes to the apparent chaos of their respective urban milieus.

Upholding a new urban tradition by following the example of Disneyland, I have for the purposes of this book labeled the four places "magic kingdoms" and "magic lands." These planned districts tended to remain lands or kingdoms unto themselves; in fact, central authorities planned and operated them as if in reaction against the largely unmanaged urban growth nearby. Each land was set off from its surroundings, and each was peopled by a more or less distinct and homogeneous crowd. Disneyland, Stanford Industrial Park, Sun City, and Century 21 can be called magical because each district helped to transform the surrounding urban landscape as well as the nation's metropolitan areas. The four districts were also magical because of their thematic designs, which both gave them greater spatial coherence and invested them with distinctly western meanings.

As regional phenomena, these four magic lands confirmed and strengthened people's identity as Westerners by helping them come to terms with unwieldy cities. They imparted a sense of community and stability to an urban region characterized by explosive growth and rapid change. By making the metropolis seem more manageable, magic kingdoms upheld the image of virgin cities that attracted and attached so many people to the West. They spoke to the pervasive belief that western urban environs should not resemble those back East.

Westerners tried—with considerable success—to set their cities and their region apart from the East. But because trends and people flowed readily across the country, the West was not simply the antithesis to the East. As national institutions, magic lands both mirrored and affected trends at work across the United States. The urban and regional growth that fueled Disneyland, Stanford Industrial Park, Sun City, and the Seattle World's Fair stemmed in large part from the nation's mobilization for world war and cold war, from federal policies and federal spending, from the decisions of national and international corporations, and from the entire country's changing attitudes toward suburbs and the environment. But western cities, and particularly their magic kingdoms, also helped to reshape Americans' urban forms and urban attitudes. Across today's United States, numerous copies of the four original landmarks attest their success in enhancing the spatial order of cities, in conveying selected messages, and in making money. They also attest the influence of the West on American culture during the twentieth century.

Studying the urban West encourages reconsideration of prevailing views of American culture after 1940, which characterize postwar American society, particularly in the 1950s, as culturally and politically and morally sterile. There is some evidence to support the view that the mid-twentieth-century United States, and urban America in particular, was in many ways a stagnant and complacent culture. But despite the country's adherence to certain arguably unprogressive attitudes after World War II, it experienced tremendous convulsions in the realms of material and popular culture that boldly challenged traditional ways, and in some instances offered creative or liberating alternatives. During the years 1940–70, inventions ranging in size from the birth-control pill and the microprocessor to the Saturn rocket and Apollo spaceship helped to usher in attitudes that sometimes differed radically from their predecessors. The American landscape experienced dramatic changes, too, facilitated by such innovations as Levittowns and fast-food franchises and a national interstate highway system.[5]

Cities were affected by the same, ofttimes liberating forces that were at work throughout American material culture. Almost inevitably, however, urban change was viewed as an unfortunate event, and the language used to describe it frequently implied some sort of decline from previous standards. The new American metropolis was depicted as "chaotic" and "formless," "sprawling" and "fragmented," a landscape in "disequilibrium" and a society infected with "anomie." Historians have often concurred with contemporary observers who assailed the reshaping of the cityscape as detrimental to the ideals of urban life. They have portrayed the recent American inner city as an economic and social wasteland, the outer city or suburb as a cultural and moral wasteland, and the entire unmanageable entity as a political wasteland.[6]

Although critics pointed to real and severe problems—environmental degradation, racial tension, urban poverty, a weakening sense of community—many of them clung inflexibly to an increasingly obsolete ideal of city life, rooted in the urban experience of the Northeast, in which strong central cities with vital downtowns dominated metropolitan areas. As the metropolis steadily diverged from this pattern, many experts viewed the change as deviation from a norm rather than as historical progression from one urban type to another.[7] In the context of the traditional understanding of the city, the new urban shape indeed looked formless and sprawling and chaotic. But in historical perspective it is easier to see changes in the city not as declension from a single ideal but as movement away from an eastern model, based on nineteenth-century technologies, toward a western model, shaped more by twentieth-century culture and by a distinctly different natural setting.

Judged in the latter terms, urban America was not so disorderly and atomistic. Critics made the changed city sound like such a miserable place that nobody would want to live there. Yet the new metropolis not only held its own but expanded, and it did so with particular speed in those western cities regarded by critics as especially disordered and rootless and atomistic. People moving to and residing in the expanding western metropolis clearly did not agree that all urban America was one kind of wasteland or another. Indeed, one historian claims to have found America's "*most* comprehensible cities" in the Southwest.[8]

The ability to perceive coherence in cities depends at least in part upon viewpoint. Sociologist Peter Orleans warns, in this regard, that the perceptions of urban "analysts" should not be taken "as representative of the population at large. Urban life has the reputation of being essentially alienating and disorganized, even though . . . upon close examination, order often emerges from chaos."[9] Critics have tended to approach the new metropolis from the perspective of either spatial organization or political management. As a result, much of the literature has adopted the dissatisfied viewpoint of either the planner or the reformer. These avenues of investigation have proven rewarding, but a third path has received less attention. This approach attempts to learn how average individuals have come to terms with their city.[10] It begins with the assumption, to employ Amos Rapaport's terms, that "users" and "designers" of the built environment frequently derive different "meanings" from the same setting.[11] In other words, the views of those who planned, or who would plan, the urban environment did not always correspond with the views of those who lived, worked, commuted, or played in it.

In contrast to what might be called the macro view of planners and reformers, this study relies heavily on a micro view of the western city in an attempt to understand how average people created, and were affected by, a mid-twentieth-century urban culture. It relies especially on two types of information. First, it seeks to understand how specific controlled environments were planned, built, managed, and used. Instead of looking at cities as wholes, the following pages focus primarily on smaller parts of cities to see how designers created them and to see how people experienced them—which was often in ways their designers had not anticipated. Because of their smaller scale, to average citizens these special environments seemed more comprehensible than entire cities. They may also seem more comprehensible to historians who examine them inductively as evolving artifacts that provide clues about the urban culture of region and nation.

The second level of micro analysis requires an examination of how inhabitants may have made sense of the cities in their minds. Westerners embraced magic kingdoms not only because they were high-quality environments but also because they made the surrounding metropolis seem more legible and more congruent with regional ideals. Carefully planned districts stood out boldly in the urban images developed by citizens as tools for comprehending, and finding their way through, a city. Average people proved adept at drawing mental maps that found coherence in urban settings which struck others as chaotic.[12]

Looking at the frames of reference of both the users and the designers of magic kingdoms may help to explain how residents of the urban West came to terms with the disorder that seemingly characterized not only cities in their own region but also urban America as a whole during the mid-twentieth century. Historical evidence of how western urbanites came to terms with the city around them is, however, elusive. There are no archival collections of mental maps, and few reliable first-hand accounts of what urban settings meant to people. Users have almost invariably left little record of their experiences with the built environment. Designers, planners, and critics of the larger urban scene have left more records of their activities and their intentions. The designers of magic kingdoms did survey their customers frequently in order to find out how to keep them happy; such market research provides a glimpse of how people responded to certain settings.

There are other forms of indirect or circumstantial evidence that offer traces of the meaning of certain cities and city districts for Westerners. Significance can be inferred, using a variety of rather crude measures, from how, and how frequently, people incorporated a particular setting into the routine of their lives. Another kind of circumstantial evidence pertains to the backgrounds and mindsets of the users of magic lands. By asking what the inhabitants of the urban West expected of the region, we may gain a better sense of the mentality that guided their interactions with the built environment.

In trying to explain how Westerners made sense of metropolitan areas, I do not mean to suggest that cities seemed equally coherent to all people. To assert that the designers and users of special environments were able to come to some terms with the explosive city is not to claim that most urban problems had been solved. In fact, something like the opposite may have occurred. Many Westerners arrived at some sort of understanding of the metropolis only by simplifying it through mental maps, by designing away contradictions in the cultural landscape, and by walling themselves off from the complications of city life. Magic kingdoms attempted to exclude diversity and misery from their idealized settings, substituting in their stead a world indexed to the middle-class standards of an affluent society. An understanding of these special environments, and of their respective urban contexts, requires recognition of their implications for those minority and working-class groups who made up a large part of the population of the western metropolis.

Westerners also often excluded from their magic kingdoms much awareness of the escalating costs of the region's pattern of urban growth. They tended to treat carefully planned districts as refuges from the aesthetic and ecological realities of cities. Only belatedly did they begin to perceive the detrimental implications of rapid expansion, and even of magic kingdoms, for the special regional environment. Cities that had seemed virgin in 1950 or 1960 were by 1980 struggling to overcome severe, unforeseen problems. Planned districts that had seemed almost utopian in the years 1953–62 offered much less room for optimism after the mid-1960s.

If the cities of the American West did not get exactly what had been planned and hoped for, the future of Disneyland, Stanford Industrial Park, Sun City, and the Seattle Center nonetheless seemed assured. Magic kingdoms of the urban West helped to define a new standard for what was normal on the American cityscape, and their proliferation sustained at least some of the thinking that had helped to create them during the postwar years. To analyze them is to heighten our understanding of the development of mid-twentieth-century American culture, and to increase our appreciation for the role of western cities in that culture.

In the pages that follow, the West is defined as a place, a process, and a state of mind. First, it is understood to include the eleven Mountain and Pacific states as defined by the U.S. Bureau of the Census, but not Alaska and Hawaii. When considered for its economic, demographic, and cultural trends, the region is often contrasted to either the United States as a whole or to the northeast, north central, and southern sections of the country, again as defined by the Census Bureau. The region has also been conceptualized here as a place where the experience of moving to and living in its cities and suburbs contributed significantly to regional identity.

Finally, the West is understood to be the place that its inhabitants *thought* it was. This place of the mind was defined in large part by the efforts of Westerners to contrast their region to a pervasive but rather ill-defined perception of the East. Seattle and Phoenix and Denver were all different from one another, yet they shared not only their far western location and certain processes of growth and change, but also their inhabitants' tendency to identify with one region by explaining their presence there as the rejection of another. The West's reputation for virgin cities depended heavily upon negative images of cities elsewhere.

The urban West may have diverged from other sections of the country, but it was not itself uniform throughout. The present study relies on evidence from four metropolitan areas (or five Standard Metropolitan Statistical Areas, as identified by the Census Bureau) for most of its information about the region: Los Angeles and Orange counties in southern California (the Los Angeles and Anaheim SMSAs); Santa Clara County in northern California (the San Jose SMSA); Maricopa County, Arizona (the Phoenix SMSA); and King and Snohomish counties, Washington (the Seattle SMSA). These cities were neither entirely representative of the urban West nor exactly alike.

The Orange County, San Jose, and Phoenix metropolitan areas were the most similar. Growing with extraordinary speed after 1940, and recognized as emblematic of the new urban pattern of the Pacific coast, each of these metropolitan areas belonged to a distinctive subregion of the West that might be called "Greater California." Although many in the region were reluctant to admit it, Greater California dominated the Far West demographically, economically, and culturally. This warm, arid, and exceptionally creative corner of the country produced, besides Disneyland, Stanford Industrial Park, and Sun City, such other magic kingdoms as the Las Vegas Strip, Dodger Stadium, the Los Angeles freeway system, the planned community of Irvine, and the San Diego Zoo.[13]

Seattle had much in common with urban California, yet its residents flatly denied any similarity between the damp, green Northwest coast and the dry Southwest. Their city changed in less obvious and less influential ways than California towns. Confined by its relative isolation and its hilly and watery terrain, it grew more slowly. Consequently, like Portland or San Francisco, it was better able to retain the traditional downtown focus that it had acquired in the pre-automobile age. In fact, unlike the other controlled environments under consideration here, the Seattle World's Fair appeared not on the fringes of the urban area but adjacent to the central business district.

Yet Seattle was affected by the same processes that reshaped other cities throughout the West after 1940, and the changes were nowhere better illustrated than in the creation and impact of the Century 21 Exposition. The 1962 World's Fair not only highlighted in Seattle the same aerospace and suburban orientations that were guiding development throughout the metropolitan West, but also brought to bear upon the Northwest the direct influence of southern California by recruiting veteran workers from Disneyland to help lay out the fairgrounds. A variation on the postwar pattern in the urban West, Seattle provided evidence of the influence of magic kingdom design on cities not just in California but across the country.

More perhaps than any other factor, rapid demographic and economic expansion unified the postwar West. Chapter 1 explores how this growth led to both a sense of fulfillment and a perception of chaos. Westerners initially planned for and celebrated expansion because it seemed to imply the realization of long-standing hopes for their cities and region. Ultimately, however, growth became so explosive that the city appeared out of control: populations increased dramatically; municipal boundaries changed incessantly; people and autos moved about ceaselessly. In such a milieu, many doubted that a shared sense of community and culture could be achieved.

The success of magic lands, however, suggested that, for many, culture and community in western cities were not as elusive as the critics had feared. Chapters 2 through 5 present a history of Disneyland, Stanford Industrial Park, Sun City, and the Seattle World's Fair. They trace the origins and evolution of each planned cityscape, and they place each in its specific urban setting in order to assess its significance for the surrounding metropolis. To explore the extent of innovation in the urban West, each chapter also reviews the institutional context for a particular cityscape: Stanford Industrial Park is considered against the backdrop of postwar industrial land use, for example, whereas Sun City is considered in terms of the evolution of retirement and retirement communities in America.

Chapter 6 closes the book with the argument that magic kingdoms epitomized the process by which people came to terms with their ever-changing cities in a manner that contributed to their identity as Westerners. Magic kingdoms played a key role in reconciling city-dwellers to fluid settings. They acted as landmarks that heightened the legibility of the urban scene, and they accelerated the growth of a feeling of maturity in relatively new cities by strengthening the sense of cultural attainment. In addition, designers and operators of controlled environments touted their contributions to the formation of community in new settings. They claimed that the carefully planned districts both enhanced the appearance of the urban surroundings and evoked better behavior from residents and guests of the western city. By making both the cityscape and its inhabitants seem more manageable and by celebrating the economic and cultural underpinnings of expansion, magic kingdoms offered reassurance that the urban West could live up to the hopes that both newcomers and old-timers had for the region.

People frequently contrasted magic kingdoms, like their respective cities, with less satisfactory eastern counterparts. The comparison usually suggested that the urban West could continue to grow and at the same time retain those virtues that distinguished it from the metropolitan East. Magic kingdoms indicated that growth need not always imply disorder. They held out hope that if the *quality* of urban development on a small scale could be raised significantly, then its *quantity* would not matter so much on the larger scale. Support for this proposition diminished after the mid–1960s, as advocates of "limited" or "managed" growth came to the political forefront in western cities and began to address urban problems that had once been associated only with the East.

By 1970 the optimistic and creative milieu that had produced magic kingdoms had begun to change. Yet heightened awareness of urban ills only enhanced the importance of controlled enclaves. Each magic land increasingly served less as a natural extension of the city and more as a refuge from it. Even as their meaning changed, then, special western cityscapes continued to exert substantial influence over both the surrounding metropolis and the nation. And although they are presented in these pages in the past tense, their influence persists today.

CHAPTER ONE

The Explosive Metropolis: Urbanization in the Far West After 1940

Until 1970 or so, the watchword of Anglo-Americans heading to and living in the American West had been "growth." "Growth" customarily meant an increase in population and wealth, and it implied not only change but also progress. Growth would tame nature, spread "civilization," build societies, and make fortunes.

Before the mid-twentieth century, most Anglo-Americans in the West, besides agreeing on the desirability of growth, also agreed that the West had not gotten its rightful share. They tended to view their section of the country as a colony of the East, subservient to businessmen and politicians from the Atlantic seaboard, and they believed the West could not control its own destiny so long as it remained underdeveloped—that is, so long as it failed to grow sufficiently. This feeling of inadequacy crested during the years after World War I, when the western economy slumped, pushing the West toward hard times about a decade before the rest of the nation experienced a severe downturn. By the 1930s, when nationwide depression had compounded regional feelings of helplessness, the atmosphere of opportunity that had long pervaded the West had vanished.[1]

At the height of the Great Depression, historian Walter Prescott Webb articulated the western malaise. Until 1890, he wrote, the westward movement had nurtured democracy, equality, individualism, and self-reliance in America. But "if the frontier *was* a dominant force until 1890, the *absence* of the frontier has been just as dominant *since* 1890."

The open West had represented a safety valve, Webb argued. When that valve closed, the modern corporation of the industrial Northeast had risen to a position of supreme influence. Webb denounced "the economic imperial control by the North over the South and West." He suggested that the South and West should make common cause against the northeastern elite, for their "political interests . . . are practically identical. Both sections are rural and agrarian, and both stand in an attitude of protest against the forces that have come to dominate them."[2]

Even as Webb wrote, however, events had begun to alter the West in ways that rendered his argument obsolete. First, during the 1930s the American West received more than its share of federal aid, as New Dealers attempted to make the region more self-sufficient. Second, even though the Great Plains region (on which Webb focused) lost population between 1935 and 1940, the Rocky Mountain and Pacific states experienced relatively rapid growth. Finally, with mobilization for World War II and then the cold, Korean, and Vietnam wars, the modest growth of the later 1930s evolved into a full-scale, long-term boom.[3] The unparalleled expansion from 1940 to 1965 at long last brought to the West growth on a scale that matched its lofty aspirations.

This postwar growth was concentrated in cities. Rural and agrarian areas, the focus of Webb's concern, in fact remained in relative decline. Indeed, Webb had underestimated the importance of cities to the region (just as he had underestimated the influence of big business before 1890). Since the mid-nineteenth century, major cities had dominated the economy and society of the Far West, each developing its own large hinterland. San Francisco and, to a lesser extent, Portland ruled much of the Pacific slope well into the twentieth century; Alaska became a "suburb" of Seattle not long after 1890; and Denver became a hub for the Rocky Mountain states.[4]

Western growth after 1940 thus built on a well-established urban system. But the pattern shifted. The rate of growth in older cities—San Francisco, Portland, Seattle, Denver—lagged behind that in the booming metropolitan areas of San Jose, Orange County, San Diego, Las Vegas, Phoenix, and Albuquerque. These southwestern cities had numerous traits in common with such rapidly expanding towns as Atlanta, Miami, Tampa, and Orlando in the American South. In fact, the urbanizing West and South together shed their reputations as colonies of the Northeast and became known as one super-region, the Sunbelt.

But the urban experience was quite different for the two sections. They differed in geography, racial and ethnic mixture, and cultural traditions. Equally important, the West began with more large cities than the South, and it attracted more settlers from other regions.[5]

This economic and population growth after 1940 gave Westerners greater self-assurance. In cities of the Rockies and the Pacific slope particularly, it was seen as a creative process that liberated the West from its inferiority by generating new societies, new ways of living, and new attitudes. Economic and demographic gains thus translated into cultural accomplishment. "Contribute regionally to the national culture?" the novelist Wallace Stegner responded to a query about California's place in American life. "We *are* the national culture, at its most energetic end."[6] The recent growth had seemingly solved the quest of generations of Westerners for a level of progress and achievement that would put them on a par with—maybe ahead of—the East.

But the region soon learned the truth of Oscar Wilde's quip, "When the gods wish to punish us they answer our prayers." Within a remarkably short period at least some Westerners had discovered that growth, particularly in urban areas, was not the uniformly positive process they had long assumed it to be. This realization dawned gradually and incompletely; it emerged sooner in older towns like San Francisco and Portland, later in newer cities like San Jose and Phoenix. But everywhere the conclusion seemed inescapable as Westerners watched the deterioration of their natural environment, the development of transiency and conflict in their society, and the disarrangement of the city itself.

Most disturbing of all, growth, and particularly urban growth, appeared to be out of control. Westerners had believed that rapid expansion would make them the masters of their own fate. But precisely the opposite seemed to have happened. In the minds of many, unmanageable growth had bred a kind of powerlessness over the urban scene. The growth that was to have been the region's salvation from colonialism had become, at least according to some critics, its downfall by prolonging Westerners' inability to control their own destiny.

Both the character and the sources of growth helped to make it seem at first beneficial and then uncontrollable. Growth fostered a sense of maturity and achievement, but it simultaneously transformed cities as well as their inhabitants in a manner that seemed to heighten instability and disorder. And it proved too formidable an opponent for city planners, the only local agency that might have restrained expansion.

Growth and Its Discontents

How we see the West has always depended on where we stand to view it. Walter Prescott Webb surveyed the scene from the Texas prairie, and from there the conviction that the West was agrarian could survive unchallenged. At about the same time, a Pacific coast perspective produced a different picture. In 1940 the American radical Anna Louise Strong, touring her native land after years in the Soviet Union, wrote, "Life boils in California."[7] If this described the West on the eve of World War II, it applied with even greater force during the decades after Pearl Harbor. Mobilization for war turned up the heat on society in the American West by igniting an economic boom and directing millions of newcomers to cities in the coastal states. A virtually all-new civilization suddenly bubbled over the old one, remaking towns and preparing the way for an unprecedented mixture of cultural ingredients.

The region had grown quickly before, to be sure, but never on such a massive scale. Between 1940 and 1970 the chief fact of life in western states was the prodigious expansion of the population and the economy. It had taken thirty years, from 1840 to 1870, for the lands that became the eleven far western states to attain their first million non-native people. In the next hundred years, the region acquired a population exceeding 13 million. Then the West accomplished again in two decades what had taken ten decades before, and, finally, between 1960 and 1970 it added still another 7 million, making a total increase since 1940 of 20 million people. For every one person who settled in the West between 1840 and 1870, then, twenty had come a century later, and for every three who arrived before 1940, five more arrived in the next thirty years.

Most of the newcomers headed for urban centers, especially the coastal centers. But western cities did not expand at equal rates. The metropolitan areas of Portland and San Francisco barely doubled in population between 1940 and 1970, lagging behind the regional mean for urban growth. In southern California, by contrast, although Los Angeles County expanded "only" about two and a half times—that is, at about the same pace as the urban West as a whole—adjacent metropolitan areas multiplied even more quickly. San Diego's population increased more than fourfold, Oxnard's more than fivefold, San Bernardino's more than sevenfold, and Orange County's almost elevenfold.

Other parts of the urban West showed equally startling growth. The population of the San Jose metropolitan area multiplied six times, overtaking San Francisco as the most populous metropolis in the Bay Area; the population of the Phoenix metropolitan area increased more than five times, by 1970 containing almost 60 percent of Arizona's residents. Albuquerque's population increased almost five times, Denver's more than three times. In the West's twelfth state, Texas, the Houston, Dallas, and Fort Worth metropolitan areas each expanded between three and four times in population; in the opposite corner of the region, the metropolitan area of Seattle increased nearly threefold.[8]

Such dramatic increases made the West not just the fastest-growing section of the country but its most rapidly urbanizing region as well. Whether measured by absolute numbers or as percentage gain, the West contained two-thirds of the thirty fastest-growing metropolitan areas in the country between 1950 and 1960. Between 1960 and 1970, half of the thirty fastest-growing urban areas were western ones. Orange County, California, ranked first in percentage gain during the 1950s and continued to hold that distinction during the early 1960s. At the same time, Santa Clara County and Maricopa County ranked second and third, respectively. By 1970 the West had surpassed the Northeast as the most urbanized section of the country.[9]

International conflict stimulated much western expansion. World War II precipitated rapid change by mobilizing the western economy on behalf of national defense. New Deal programs had laid a foundation for defense work by erecting dams, power lines, and other public works projects, and by giving the region a taste of federal planning and subsidy on a large scale. But during the early 1940s, the intensity of national interest and the scale of economic advancement surpassed anything that had come before. Military bases and defense industries came to dominate local development in city after city, and they remained influential for decades as cold war crises followed the close of the World War. Moreover, the West's share of the nation's defense-based economy continually expanded. During World War II the region, while making extraordinary gains in almost every other area, received a smaller percentage of prime military contracts than any other part of the United States; by the 1960s and 1970s it consistently won a larger number of contracts than any other region. Its cities were true defense enclaves.[10]

Mobilization brought industrial maturity to the West. While other parts of the country converted existing factories to wartime production, the Pacific coast acquired altogether new industries. Furthermore, the war attracted both a new industrial work force and millions of soldiers and sailors who were seeing the region for the first time. Hundreds of thousands of these servicemen ultimately returned as settlers, thus prolonging the wartime boom into the postwar era in every major city.[11] In Phoenix, for example, many veterans and defense workers either remained or returned after the war, helping to attract to the city such companies as Motorola and General Electric. In Seattle the World War ushered in the "Boeing years" by linking the city tightly to the fate of commercial and military aerospace.[12]

No state profited more from World War II than did California, which had received federal funding of $35 billion by 1945. Although the federal money flowed throughout the state, its long-term impact varied from place to place. Shipbuilding prospered in San Francisco and Oakland during the war, but its benefits did not linger. On the other hand, the cities of the Santa Clara Valley and southern California witnessed the wartime expansion of more forward-looking defense manufacturing, such as aviation and ordnance, which underwrote quite dramatic urban growth over the next three decades. California would continue to garner more than its share of federal dollars spent on defense and space. These monies in turn spurred repeated, rapid population increases in metropolitan areas.[13]

California demonstrated how military spending could prime the pump for civilian markets and manufactures. More than in most states, California defense dollars went to procurement. NASA and the Department of Defense drove the development of the electronics industry, for instance, until the civilian market matured after the 1960s. California, and especially its newer cities, capitalized on federal outlays but at the same time diversified sufficiently so as not to suffer too seriously during periods of government reductions.[14] The overall result was a state economy that, as Californians liked to point out, ranked "sixth among the *nations* of the world" in 1967—even, for the time being, ahead of Japan.[15]

California's urban growth exemplified both the blessings and the bane of the "economic miracle" of the mid-twentieth-century American West. In a 1964 campaign speech in Los Angeles, Lyndon B. Johnson described the Golden State as "the greatest educational State in the Union . . . the greatest space and the greatest aeronautical and the greatest missile, the greatest technological state in the Union."[16] The president's statement correctly described the exalted cultural and economic role California played in the West and the nation. Its growing population helped to explain its importance. In 1962 California passed New York to become the most populous state, and shortly thereafter it surpassed New Jersey as the most urbanized state. Almost 60 percent of the inhabitants of the eleven western states lived in California, and 25 percent of them resided in or around Los Angeles.[17]

Los Angeles exerted enormous influence on the West. Even before World War II, as the Hollywood mogul Cecil B. deMille had remarked, the motion picture industry had "taken Los Angeles to the world on wings of celluloid." Now, in matters of intellectual and technological achievement, education, fashion, arts and architecture, and urban design as well, the influence of Los Angeles, like that of the entire state, grew out of proportion even to its swelling size.[18] Its rapid growth gave the city its cultural authority in ways that went beyond sheer numbers. Such swift change nurtured a distinctive mindset. Southern Californians were, to quote architect Richard Neutra, more "mentally footloose" than people elsewhere, because as migrants to the West they had broken more ties to tradition and opened their minds to new cultural forms.[19]

If California and its metropolis of Los Angeles dramatized the promise of the changes affecting the West after World War II, they also dramatized the peril. Explosive growth seemingly led in two directions, one destined for a wondrous tomorrow and the other headed down a dead end for civilization. The "mentally footloose" character of the region had its disadvantages, as commentators had noted for decades. The flaws in the new California attracted comparatively little attention in the early postwar era. By the 1960s and 1970s, however, many people saw the state and the city as epitomizing many of the evils associated with modern American society, and all the problems of the West as well. In southern California, the race riots in Watts, the chronic pollution, the congested freeways, the over-reliance on military spending, the high rates of transiency, and the success of right-wing politicians all seemed to characterize a people with no past, no aesthetic standards, no solid economic base, and no shared set of healthy values. "I have seen the future," Harrison Salisbury noted of Los Angeles in 1959, "and it doesn't work."[20]

In California and throughout the West, rapid growth had tended to obliterate continuity between past, present, and future. Like their eastern counterparts, each western city had a substantial history, dating back as far as 1777 and 1781 in the cases of the Spanish *pueblos* of San Jose and Los Angeles. But the local past vanished under the onslaught of population after 1940, which effectively remade the cities again and again.

Westerners welcomed growth because it liberated them from eastern colonialism, but they also came to see that the spigot of growth was turned on and off primarily by people outside their cities. Federal and local policies combined, often unintentionally, to accelerate urban expansion. The impact of defense spending was supplemented by such federal programs as the interstate highway system and the mortgage reinsurance of the Veterans and Federal Housing administrations, and by the treatment of real estate in the tax code. State policies in such areas as annexation and highway development frequently bolstered the effects of federal intervention.[21]

National and state governmental influence on local growth sometimes severely compromised citizens' control over their own destinies. In the middle decades of the century, however, Westerners did not appear to mind. The encouragement of growth by higher levels of government would be perceived as a problem only after the mid–1960s, when expansion itself came to be questioned. Until then, the region generally saw government policies in positive terms, as a source of venture capital that would promote growth and prosperity, and regional representatives lobbied in state and federal offices for even more funding.[22]

If federal and state efforts during and after World War II provided opportunities for accelerated growth, Westerners toiled to maximize that growth by modernizing urban governments. Voters throughout the region replaced supposedly complacent leadership with self-styled reformers whose growth-maximizing formulas dominated municipal politics through the 1960s.[23] In San Jose the formation of the Progress Committee in 1944 marked the emergence of a leadership devoted to aggressive growth. The committee's agenda reached fruition between 1950 and 1970 under the administration of A. P. Hamann, the city manager, who sought to make San Jose "the Los Angeles of the North."[24] In Phoenix, Charter Government was a municipal leadership devoted to aggressive growth. This bipartisan elite of professionals and businessmen that included a department-store owner named Barry Goldwater came together in 1949 to make city government more efficient at annexing outlying districts and attracting new industry.[25] In Seattle new leadership emerged from among downtown businessmen during the 1950s. One of their great successes was the Seattle World's Fair of 1962, conceived as a tool for consolidating and perpetuating growth.

Such municipal elites focused their efforts on economic and territorial expansion. Western cities of the 1940s and 1950s had relatively few grave inner-city problems, obsolescent land-use patterns, decaying infrastructures, or burdensome municipal debts. They could devote their resources to the traditional mission of growth-minded western towns: attracting new businesses and accelerating land development. Leaders employed a variety of strategies to achieve these goals. They kept tax rates low, developed amenities that seemed likely to lure corporations, and annexed land and installed infrastructure on it well in advance of residential or industrial construction.[26] Such activities naturally pleased business interests. The owner of the *San Jose Mercury-News*, when asked why he supported the runaway growth which was uprooting the trademark orchards of the Santa Clara Valley, replied, "Trees don't read newspapers."[27]

Until after the mid-1960s, when citizen demands for controls on expansion became forceful, pro-growth leaders remained influential, ensuring that those who profited most directly from expansion would receive primary consideration in municipal politics. Like federal and state governments, these local elites had a strong hand in steering the course of the postwar urban West. Perhaps their concerted power contributed to the growing perception of growth as inevitable.

Technology contributed to this perception, too. In large part because of timely federal investments, the economies of western cities depended heavily upon industries that revolved around sophisticated technologies. Intimate association with such fields as aviation and space, advanced weaponry, petrochemicals, computers, and electronics reinforced among Westerners a long-standing fascination with the technologies they required to master the resources, distances, and extremes of a formidable environment. Two not-so-high technologies, the air conditioner and the automobile, also made a pronounced impression on the West after 1940, facilitating the settlement of lands that had once seemed unsuited for city development.

Again, like growth itself, these tools of urbanization were not initially regarded with much skepticism. Rather, they elicited a confidence which helped persuade Westerners that the future as foreseen in the mid-twentieth century presented few barriers. Residents in and around Seattle counted on a never-ending supply of hydroelectric and atomic power. Southern Californians counted on elaborate technologies to bring them the runoff from the Rocky Mountains and the Sierra Nevada, to reroute southward the Columbia, Eel, Trinity, and Klamath rivers of the Pacific Northwest, and to remove salt from seawater.[28] Thanks to technology, the West's supply of resources seemed plentiful.

If technology initially inspired optimism about the future of the region, however, it provoked doubts once the limits to the environment became more apparent. The same pipelines or freeways that some saw as nurturing cities, others saw as strangling them. Faith that technology could perpetuate unlimited use of natural resources diminished. When growth was translated into environmental terms, people looked more critically at it. California averaged a net gain of almost 1,500 newcomers daily during the later 1950s and early 1960s; every one of them, according to a 1957 estimate, meant the loss of one-sixth of an acre of farmland, and each created more than 100 gallons of wastewater daily.[29] Within Los Angeles County the quickest growth occurred in the San Fernando Valley, where the population multiplied from 150,000 people in 1945 to 739,000 in 1960. Such expansion almost justified developers' claims that they built one new town every month and uprooted 1,000 orchard trees daily during the 1950s.[30] Cast in such terms, growth seemed less than a blessing.

Also dimming confidence was the sense that expansion represented an invasion by strangers from distant places, over whom Westerners had little control. Westerners had spent decades trying to recruit tourists and new residents to the West, but by the 1940s they began to realize that "the initiative has long since passed to the migrants. It is the migrants who are planning to come to California," Carey McWilliams explained, "not California that is planning to receive them." The rising "tide of new arrivals does not seem to stop," observed another Californian as he contemplated the proliferation of suburbs "from Santa Barbara to San Diego."[31]

People and Cities in Motion

The postwar West could not divorce itself from trends that affected the entire country. Twentieth-century Americans have tended to move from rural to urban locations, from zones of economic stagnation to zones of expanding opportunity, and between large metropolitan areas. These tendencies uniformly favored the West as a destination. Americans' increasing desire for climatic and scenic amenities, and the boost given to western industry by military spending, placed the region in still greater demand.[32]

Throughout the urban West, the newcomers far outnumbered the newborn. In Santa Clara County, for example, increase by migration accounted for more than three times the growth caused by natural increase during the 1950s, and in the following decade the ratio was still more than two to one. Because typical westward migrants in the modern era were relatively young people, they did bring with them the makings of another, more gradual population boom in which natural increase was to play a larger part. During the 1970s in Santa Clara County, natural increase actually exceeded growth by migration. Until that new generation came of age, however, western cities would seem peopled not by native-born residents but by those who came from elsewhere.[33]

The composition of western populations varied from town to town and from decade to decade, but the overall pattern was one of increasing diversity. Mexican and African Americans comprised the largest minorities. Native Americans, too, became urbanized more rapidly after 1940 than before, and the Asian-American population increased in absolute terms. Los Angeles epitomized the region's growing heterogeneity. Among the ten most populous cities in the nation in 1965, Los Angeles ranked "first in the number of American Indians, Japanese, Filipinos and Mexican Americans, second in Chinese and sixth in Negroes."[34]

People of Mexican descent outnumbered all other minorities both in Los Angeles and in the Southwest as a whole. Their centuries-old patterns of settlement were modified significantly after 1940. One key change was simple increase. California had perhaps 354,000 Spanish-speaking residents in 1940; by 1950 the census counted more than 760,000 people with Spanish surnames in the state. In 1943 an unofficial count estimated roughly 2 million Hispanics in the five states of Texas, New Mexico, Colorado, Arizona, and California; by 1960 there were 3.3 million Mexican Americans in the those states, and by 1970 more than 5 million.[35] Equally important was the movement toward cities. In 1940 most Mexican Americans resided in rural areas; twenty years later, 79 percent of the Spanish-surname population of the Southwest—including many employed in agriculture—dwelled in urban areas. A third significant change was the shift from the other four southwestern states, especially Texas, toward California, whose cities offered more opportunities and options than were available elsewhere.[36]

Substantially fewer African Americans than Mexican Americans migrated to western cities. Whereas people with Spanish surnames made up between 10 and 20 percent of the populations of Orange, Maricopa, Santa Clara, and Los Angeles counties in 1970, African Americans accounted for between 1 and 11 percent. Of the urban areas under scrutiny here, only Seattle had more African Americans than Hispanics, and there the two groups together amounted to less than 10 percent of the population. Nonetheless, like Mexican Americans, African Americans in the West concentrated in cities. During the World War the region's population of African Americans spurted from 171,000 in 1940 to 620,000 in 1945. The rate of increase then slackened, but never ceased. As the population of Los Angeles County nearly tripled between 1940 and 1965, its African-American population grew more than eightfold, from 75,000 to 650,000.[37]

No matter what their racial and ethnic background, newcomers to western cities shared certain traits. They generally brought skills and ambitions that contributed to the region's prosperity and helped shape its attitudes. Both Mexican and African Americans, like Anglo-Americans, looked to the Far West for economic and social opportunities that did not exist elsewhere. If opportunities played a key role in attracting migrants westward, however, it is equally true that the migrant population itself represented an enormous economic boon to the West. A student of American migration has pointed out that when one region loses population to another it tends to suffer "a disproportionate outflow of ability, industrial energy, technical skills, and innovative dispositions from its younger generation." And, indeed, those who moved to the American West—including African Americans from the South, immigrants from Mexico, and World War II veterans—tended to have more skills and education than the people they left behind. They helped to make the population of the West the best-educated in the country. Newcomers adapted well to the variety of opportunities available in western cities, and they created or took jobs that tended to be more white-collar in status than those they would have held in other American cities.[38]

Strong correlations held between the influx of people and regional affluence. Migrants who represented an economic drain on source regions represented an economic asset to destination regions. "Whether these new residents want to or not," one Stanford professor pointed out, "they usually spend as much in the first six months of getting settled as the old residents spend in six years." The economy grew to keep pace with the expanding population. During the 1950s the state of California by itself "captured more than one out of every four new

Figure 1. Thousands of military veterans and defense workers either returned to or remained in the Far West after World War II. Like other newcomers, they brought assets—including housing loans and other benefits from the G.I. Bill—that helped to fuel the region's postwar boom. Kaiser Community Homes, builder of these 1947 model houses on Victory Boulevard in the San Fernando Valley, gave veterans first chance to buy. Reproduced by permission of The Huntington Library, San Marino, California (Whittington Collection #2024).

jobs in the United States."[39] Western urban economies increasingly revolved around sophisticated technologies and ever more profitable manufacturing. These developments were possible in part because the newcomers had the education and skills needed in high-tech industries.

Rapid growth also made over the urban West through a continuing series of construction projects. Crucial to both the region's newly arrived residents and its newfound prosperity was the effort to house the swelling population. Each major city witnessed the rapid rise of outlying residential subdivisions where the homes were newer and the families younger and more affluent (see Figure 1). Los Angeles led the way. Its recent arrivals tended to come from areas that favored single-family, unattached housing, as well as commuting to work by automobiles, and those preferences reinforced the tendency toward suburban settlement. Between 1946 and 1957 the county gained an average of almost 37,700 new subdivided lots each year. In large part because so much of the housing was relatively new, it tended to be of better quality in the West than in the remainder of the country. And the newer tracts for the most part consisted of owner-occupied, single-family, detached homes.[40]

The proliferation of outlying housing tracts constituted not only a quantitative but also a qualitative change for the urban West. As suburbs grew they attracted commerce and industry, which made them less subordinate to central cities. Orange County provided a particularly clear example of the character and consequences of rapid growth in the postwar West. The area had long been peripheral to, and dependent upon, its neighbor Los Angeles, and as a result had seemed rather provincial. As late as 1950 it contained barely 200,000 residents. Much of its terrain consisted of orchards and cropland, and its largest city was the county seat of Santa Ana, with 45,000 people.[41]

Thereafter Orange County began to grow at an "almost inconceivable" pace; by 1987 its population had reached 2.2 million.[42] Both the extent and the form of the metropolitan area's growth helped to set it off from its neighbor. The bulk of Orange County's population was initially clustered in a series of bedroom communities located along the two freeway routes into Los Angeles, but after 1950 this northern tier of towns began to develop an independent economic base. The county also began to develop its own cultural attractions, including the Knott's Berry Farm amusement park in Buena Park, the Crystal Cathedral drive-in church in Garden Grove, and a number of popular shopping malls. Disneyland epitomized the new trend, helping to make Anaheim the leading city of the county. During the 1960s the Irvine Ranch, a rural stronghold that occupied about 20 percent of the county's land and impeded its urbanization, was developed into another nucleus for high-technology industry in southern California.

One of the fastest-growing and wealthiest counties in the country, Orange unofficially earned its independence from Los Angeles when the U.S. Census Bureau declared it a separate SMSA in 1963. At the same time, the state awarded the county its own branch campus of the University of California, at Irvine. Orange County had risen from the shadows of a greater metropolis to gain its own identity. Moreover, as Los Angeles seemed to be losing its value as a barometer of tomorrow, the "affluent technocracy" emerging in Orange County struck one observer as a more fitting "showplace of America's future."[43]

One appropriate measure of changes in Orange County was retail sales. While the old business districts of such cities as Santa Ana and Anaheim decayed, it seemed as though a shopping center sprang up at every freeway off-ramp, anchoring the retail segment of an economy that by the mid-1980s would have ranked forty-sixth among the nations of the world. One especially popular mall, South Coast Plaza, generated more sales annually than downtown San Francisco did. Developers attested its importance by building a new performing arts center nearby.

By 1977 Orange County had acquired the highest density of settlement of any county in the state except San Francisco, yet it lacked a dominating central business district or any other traditionally shaped, central urban focus.[44] Furthermore, even if the county had started out with some kind of conventional nucleus, the tide of new residents, new jobs, and new construction would probably have swept past it anyway.

Throughout the West, municipal boundaries raced outward to accommodate the growing numbers of inhabitants, and in the process many towns, like those in Orange County, lost their customary shapes and orientations.[45] The figures tell a remarkable story. Between 1940 and 1970 the population of Phoenix multiplied nine times, but the area inside the city boundaries multiplied twenty-six times, so population density per square mile decreased threefold, from 6,814 to 2,347. The population of the city of San Jose increased more than four times between 1950 and 1970, while its area multiplied eight times and its density fell by almost half, from 5,605 to 3,190 per square mile.[46] Quickly as the population of the metropolitan West increased, the extent of urbanized areas increased even faster.

Figure 2. South Coast Plaza, in the town of Costa Mesa, became a major
retail center and community focal point for booming Orange
County. The shopping center, shown here in 1968 shortly after
completion, was built atop farmland located next to the new San
Diego Freeway. Copyright, Whittington Collection, California
State University, Long Beach (neg. #87–54-A34).

The numerical and areal expansion of urban settlement significantly
altered agrarian society, for much of the newly arrived population came
from western hinterlands. Cities generally gained in importance at the
expense of rural areas. In 1940 about one-third of the population of
Arizona was urban; by 1970 the metropolis of Phoenix alone contained
more than half of the state's residents—and, needless to say, most of its
economic and political power.[47] The growth of cities also compromised
the often quite vital rural life that bordered urban areas. In Los Angeles,
Orange, and Santa Clara counties in California, and in Washington's
King County and Arizona's Maricopa County, the new arrivals ultimately overwhelmed once vigorous farm economies (see Figure 2).
The newcomers' impact on citrus-growing, one southern Californian

recalled, made it "readily apparent that agriculture and urbanization were not compatible."[48]

As metropolitan regions of the West steadily became less rural and more suburban in appearance, their inhabitants commonly looked with favor upon the annexation of farmlands as another form of growth. And as the legal line between central city and suburb was repeatedly redrawn, the visual distinctions gradually disappeared. The low-rise, scattered look of the suburb became the prevailing image of entire cities, and central city districts blended into peripheral neighborhoods.[49] The new look doubtless confused those accustomed to bold skylines, striking landmarks, and clear-cut divisions between central city and suburb. Daniel Boorstin, along with many others, identified Los Angeles as "one of the least 'legible' of the great settlements of the world." In San Jose during the early 1960s, annexation, new development, an absence of landmarks, and rapid population growth so conspired against an accurate sense of the city that many new residents often lost their way home.[50]

The new urban area contrasted sharply with older cities in the West. Between 1850 and 1900, San Francisco, Oakland, Alameda, and Berkeley had contained more than half of the urban population of California and more than four-fifths of the population of the San Francisco Bay Area, and they played a disproportionately large role in shaping California politics and culture. Their prominence faded during the twentieth century with the urbanization of southern California, the Central Valley, and the Santa Clara Valley. By 1960 they no longer contained even a majority of the Bay Area's population; newer settlements in Contra Costa, Marin, San Mateo, and Santa Clara counties increasingly dictated the politics and culture of the subregion, making it seem ever more similar to southern California.[51]

The older cities of northern California had first taken shape in the days of rail transportation, when a strong downtown and a high population density created a vertical urban form. They paid comparatively little attention to annexation, expecting to expand up rather than out. Western cities that experienced most of their growth in the twentieth century adopted different attitudes that mirrored their attachment to new means of transport. They anticipated extensive rather than intensive growth, and as a result they kept alert to opportunities for annexation. Their policies honored, not the old downtown, which too easily became congested with cars, but the many built and unbuilt subdivisions on the periphery, which promised a different kind of greatness.

The city of Seattle combined the old and the new urban forms. Its vital central business district and its natural barriers to outward sprawl helped to preserve its character as a high-density central city. Moreover, unlike San Francisco, Seattle did not face any serious challenge to its supremacy as a population center on Puget Sound. But its downtown leaders nonetheless felt threatened by outward expansion; the 1962 World's Fair was in part their response to suburban sprawl. Also unlike San Francisco, Seattle did have room to grow through annexation, and thus it could absorb some of the peripheral growth. When the population grew by 19.1 percent between 1950 and 1960, virtually all of the increase resulted from annexation of suburban tracts, rather than from natural increase or migration to the old central city.[52] Seattle thus retained its vertical core, but at the same time it incorporated outlying districts within its borders.

Southwestern cities generally had less-well-established downtowns, fewer natural restraints on sprawl, and more intense population growth. As a result, no balance between the old and the new seemed possible for them, and annexation played a critical role not only in cities' spatial growth but also in their demographic growth. In Phoenix, where annexation was seen by some as the central goal of postwar urban planning, 75 percent of the population in 1960 lived in neighborhoods that had been added to the central city since 1950. Between 1941 and 1954, towns in Los Angeles County annexed 458 separate parcels, and those in Orange County annexed 235 parcels.[53] In every case, the reality or the prospect of annexation detracted from the power of the city center, lowered the density of settlement, increased the size of the population, and prevented municipal borders from becoming fixed and recognizable.

Annexation occurred in every western metropolitan area as urban settlement spread outward, but nowhere did it have a greater impact than in San Jose. Determined that their town become the focus of urbanization in the southern San Francisco Bay Area, even if it lost its own downtown focus in the process, the leaders of San Jose pursued aggressive policies that increased the size of the city from 11 square miles in 1940 to 137 square miles in 1970.[54] The town absorbed surrounding orchards and farms through quite calculating methods. It acquired districts that actually lay at some distance from existing city boundaries by annexing roadside strips and using them as tentacles to make outlying tracts contiguous. In the process, the city outflanked closer unincorporated districts, making their eventual annexation and urbanization much more likely. City leaders also pressured residents of unincorporated areas by demanding that they agree to annexation in return for connection to the San Jose sewer system. Finally, planners officially designated outlying tracts as within "the City's sphere of annexation influence."[55]

Annexation allegedly served to increase San Jose's population, strengthen its economy, and preserve its autonomy. Officials proposed to acquire outlying parcels of land for parks, roads, reservoirs, and other municipal purposes before it was needed or built upon, because it would be cheaper that way. They also planned for the construction of shopping centers—with an eye toward capturing their sales tax revenues—and they hoped to claim possible industrial sites in order to collect their taxes as well. Annexation held out the additional promise of consolidating local bureaus under one governmental rubric. The opportunity to get help in paying for new infrastructure by incorporating potential users and taxpayers into the city also justified annexation. Finally, San Jose needed to protect itself from the designs of other nearby communities, as George Starbird, one growth advocate, reasoned:

[I]f you wanted to grow and be able to pay the bill, you had to annex surrounding areas to the city. To do that you couldn't sit on your hands. Pretty soon you would become like Bakersfield and St. Louis, an enclave circled by small incorporated cities or special service districts that would tie you up forever. If you got bottled up, your tax rate would put you out of the running for new industries.[56]

Although annexation catered to Westerners' fondness for uninhibited growth, critics condemned it in San-Jose as unnecessarily expensive as well as injurious to residents' sense of community. Continuous annexation made people unsure of where the city began and ended and what its character was. Its identity changed as quickly as its boundaries and land uses did. Rapid urbanization and aggressive annexation in the Santa Clara Valley uprooted stable farm communities and compromised some of the nation's best agricultural land (see Figures 3 and 4). Despite the vigorous efforts of county planners to preserve farms and orchards, San Jose and other valley towns grew so quickly and recklessly that they paid little attention to protecting their rich soils. Between 1940 and 1973, the number of acres devoted to orchards in Santa Clara County fell from 101,666 to 25,511. Urban expansion placed heavy burdens on growers, who often had no other recourse than to sell out to developers who then, ironically, portrayed the doomed farmland as a greenbelt subdivision suitable for "country living." By 1980 only the developers' nomenclature—such as the PruneYard shopping mall or Orchard Technology Park—recalled the

Figure 3. Urban growth in the Santa Clara Valley came at the expense of its once ubiquitous fruit trees. Developers bulldozed entire orchards to make way for residential housing, shopping districts, and new industry. In the process they paved over some of the world's richest soil. Photograph, 1960, courtesy of the Department of Planning and Development, Santa Clara County.

agrarian heritage of specific sites. Meanwhile, afraid of being swallowed up by San Jose, wealthy smaller communities in the county resorted to such defensive measures as incorporation and counter-annexation, racing to beat San Jose at its own game. By the late 1960s and early 1970s, the whole contest struck many observers as a wasteful and foolish process that dramatized the erosion of a sense of community and the absence of effective planning.[57]

Cities out of Control

Rapid population growth and territorial expansion distorted the proper shape of the city, according to accepted wisdom.

Figure 4. New houses, such as these going up in 1957, sprouted where orchards had fallen in the Santa Clara Valley. This builder left a few cherry trees standing, perhaps to persuade prospective buyers that the new subdivision offered "country living." Photograph courtesy of the Department of Planning and Development, Santa Clara County.

Conventional urban form, based upon the nineteenth-century American experience, might be pictured as a magnetic pole that kept particles in a tight orbit around a distinct nucleus. In the newer portions of the western metropolis during the mid-twentieth century, the particles increased in number too quickly to be held by the pull of the center. Rather than accumulating vertically, they escaped the magnetic field and formed orbits around new nuclei that competed against the attraction of the traditional center. Moreover, the particles increasingly became supercharged. They moved about the metropolis far more quickly and freely than before, and they adopted new paths that further weakened the coherence of the older form.

The heightened kinetic energy of life in the urban West derived from several sources. Most important was the steady arrival of newcomers, which gave the region a less rooted population. In Phoenix during the late 1950s, almost one-quarter of the population had arrived within the previous two years, and about another third had been there less than ten years. San Jose had fewer than seven out of every thousand residents of American metropolitan areas during the 1960s, but it attracted fifty-five out of every thousand net migrants to metropolitan areas during the same decade.[58]

Moreover, throughout the region the newcomers tended to be youthful and, in the words of one demographer, "chronically mobile." They had scarcely settled down in one place before they moved on again. In Los Angeles, Carey McWilliams reported in 1949, "an address or telephone number is good, on an average, for only three or four months." A study of the California population found that those who had changed residences during the year 1965 were three times more likely than non-movers to do so again in 1966. In the Santa Clara Valley during the 1960s, there were twenty-one new arrivals and seventeen fresh departures *annually* for every hundred residents of the metropolitan area, and one-third of all recent arrivals stayed less than a year.[59] The incessant movement of Mexicans back and forth across the international border added to the atmosphere of change.

Despite appearances, the perpetual motion between western cities was not altogether random. Some urban areas served primarily as way stations, others as destinations. Newcomers to California tended to move initially to San Francisco, Los Angeles, and San Diego on the coast. From these beachheads they went to such inland towns as San Jose, Sacramento, and Fresno, which received most of their newcomers from within the state.[60]

Transiency prevailed at the intra-metropolitan level as well. It was fueled by the speculative inclination that had long characterized western land development. Westerners moved restlessly about their cities, exchanging one home for another almost as easily as they sold and bought cars. Between 1955 and 1960, about a third of the populations of Seattle and Los Angeles changed houses within their county of residence. Between 1965 and 1970, 40 percent of the population of the San Jose metropolitan area changed dwellings within county limits.[61] Western cities offered little that was old or fixed; everything about them seemed to have arrived recently, and that included the family next door.

By dominating western transportation networks, automobiles heightened the impression of an atomistic society. Older cities depended heavily upon fixed routes of travel focusing on city centers; the newer cities offered more options, particularly to individuals in private autos who could ignore rail and bus routes as well as the downtowns through which such routes customarily passed. Although Los Angeles had long been seen as "the supreme automobile metropolis," other southwestern towns too now earned such titles as "Auto City" and "the automobile city *par excellence*."[62]

Just as territorial growth outpaced percentage gains in population, so the number of cars ballooned more rapidly than the number of residents. Between 1950 and 1974, motor vehicle registrations in Santa Clara County accumulated at an annual rate 1 to 2 percent faster than people; during that period the ratio of persons per auto dropped from 2.6 to 1 to 1.8 to 1. In Orange County there were 2.4 individuals for every car in 1950, 1.7 in 1974.[63] Census data from 1960 and 1980 indicate that, although the percentage of other Americans relying upon private vehicles for commuting to work began to catch up to that of Westerners, the proportion of residents commuting to work by car still remained higher in the urban West than in the rest of the country.

Automobiles did not rise to dominance unopposed, but, rather, prevailed over other means of urban transport. During the 1920s and 1930s they began to win riders away from streetcars. In the years surrounding World War II, streetcars made their last runs in San Jose (1938), Seattle (1940), and Phoenix (1948), and although they lasted longer in Los Angeles (1963), their fate had also been decided there.[64] The heyday of rail transit had passed for almost every western city, at least for the time being, and the era of the highway had arrived.

Some owners of electric railways replaced the streetcars with private bus lines, but the buses failed to challenge the dominance of cars. During the 1950s, in city after city, bus systems lost riders. Cities like San Jose and Los Angeles and Phoenix had nothing "that deserves to be called a public transportation system," in the words of Los Angeles mayor Norris Poulson. The rapid dispersal of population made efficient and profitable service virtually impossible. By the 1960s a generation had matured, as one observer commented, with "no significant experience with public transit."[65] Cars ruled the day.

Auto hegemony did not prevent civic leaders from visualizing transit alternatives, especially ones that seemed suitably futuristic. In the 1940s industrialist Henry J. Kaiser proposed commuting by private plane, in the 1950s planners in the Los Angeles and San Francisco areas considered the use of helicopters for commuting, and in the 1960s Seattle flirted with the idea of a monorail system.[66] Portland, San Diego, Los Angeles, and Santa Clara County finally began work on light rail projects during the late 1970s and early 1980s, but mass transit systems generally failed to win decisive popular support. Rail transit suited older northeastern cities, not postwar western ones.

The Bay Area Rapid Transit system (BART), centering on the region's premier nineteenth-century central business district, was the principal exception to that rule. BART was conceived in large part to "protect and strengthen the economic vitality of downtown San Francisco." Such a system may have appealed to San Franciscans with eastern urban sensibilities, but it seemed to offer little to the more recently settled, more highly suburbanized cities of the West. Planners in San Jose gave serious consideration to the idea of bringing BART service to their city, but in 1958 they decided that

a radial and circumferential system of freeways and thoroughfares for the entire San Jose metropolitan area may be of greater value and significance than participating in a rapid transit system which can serve only to shorten the distance between the San Jose urban center and San Francisco by a few minutes at best.[67]

The automobile promised to deliver what streetcars, buses, and rapid transit could not—greater speed, convenience, and range in getting around the new urban areas. But to fulfill that promise, it needed proper highways and streets, so people made sure that the auto would have a smooth ride. Western cities became cities on wheels where the perpetual auto-motion reinforced other forms of mobility.

Over the decades of the mid-twentieth century, Westerners' attitude toward cars, like their attitude toward growth, grew more ambivalent as the costs began to surface. One problem was air pollution, for which the Los Angeles area became notorious. Another was traffic congestion, and still another was the isolation imposed upon those, particularly in minority communities, who could not afford their own vehicles. One of the most visible consequences of autos was their impact on the downtown centers. They tended to heighten the importance of larger cities at the expense of nearby smaller towns, while within the metropolis they weakened the power of the central business district. Rapid growth, population dispersal, and urban annexation had already begun to erode the primacy of downtowns; cars added their horsepower to the work and intensified the damage to the traditional urban core. Throughout the West old central business districts diminished in appeal as new office, shopping, and government centers flourished away from midtown.[68] The ironic outcome of the increased auto use was that many of America's newest cities undertook hasty redevelopment schemes to save their downtowns.

The story of San Jose's central business district exemplifies the problem. The downtown had long stood as the most important point in the southern Bay Area; key railroad and streetcar junctions attested its status. But after World War II, highways were built that bypassed the district, and civic leaders focused attention on outward expansion rather than maintenance of the central district. The vitality of the downtown steadily drained away. At the beginning of the 1950s the district earned more than half of the retail income in the county, but twelve years later it accounted for less than one-eighth. In the same period, the number of shopping centers in the county climbed from two to sixty-eight. Commercial strips and malls now got the lion's share of business, in large part because they better accommodated auto traffic. Meanwhile, downtown became known to planners as an area of "severe blight." Car dealers, department stores, the leading newspaper, and even the city hall abandoned the district for outlying sites, leaving behind a poorer residential population, high-volume discount stores, and increasingly derelict buildings. Twelve thousand people still worked in central San Jose as late as 1966, but the higher their incomes the less they supported downtown business. Commuters fled the "wasteland" after working hours, not to return at night or on weekends for whatever entertainment or shopping the district continued to offer.[69]

Although cars had contributed to the deterioration of downtown San Jose, they were promoted as tools for redeveloping the central business district. In the late 1950s planners decided to renew the city core by making it more accessible to autos. They proposed widening the streets, increasing the number of parking spaces, regulating traffic more carefully, and linking the district more closely to a comprehensive freeway system. Predictably, these efforts failed to revitalize downtown San Jose. No form of rebuilding could enable the downtown to accommodate cars better than shopping malls, office and industrial parks, and housing subdivisions could. In some instances the effort actually made conditions worse. Minorities were particularly vulnerable to the dislocations caused by urban renewal. New freeway construction, for example, displaced a well-rooted Mexican-American barrio.[70]

The fate of the San Jose barrio illustrated the tendency for ethnic and racial enclaves to share with central business districts the burdens of the inner city while outlying areas of the metropolis reaped the benefits of growth. After 1945, many city-dwellers of Chinese and Japanese descent actually joined the migration away from central city districts.[71] As Asian Americans and Anglos moved out, African and Mexican Americans crowded into the tracts they left behind. The conditions in these communities were uniformly worse than those in white neighborhoods; the Spanish name for one barrio in San Jose—Sal si Puedes or "Get out if you can"—summarized the "substandard housing and socioeconomic problems" that beset these districts (see Figure 5).[72]

Anglo-Americans, focused on the new development that was bringing prosperity to outlying areas, found it easy to ignore the problems of minority neighborhoods. They tended to support a relatively conservative, pro-growth brand of politics and to neglect the older and needier parts of the metropolis.[73] In any case, poor neighborhoods in western cities may not have seemed true slums to whites, since they were less densely populated than their eastern counterparts and contained more single-family housing.[74] Such perceptions fed a kind of complacency about inner-city conditions.

Complacency may also have resulted from recognition that minorities had made at least some progress since 1940.[75] For example, the increasing numbers of Mexican Americans, their concentration in compact urban districts, their new political activism, inspired in part by their service during World War II, and their eligibility for veterans' benefits under the G.I. Bill all won them greater political and economic power. The election of Edward R. Roybal to the Los Angeles City Council in 1949 and the gradual migration of some Mexican Americans away from ethnic enclaves in major cities seemed to herald the arrival of a new era for Spanish-speaking Westerners.[76] However, by

Figure 5. Urban renewal projects jeopardized older housing and minority
neighborhoods in central cities. This block, shown in June 1959,
would soon be torn down to make room for the Seattle World's
Fair of 1962. One aim of fair officials was to eliminate blight from
the periphery of the central business district. Courtesy of Special
Collections Division, University of Washington Libraries (photo
by Hamilton, neg. #UW 10575).

every important socioeconomic index, Mexican Americans lagged behind Anglos. Moreover, the spreading western metropolis smothered
some Mexican-American communities located on the fringes of smaller
cities and compelled the traditional Mexican family to adjust to modern
urban ways.[77]

African Americans also found that the urban West did not live up to
their hopes. In 1925 the national secretary of the National Association
for the Advancement of Colored People had explained that the West
attracted African Americans because it offered them "a better deal." In
the years 1940–1970 the region may well have provided African Americans with more economic and political opportunities and fewer social
and educational barriers than existed for them in other sections of the
United States.[78] For African Americans even more than for Mexican
Americans, however, western cities failed to satisfy aspirations for a
better life. African Americans were more severely segregated than Mex-

ican Americans, were crowded into the least desirable neighborhoods, and had a disproportionately high rate of impoverishment. The sudden influx of African Americans doubtless seemed a threat to whites, and they often responded with increased racial hostility. The newcomers represented a threat as well to the small enclaves of African American "old settlers" in western cities, who not only worried that relations with whites would now deteriorate but also found their neighborhoods inundated by recently arrived, rural African Americans.[79] Inner cities in the West may not have looked like eastern slums and perhaps did offer more opportunity, but they offered no reason for complacency.

The Watts riots in August of 1965 shattered any illusion that western cities were free of racial problems. The number of African Americans in Los Angeles had multiplied quickly since 1940, but poverty and discrimination conspired to confine the vast majority of them to highly segregated neighborhoods and schools in the southcentral part of the city. Watts perhaps compared favorably to its eastern counterparts, but its residents must have been acutely aware that it did not measure up to the rest of Los Angeles. They resided in "the most overcrowded, substandard, and overpriced" housing in the city; experienced high rates of unemployment that were compounded by the dispersal of industry toward the suburbs; and suffered disproportionately from the inadequacies of public transit.[80] Los Angeles and other western towns may well have offered minorities "a better deal" than southern and northeastern cities, but the inability of the disadvantaged to realize their relatively high hopes for the region surely added "a special measure of frustration and disillusionment" to their lives.[81]

The Watts riots were pivotal events because they challenged the confidence that had characterized the urban West. Other cities would learn the same lessons more slowly, but all would ultimately come to pay greater attention to the inner-city costs, as well as to the environmental costs, of postwar growth patterns. Explosive slums and declining central business districts presented the enduring paradox of inner-city decay enclosed by flourishing metropolitan areas. They demonstrated how the expansion that so overwhelmed western cities contributed to the neglect of the people, buildings, and businesses in older parts of town, and they heightened people's sense that urban growth needed to be brought under greater control.

If any agency in the urban West could have been expected to ameliorate the changes resulting from expansion, it would have been city planning departments. However, planners had actually helped to create the problems; many had been recruited to serve the cause of rapid growth. Moreover, once it became clear that growth and change were undermining the traditional form of the city, planners seemed generally incapable of responding effectively to the resulting problems. In the 1960s one critic of development in Phoenix complained that the "city's planning policy was 'not to plan at all.'"[82] But it would be wrong to conclude that planning in every western city failed simply for lack of trying. In fact, some programs succeeded, and others, although they had less success, were remarkably progressive.

Urban development along the southern shore of San Francisco Bay expressed the outcome of a contest between two different planning visions. Santa Clara County possessed "one of the finest county planning staffs in the nation," according to the Ralph Nader Study Group on land in California. It was headed by Karl J. Belser, a highly respected planner and one of the region's most articulate opponents of urban sprawl. Trained in the East and in Europe as an architect and urban planner, Belser led eminent fights to protect farmland from urbanization, save open spaces, fight commercial over-zoning, and integrate the poor into the urban mainstream. Belser's efforts conflicted, however, with planning by the municipality of San Jose, located within Santa Clara County, which, with the assistance of permissive state laws, effectively undermined county efforts through its own pro-growth programs. San Jose's planners sought aggressively to accelerate population growth, attract new industry, annex more land, and accommodate new housing and commerce. As a result, San Jose and its nearby rivals swallowed up large, unincorporated portions of Santa Clara County. The resulting urban form was roundly condemned as "a hideous, smog-covered, amoeboid sprawl of housing tracts, freeways and shopping centers," created "needlessly and mindlessly."[83] But planning had not truly failed in San Jose; rather, one kind of planning had prevailed over another.

Conditions in Santa Clara County mirrored those throughout the region. Many critics lamented the despoliation of California and the West, with ample reason, and assigned much of the blame to the inadequacies of planning. Yet observers also realized that in certain aspects of planning California was "America's most progressive state." By the 1970s one out of every six planners employed in the nation worked for one or another public agency in California, and California was recognized as a leader in environmental action.[84] Although the problems of unplanned growth were made manifest in California, it would be mistaken to say that urbanization in the state had proceeded without the benefit of planning—in some cases quite innovative planning, such as that which influenced Los Angeles.

Because the population of southern California expected to live in a city that differed from eastern and midwestern precedents (and conceived of autos as progressive tools for shaping that better city), Los Angeles frequently proved more receptive than most American towns to novel ways of regulating land use.[85] Despite a reputation for having grown planlessly, the city actually pioneered a number of planning advances, sometimes spurred on by the pace and problems of its distinctive pattern of growth. Los Angeles anticipated the rise of zoning in major American cities by making "the first deliberate and intentional use of police power for the purpose of regulating the type and intensity of land use" during the first decade of the twentieth century. In 1920 it became the first city to authorize the use of that same police power for the protection of the single-family character of residential districts. In 1922 it created the nation's first county planning commission, and in 1930 it passed the first ordinance requiring developers of apartment complexes to provide adequate off-street parking for tenants. On these occasions and others, of course, rapid growth and feeble enforcement often undercut the power of the innovative regulations.[86] But the city nonetheless proved bold in its vision of how extensive planning might become.

In Los Angeles, as in other western cities, planning represented an effort to mediate the conflict between the quantity and the quality of urban life, between the claim that additional growth represented progress and the concern that expansion compromised the attractiveness of the area. In the years after World War II, when the quantity of growth became so tremendous and when the auto no longer seemed so progressive, achieving a balance between quantity and quality became almost impossible. Planners in Los Angeles defined their purpose to be that of making "new developments possible with the least disruption to standards of living," a formulation that favored growth over preservation.[87] To attain this goal, Los Angeles adopted policies that encouraged deconcentration, continuing the city's attachment to extensive rather than intensive growth. In this, too, Los Angeles was a pioneer. It developed innovative plans for expressways and highways and became a leader in coping with the air pollution and traffic congestion that earlier planning had inadvertently encouraged. It promoted the construction of shopping centers, both as a kind of community focal point and as an alternative to commercial strip development. And Los Angeles County devised the Lakewood Plan, which allowed smaller towns to purchase urban services from the county at an affordable price and without sacrificing their political independence.[88]

Planners did in fact influence the shape of the western metropolis, but they attempted to do so less by opposing than by facilitating or fine-tuning selected processes already under way. Consequently, despite the different levels and philosophies of planning and despite the different natural settings, since these processes were the same throughout the West the newer western cities tended to resemble one another. Each had a low-slung appearance; each depended utterly on autos and on a perpetually inadequate system of transit, highways, and roads; each featured comparatively troubled downtown and minority districts but surprisingly strong suburban centers of activity. Each city expanded prodigiously, growing so swiftly that even the best-laid plans were often undermined by the explosive increase in area, population, and prosperity. Los Angeles might have become a leader in fighting smog and devising freeway systems, but at no time did this leadership translate into effective control over the problems of automobiles.

The limitations of planning illustrated the extent to which the rapid growth and changing form of western cities had gotten out of hand. The sources for much of the growth, of course—mobilization for war, federal and state policies, decisions by national and international companies—indeed lay outside the control of any one metropolis and its planning staff. And municipal governments, even after the revitalization they underwent during and after World War II, could not have foreseen the impact of the deluge of migrants. No town had an infrastructure in place that could accommodate so many newcomers. Phoenix planners pointed out in 1960 that the city did not have a sufficient sewer system, whereas San Jose had adequate sewers but lacked almost every other important "fixture of urban life"—parking garages, street lights, parks, schools.[89] Moreover, the construction of more freeways, sewers, and schools only added to the confusion, and yet each new edifice was liable to be inadequate to meet demand by the time it was finished (see Figure 6).

Chaos, Community, and Culture in the Urban West

The problems faced by cities in the postwar West did not prove amenable to either a local solution or a new general plan. None-

Figure 6. State and local governments tried to keep up with western urban growth by building highways to accommodate the ever-increasing number of cars, yet in many cases, such as the Harbor Freeway near downtown Los Angeles (built between 1952 and 1970 and shown here in 1964), the roads were soon overcrowded. Copyright Whittington Collection, California State University, Long Beach (neg. #46–94–5).

theless, the cities themselves, or, more properly, their residents, seemed somehow to blame. They appeared to lack discipline. Karl Belser, from his perspective in Santa Clara County, summarized this critique. The pattern of western urbanization was "arbitrary," "confused," and "uncontrolled," a "random" kind of "disorder" that "blighted" the land and ignored the accepted wisdom about how cities should develop. A Los Angeles planner summarized the concern more succinctly with the word "Chaos." [90]

Underneath such commentary lay the fear that the city was out of control because the citizens could not regulate themselves sufficiently to provide the order so essential to a rich urban life. In this mode of thinking, the physical mirrored the social: a disorderly landscape implied a diseased society, and vice versa. One Seattle attorney regarded the suburb of Bellevue as "almost an unmitigated disaster, where the tasteless tract architecture and the bad shopping centers have affected the quality of thought too." Another critic wrote, "The physical shapelessness of Los Angeles is reflected in the moral anarchy of its people." [91]

Always, Los Angeles seemed to represent the worst possible case. William Irwin Thompson traveled to southern California to study this society on the "edge of history." He found that the typical resident there could "change his house, job, wife, and religion pretty much as he likes." Thompson suggested that people in Los Angeles lacked stability, tradition, and proper urban form; they possessed too much freedom and survived only by embracing such fantasies as those offered by Disneyland. [92] The chaos that prevailed on the land apparently merely reflected that which prevailed in the mind. Los Angeles represented the fate other cities should avoid at all costs.

There could never be another Los Angeles, but that did not keep people from imagining the possibility. Early in the postwar period, some had hoped to imitate the southern California pattern. A. P. "Dutch" Hamann, San Jose city manager, explained that he wanted his town to become "another Los Angeles": "I'm happy when people say that San Jose is like Los Angeles. This means San Jose is progressive." [93] But particularly after the mid-1960s, when southern California became notorious for political conservatism and the Watts riots, the idea that Los Angeles represented the city of the future diminished in appeal.

As time passed, fewer and fewer residents of the Santa Clara Valley shared A. P. Hamann's admiration for Los Angeles. As citizens of the Bay Area, they followed the lead of San Francisco in disliking the rival to the south. Yet it soon became impossible to deny that the pattern of settlement around San Jose resembled the southern California model much more than it did San Francisco. The development of the high-tech economy and low-rise downtowns of Silicon Valley heightened the contrast between the two cities by the bay. By the 1980s Steve Wozniak, one of the creators of the personal computer revolution, concluded that the Santa Clara Valley was becoming "another Los Angeles. A faceless suburb, ugly houses, divided by highways on which cars are just creeping along."[94]

Los Angeles represented a threat to even the most remote places: a conservationist wondered in 1965 whether "we really want to make Alaska over in the image of Los Angeles."[95] But the concern was greatest in cities. As leaders in Seattle planned for new highway construction and a world's fair during the early 1960s, they hoped that the Puget Sound area would not come to resemble southern California. Yet a professor of urban planning at the University of Washington predicted that the metropolis would become a "little Los Angeles" by the year 2000. A *Seattle Times* editorial responded for many residents when it advised planners that "their depressing prophecy need not come true."[96] Yet it came true enough, in the eyes of later observers, to bear repetition. In the 1970s one widely read history of Seattle associated many of its faults in the postwar years with those undesirable urban elements identified with southern California. The city, wrote Roger Sale, "was not doing some of the good things Los Angeles was doing, and it was doing a great many of the bad things."[97]

Phoenix apparently resembled Los Angeles, too. Indeed, observers there took the comparison one step further. Rapid urbanization in central Arizona posed grave concerns about the selfish interests of developers, the degradation of the environment, and the absence of public planning. Many saw such problems as an "unfortunate duplication" of southern California, but one critic sounded an even shriller alarm: "The danger in Greater Phoenix is not that it will become another Los Angeles, but that it will be a lot worse than Los Angeles. Think about it."[98]

Popular perceptions of Los Angeles contained a multitude of negative images, but primary among them was the concern that city life in southern California diminished people's sense of place. "Placelessness" in Los Angeles was commonly associated with two urban processes, one qualitative and the other quantitative.[99] On the qualitative side, the *shape* of the city was being transformed in ways that seemingly made it less legible as well as less conducive to the formation of community and the enrichment of culture. On the quantitative, the *size* of Los Angeles suggested growth so rapid and uncontrolled that it denied the inhabitants any sense of stable attachment. The two processes of change became inextricably interwoven, but they were not one and the same, and they did not provoke a monolithic response.

Urban experts paid more attention than others to changes in the city's form, and they argued that the new shape kept the city from performing its central tasks of developing a shared identity and an enriched cultural life for its residents. In the view of these planners and scholars, the western metropolis as exemplified by Los Angeles discouraged a sense of community. Instead of finding "civic activism and social reform" there, critics attested to an atomistic society that put up no resistance to the greed and capriciousness of capitalists and consumers. The "mindless" form of western cities stripped city-dwellers of their urbanity, according to the critics.[100]

The malformation of the western city, critics charged, debased urban life. Phoenix and Seattle were both criticized for having an inadequate number of parks and a general shortage of open space. Everywhere the blight on downtowns and the ugliness of "an urban landscape of hamburger arches, discount shopping centers, patches and remnants of disorder" were decried.[101] The "almost irrational" attachment to automobiles exemplified for many the willful despoliation of environment and culture:

we have indeed prostrated ourselves, physically and spiritually, before the automobile, and the autocratic society. See how the finny monster dominates your life, occupies a large room of your house, eats up about 13 percent of your income, demolishes the hegemony of your town, manufactures your smog, threatens your park, recklessly sires a profusion of billboards in an already uglified world, invites the spread of slurbs.[102]

That enormous amounts of land were given over to parking spaces, garages, streets, alleys, and highways indicated a lack of appreciation for the environment; that cars sheltered people from the human contact necessary for aesthetic creativity implied a lack of sophistication. How would Los Angeles "build an intensive, well-balanced culture," wondered Sir Julian Huxley, the noted English biologist, if it was so spread out and had no vital center and no mass transit? Suburbanites, it was further argued, were too selfish and complacent and rootless to support a rich cultural life. The "outdoor living" so intrinsic to both western and suburban life, according to one New Yorker, ensured "a certain monotony for the active mind."[103]

Concern about cultural refinement was an offshoot of anxiety about the bonds that should hold city people together. The pattern of urban expansion in the postwar West appeared to work against cohesive communities; there simply seemed to be too many newcomers and too much transiency to permit social stability to develop. Observers of the western city perceived the isolation of residents in a variety of ways: in Phoenix, planners argued, inadequate controls on land use led to unstable neighborhoods; Los Angeles seemed to have "neither a center nor a discernible boundary"; critics of San Jose repeatedly lamented the "lack of community or neighborhood identity." [104]

Lacking roots and therefore lacking a commitment to place, urban Westerners apparently cared too little about others and too much about themselves. Rather than adhering to "traditional spiritual values," they avidly pursued secular and material goals. Their anomic tendencies, the argument continued, gave undue rein to individualism, which in turn helped to explain the virulent strain of political conservatism in the region. It also helped to account for the high rate of divorce, low level of donations to charity, minimal concern for the fate of the land in the hands of rapacious developers, and pervasive maladjustment. [105]

The urban character of the West truly alarmed the critics. However, few of them ever paused to ask why, if the western city was such a miserable place, so many thousands of people continued to flock to it. The obvious, if partial, answer was that the cities of the West, with all their faults, seemed preferable to those elsewhere. The most striking fact about the western metropolis after 1940, after all, was its net population increase. People migrated to and remained in the urban West because to them it seemed more promising than any other section of the country. Consequently, many of these inhabitants of western cities viewed growth more as a sign of health and prosperity than as a symptom of a society out of control. It is true that eventually even Westerners came to see that they could have too much of a good thing. But when the users did begin to criticize their habitats, it became clear that their attitudes toward and solutions for urban problems generally differed from those voiced by many urban planners and scholars.

Some experts argued that the *form* of the western metropolis deprived its residents of a strong attachment to place because it could not instill an adequate sense of community and culture. Most inhabitants of the region, by contrast, saw the *quantity* of urbanization, rather than its shape, as the key problem. When their concerns about cities reached the critical point, they responded less by trying to alter the pattern of the cityscape than by attempting to limit or halt growth. Westerners' reaction assumed that undesirable changes in urban areas resulted not from deficiencies in form or in themselves but, rather, from too rapid and seemingly uncontrollable expansion, which created communities that were too new and unsettled. Growth also threatened those amenities that gave the West its appeal. Southern California's smog served as the leading example of blight, but water pollution, vanishing open spaces, crowded highways, mass-produced housing, and other scars on the landscape were also denounced. By the 1970s such concerns had nurtured in the region a sizable movement to bring expansion under control.

Yet Westerners found it difficult to kick the habit of growth completely. Even as they began to comprehend that increases in population and economic activity endangered their rather fragile sense of place, they retained their strong attachment to the idea of growth as a desirable end in itself. To many people in the urban West, the gains made after 1940 represented the almost instantaneous gratification of long frustrated hopes. For decades, growth had been the indispensable but elusive ingredient in the area's formula for success. By the mid-twentieth century, rapid expansion had finally given the West an edge over the East, and many were determined to hold on to that advantage. Much as people talked about their city becoming another Los Angeles, they seemed even more afraid that it would become another St. Louis—an oft-cited "eastern" town whose urban problems were attributed to its inability to grow during the twentieth century.[106]

Growth was inextricably associated with the vitality, creativity, and appeal of the region; in other words, it in fact contributed to a western sense of place. Thus, at the same time that it was argued that each new resident made the West more similar to the East, it could also be said that once the West stopped expanding, the region would no longer be so different from, and so preferable to, the East. Growth represented both problem and promise, and as a result it took many years before most Westerners could seriously challenge the idea that more was better. Only after 1965 or so did calls to manage or limit urban growth fall upon receptive ears.

Even when western urbanites began to question the value of growth, they did not generally challenge the pattern on the land that recent growth had produced. Cityscapes that seemed irrational to many critics commonly made sense to the residents of western cities. Among other things, the new spatial patterns helped to channel urban expansion in relatively acceptable directions. They helped to make the metropolis manageable, in the minds of its users, and thus helped to fulfill people's expectations about a certain kind of region and a certain type of city in the West.

Magic lands epitomized the influence of the new spatial patterns. They demonstrated how the careful design and intensive supervision of selected new urban forms generated a semblance of order and coherence in a region experiencing enormous change. Nobody could plausibly suggest that Disneyland was disorganized or blighted or out of control. And few could deny that Disneyland's ability to create order out of chaos affected the urban patterns outside its walls.

CHAPTER TWO

Disneyland:
The Happiest Place on Earth

If an organization's ability to affect language is any measure of its influence, then the Walt Disney company has been one of the most influential organizations in the English-speaking world. During the 1930s the phrase "mickey mouse" entered American usage as an informal synonym for "trite and commercially slick in character," useless, trivial, or petty. Soon thereafter, "Disneyesque" gained currency as meaning "having the characteristics or resembling the style of an animated cartoon made by Walt Disney or his company."[1] No Disney idea or product, however, has accounted for so many neologisms as Disneyland, which opened in Anaheim, California, in 1955.

Over the years the Walt Disney company has attempted to guard against indiscriminate or inappropriate use of the term "Disneyland," which is a company trademark subject to legal protection.[2] Yet the name of the theme park quickly fell into general use. As early as 1956, it had come to mean "any fantastic or fanciful land or place; a nevernever land." "Disneyland" also signified "any large, bustling place noted for its colorful attractions" and "a land or place of make-believe."[3]

Applications of the term proliferated immediately. Since the theme park was billed as an enjoyable experience for children, it seemed natural to use its name to characterize other places catering to other groups. The phrase "Disneyland for Adults" was invoked to publicize (and sanitize the images of) both Hugh Hefner's Playboy Clubs and the gambling resort of Las Vegas. Observers dubbed Sun City, Arizona, a "resident Disneyland for old folks" and the Houston Astrodome "baseball's Disneyland." Publicists for the Cedar Point amusement park tried to entice customers by calling it "Ohio's Disneyland."[4]

Not all uses of the metaphor were favorable. Over time, Disneyland came to connote negative as well as positive qualities. Environmentalists in the Pacific Northwest, for example, criticized tourist attractions in wilderness areas by likening them to Disneyland. To a certain extent, people used the idea of "another Disneyland" as they did the notion of "another Los Angeles." Indeed, in the minds of some, the theme park stood for all the ills perceived to be concentrated in southern California.[5]

Disneyland inspired terminology apart from the use of its name as a metaphor for other places. By 1982 the venerable adjective "Disneyesque" no longer suggested similarity to a Disney movie; now it meant "resembling Disneyland." Slang usages further attested the park's impact upon the language. "Disneyland daddy" connoted a "divorced or separated father who sees his children rarely"; the term "E ticket," the name of the kind of coupon once needed for admission to the best rides in the park, came to mean, particularly to younger people, an especially thrilling experience or "trip."[6] For some critics the theme park typified recent trends in American life. Anthony Haden-Guest and Edward Relph have written disparagingly about the "Disneyfication" of the landscape, and David Lowenthal has noted the "sanitized, Disneyfied heritage" that passes for history at numerous sites.[7]

The English language is only one of many areas in which Disneyland has altered the way we see and act. Most obviously, the Disney company modified thinking about commercial, outdoor recreation by spawning an amusement park that has been imitated and promoted the world around. As both the first thematically organized amusement park and the first park to be marketed nationally, it revolutionized the nature of the business.[8] More subtly, Disneyland altered both the design and the perception of all sorts of landscapes. In 1963 the renowned American developer James Rouse described Disneyland as "the greatest piece of urban design in the United States today." Those concerned with the layout, architecture, and construction of the built urban environment have taken Disneyland as a model for such projects as shopping malls, public and private buildings, sports stadiums, and historic preservation efforts.[9]

Portrayals of Disneyland as an institution that both influenced and expressed the American culture of its time are generally accurate.[10] But in order to appreciate Disneyland fully, it is necessary to understand

that its origins and influence also possessed a distinctly *western* character. Above all else, Disneyland was a product of southern California's
motion picture industry. It could not have appeared without the skills
and marketing associated with feature filmmaking. At a time when
Americans spoke about the demise of motion pictures, Walt Disney
ensured that, through theme parks and through television, Hollywood
and the West became not less influential but more so.

Disneyland's success as a cultural landscape also derived in no small
part from the urban and environmental context of southern California.
Disneyland started out as a celebration of southern California, yet by
the 1970s it was regarded as an aberration on the landscape. Either way,
its identity became intertwined with that of the surrounding metropolitan area. After 1955, Disneyland and Los Angeles became synonymous to Americans across the country, even though the theme park was
located outside both the city and the county of Los Angeles. Similarly,
Disneyland became identified with the Far West. Its commercial success
depended first and foremost on the patronage of Californians and other
Westerners.

Disneyland's influence was particularly concentrated in its home of
Orange County, where it added to a distinctive suburban identity. The
nation's original magic kingdom helped to transform Anaheim, a small
and subordinate town on the fringes of Los Angeles, into the equivalent of a central business district for urbanizing Orange County. In
large part because of Disneyland's presence, Anaheim acquired such
assets as a major convention center and hotel-motel complex, and a
big-league stadium that attracted both professional baseball and professional football teams. These facilities made Anaheim the leading
"downtown" in Orange County and thus helped to bring cohesion to
its seemingly disorganized sprawl.

Although Disneyland can be analyzed as a product of the West and
as a significant force in both regional and national culture, Walt Disney
liked to think that the theme park permitted people to escape the here
and now. Its visitors by and large tended to agree. Disneyland was designed to wall people off from the outside world. It was intended *not*
to resemble a particular site or region—least of all a large and confusing
metropolis. In a way, it was supposed to be placeless, even though it
was very much the product of a particular place and also an influential
force in the reshaping of that place.

Similarly, the park was supposed to be timeless. "In Disneyland,"
publicists explained, "clocks and watches will lose all meaning, for there

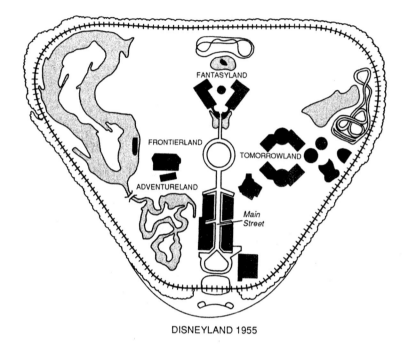

FANTASYLAND

FRONTIERLAND

TOMORROWLAND

ADVENTURELAND

Main Street

DISNEYLAND 1955

Map 1. The lands of Disneyland, 1955.

is no present. There are only yesterday, tomorrow and the timeless land of fantasy."[11] Customers escaped from today and visited a better world. They found the past in Frontierland and on Main Street U.S.A.; they visited the future as envisioned in Tomorrowland; in Adventureland they sampled the excitement of faraway places and times; and in Fantasyland they walked among the fairy-tale characters and stories that Disney had featured in animated films (see Map 1).

Again, however, just as Disneyland was actually the product of a specific place, so it was also the product of a definite time. It succeeded not so much because it allowed people to escape from the present as because it capitalized so brilliantly on postwar tastes and trends. It enshrined the cold war and all the things for which it stood—competition with the Soviets in productivity, in space, in ways of life. It celebrated corporations and in fact made them integral partners in the park. Disneyland's work force behaved in ways that paralleled contemporary depictions of organization life and white-collar work. And the park embodied the optimism and the suburbanization that accompanied the emergence of postwar affluence in America. Like other aspects of material culture in the Far West, the theme park was both ahead of its time, in its innovations on the landscape, and perfectly in step with its time, in the values and assumptions built into the park. It was different enough to be novel, but not so unusual that those who paid to visit it or who wished to adapt its innovations to other places and contexts found it strange or intimidating.

The Urbanization of Disneyland

The development of Disneyland replicated in microcosm the dilemma of urbanization in the West after World War II. From opening day the theme park succeeded beyond all reasonable expectations, becoming an experience shared by millions of people as well as a tremendously influential landmark. But in order to maintain both its growth and its distinctiveness, Disneyland, like the remainder of the urban region, had to surmount such problems as overcrowding and pollution, which were largely a by-product of its success. More than the rest of southern California, Disneyland succeeded in retaining its uniqueness; the quality of its built environment remained appealing despite the enormous quantity of people it attracted.

The proprietors of Disneyland had a great interest in ensuring its lasting appeal. Until 1955 they had made their reputation and fortune primarily from motion pictures. After the opening of Disneyland, however, they grew steadily more dependent on the theme park. In 1954 Walt Disney Productions earned $11.6 million in gross profits, primarily from films. Fifteen years later it earned $143.3 million in gross profits; less than 40 percent came from movies, and almost 50 percent came from "the Anaheim goldmine." Ten years after the opening of Walt Disney World in Florida in 1971, theme parks earned almost 70 percent of all revenues for the company, whereas its reputation for making movies had steadily declined.[12]

Disneyland did not represent the demise of the company's filmmaking; rather, in Disneyland the company applied filmmaking skills, ideas, and methods to a three-dimensional medium. Such an innovation could have been born only in southern California, the capital of the movie industry. During the initial decades of the twentieth century, filmmak-

ers first trickled and then streamed into the area, attracted by its isolation, climate, topography, and society. Southern California shaped both
the motion picture industry and the content of its films. The movies in
turn promoted Los Angeles around the world, helped form the city's
identity and style, and made it into the first American cultural hearth
west of the Mississippi River.[13] The road to Disneyland began in Hollywood.

Disneyland resulted from efforts by Walter Elias Disney to expand
his creative and commercial empire. In the early 1920s, Disney decided
to seek his fortune in motion pictures. He left Kansas City and moved
to Hollywood. By the 1940s, having mastered the animated motion
picture, he turned to "live action" and nature films, and he grew increasingly curious about forms of commercial entertainment other than
movies.[14] Amusement parks presented an intriguing challenge.

During the 1930s, Disney had been bored by the amusement parks
he visited with his daughters. By 1951 his reaction had crystallized: he
thought of building a "Kiddieland" that would teach children about
their nation's heritage. He also envisioned a traveling show for schoolchildren called "Disneylandia"; it would present, in miniature, animated scenes from American history and folklore.[15] Neither Kiddieland
nor Disneylandia ever panned out, but elements from each persisted in
attempts to create a more uplifting and engaging kind of amusement
park.

Disney began to evaluate specific plots of land in southern California. In 1952 he announced plans for a small venture called Disneyland,
to be built on eight vacant acres adjacent to the Walt Disney Studios in
Burbank. As Disney visualized it, his employees and their families
would visit this park, and studio artists would exhibit some of their
works there. The park might also attract some of the large numbers of
tourists in southern California who wanted to visit a Hollywood studio. For children it would feature three-dimensional versions of many
of the characters presented in Disney's animated films. The proposed
park would create and publicize new products: "Disneyland and its activities will be transmitted by television throughout the country. A
complete television center with theater, stages, sets and technical equipment are [sic] planned."[16]

That Disneyland was initially intended to perform so many tasks
indicates the variety of Disney's motives. That it would have so many
functions also meant that eight acres would not be able to contain it.
When he realized this, Disney hired the Los Angeles office of the Stan-

ford Research Institute (SRI) to find another site for his project. It had to be at least a hundred acres, somewhere in the Los Angeles basin. In a report of August 1953, SRI recommended a tract of approximately 140 acres of orange groves near the small town of Anaheim in Orange County. This parcel, located twenty-five miles southeast of the Los Angeles city center, suited Disney's criteria that it have no "intensive improvement and buildup," no nearby oil fields, and little adjacent land under "government control." Anaheim had fine weather for outdoor entertainment, with less extreme temperatures, less rainfall, and less "haze" than other eligible parts of the Los Angeles basin. Moreover, it lay right beside the projected route of the Santa Ana Freeway from Los Angeles, then under construction. Disneyland would adjoin a major transportation corridor capable of bringing customers to its doorstep. The anticipated completion of the freeway would accelerate residential growth in Anaheim and surrounding towns, placing Disneyland in the middle of a rapidly expanding population of potential employees and customers. Persuaded of the attractiveness of Orange County, Disney purchased a parcel of land in Anaheim in spring of 1954; by summer, construction had begun.[17]

The SRI investigators, in addition to evaluating available properties, had explored the market for Disneyland by examining such outdoor attractions as fairs, zoos, gardens, amusement parks, and Forest Lawn Memorial Park cemetery in Glendale (before Disneyland, Forest Lawn was the most popular tourist attraction in greater Los Angeles). Interviews with the operators of existing amusement parks produced some discouraging words. Disneyland's costs and risks would be too high, they said, and its profits and capacity too low.[18] In retrospect, it seems likely that these critics never understood what Disney intended to build and that they underestimated the ability of his previous creations to lure a ready-made market to the theme park. Both Disney and his customers viewed the park as an extension of his enormously successful movies.

Even more important, in initial planning Walt Disney was not overly concerned about the bottom line at Disneyland, because he did not yet envision it as a "commercial venture."[19] As late as June of 1954, newspapers reported that entrance would be free. By opening day one year later, the high cost of construction had made it necessary to charge an entrance fee of one dollar, but even then Disney and his corporate partners did not expect their profits to come primarily from theme park customers. Rather, they saw Disneyland both as a "vehicle for promot-

Figure 7. Walt Disney proudly introduced his plans for Disneyland to a national television audience in 1954. He aimed simultaneously to revolutionize the concept of the amusement park, to translate his movies into three dimensions, and to join the television age. © The Walt Disney Company (954–8045).

ing their products and services" and as a studio for new Disney programs.[20]

Initial plans showed the park as less a tourist destination than an adjunct to the Burbank studios as Disney moved into the television age. One 1953 description of the project listed three separate TV series to be filmed at Disneyland, and the SRI report included among the virtues of Anaheim the fact that it offered "a direct line of sight" to "master transmitters" on Mount Wilson.[21] Many have equated the advent of television with the decline of motion pictures, but Walt Disney thought otherwise. In Disneyland he saw "a living set for television" that fans and customers could visit, and in television he saw the means "to create a new motion-picture theatre audience and to encourage the fullest box-office patronage for our forthcoming pictures" (see Figure 7).[22]

Television was crucial not only to the initial conception of Disney-

Figure 8.   Disneyland under construction in 1955. Courtesy of Anaheim
History Room, Anaheim Public Library (P7298), and © The Walt
Disney Company.

land but also to its financing. In part because the project was so novel,
Disney had difficulty finding investors. He turned to leading American
companies as one source of capital, leasing them space for exhibits that
would serve the purposes of corporate public relations, and thereby he
inaugurated a lasting partnership between the theme park and big business.[23] But industry did not provide enough additional capital, particularly as costs skyrocketed from an early estimate of $4 million to a
total expenditure of $17 million by opening day (see Figure 8). Con-
sequently, after he had invested much of his personal wealth, Walt Disney turned to television for help. In the spring of 1954 he became "the
first leading Hollywood producer to enter into formal alliance with
television" by striking a deal with the American Broadcasting Company
(ABC) that raised $5 million to be used in building the park. ABC,
struggling to catch up to the other major networks, in return received
a 35 percent interest in the theme park as well as a promise from Disney

to produce a weekly series. Also titled "Disneyland," the program began in 1954 and conformed closely to Disney's aspirations for a vehicle to publicize his other creations. It played some of the studio's backlog of motion pictures, promoted new feature films, and broadcast "constant bulletins" on the progress of construction in Anaheim. Disneyland truly was "the playground television built."[24]

Considering the contemporary estimate of Disney's deal with ABC as "the most important development to date in relations between the old and the new mass entertainment form," it was fitting that the preview of Disneyland on July 17, 1955, became a historic moment for television. The network assigned "the greatest concentration of television equipment and operating personnel ever assembled in one place" to the show.[25] The climax of a year of promotion on Disney's weekly series for ABC, the public debut of the park was given an hour and a half of live, prime-time coverage. Art Linkletter, Bob Cummings, and "Ronnie" Reagan hosted the show, which featured numerous Hollywood celebrities among the estimated 25,000 guests.[26]

The staging of the opening of Disneyland demonstrated Hollywood's lack of experience with made-for-television events. In dedicating the park, Walt Disney promised that "Disneyland will never be completed." He meant that he would continuously improve and update the park, but his statement may well have been taken in quite another sense, for Disneyland was only about three-quarters finished on opening day. The long-standing commitment to a live broadcast forced the company to invite customers to Disneyland, but the park was not in fact ready for them. Parking lots and roads could not be prepared in time to accommodate the bumper-to-bumper traffic. Women lost high heels to asphalt that had been poured just hours before. There were no drinking fountains and too few restrooms. These and other problems— long lines, mechanical breakdowns, unsightly grounds, ongoing construction—plagued the park during its initial months. As a result, many reporters at first panned Disneyland.[27]

Although the park steadily put its early shortcomings behind it and carefully cultivated the goodwill of the press, the difficulties of opening day in some ways foretold its future. Selecting the grounds for Disneyland had been a matter of finding a spot at once isolated from intensively built-up areas and yet convenient to developing roadways and subdivisions. Located amid orange groves in a district regarded primarily as a rural buffer for Los Angeles, the Anaheim site initially suited Disney's purposes. After opening day, however, Disneyland continually had to adjust to the urban problems it had itself created. Success presented management with the difficult task of expanding without seeming to expand, of adapting Disneyland to its changing surroundings without seeming to change it. In spatial terms, Disneyland had to remain a suburban enclave even as it became urbanized. It needed to coexist with congestion outside its earthen wall or "berm," as the company called it, and with development that conflicted with the character of the park. Inside, it had to preserve its orderliness as it added attractions, updated or replaced others, and admitted the steadily growing crowds.

Disneyland's popularity severely tested the magical qualities in its design. In six months of operation the park attracted its first million customers; within three years it had become "the biggest tourist attraction in California and the West, among the biggest in the nation."[28] By the early 1960s the annual number of visitors hovered around 5 million, and in 1970 it topped 10 million for the first time. In the same period, the average length of a day's visit grew from less than five hours to about eight hours. To serve so many customers for so long, the number of employees at Disneyland climbed from 1,280 in 1955 to 6,200 in 1970.[29]

The designers of the theme park were unprepared for such large and devoted crowds. In fact, having spent nearly all their money by opening day, they hired their first musicians and vendors on short-term contracts because they could not afford to guarantee them steady employment.[30] But they soon recognized that they needed more entertainment and rides in order to keep customers happily occupied. Thus, almost immediately, began the elaboration of Disneyland during which the number of major attractions (not including free exhibits and shows) grew from twenty-two in 1955 to fifty-two by 1967 (see Figures 9 and 10). The park also added two new theme areas to the original five—New Orleans Square in 1966 and Bear Country in 1972.[31]

Publicists explained that these additions were made in order to give the customers what they wanted, and Walt Disney himself consistently denied that he reinvested in the park primarily to increase revenues.[32] But in fact the additions proved profitable in a number of ways. Jack Sayer, the general manager of Disneyland, confided in 1958 that Walt Disney's personal tax situation virtually forced him to reinvest earnings in the park. Moreover, each new feature provided management with a new marketing opportunity. In 1959, for instance, promoters touted the addition of the first working monorail line in the United States; a roller coaster called the Matterhorn Bobsleds, which climbed and descended a mountain scaled at one-hundredth the size of the original Alp; and a fleet of "atomic" submarines. Such publicity paid off handsomely, partly because it reminded customers that Disneyland offered them something different every time they returned. Each major new ride, it was estimated, "boosted attendance" by 10 percent during its initial year of operation, so that "revenues increased more than proportionately to the added capital."[33]

The popularity of each new feature reaffirmed the success of Disneyland, but it also contradicted the designers' expectation that the added attractions would occupy customers who would otherwise be waiting in line. New "adventures" contributed to congestion in the park both by consuming more space and by creating new queues of waiting customers. Promoters tried to put the best light upon such growth, as the number of acres inside the berm grew from about sixty in 1955 to seventy in 1968 and about eighty by the late 1980s.[34] Yet both the operators and the customers of the theme park were aware of the threat of congestion.

Walt Disney himself expressed concern that Disneyland had grown too crowded. Having seen expansion beyond the original acreage set aside for it, he concluded, "I've got to build down now, and up."[35] Some new rides, such as Pirates of the Caribbean, were located beneath ground level, while others, such as Space Mountain, joined the Matterhorn Bobsleds in the sky over the park. Vertical development, however, did not entirely ameliorate the crowding, as more than one observer remarked. A newspaper columnist described the increasingly cluttered park as a "dizzying" place, and another writer suggested that its crowds imperiled fantasy by interfering with visitors' ability to suspend their disbelief.[36]

Yet the congestion at Disneyland did not drive customers away. In 1965 one journalist summarized a widespread impression by saying that although Disneyland then covered only about 65 acres, "every inch of space is used in the most tasteful manner imaginable. It is not crowded."[37] In ten years the theme park had become appreciably more urbanized than it had been on opening day, but for at least three reasons it was still not generally experienced as a chaotic or overwhelming place. First, compared to the world outside, and especially to increasingly unwieldy Los Angeles, Disneyland seemed to be a manageable environment. Second, customers, with guidance from Disneyland publicists, proved remarkably adept at screening out flaws in the theme park and focusing on its virtues. Third, that Disneyland remained an orderly place in visitors' minds attested to its designers' ability to create

Figures 9 and 10. Disneyland grew dramatically between 1955 and 1967.

Figure 9. In the first days after the park opened, the rural ambience persisted
in Anaheim, the parking lot remained uncrowded, the Santa Ana
Freeway was still under construction, and an ample amount of
open space remained within the berm. Courtesy of Anaheim
History Room, Anaheim Public Library (Aerial #32), and © The
Walt Disney Company.

an environment that minimized urban problems. Their success was
hardly accidental. Those who built Disneyland specifically planned it in
opposition to selected urban models. The park could claim to be "the
happiest place on earth" only if it did not repeat the flaws that characterized American cities, particularly those back East.

A Controlled Western Environment

Conceived largely in reaction against the confusion and
disorder perceived at amusement parks and world's fairs, the design of
Disneyland conveyed a none-too-subtle critique of its predecessors. In

Figure 10. A dozen years later, cars frequently filled the enlarged parking lot, larger crowds found many more attractions, and Disneyland underwent continual redevelopment—here growing to incorporate two new attractions, the above-ground Haunted Mansion (left of center) and the subterranean Pirates of the Caribbean (center), both in the recently added New Orleans Square. Courtesy of Anaheim History Room, Anaheim Public Library (P13029), and © The Walt Disney Company.

words that echoed Walt Disney's own estimate, *New York Times* reporter Gladwin Hill explained that the Anaheim park marked a distinct departure from "the traditionally raucous and ofttimes shoddy amusement-park field." It had been "designed not as a place where anyone would go casually to take a roller-coaster ride or buy a hot dog, but as the goal of a family adventure." Disneyland indeed encouraged little that could be considered casual. It meant to attract customers for an entire day of amusement, during which they would never become distracted or lost or bored. It proposed to dispense with the spatial disorganization, "surly attendants," unkempt grounds, and "'carny show' hard sell" that reportedly prevailed at conventional amusement parks. Most important, Disneyland subordinated the identities of individual rides, exhibits, and other features to the larger, thematically coordinated environment. The result, Hill summarized, was "less an amusement park than a state of mind."[38]

Advocates of Disneyland regularly illuminated its distinct virtues by contrasting it with Coney Island, New York City's venerable amusement district. The best known amusement park in the country before 1955, Coney Island dated from the previous century, and thus comparisons between it and Disneyland were not entirely fair. For one thing, they neglected to point out that in the late nineteenth century, Coney Island itself had represented an attempt to reform and improve upon contemporary forms of commercial recreation. For another, Coney Island had suffered significant physical decline since 1900, partly as a result of the rise of radio and movies, so that by the mid-twentieth century it had lost much of its original luster. This latter defect, however, only made it all the more useful as a point of contrast to Disneyland. When Walt Disney visited the dilapidated Coney Island in the course of planning his theme park, he recoiled from its "tawdry rides and hostile employees." The New York amusement park, others added, had a "diffuse, unintegrated layout," in contrast to Disneyland's thematic, coordinated design. As a result, customers became less engaged at Coney Island, and they spent less money there. To cap it off, observers regarded the Coney Island grounds as dirty and its patrons as rude.[39]

Coney Island made an ideal foil. It represented the outmoded past of outdoor recreation while Disneyland stood for the future. Or, phrased in regional terms, Coney Island symbolized the East and its major metropolis. It belonged to an environment of extreme temperatures, dense traffic, and industrial "smoke and dirt," all of which were regarded as anathema to Disneyland. Moreover, some designers of Disneyland doubted whether those who resided in such an environment—that is, the kind of people who patronized Coney Island—could truly appreciate such a western phenomenon as Disneyland. When the idea of building another theme park in the New York City area was proposed to Walt Disney, he rejected it, in large part because he doubted that New Yorkers would embrace anything like the Anaheim park. "He said *that* audience is not responsive. That city is different."[40]

The Disney organization was later to change its mind about New York City and the eastern audience, but it nonetheless continued to take upon itself the mission of surpassing the East by creating improved urban environments that both reflected and effected a better type of citizen. This sense of superiority was reiterated in 1966 upon the completion of New Orleans Square, the first theme zone in the park to be based on an urban model. During the opening ceremonies, when the mayor of New Orleans praised the area by saying, "It looks just like home," Walt Disney rather smugly replied, "Well, I'd say it's a lot cleaner."[41]

Disneyland's improvements over eastern models were expected to appeal to a western, rather than an eastern, audience. As early as 1953 Walt Disney stressed that his theme park would "be a place for California to be at home, to bring its guests, to demonstrate its faith in the future." Its designers also described certain portions of the park as particularly well suited to greater Los Angeles. The miniature, gasoline-powered cars of Autopia in Tomorrowland were initially publicized as "the perfect place" to teach local children how to "drive safely on the rapidly growing freeway system."[42]

Disneyland offered a California-based critique not only of specific eastern urban models but also of certain flaws in American civilization that eastern cities had helped to create. Coney Island's New York, in the eyes of Disney, was perhaps no more than the most extreme case of a broad national malaise: people had lost all sense of spontaneity and play. The average citizen, he said, "is a victim of a civilization whose ideal is the unbotherable, poker-faced man and the attractive, unruffled woman."[43] One of Walt Disney's closest associates, designer John Hench, attributed these unnatural traits to the danger and chaos of urban life:

[I]n modern cities you have to defend yourself constantly and you go counter to everything that we've learned from the past. You tend to isolate yourself from other people. . . . You tend to be less aware. You tend to be more withdrawn. This is counter-life . . . you really die a little. . . . I think we need something to counteract what modern society—cities have done to us.[44]

Disneyland was intended as an antidote to the perceived urban malaise of the day. In being transported to some not very well defined golden age—perhaps the period 1900–1910 as presented along Main Street U.S.A., or the pioneer era as suggested in Frontierland—and in touring "lands" devoted to fantasy, adventure, and the future, visitors could escape their unnatural present day cares, "drop their defenses," and "become more *like themselves.*"[45]

Advocates of Disneyland felt confident that it could recapture and nurture a better human nature. The keys to creating such a magical place lay in controlling the movements of people and in managing their interactions with each other and with their surroundings. The Disney organization saw the challenges of organizing space in ways that controlled the flow of the crowds and of building overall themes and messages into the design as a job neither for city planners nor for traditional amusement park operators, both of whom were all too often responsible for settings that seemed disorganized and unfriendly. Rather, it was a task for moviemakers like themselves, people already trained to cue audiences from scene to scene and to entertain them by telling stories. Their plan was for Disneyland to be a three-dimensional extension of Walt Disney's films, complete with many of the characters featured in both his animated and live-action movies. It would have rides like other amusement parks, but rather than starring in the park, they would play supporting roles that contributed to the development of overall themes within Disneyland. And these themes would entail for customers the same suspension of disbelief required of moviegoers.[46]

The skills and stories brought to bear in Anaheim had been developed and mastered at the Disney studios in Burbank, where the theme park was planned. In order to develop commercial opportunities outside of motion pictures, in 1953 Walt Disney had created WED Enterprises, Inc., which became "the designing and engineering arm for Disneyland." WED recruited employees from the Disney studios and from other Hollywood studios, in particular Twentieth Century Fox. "Movie studio art directors" thus became the chief designers of Disneyland, and they were supported by architects, writers, special-effects artists, and others who had worked in the motion picture industry.[47]

The specialists employed by WED Enterprises applied their moviemaking skills to the three-dimensional setting of the theme park. One technique they used was that of scaling down the size of the park and its various features. Disneyland seemed a cozy and friendly place, particularly to children, because it was somewhat less than life-size. The trains running around the park on narrow-gauge track, the horseless carriages on Main Street, and the *Mark Twain* paddle-wheel steamboat were all built at approximately five-eighths scale.[48] Designers also used the technique of forced perspective, "a device well known in motion picture circles," which tricked the eye into seeing structures as taller than they really were. Sleeping Beauty Castle in Fantasyland and the Matterhorn Bobsleds roller coaster, both proportionally larger at the bottom and smaller toward the top, generated an illusion of greater height. Stores and offices along Main Street U.S.A. were scaled at about 90 percent of full size on the first floor, 80 percent on the second floor, and 60 to 70 percent on the third floor.[49] The overall effect of the built environment was impressive but not intimidating.

Crucial to the effectiveness of the Disneyland environment were the story lines built into it. At three separate levels—the individual rides, the several lands, and the overall park—designers stressed selected themes, most of which derived from Disney films. In 1948, for instance, Walt Disney began making "True Life Adventure" films about nature, and these formed the bases for attractions in Adventureland. A popular television series about Davy Crockett inspired keelboat rides in Frontierland; the Disney film *Grand Canyon* provided the beginnings of the Grand Canyon Diorama seen by riders on the Disneyland and Santa Fe Railroad; and the idea of a roller coaster based on the Matterhorn stemmed from *Third Man on the Mountain*, a Walt Disney film about the European peak.[50]

As if making movies, the designers of Disneyland stressed the transition from scene to scene. Rather than clash, the ideas built into the various zones or rides presented "an orderly sequence of messages."[51] Attractions relating to the historic American West were grouped together in Frontierland, and images and figures from fairy tales came together in Fantasyland, which contained the greatest concentration of characters from Disney's classic animated films. Actors costumed as Mickey Mouse, Donald Duck, and other cartoon creations roamed throughout the park, but they were found most often on Main Street U.S.A., where they helped to welcome customers.

By providing a familiar and predictable environment while minimizing the number of distractions or interruptions, Disneyland designers intended to reassure customers. In this regard they followed Disney movies very closely. Walt Disney took great pride in the ability of his films to emphasize the clear triumph of good over evil. He desired neither ambiguity nor contradiction in his motion pictures, and he resented those arty and academic types who insisted on seeing the darker side of the stories he told.[52] The Anaheim theme park similarly tried to present an undilutedly rosy view of the world; contradiction or confusion were qualities the planners of Disneyland associated with the defective, poorly planned, conventional amusement park.[53] They believed that Disneyland offered an enriched version of the real world, but not an escapist or an unreal version. To achieve "Disney Realism," they explained, "we program out all the negative, unwanted elements and program in the positive elements." The result, they insisted, was not a distorted reality but a recaptured one: "[W]e've taken and purified the statement so it says what it was intended to," asserted John Hench.[54]

Disneyland was "much more real" than life in general, it was argued further, because it evoked the truer human nature of the past, before mid-twentieth-century urban malaise had set in. Walt Disney himself explained this in a possibly apocryphal conversation with evangelist Billy Graham. Wounded when Graham said he had at Disneyland "a nice fantasy," Disney replied:

You know the fantasy isn't here. This is very real. . . . The park is reality. The people are natural here; they're having a good time; they're communicating. This is what people really are. The fantasy is—out there, outside the gates of Disneyland, where people have hatreds and people have prejudices. It's not really real![55]

The contrast between conditions inside the theme park, where everything seemed to work, and conditions outside, where nothing seemed to work, led many to conclude that the world ought to model itself as closely as possible after Disneyland. And publicists for the park, besides billing it as an escape from the troubled world of the present, indeed promoted it as a model for society to follow. Despite its implicit critique of the present, Disneyland remained confident of Americans' ability—and especially the ability of businesses that were creating new technologies—to pave the way for a better age. Believing that "mankind could lick any problem, if the right information was available at the right time," Disney officials viewed the theme area of Tomorrowland as a demonstration "that tomorrow's world can be achieved today through the imaginative use of current technology."[56] In 1956 one Disneyland film heralded "the theme of progress" by depicting the "Atomic Age in Action"; in the mid-1960s a ride simulating a 1970 moon voyage ended with the "captain" telling his passengers that "Smog was eliminated in North America some time ago."[57]

Prominent American corporations, eager to be associated with Disney and to pronounce to their public how they would improve the world of the future, sponsored their own displays in the style of Capitalist Realism. The Monsanto Chemical Company built a Hall of Chemistry for Tomorrowland when it first opened. Two years later it erected an all-plastic House of the Future which contained such features as a microwave oven, an ultrasonic dishwasher, and "electronically controlled modular bathrooms."[58] The General Electric Company planned exhibits to dramatize progress through electricity. First in unrealized proposals for an "Edison Square" and then in the Carousel of Progress, G.E. identified itself with a future of spaceships landing on Venus, interplanetary television, electrically powered rapid transit, nuclear power, and enclosed, climate-controlled downtowns.[59] Observers took such predictions seriously. When Vice President Richard Nixon officiated at the opening of the Disneyland Monorail in 1959, he joined reporters in viewing it as a plausible solution to "grave traffic problems in urban areas."[60]

Promoters of Disneyland treasured such publicity because it added a measure of seriousness to their creation. It suggested that the theme park provided not merely amusement but a model for the future. But they also eventually realized that their predictions became dated rather quickly. Of all the zones inside the park, Tomorrowland gave management the most problems, because it continuously grew obsolete.[61] Between 1964 and 1967 the company spent a widely advertised $20 million to demolish and rebuild Tomorrowland. In the reconstruction it de-emphasized atomic power and space travel.[62] About the only element that remained constant from the start in Tomorrowland was Autopia's miniature highways, which expanded quickly to meet customer demand. Billed as the "the freeway of the future" when it opened for business in 1955, Autopia's enduring popularity resulted less from its ability to predict tomorrow than from its ability to provide youngsters with a dose of the automotive world that seemed so pervasive outside the gates of Disneyland.[63]

The fate of Tomorrowland loomed large because it dramatized Disneyland's lack of control over the future. The success of the theme park was predicated on complete mastery of its world, but the future refused to cooperate, and thus it compelled the theme park to make constant adjustments. By undermining the messages presented inside the park, the future could smuggle contradiction and ambiguity into Disneyland.

The purity and coordination of themes faced two other critical threats. One was nature, and the other was human nature, as embodied in the park's employees and visitors. Representations of the natural world were crucial to many parts of the Anaheim theme park, but they had to be carefully conceived and controlled. For Adventureland's Jungle Cruise ride, for instance, Disney designers built not an accurate copy of nature but a "Hollywood jungle" that conformed to people's untutored expectations for the setting. Yet instead of admitting that the net effect was unnatural, WED designers described their work as "a *concentrated form* of nature."[64]

In the minds of the studio artists who designed Disneyland, a

Figure 11. Disneyland's mastery of the environment began in 1954 with the bulldozing of orange and walnut groves. Starting tabula rasa, the creators of the theme park recreated and reinvented nature in Anaheim according to their own Hollywood script. Courtesy of Anaheim History Room, Anaheim Public Library (P1160).

version of nature that was rigidly distilled and controlled was essential to their ability to present an undiluted, purified experience to customers. They spoke of unmanaged nature as a source of "accidents," rife with potential "contradictions" to the messages of the theme park.[65] Like the future, it was something that they could not entirely control—but not for lack of trying. Anaheim had been chosen as the home for Disneyland because it offered nearly ideal weather for a theme park: rain, smog, and excessive heat were minimal. In addition, Disney appreciated the flatness of the site, because he wanted to manufacture his own hills and valleys. The company bulldozed and burned the orange, walnut, and eucalyptus trees on the parcel, creating a blank slate for themselves (see Figure 11). "No distinguishable landmark remained," one Anaheim official remembered; "the neighborhood was obliterated."[66]

The operators of Disneyland exerted precise control over the ecology within the park as well. By 1980 they had installed seven bodies of water (lakes, rivers, waterfalls) using 18.5 million gallons and requiring a comprehensive mechanical system for recycling and water treatment. When air pollution became severe, Disney officials converted internal-combustion engines to natural gas and, during periodic smog alerts, even closed some rides. They also continuously replanted flowers, trees, and lawns in the park, lending to Disneyland an artificial changing of the seasons that was much more pronounced than in surrounding parts of southern California.[67]

In the hands of Disney's special-effects experts, mechanization offered another important tool for managing nature. Using a technology dubbed Audio-Animatronics, Disneyland brought film-style animation to three-dimensional creatures in the park. Both in the various rides incorporating animals and in displays such as the Tiki Room, the theme park presented lifelike figures that moved and made noise. The same technology enlivened Great Moments with Mr. Lincoln, an exhibit wherein a robot portrayed Walt Disney's favorite president. Management praised such robots as superior to real-life animals and actors because they would "never forget a line or miss a cue." They provided a completely predictable show at a relatively low, fixed cost.[68]

Machines promised to minimize those accidents and contradictions that can result from the capriciousness of nature. But human nature proved even more unpredictable, and robots could not supplant all people in the park. Disneyland required thousands of employees. "Like the architecture, landscaping and other major elements," however, these people had to fit perfectly into the thematically organized settings and activities without causing contradictions or accidents.[69] To achieve this required an immense and precise program of hiring, training, and supervising workers. It entailed the development of an elaborate set of uniforms for each theme area, the publication of a plethora of handbooks and inspirational literature for employees, and, by 1960, the establishment of a rigorous course of training. Workers in the magic kingdom would be programmed as thoroughly as possible.

Walt Disney had noticed the lack of satisfactory service at Coney Island and other amusement parks. In 1955, however, he did not have enough money to hire and train all his own employees, so other established companies were recruited to sponsor and staff exhibits, and vendors were hired to run many of the park's concessions and provide security. Disney soon regarded such use of outsiders as mistaken, however, and asserted his organization's control over all concessions as well as over the selection, education, and supervision of all workers, including those employed by his corporate co-investors. "I couldn't have outside help and still get over my idea of hospitality," he later recalled. "So now we recruit and train every one of our employees."[70] In order to educate both new and continuing employees in the Disney way, management created the University of Disneyland. It taught the history of Walt Disney and the park and prepared trainees to answer all sorts of customers' questions. It offered arithmetic courses for people who had to handle money, and public speaking for those who met the customers. It also prepared textbooks for virtually every type of job in the park, thus standardizing each employee's activities.[71]

Highly selective policies for recruiting workers further shaped the work force. Disneyland mainly employed attractive, white, young men and women who could easily be assimilated into the company's designs. It preferred relatively mature "college students, graduates and teachers," and not just because they tended to be available to work on a weekend or seasonal basis. Those involved in education exemplified the type most desirable in managers' eyes—"intelligent, aggressive nonprofessionals who could learn rapidly without having to unlearn the mistakes of past generations." Disneyland wanted employees who liked working with people and who responded well to training. It generally avoided hiring those with "previous experience in an amusement park, fair, or circus," believing that they had been tainted by association with inferior forms of commercial recreation. It took great care to recruit employees who possessed the "Disneyland look" and accepted the "Disneyland way."[72]

The rules governing workers' behavior, like those that guided the park's physical design, evoked the motion-picture industry. Employee manuals spoke of work at Disneyland as a continuous form of live theater. The park itself was called "the show," and its employees were reminded constantly that they were in "show business." Performances at Disneyland began in the "outer lobby" or parking lot, passed through the "inner lobby" or main entrance, and culminated on "center stage" along Main Street U.S.A. Upon entering Disneyland, employees were to consider themselves actors and actresses, whether they worked "backstage" in service areas or "onstage" in direct contact with customers.[73]

Disneyland management instructed its workers that their ultimate purpose was that of "show people throughout history": to "create happiness" for customers, for the theme park had brought into being "a new industry with *happiness* as its principal product."[74] To meet production quotas, workers needed to understand the true nature of their job. Creating happiness was "a highly disciplined type of work. It is all service to others." It required a great deal of deference: "At Disneyland, the *guest* is *always* right, and we are quick to point out our own mistakes to guests and supervisors." So that employees would not come to resent such subservience, Disneyland reminded them that customers deserved and expected precisely that kind of treatment. "The Guest pays Us to make him happy." But, in turn, service at Disneyland offered rewards beyond a mere paycheck. University of Disneyland manuals explained that by making others happy the employees made themselves happy: "Creating fun is our work; and our work creates fun—for us and our guests."

Those who trained and supervised employees at Disneyland assumed that they had brought into being a new and fulfilling kind of labor.[75] But in fact their "actors" and "actresses" closely resembled the white-collar, other-directed, organization men and women described by social critics during the 1950s. "When white-collar people get jobs," C. Wright Mills had argued, "they sell not only their time and energy but their personalities as well. They sell by the week or month their smiles and their kindly gestures, and they must practice the prompt repression of resentment and aggression."[76] David Riesman concurred: those whose product was personality, he wrote, aimed both to evoke "some observable response" and "to conciliate and manipulate a variety of people." Doing so often required such extensive acting that "the other-directed person tends to become merely his succession of roles and encounters."[77] Yet according to the ethos of the era, "[b]usiness is supposed to be fun," both for employees and for their customers. Service provided important psychic rewards. As William H. Whyte explained, managers were encouraged to think that "[b]usiness is *people*, and when you help people to rise to their fullest you make them fulfill themselves, you create more and better goods for more people, you make happiness."[78] In other words, as one Disney spokesman explained, you make them more *"like themselves."*

Of course, the organization itself was essential to all this fulfillment. Walt Disney and the University of Disneyland echoed the maxims of the "organization man" when they spelled out for employees the need to display a certain type of personality and to create happiness for customers. The "organization way of life," as William H. Whyte explained, assumed that "groups are the sources of creativity" and that individuals could achieve satisfaction on the job only through the group. Disneyland employees were similarly instructed that the company needed their efforts as a group, not as individuals.[79] Success occurred solely through "teamwork": "Your every effort lies in your ability to work with others in our cast" (or, as Whyte put it, "working with others through others for others"). Like other exponents of the organization-man philosophy, Disney wanted no "geniuses," and particularly none of the "highbrow" variety. "We all think alike in the ultimate pattern," he explained.[80] Disneyland handbooks told new employees, "We hope that you enjoy thinking our way."

Ironically, the extensive quotations from Walt Disney which permeated every employee manual clearly implied that there *was* in fact a governing genius. Walt Disney's words always stressed the importance of the organization, but the organization itself bore his name and his imprint. "Everything here is a team effort," Disney said, but the team succeeded in large part because it tended to "think as Disney does" and "see things the way he does."[81] Invoking the wisdom of the revered founder as a kind of scripture intended to instruct and motivate employees served both to glorify Walt Disney and to solidify his organization, even after his death in 1966.

Besides inculcating workers with proper respect for their employer, Disneyland handbooks introduced them to a distinct corporate culture. The park had its own terminology. Employees were to refer to themselves as "hosts and hostesses" and, because "'customer' is a bad word," they were to speak of visitors to Disneyland as "guests." There was to be no crowd at Disneyland, only an "audience"; no uniforms, only "costumes"; no jobs, only "roles"; no rides (because the term connoted a conventional amusement park), only "attractions" and "adventures." Verbal spontaneity was to be minimized. Those who talked with customers in the park "have to be able to learn a script and stick to it," explained Disneyland executive Dick Nunis. "Any ad libs must be approved before use."[82] In other words, there were to be no ad libs.

The managers of Disneyland used language to reinforce a certain style of work. They insisted on an ostensibly egalitarian informality, appropriate to show business: "At Disneyland, we operate on a first name basis. . . . We believe that everyone in our organization is important. We soft-pedal job titles, and we feel that one activity is just as important as another." But Disneyland's informality did not extend to giving employees much flexibility in how they went about their work. They were expected "to give a pleasant, happy performance" always, with no variation in content. Customers were to receive "what Disney called 'the same consistent show'" on every occasion.[83] The theme park offered a studied casualness. Its trains, like all its rides and its employees, were to run exactly on time, but their passengers were not to feel harried.

The same sort of relaxed precision prevailed in the appearance of hosts and hostesses. Disneyland assigned color-coordinated costumes to its employees, and it expected them to adhere to explicit standards of personal grooming. "Into each life some conformity must fall," one handbook explained, "and quite a bit falls into yours when it comes to your 'stage' appearance." Employees were regularly advised, "Be yourself," but at the theme park their selves had to have a "neat and natural" or unadulterated look. Hosts and hostesses were expected to wear no more than modest amounts of jewelry and makeup, to sport conservative hairstyles and short sideburns, and never to wear beards, mustaches, heavy perfume, or casual shoes. All of this, of course, added to both the employees' and the customers' happiness: "We *feel* better when we look our *best*."[84]

Disneyland coached its employees to be as friendly as possible, to each other as well as to customers. It expected its workers to continue smiling even when they were off duty, since they never ceased to represent the organization. Working for Walt Disney, they were told, meant that their lives would constantly be "under close observation" by outsiders: "What you say and how you act reflects upon our entire organization." Employee manuals designated the workers' time away from the theme park as "off stage," but in fact all the world was Disney's stage, and his employees were expected to uphold company standards at all times.[85] It was only inside Disneyland that management strove to control physical nature. The quest to control the human nature of its employees, however, extended beyond the park's wall and into their personal lives.

To Soothe and to Sell: Managing Customers at Disneyland

Although Disneyland trained employees to treat the customer as if he or she were always right, its designers were convinced that the customer, at least upon entering the park, was not quite right and needed a little help from the employees and environment of Disneyland. Like workers inside the park, customers were seen as actors who shared the Disneyland stage. But it was up to the employees, the environment, and the publicists at Disneyland to make sure that visitors played their proper parts.[86] Disneyland intended that when customers left the park they would be more nearly right than when they came. And making the customers feel better proved profitable. Designers steadily refined the workings of the park, certain that better treatment of the customer translated into greater revenue.[87] Disneyland managed both to soothe and to sell at the same time; indeed, one could say that the act of consumption was part of the Disneyland therapy.

Park promoters saw the outside world as an unhappy place that drove people to the therapy of Disneyland. A year before opening day, Hollywood columnist Hedda Hopper explained that Walt Disney's "central aim is to take people from this tense, nerve-killing world of today into a dream one of yesterday and tomorrow." With so much seemingly so wrong with life, as John Hench reiterated two decades later, "Disneyland is symbolic that all is right with the world. There, the guest walks through an atmosphere of order and cleanliness and comes away feeling that things must be all right, after all."[88]

One purported key to Disneyland's curative powers was the identification of its designers with its audience. Walt Disney professed not to care about intellectual critics of his films. "Rather than being concerned with 'expressing' myself with obscure creative impressions," he explained, he made movies that provided the wholesome entertainment most Americans desired.[89] The park, like Disney movies, supposedly offered the people precisely what they wanted and needed; its designers tried to respond to its customers' preferences, both conscious and unconscious. "Whatever failed to meet the public need," as understood by the Disney organization, "was changed—replaced by a better idea."[90]

Disneyland allegedly succeeded because its designers, like good therapists, understood people better than they understood themselves. The task of the park's planners was not simply to entertain people but to improve them. This implied not simply reacting to the needs of customers but actually inducing them to think and behave in the way that Disney knew was best for them. John Hench explained that Walt Disney knew how to make people "feel better about themselves" because he could make them "believe about themselves the way he felt about them." If Disneyland could communicate effectively, its guests would *"respond correctly."*[91]

The park's design and employees spoke most directly to the audience, but guests' schooling in the Disney way began long before they arrived in Anaheim. The company assembled a powerful promotional machine that prepared visitors by bombarding the country with information about Disneyland. Advertising campaigns probably had their greatest success in defining the park during its early days; in later years the majority of park business came from repeat customers whose understanding derived in large part from direct personal experience of the park.[92] Nevertheless, Disneyland publicity continued to convey the company line to potential visitors and, in so doing, illuminated some of the Disney thinking about customers.

Advertisements for Disneyland in many respects paralleled the ideas designed into the theme park and impressed upon employees. There emerged an overall sameness in messages about the park; slogans coined even before the park was built were reiterated year after year by publicists.[93] The consistency of the phrasing exemplified the effort to eliminate contradictions and distractions in conveying ideas.

Promoters reached both near and far. They advertised incessantly in southern California newspapers. They published magazines such as *Disneyland Holiday* and *Vacationland* and distributed them to motels and hotels throughout the Southwest in an attempt to reach travelers on their way to Los Angeles. To publicize Disneyland's tenth anniversary in 1965, the company invited travel editors and reporters from around the country to visit the theme park, the studios, and WED Enterprises.[94]

No doubt the most effective promotional medium of all was television, as Walt Disney had foreseen. His various weekly programs, including "The Mickey Mouse Club" and "The Wonderful World of Color," regularly highlighted new developments and special events at the theme park. One critic complained in 1965 that a show devoted to Disneyland's tenth anniversary amounted to little more than an hour-long commercial for the theme park.[95] Most people were not so annoyed by Disney programs, but they agreed that they were effective at publicizing the park. As one parent explained: "Disneyland may be just another damned amusement park, but to my kids it is the Taj Mahal, Niagara Falls, Sherwood Forest and Davy Crockett all rolled into one. After years of sitting in front of a television set, the youngsters are sure it's a fairyland before they even get there."[96]

Observers often spoke as if television primarily influenced youngsters, who then persuaded their parents to take them to Disneyland. This idea agreed with the notion, encouraged by publicists, that the theme park was for children, or at least for the "young at heart." And indeed Disneyland had to be, in some sense, child-oriented if it was to offer relief from the adult troubles of the outside world. But, as one newspaper columnist pointed out, Disneyland was "a children's wonderland artfully geared to adult tastes."[97] After all, it was the adults who most needed the relief. Even more important, it was not the children but their parents who decided to take the trip, who drove the cars, and who paid the costs. And it was the adults who most appreciated the park's nostalgia and its allusions to classic Disney movies. Parents, more than kids, saw Disneyland as an ideal place for their children's and their own amusement. Youngsters' enthusiastic response was no doubt genuine, but it was only a confirmation of what parents had led them to expect.

Walt Disney had grasped this economic and psychological reality from the start. Shortly before the park opened he predicted that 80 percent of its customers would be adults, and in the first five years adults did outnumber children by four to one.[98] Disney often reminded people that he had first thought of a theme park because he had been bored in a conventional amusement park. He declared simply, "We don't design for children. . . . If the adults like it, the children will like it."[99]

Disneyland's advertisements frankly appealed to adults. Publicists during late 1955 stressed that "Smog-Free Disneyland" was "Easy to REACH! Easy to PARK! Easy to ENJOY!" Two years later, ads urged fathers to "become a hero in your home" by taking the family to Disneyland. The following year, at the dawn of the space age, publicists told fathers: "Don't promise them the moon . . . take them there!" In doing so, fathers were assured, they would improve relations with their children: "Disneyland, USA; Dedicated to the Happiness of Your Family."[100] By the late 1950s it had become a cliché that Disneyland catered more to parents than to children.[101]

Extensive publicity not only prepared visitors for Disneyland. It targeted a particular kind of customer—primarily the family-oriented middle class. The park catered to those who owned televisions, watched movies, subscribed to newspapers, took vacations, and accepted the domestic values of mainstream America. It promoted special nights for seniors graduating from high school (as opposed to dropouts) and for couples out on dates (rather than singles or same-sex groups). Disneyland generally welcomed other kinds of customers, too, provided they could afford the cost of admission; but once inside the park they would be expected to conform to the middle-class, family-oriented mores scripted by its designers.

The entrance to Disneyland continued the selection and preparation of customers. From the start of planning, designers had sought a means of ensuring a select crowd. Before construction costs became so high as to require a significant entrance fee, one early official recalled, "[t]he *only* reason for *any* price was to keep undesirables out." The cost of admission for adults grew from twenty-five cents in later 1954 to one dollar in 1955, two dollars in 1965, and five dollars by 1980.[102] The costs of rides, food, and merchandise, not to mention travel for those from outside southern California, grew correspondingly. As many observers commented, Disneyland was not an inexpensive proposition. The cost of a visit no doubt helps to explain the air of prosperity Disneyland's clientele displayed. Management reminded the other companies that participated in the theme park that their audience belonged "primarily in the middle and upper income brackets . . . the heart of the consumer market for major corporations."[103]

Disney preferred to attract people with ample money to spend, but over the years increasing care was taken about when and where that money changed hands. In the early days customers paid to park their cars, paid to gain admission at the main gate, and then paid inside the park for tickets to each ride. This system proved troublesome for a number of reasons. On days with heavy attendance, the park did not reap maximum profits, because people were waiting in lines when they could have been spending money on other attractions.[104] Besides, they patronized the larger, more expensive rides to the neglect of the smaller and cheaper ones. Finally, as one veteran of Disneyland explained, the continuous exchange of cash presented "a psychologically bad situation."[105] The sense of constantly spending money fostered complaints that the park was too expensive.

The operators of Disneyland soon countered these problems by rating each ride according to its size and excitement (A rides were cheapest and tamest and C rides most expensive, until D and E attractions were built), and then selling at the main entrance discounted books of tickets that contained some coupons for each category of ride. Visitors paid one lump sum at the start and did not have the unpleasant sensation of digging into their pockets for each adventure. Moreover, because they had already paid for tickets to smaller rides they were more willing to try them, if only to get their money's worth, thus easing the pressure at bigger attractions. And Disneyland received upfront a single substantial sum from many customers on even the busiest days, thus protecting itself against shortfalls resulting from long lines and slow turnover. Some (but not all) visitors saved their unused tickets for return trips, but of course they would have to pay general admission all over again. This whole system was further refined in 1982, when Disneyland did away with all single tickets, ticket books, and categories of rides. All customers now purchased "passports" for $12.00 at the entrance, which entitled them both to all-day admission and to unlimited access to all major attractions in the park.[106] Numerous restaurants, stores, and arcades still dealt in cash or credit cards, but the primary exchange of money now occurred but once, at the entrance. Another "psychologically bad situation" had been banished from the park to the outside world where it belonged.

The main entrance to Disneyland filtered out both an unwanted set of feelings about the park and an undesirable kind of customer. The entrance permitted security personnel to scrutinize visitors to make sure that, like the hosts and hostesses onstage and backstage, they conformed to Disneyland's "good grooming code," as well as to ensure that nobody gained entrance who might cause problems for the park and its other customers. To "restrict undesirables" and generally intimidate troublemakers, Disneyland recruited a special type of security guard. Instead of hiring jaundiced ex-policemen, it sought out high school coaches and physical education teachers who were used to handling young people. It looked for men who stood at least six feet tall and weighed at least two hundred pounds. Such measures, one park spokesperson explained, were necessary to protect the "wholesome family"

Figure 12. Crowd management within Disneyland began at the main
entrance, shown at the bottom of this 1965 photograph, where
customers purchased tickets, passed through turnstiles, and
funneled into the park. Then Main Street U.S.A. took over,
guiding guests toward the hub at the center of Disneyland, from
which paths led into each of the other theme areas. Courtesy of
Anaheim History Room, Anaheim Public Library (P844) and ©
The Walt Disney Company.

orientation of the park. They also helped to ensure that even the most
desirable kind of customer did not respond "incorrectly" to the built
and human environment. In 1967 one anonymous official justified ban-
ning "hippies" from Disneyland as a measure to ensure the other guests'
good behavior: "If we allowed people in weird outfits into the park,
that might cause other patrons to make derogatory remarks, and that
could lead to trouble. So we avoid trouble by not letting the hippies
inside."[107]

The entrance to Disneyland thus performed several important functions (see Figure 12). It became the chief site of Disneyland's very profitable financial transactions. As the park's chief point of contact with

the outside world, it admitted those prosperous types who seemed most amenable to the therapy that Disneyland offered, while screening out those denizens of the outside world who either would not appreciate or might disrupt the atmosphere of the park as refuge. It also took care of certain unseemly tasks—security and commerce—to keep them from intruding upon the experience inside.

In addition to serving as the chief point of contact with the outside world, the entrance to the park was part of an internal system for monitoring the movement and mood of the audience. Other amusement parks, Disney had noticed, had more than one entrance and exit, which disrupted the even flow of crowds and prevented effective control over the influx and egress of customers. Disneyland, by contrast, had only a single path by which visitors came and went.[108] This route led to a system of circulation that, using moviemakers' cues, subtly guided people around the park. The system exposed visitors to as many attractions, restaurants, and shops as possible, without wearing them down, confronting them with difficult choices, or disorienting them. The major "rule," according to director of marketing Ed Ettinger, "is to figure out what could worry anybody, and remove it." Walt himself had promised that Disneyland would "be a place where you can't get lost or tired unless you want to."[109]

Within the pattern of Disneyland, one official explained, Main Street U.S.A. acted as "an entrance corridor" that "absorbs large masses of visitors in a short period of time" (see Figure 13). Customers moved along the route toward "a large hub from which the other 'lands' radiate out like spokes in a wheel." Each theme area had a major landmark— Sleeping Beauty Castle in Fantasyland, the Rocket to the Moon in Tomorrowland, the stern-wheel riverboat in Frontierland—that drew visitors farther along. Inside each theme area, smaller patterns of circulation kept the crowds headed in the right direction: "Each 'land' is easy to enter and easy to exit, because everything leads back to the central hub again. The result is a revelation to anyone who has ever experienced the disorientation and confusion built into world's fairs and other expositions."[110]

The management of lines inside Disneyland, like the layout of its walkways, was skillfully planned to keep customers moving, smiling, and spending. Designers would have liked to dispense with queues altogether, but they were a frequent fact of life in many parts of the park. The problem of waiting in line seemed so important, in fact, that designers addressed the question of getting customers into and out of a

Figure 13. Walt Disney stood at the foot of Main Street U.S.A. on opening
day in July 1955, watching a workman apply the finishing touches
to the park. The buildings along the walkway were designed to be
unintimidating, and at the end of the vista Sleeping Beauty Castle
served as a visual magnet to lure people into the park. © The Walt
Disney Company (857–530).

proposed new attraction before they worked out its many other details,
so that they could keep the lines to a minimum. Those people who did
have to stand in line were kept as calm as possible by "fences and rail-
ings which double back and forth in maze patterns, preventing crowding and without policing," and encouraging the "illusion of several
short, fast-moving lines instead of a single long one." Roaming entertainers, passing crowds, and a multitude of other sights and sounds also
distracted people from the tedium of waiting.[111]

The behavior of guests was influenced by the tremendous cleanliness
of the park, which discouraged littering. Furthermore, when hiring
performers the Disney organization did all that it could to uphold a
pristine image. In an effort to attract more youthful guests at night,
Disneyland scheduled its first rock music bands for the summer of
1965. But, as the director of entertainment explained, only "reasonably
scrubbed and barbered" musicians would be hired. "The long hair, sick

looking group just won't be booked." And in the same way that the park controlled the terminology used by its employees, it controlled the image of the bands' performances by insisting that they be called Humdingers instead of "rock 'n' roll shows." Once again, each aspect of the Disneyland environment was designed to elicit people's better instincts and thus to increase the likelihood that they would "respond correctly" to it.[112]

That Disneyland might control not only its customers' mood but also their behavior seemed crucial to its designers. The company often said that the guests at Disneyland, unlike the movie audience, had an active part to play. The park offered no mere "idle" or "vicarious" amusement but, rather, promised "actual physical involvement" in the show. One 1965 advertisement explained, "[Y]ou are an *active participant* in the fun, the imagination, the adventure and entertainment of Disneyland."[113] The psychological engagement of customers was crucial if the park was to succeed in improving its guests, John Hench explained. Visitors encountered assorted theatrical threats, but by overcoming them they learned how to have greater mastery over their own fears and gained the "reassurance of survival." Disney's theme park made people "feel better about themselves and they are better for it. He's given them a concept . . . that . . . offers a lot more life awareness, and well being. It does reduce fear I think, a great deal."[114]

Although Disney and his planners believed the fun provided in the park "had to be pointed toward some beneficial result that people were going to get,"[115] they were careful that the park not appear too highbrow for their guests' tastes. "Culture will kill you," warned Jack Sayer, Disneyland's general manager. But Walt Disney, who felt he knew his customers better than they knew themselves, was determined to edify them for their own good—albeit in as painless a fashion as possible. As John Hench explained, "He said you can't let people know you're talking to them—you entertain them. You've got to understand how people work. They want entertainment—they don't want to be lectured to. You can teach them at the same time."[116]

Disneyland's attempt to improve customers set it apart once more from traditional amusement parks. The Coney Island of the late nineteenth and early twentieth centuries, although billed as a morally superior form of commercial recreation, had not functioned to edify its customers. It provided them instead with a release from their inhibitions, particularly those based on social status. Coney Island encouraged people to feel less constrained by the proprieties governing behavior between the classes. From its heterogeneous crowds it elicited "vulgar exuberance."[117] Contemporary critics, like Walt Disney in later years, objected to the vulgarity. In 1897 the landscape architect John C. Olmsted, stepson of the great Frederick Law Olmsted, incorporated this reaction into his opposition to including athletics, parades, and commercial amusements in "landscape parks." These urban spaces, he explained, were meant to allow the masses to

"enjoy beautiful natural scenery and to obtain occasional relief from the nervous strain due to the artificiality of city life." Park commissions should not cater to demands for cheap thrills of the "Coney Island" type from those who "do not know what is good for them when they go to a park to look for more exciting pleasures. They should be gradually and unconsciously educated to better uses of large public parks and not have their crude demands alone catered to."[118]

Walt Disney, in building for the masses an attraction that was decidedly not a landscape park, nonetheless adhered to the preferences of John C. Olmsted and his stepfather. Disneyland, too, represented a counterpoint to the malaise of city life as much as to the cheap thrills of Coney Island, and it similarly proposed to improve its guests without them knowing it. Furthermore, like parks landscaped by the Olmsteds, the Disneyland environment had been planned subtly to direct, control, and impress urban crowds without pandering to their baser instincts. Designers in both instances were as concerned with preparing audiences to receive cultural messages correctly as they were with the content of the messages being transmitted.[119]

In certain key respects, however, Disneyland departed from the example of its Olmstedian predecessors. For one thing, Disneyland catered to Westerners and expressed a regional state of mind regarding the city. For its magic, furthermore, it counted not on carefully controlled nature, which struck moviemakers as unreliable, but on technologies that improved upon the natural world. And it aimed at a different audience. During the last half of the nineteenth century, American culture had become somewhat bifurcated into "highbrow" and "lowbrow" segments, a fact with which landscape architects had to contend. Frederick Law Olmsted intended that New York's Central Park would "harmonize and refine" the lower orders of society.[120] But Disneyland did not necessarily intend even to admit the lower classes. It aimed instead to harmonize and refine the respectable middle classes with middlebrow culture.

Finally, whereas the Olmsteds wished to divorce their parks from the trappings of the business world, Disneyland was a commercial proposition from start to finish. In fact, by distancing guests from the anxieties and distractions of the outside world, by engaging them actively as members of the cast, and by encouraging reassurance and relaxation, Disneyland prepared its customers both consciously and unconsciously for the commercial information it transmitted. The managers of Disneyland described the audience to its corporate co-investors as "in a mood to enjoy themselves, to be impressed, and to carry away with them lasting impressions and memories." The park, in other words, lulled guests into being less critical; it suspended their disbelief in matters not only of fantasy but also of advertising and commerce. "In this environment, visitors are more susceptible to the messages of institutional sponsors."[121]

According to its designers, the carefully planned and managed environment of Disneyland performed two major tasks with regard to customers. First, it offered a sort of therapy by providing not only temporary escape from the outside world but also a more lasting sense of reassurance about the individual's ultimate fate in that world. Second, it earned revenue for management and its corporate co-sponsors by maximizing turnover and providing good publicity. Remarkably, the tasks of edifying, entertaining, and advertising seemed perfectly congruent. What seemed efficient from a business point of view was generally deemed pleasing to customers as well. The management of Disneyland not only felt that it truly identified with visitors, but it also generally saw its own and its co-sponsors' interests as entirely in agreement with its guests'. And for the most part the customers concurred.

Disneyland in the Customer's Mind

Visitors to Disneyland rarely belabored its faults, but they were not blind to them. For example, they conceded that Disneyland got rather crowded and that it could be expensive. They also realized that it made for an incomplete refuge from the outside world. Many guests did not experience Disneyland precisely as its designers intended, but their perception of it nonetheless agreed closely enough with that of the designers to make the theme park a tremendous success.

Like Walt Disney and his employees, most Disneyland customers lived in the urban West and came primarily from the middle and upper-middle classes. Surveys showed that visitors were disproportionately well educated, well paid, and well positioned compared to American society as a whole. Disneyland described them as "discriminating" consumers who appreciated "the better things in our American economy." A 1958 survey found that 74 percent of the families that paid admission to Disneyland also owned "1955 or newer cars" and 69.8 percent owned their own homes. "And they have . . . 10.2 electrical appliances . . . 1.8 radios . . . 1.67 television sets . . . 1.3 automobiles."[122]

The 1.3 automobiles belonging to each household loomed especially large, because they served as the principal means of transport to Disneyland. Roughly three-fifths of all visitors between 1955 and 1980 came from residences in California. About half of all guests came from the southern part of the state; most of these were repeat customers, and almost all of them arrived in cars.[123] Visitors from out of state also tended to arrive by car, although the number of those traveling by plane increased steadily over the years. The numbers of these tourists peaked during the summer, when vacationers included Disneyland in trips throughout the West. Predictably, the largest eastern states—Illinois, New York, Ohio—sent many tourists to Anaheim, but the majority of out-of-state guests lived west of the Mississippi River. This tendency became even more pronounced after the opening of Walt Disney World in Florida in 1971 siphoned off some of the East Coast trade.[124]

Because so many guests came from the West and stopped in Anaheim during vacations in which they also visited other regional attractions, it seemed natural to identify the theme park with the region. One Kansas reporter conceded that Disneyland could be rather artificial, but lumped it nevertheless with "Grand Canyon, Pike's Peak, Old Faithful and the rest" as one of "America's great wonders." The *Anaheim Bulletin* similarly linked the wonders of Disneyland to the natural attractions of Yosemite and the Grand Canyon, as well as to unnatural Las Vegas, in depicting a tourist's West.[125] Visitors appeared to share the regionalism of the Disney organization when they joined in contrasting the theme park with its eastern predecessors. "Certainly Disneyland is not just another amusement park," reported the travel editor for the *El Paso Herald-Post*. "It's as different from the Coney Island type of park as Walt could make it."[126]

In likening Disneyland to national parks and contrasting it with Coney Island, visitors identified the theme park with the West. Moreover, they identified themselves with Walt Disney. In fact, some writers seemed so thoroughly prepared to accept Disney's message that they never challenged publicity generated on behalf of the park. Company press releases often found their way into print as fact, helping to present the park in the most favorable light.

But the overwhelmingly positive response to Disneyland was not solely, or even primarily, the work of publicists. The park consistently charmed even the most skeptical observers. Journalists writing for such publications as the *Nation*, *New Yorker*, and *New York Times* visited it and, although they did not approve of everything they saw, they almost uniformly agreed that Disneyland was the real thing, that it worked as well as its designers had promised. These writers acknowledged the standard, obvious criticisms—that Disneyland was plastic and commercial, manipulative and conformist—but they emphasized that the theme park lived up to its billing.[127] In 1965, science-fiction writer Ray Bradbury praised the layout of the park in terms that Disney publicists would only later echo. Disneyland, he wrote, proved

that the first function of architecture is to make men over, make them wish to go on living, feed them fresh oxygen, grow them tall, delight their eyes, make them kind. . . . Disneyland liberates men to their better selves. Here the wild brute is gently corralled, not vised and squashed, not put upon and harassed, not tromped on by real-estate operators, not exhausted by smog and traffic.[128]

Overall, the response to Disneyland was one of open-eyed acceptance. Customers knew about the crowds and their control at the park. They conceded that "the place is jam-packed" and that visitors waited in long lines. Many travel editors urged readers to avoid the afternoon crunch when the park became "wall-to-wall humanity." They also acknowledged that Disneyland manipulated the crowds inside its walls: one headline dubbed it "The People Trap That a Mouse Built."[129] But at bottom neither the crowds nor the techniques by which Disneyland managed them truly annoyed most customers. In fact, the park's subtle controls earned repeated praise as the only way to present an enjoyable experience to masses of people. "Despite the tremendous audience," wrote one Delaware visitor, "there is no impression of crowds or of hurry." At Disneyland, a *New York Times* correspondent reported, one "can put in a full and, curiously enough, not exhausting day." Parents claimed that the park elicited good behavior from children.[130]

Observers' comments about the expense of Disneyland displayed the same combination of knowledge and acceptance. They typically remarked that "the entire enterprise is extremely commercial" and that "a fat wallet is essential" for visitors.[131] Some compared Walt Disney to the great nineteenth-century huckster P. T. Barnum.[132] Yet customers did not object to the considerable expense of the park, because they got good value in return. One travel editor from Maine summarized a widespread sentiment: "Disneyland is a commercial proposition from start to finish, so don't go with an empty pocketbook, but it's worth all you care to spend."[133] Marketing studies confirmed the high level of visitor satisfaction: 93.7 percent of the customers surveyed during the first year said they got their money's worth, and 77 percent planned to return. Three years later the level of satisfaction was up to 98.6 percent, and the number of guests intending to make a repeat visit had jumped to 83.0 percent.[134]

If, in the matters of crowds and costs, customers generally concurred with designers and operators that Disneyland did its job well, they did not accept so fully the claim that the park served as a refuge. Disneyland served not so much as an escape from the rest of the world as a foil for it. The park allowed customers to gain perspective on life but not truly to forget its problems. Indeed, publicists for Disneyland invited observers to contrast what they found inside the park with the world outside. One Baltimore columnist reported, "[I]t is pleasant to sit in Mr. Disney's shaded and leisurely town square and know that it is in no danger of being overtaken by expressways, urban renewal and rotary-traffic signs." Another journalist promised, "A visit to Disneyland will act like a tonic in restoring your faith in the things to come, despite the threat of atom bombs and guided missiles and come-what-may."[135]

Disneyland in some ways typified popular culture in postwar America. The designers and managers of Disneyland emphasized its ability to make guests forget day-to-day concerns and at the same time to reassure them that they could thrive in the outside world. In a parallel fashion, Roland Marchand has argued that "popular culture reveries" in the period 1945–1960 provided both an escape and a compensation for "Americans beginning to suffer from a vague closed-in feeling, a restless frustration stemming from Russian threats abroad and the restraints and manipulations of large organizations at home."[136] Of course, one's ability to escape, at least in Disneyland, was dubious, for the sources of the supposed national malaise were intrinsic to the theme park. The large corporations that seemed to threaten personal autonomy played an integral role as partners at Disneyland, and the Disney company itself was a large organization that restrained and manipulated its customers. Nonetheless, few visitors felt a need to escape the controls of the theme park.

The cold war was even more clearly on display at Disneyland; again, the alleged source of malaise had been built into the environment. Indeed, it could already be detected in abundance on opening day. On July 17, 1955, Walt Disney announced, "I don't want the public to see the world they live in while they're in the park. I want them to feel they are in another world." Yet the ceremonies that followed his remarks offered reminders of this world's tensions. After Disney dedicated the park "to the ideals, the dreams and the hard facts which have created America," Goodwin Knight, governor of California, identified the park as an artifact of the cold war by describing it as "all built by American labor and American capital, under the belief that this is a God-fearing and God-loving country." The national anthem played, jet fighters streaked overhead, and the Marines led a parade down Main Street U.S.A.[137] Opening day at Disneyland celebrated the American way at a time when competition with the Soviet Union was an inescapable fact. Both the region that hosted the park, which depended heavily upon military spending, and the movie industry that built it, which had been mobilized for the anticommunist crusade, doubtless regarded the cold war trappings with pride.

In its early years the theme park never moved far from cold war concerns. A 1956 promotional film explained that "Disneyland could happen only in a country where freedom is a heritage and the pursuit of happiness a basic human right." In 1957, on the eve of the space race, Walt Disney justified Tomorrowland as more than an amusement zone by saying that he intended it to inspire children to study science. The following year, after the Soviet Union launched *Sputnik I*, Disneyland's Rocket to the Moon inspired a Texas reporter to suggest, "If the Russians get much further ahead in the race to explore outer space, our government may have to hire Walt Disney to catch up."[138]

Disneyland spoke most vehemently to cold war concerns in 1959 when Nikita Khrushchev was denied permission to visit it. Like an increasing number of foreign visitors to the United States, the Soviet premier put the theme park near the top of his list of sights to see. But upon his arrival in Los Angeles the local police and the officials responsible for his tour told him that he could not visit Disneyland because they were unable to guarantee his safety there. Khrushchev exploded in angry disbelief: "What is it, do you have rocket-launching pads there?" The episode provided irresistible ammunition for cold warriors intent upon contrasting free and unfree societies. One Missouri columnist wrote an open letter to the Soviet leader: "[Y]ou missed out on seeing a great big chunk of America. Even though you are the dictator of what may be the most powerful country on earth, you are deprived of viewing the things that any American youngster can see if their [*sic*] parents pay a relatively moderate admission price." [139]

During the 1960s Disneyland's prominence as a symbol of international tension subsided, but it remained intimately associated with cold war technologies. "For all its playfulness," one reporter explained in early 1965, "Disneyland is as sophisticated as a missile control system and as tightly organized as a computer." [140] Both similes came near to the literal truth. Later that year Disney introduced Great Moments with Mr. Lincoln, a show in which a robot looked, moved, and spoke like the sixteenth president. The technology behind the performance was borrowed from the nation's space and missile programs. At the same time, Tomorrowland included rides that simulated a rocket to the moon, a flying saucer, and atomic submarines. Two years later, when the future according to Tomorrowland was updated, the Monsanto Company introduced a new ride, Adventures Thru Inner Space, in which customers traveling in Atomobiles learned about molecular structure. Monsanto intended the attraction to publicize its work in atomic energy and atomic weapons. [141] Disney and his corporate partners aimed to put the best possible face on the complexities of the outside world, but they never tried to exclude them from the park altogether.

In attempting to relive yesterday and predict tomorrow, too, Disneyland found it impossible to wall itself off from today. In fact, the effort backfired at times. Forecasting a future of atomic power and rockets for everyone proved to be difficult. Predictions of space travel that seemed at the same time reassuring and adventuresome and urgent in the mid-1950s lost some of their punch after the Soviets launched *Sputnik* in 1957, and by 1965 they had become thoroughly outdated.

Representing life in the past could be equally tricky. Over time the assumptions and stereotypes of the Disneyland version of yesterday became increasingly less acceptable to its audience. Frontierland in its early years contained two particularly revealing examples of history according to Disney. Wanting authentic Native Americans to paddle canoes full of guests around the rivers of the theme area, Disneyland recruited employees from southwestern tribes. These Indians, of course, came from the desert rather than a riverine or lakes environment, so they had to be taught how to paddle canoes by white employees of the park who had learned the skill at summer camp.[142] Only then were the Native American hosts deemed authentic enough to meet customers.

Initially, the public role of African Americans in the park was even more limited but just as contrived. When Disneyland opened in 1955, the Quaker Oats Company sponsored a restaurant called Aunt Jemima's Pancake House. The restaurant belonged within the ostensibly western realm of Frontierland, but its designers intended it to help customers relive the days of the "Old South." The namesake and hostess of the restaurant was played by an older black woman whose role as Aunt Jemima, a plantation cook, cast her as a mammy with "warmth of heart and good feeling."[143]

Other stereotypes of blacks existed in the park, such as the panicky Africans "on safari" in the Jungle Cruise, but for the most part Disneyland included very few blacks at all in its early years. Great Moments with Mr. Lincoln initially made no reference to emancipation or equality for African Americans, and the park itself only reluctantly hired black hosts and hostesses. In 1963 the Congress on Racial Equality pressured Disneyland to hire more African Americans, but only in 1968 did the park place its first black in a "people contact" position.[144] Race relations inside the theme park were far from futuristic.

In reflecting more of its own time than it intended, Disneyland illustrated how postwar society was caught between old and new ways.[145] While it championed the individualism of traditional America, it mastered the economics and media of mass culture. The park was organized along industrial lines for a type of mass-production, but it produced "happiness" instead of any durable good, and its work force exemplified the movement of labor away from extractive and industrial jobs toward the service sector. It recalled an age of small business and entrepreneurialism, but in order to do so it joined with multinational corporations and hired organization men and women.

Disneyland conveyed mores that were associated with America's preindustrial and industrializing past by using techniques specific to America's postindustrial present and future. The distinction between a traditional, producer-oriented America and its modern, consumer-oriented successor was never rigid. Nor were tensions between the two altogether new in 1955. But both were featured prominently and inextricably within Disneyland's walls.

Preindustrial, industrial, and postindustrial themes took on spatial connotations at the theme park. Disneyland represented for some a rejection of the industrial city as it was understood to exist in the north-eastern United States. On the one hand, the desirable alternative to the grit and tension and confusion of the industrial metropolis was the preindustrial small town of the American past. Thus the lands of Disneyland, especially Main Street U.S.A., were valued because they scaled urban life down to a more manageable size and recreated the supposedly more orderly village of bygone years. On the other hand, the theme park stood beside a freeway intersection in suburban Anaheim, which itself represented a postindustrial solution to the problems of the industrial city. To many, the Los Angeles metropolitan area was the urban Tomorrowland of the midcentury United States. Disneyland, with its Autopia expressways, monorail, and space-age technologies, belonged as much to this city of the future as it did to small towns of the past.

Disneyland and Southern California

Disneyland's relationship to the surrounding urban region was profound but fickle. Greater Los Angeles provided Disneyland with its inspiration, its setting, its cast, its models, and the majority of its customers. The park's preoccupation with frontiers, fantasy, the future, and assorted modes of transportation tied it to the mentality and history of southern California. And it depended on local amenities, including good weather as well as other tourist attractions, to bring customers to Anaheim. In short, Disneyland originally might well not have been possible outside the Los Angeles area. Over time, however, some began to wonder whether the surrounding metropolis might not suffocate the theme park.

When promoters first spoke about Disneyland as a way to escape from everyday cares, they did not include southern California as a part of that outside world from which customers needed relief. Publicists linked Disneyland to such nearby attractions as the ocean beaches, Hollywood, Knott's Berry Farm, Forest Lawn Memorial Park, Marineland, and the San Diego Zoo.[146] They even portrayed freeways favorably. Working on the assumption that out-of-state customers would not have the motoring skills of Californians, Disneyland's promotional magazines coached visitors about the essentials of driving in Los Angeles. A 1959 article titled "Freeway Driving Can Be Pleasant" offered advice from the California Highway Patrol, and a 1964 article called freeways the "Gateway to Vacationland."[147]

The theme park initially worked with rather than against the rest of southern California. Rival businesses worried about competition from Disneyland, but it actually seemed to increase attendance at other local attractions rather than keep customers to itself, thus spurring tourism to new heights. A survey made during late 1963 and early 1964 reported that the average party of out-of-state guests at Disneyland spent more than two weeks and more than $300 in southern California—mostly *not* in Anaheim.[148] The region and the park reinforced one another's appeal.

Over the years, however, the surrounding metropolis came to be viewed less as an extension of or supporting context for Disneyland and more as a part of that outside world from which customers needed relief. As early as 1958, out-of-state reporters began to make invidious comparisons between the compact sanity of Disneyland and "the sprawling madness of Los Angeles." Journalists based in San Francisco, where condemnation of Los Angeles thrived as an art form, made the most of the comparison. They regarded the theme park as more "real" and "permanent" and "believable" than the city of Los Angeles, and they contrasted its well-ordered and stimulating environs with the "smoggy" and bland tracts surrounding it.[149] Travel writers from across the country soon adopted the formula. Disneyland, they reported, was "an incredible pearl" amid "neon ugliness," crowded freeways, and phony people. They went on to label the park "perhaps the only truly good thing about the entire smog-bound metropolis" and "the real attraction" of the region.[150]

Southern Californians were slow to echo the unfavorable comparisons. Instead, they looked to the theme park for ideas as to how Los Angeles could adapt to the future. Ray Bradbury had suggested Walt Disney for mayor in 1960 because he seemed like the only man who could provide rapid transit for the metropolis, and in 1964 he wrote that Disney was perhaps the only person who could "save us from our own self-destruction": "Disney is a city builder. He has already proven his ability to construct an entire community, plus rivers, plus mountains, from the gaslines up. He has already solved, in small compass, most of the problems that beset Los Angeles."[151]

By the later 1960s and the 1970s, however, many Angelenos concurred in viewing the theme park as the antithesis to Los Angeles. Ignoring the fact that Disneyland had originally celebrated southern California and had capitalized on its freeways and cars and suburbanization, the Disney organization joined in the refrain. A 1984 publication explained that Walt Disney had included Main Street U.S.A. in the park as a counterpoise to "the rootless society and ugliness" of Los Angeles. "It would only be natural for Walt Disney to want to create a place where those who were raised under a blanket of smog, in tract homes, near noisy freeways, might see how life in Midwest America was . . . or might have been."[152]

In later years it became standard to view the theme park not as a natural outgrowth of Los Angeles but as an aberration and an antidote to it. In reality, of course, it was both. As the years passed the fact that Disneyland truly was an exceptional landscape within the larger metropolitan area increased in importance, and visitors tended to overlook its close ties with many dimensions of southern California. The offhand remark of one customer summarized tourists' estimation of the theme park and southern California: "To our children Los Angeles is merely a suburb of Disneyland."[153] This comment, however, unwittingly conveyed the important point that, within the urban context of southern California, and particularly within Orange County, Disneyland had assumed some of the functions traditionally performed by downtowns.

The theme park helped to bring some order to the apparent chaos that preoccupied visitors in Los Angeles. As the architect Charles Moore explained, Disneyland was "singlehandedly . . . engaged in replacing many of those elements of the public realm which have vanished in the featureless private floating world of southern California."[154] Somewhat like local beaches and shopping malls, Disneyland filled the functions of pedestrian meeting place, public square, and city park. It also made the spatial pattern of Orange County more cohesive by providing an important nucleus of activity in a region that seemed to have no center of its own. The park transformed the city of Anaheim into a cultural capital for surrounding towns. In an urban region without commanding central business districts, a place such as Disneyland could wield surprising power as a center for the landscape, even as it presented itself as the antithesis to the conventional central business district.

Before 1955 Orange County had few centers of activity. Santa Ana ranked as the leading city in 1950 with a population of 45,533, more than three times that of Anaheim. Although it was the county seat, Santa Ana did not serve as the dominant core city of the region. In fact, as one study remarked in 1958, "there is no natural reason why a truly dominant municipality should emerge. Santa Ana exercises only limited hegemony over other areas, and no basis exists upon which supremacy could be established." The true core city for Orange County was Los Angeles—which of course itself lacked a core.[155]

In 1950 there had been no reason to think that Anaheim could do anything about either Orange County's centerlessness or its subservience to Los Angeles. The town had long depended upon a primarily agricultural economy. As World War II drew to a close, local leaders, like other city officials throughout the Far West, had worried that their community would return to the doldrums of the 1930s and had therefore begun planning a future of economic change. They set their sights on attracting factories to supplant local farms and ranches, and they predicted that the proposed Santa Ana Freeway, connecting Anaheim directly to Los Angeles, would help their cause.[156] By the time Disneyland opened, Anaheim had begun to transform itself. Yet there was no certainty that the new freeway would bring either new industry or a new independence to the town. Without Disneyland, Anaheim might have become another residential suburb of Los Angeles in which housing subdivisions replaced cultivated fields.

The new freeway did import fundamental changes. By 1955 Anaheim's population had more than doubled over the previous half-decade, from 14,556 to 30,059. Yet the most important newcomer attracted to Anaheim by the freeway was Disneyland, and after 1955 it was not the interstate highway but the theme park that became Anaheim's fount of growth. After Disneyland opened, the population grew by about 18,000 people in each of the next two years. By 1960 it had reached 104,000, making Anaheim "the fastest growing city in the fastest growing county in the nation" during the 1950s. Anaheim had surpassed Santa Ana in population and, as the two cities continued to grow over the following decades, it maintained its narrow lead. By 1980 Anaheim had 219,311 residents; Santa Ana, 203,713.[157]

After Disneyland arrived, Anaheim expanded its borders and its economy as well as its population. Before construction of the theme park the town had contained about four square miles, thirty-four restaurants, and perhaps as many as eighty-seven hotel and motel rooms. Thereafter, Anaheim began to annex territory aggressively, bringing its total area to 35 square miles in 1971. These annexations were one cause of the dramatic population growth. Moreover, by 1973 the city had attracted 125 motels and hotels, for a total of 6,500 rooms within a five-mile radius of the theme park (see Figure 14). By 1980 the city of

Figure 14. In 1964 some orchards and farms still bordered Disneyland, but housing subdivisions, industrial low-rises, parking lots, and motels had sprung up around the park, particularly along Harbor Boulevard, to the right of the park, and Katella Avenue, in lower right of photo. Courtesy of Anaheim History Room, Anaheim Public Library (P10677), and © The Walt Disney Company.

Anaheim offered over 12,000 rooms and more than 400 restaurants.[158] Nobody attributed all of this expansion to the presence of Disneyland, but nearly everyone who commented on Anaheim's phenomenal boom identified the park as its major catalyst.[159]

Revenues generated by the park brought unprecedented local affluence. In 1959, 96.5 percent of the park's 3,650 employees lived in Orange County, and about 85 percent of its payroll was spent there. Disney officials asserted that theme park employees made highly desirable neighbors.[160] And they pointed to the windfall brought by their customers; in 1971 guests spent "much more outside the park than in. We estimate that Disneyland pours over $250,000,000 each year in to the local Anaheim economy. . . . The park gets only about 25 percent of the expenditures it actually creates." In 1974, according to company figures, the park itself spent $45 million in Orange County for such items as maintenance and supplies. Over the first two decades of operation, it paid $22.9 million in local taxes.[161]

Disneyland created a new economic base for Anaheim. In fact, tourism became so predominant that it may have inhibited the growth of local manufacturing. The city of Anaheim quickly understood just how valuable the theme park could be, and it did all that it could to encourage and support its leading industry. Before construction even began, the city annexed Disney's parcel of land. Once the site was incorporated into Anaheim, city officials guaranteed fire and police service, provided new public works, closed an existing road, and rezoned nearby blocks. Before the park opened its gates, local leaders advised town businessmen to spruce up their shops in anticipation of new visitors. And over the years assorted local boosters and officials continued such accommodating treatment.[162]

Anaheim was not the only town in Orange County to benefit from Disneyland, for park customers frequently visited other nearby attractions. But Anaheim gained the most from Disneyland and was able to make itself into an urban nucleus for Orange County in ways that other towns could not match. One reason was publicity. Because Disneyland was located there, Anaheim got unrivaled attention.[163] Its reputation paid off handsomely in the acquisition of two other tourist attractions, which further bolstered Anaheim's leading role in the area.

In 1964 Anaheim's governing elite decided to raise $21 million to construct a major-league sports stadium two miles from Disneyland. It then proceeded to raise another $14 million for a convention center situated virtually next door to the theme park. When the stadium opened in 1966 its major occupant was an American League baseball team. The Los Angeles Angels had played for several seasons at Dodger Stadium, but they had been unable to make much money or acquire much of a following there. The move to Anaheim rejuvenated the franchise and recruited more, and more loyal, fans. Part of the Angels' new appeal was the stadium's proximity to Disneyland.[164] The baseball team disappointed its host city by calling itself the California, rather than the Anaheim, Angels. Nonetheless, Anaheim could rightfully call itself a major-league city, the only one in Orange County. With the stadium and the team it had distinguished itself further from Los Angeles while becoming more nearly its equal as a major-league town. To most residents of Anaheim, the new status represented astonishing progress for a town which, barely fifteen years before, had claimed fewer than 15,000 residents and little more than a rural economy.

The Anaheim Convention Center, completed the year after the stadium, also inflated the city's reputation. By arranging with the operators of Madison Square Garden to bring New York shows and events to the new center, Anaheim secured for Orange County a more cosmopolitan cultural life. However, the convention center was mostly viewed as an adjunct to the theme park. Civic officials intended it to ameliorate downswings in the tourist trade by attracting visitors during Disneyland's off-season. Big hotel chains soon increased the appeal of the center by building large inns next door. The combination of Disneyland and convention facilities proved to be a powerful draw. By 1980 Orange County ranked second only to San Francisco among West Coast convention sites.[165]

Disneyland's influence on the stadium and convention center extended even further. The city of Anaheim adopted Disneyesque techniques of treating customers. At both the stadium and the convention center, "an attractive and smiling staff, nattily dressed, greets visitors while porters scurry about sweeping up the tiniest scraps of paper." City employees followed Disneyesque rules of grooming and adopted a "Disneyland vocabulary," banishing the terms *employees, fans,* and *conventioneers* in favor of *hosts* and *hostesses, cast members,* and *guests.* The town even set up its own academy, modeled after the University of Disneyland, to teach "the Anaheim Way."[166]

Disney officials realized that the park's impact upon the town and its self-image had been enormous. Its contributions had above all been economic ones. Income from Disneyland helped to offset slumps in the county's aerospace industry. Even more important, it provided capital, which was used to transform itself into something much larger. How else, Walt Disney asked in 1966, could a "little city of 150,000 afford a $20 million baseball stadium and a $15 million convention center?" Disneyland encouraged what had recently been "a small quiet agricultural-oriented settlement" to imagine its future on a much grander scale than before.[167]

Disneyland changed the very skyline. When an artificial Alp was erected in 1959 as the site of the Matterhorn Bobsleds, at 147 feet it was the tallest man-made object in the county. It became a prominent landmark in the low-rise landscape, joined within several years by the 230-foot-high scoreboard at Anaheim Stadium and the 252-foot-high Tower of Hope atop the drive-in Garden Grove Community Church.[168] These structures, Orange County's equivalent of downtown skyscrapers, performed an important centering function.

People paid little attention to the edges of communities in Orange County; Anaheim blended seamlessly into Garden Grove and Santa Ana. Major pathways through the county—its ubiquitous freeways and boulevards—gained wider recognition, but they cut through towns in a linear fashion without creating nodes to anchor mental maps of Orange County. Such districts and landmarks as Disneyland, Anaheim Stadium, the Anaheim Convention Center, the Garden Grove Community Church, and leading shopping centers provided suburban alternatives to traditional downtowns.[169] Appropriately for the postindustrializing era, these landmarks were more devoted to consumption than was the conventional, production-oriented, central business district. Each became a nucleus for urban activity and thus heightened people's sense of place within Orange County.

Like traditional city centers, Disneyland lent a sense of refinement to Anaheim by enriching its otherwise sparse cultural life. "Where else in the county," one local booster asked, "has there been a place to hear the very top musical entertainers in the business, year in and year out?" The park had attracted to "rural Orange County" the kinds of performers and events and restaurants that had previously been associated in southern California only with Los Angeles or Hollywood.[170] Yet ostensibly it attracted none of the film colony's dubious morality. Orange County residents valued the cultural accomplishments of Disneyland in part because they were not too risqué for family consumption. Anaheim's leaders praised the theme park as an uplifting influence on surrounding districts.[171] With its kind of virtuous sophistication, Disneyland gave to Anaheim the hope of combining a suburban moral tone with the cultural riches of a central city.

Thanks in large measure to Disneyland, residents of Orange County no longer had to feel subservient to Los Angeles. In their economy, culture, and sense of identity, they had both achieved relative autonomy and attracted some of the activities that signaled urban maturity.[172] The theme park had helped to redraw mental maps of Orange County by making Anaheim the nucleus of a number of hubless towns, but without directly challenging the county's suburban attitudes.

However, the transformation of Anaheim took place so thoroughly and rapidly that some urban problems were inevitable. These caught both Disneyland and the surrounding communities unprepared. In 1955, before Disneyland's immense success and its implications could be foretold, an editorial in the *Anaheim Bulletin* had welcomed the new tourist attraction unconditionally: "Any business established to bring happiness cannot develop into a detriment to the community in which it is established."[173] Within a decade, however, some residents of Anaheim had come to feel that Disneyland was too much of a good thing. As in other communities given over to tourism, at least a few began to wonder whether the happiness acquired by visitors at Disneyland did not come at the cost of the hometown's own well-being.[174]

One complaint concerned the problems that accompanied growth. A critic contrasted Anaheim "since Disneyland" with its predecessor— a "small, rural, closely knit, very comfortable community where . . . everyone seemed to know everyone else."[175] That idyllic town, if it ever really existed, would have been endangered whether or not Disneyland came to Anaheim, but its downfall was most readily attributed to the theme park. Similarly, although Anaheim's central business district had no doubt also been doomed by the advent of freeways, commercial strips, and shopping malls, one small businessman charged that the arrival of Disneyland, along with other changes, drained downtown Anaheim of its vitality.[176]

More realistically, the citizens of Anaheim worried about the strip development along Harbor Boulevard next to the park. The unattractive commercial buildings, intense traffic congestion, and influx of prostitutes all earned for the district comparisons to Las Vegas.[177] The governing elite of Anaheim, of course, continued to stress the advantages of having the park inside the municipal boundaries. However, as the years passed, the early, rosy estimates of Disneyland's impact gave way to awareness of a more complicated reality.

In addition to encouraging troubling growth along Harbor Boulevard, Disneyland compromised Anaheim's political autonomy. The growing influence of the Disney organization was one indication that the town had become more impersonal and, in some respects, less manageable. The business leaders who had previously prevailed in local politics may not have always proven sensitive to their constituents, but they had at least been Anaheim's own elite. With the opening of the theme park, a big corporation with headquarters outside the city limits came to play a powerful role in local affairs. The people behind Disneyland flexed their political muscles on several occasions. Once they protested a city council proposal to implement an entertainment tax in Anaheim, and another time they urged the closing of a topless revue in a theater near Disneyland, in order to protect the park's "family concept."[178] But their most revealing foray into local government occurred in 1963–64 when they challenged plans for a high-rise hotel.

High-rise architecture, like traffic congestion, seemed an inevitable by-product of the park's success. Disneyland exerted enormous influence on commercial real estate in Anaheim. By attracting so many customers it created a great demand for new motels and hotels and restaurants. These establishments, along with the Anaheim Convention Center, increased the appeal of the park by providing convenient accommodations for visitors. At the same time, the presence of Disneyland drove up the price of land in the vicinity, which in turn encouraged builders to erect high-rises that made more efficient use of the expensive property.

Following this economic logic, the Sheraton Hotel company announced in 1963 that it would build a twenty-two-story hotel within a half-mile of the park. Because the proposed edifice would be visible from within Disneyland's walls, the Disney organization protested to the Anaheim city council. This "intrusion" on the park's view would violate its visual integrity, Walt Disney explained, and would undermine its ability to distance visitors from the outside world.[179] Park visitors spotting the hotel would presumably have lost their sense of fantasy. The company's position was somewhat paradoxical. Its 147-foot Matterhorn, which could be seen from outside the park, constituted a landmark that helped bring visual order to Orange County; Anaheim residents did not complain that the model Alp intruded upon their view. But it was not acceptable, according to Disney, for others to build their own landmark structures that could be seen from inside the park. The skyline belonged to Disneyland alone.

Some neighbors regarded this stance as arrogant. In notoriously conservative Orange County, it was not surprising that one local editor defended Sheraton's property rights: "To say that owners of land almost a half mile away cannot build a fine and gracious structure on that land because people might look at it while buying hotdogs or riding the merry-go-round in Disneyland is an unreasonable and immoderate intrusion of government in the private business of those landowners."[180] But city government sided with Disneyland. It required Sheraton to reduce its planned hotel to sixteen stories and, using Disneyland's recommendations as guidelines, passed an ordinance prohibiting construction of buildings over seventy-five feet high in the thousand-acre "commercial recreation zone" around the park.[181] Anaheim could not afford to permit challenges to Disneyland's hegemony.

In restricting the height of the hotel, Anaheim did not justify its decision on the basis of a policy to limit growth; such thinking still lay in the future for Orange County. In fact, protecting Disneyland was seen as the best method for perpetuating local expansion. The city identified its fortunes very closely with the theme park, and it did not wish either to annoy the park's owners or to diminish Disneyland's appeal. A former city manager explained the prevailing attitude: "The [city] council and the bulk of the property owners nearby seemed to understand eventually that what was vital to Disneyland was good for the rest of us."[182] This was the local equivalent to that famous remark, uttered by Charles E. Wilson, the former head of General Motors, during his confirmation hearings as President Dwight D. Eisenhower's first secretary of defense, when he was asked about a possible conflict of interest between his old and his new employer: "I cannot conceive of one because for years I thought what was good for our country was good for General Motors, and vice versa."

A Disney World

By the 1980s conventional wisdom held that Walt Disney had both built Disneyland and planned Walt Disney World in Florida out of his concern for urban problems generally and his dissatisfaction with "the unplanned sprawl of Los Angeles" in particular.[183] Little evidence exists, however, that suggests that Disney originally intended the Anaheim park as a model by which to reform urban planning. It *was* conceived as an improvement over New York's Coney Island and other amusement parks, and it was regarded as an appropriate innovation for California and the West. But in the 1950s Walt Disney did not directly address the nation's urban problems, and least of all those in greater Los Angeles. In fact, by choosing a site next to a proposed freeway and new residential development, he tacitly embraced the characteristic sprawl of southern California. Only in retrospect was it decided that he had conceived Disneyland in reaction against Los Angeles.

In the case of Walt Disney World, Disney may indeed have seen his new venture as a response to urban problems. The East Coast would get its theme park, modeled, naturally, after Disneyland, but Walt Disney also proposed to build the Experimental Prototype Community of Tomorrow, or EPCOT, which would "show how many of today's city problems can be solved through proper master planning."[184] EPCOT developed into something quite different from what Disney had envisioned, but it grew in part out of a concern about city planning which had a significant impact upon the development of Walt Disney World in Florida.

Walt Disney's sense of which urban problems ought to be addressed was highly selective. He, and those who interpreted his intentions after his death, spoke about the general malaise of urban life, about cities being too impersonal. Worried about the fate of the family, they hoped to address "the young adult problem" by designing urban spaces where teenagers could be "properly controlled" and occupied while being permitted to express themselves.[185] The Disney organization also wanted a town where the private sector could develop technologies capable of solving such problems as traffic congestion and pollution.

The Disney program paid virtually no attention to many other urban dilemmas, including those that preoccupied the nation during the initial planning for EPCOT—the African-American uprisings in cities across the country, and the problems of slums and ghettos, sanitation and health, poverty and unemployment. Disney no doubt expected EPCOT to suggest solutions to some of these dilemmas, but they were not among the ones to which he assigned top priority. In fact, his own and his company's approach to city planning, emphasizing high-technology and private-sector design, may have been particularly unsuited to addressing America's urban crisis.

Walt Disney recognized "the ills of old cities" but he did not want to locate EPCOT near them. Rather than take his initiative to Watts, for example, where urban problems were most acute, he argued that "the need is for starting from scratch on virgin land."[186] This attitude followed an old tradition in Americans' westering experience, dating back to the Puritans of Massachusetts Bay Colony in the early seventeenth century. Rather than solving problems where they are, it has often seemed more logical to move on to new territory where the same problems do not exist, and there to build a "City upon a Hill" from which others may learn. Disney's response was equally appropriate within the context of the twentieth-century motion-picture industry, wherein filmmakers could begin with an equally blank slate. "Walt saw building a city very much like a movie," John Hench explained. "You start with scene one, which relates to scene two and scene three. And you don't leave out any of the parts."[187]

The keys to EPCOT's success were assumed to be to start afresh and to maintain absolute control over script and set. In this respect, the experience gained at Disneyland loomed large. It had taught a company of moviemakers how to apply their skills in a three-dimensional setting, and it had also taught them that they needed to keep control not only over their main stage but also over peripheral environs that might affect the quality of the show. Walt Disney's thinking about urban planning probably stemmed more from lessons learned along Harbor Boulevard than from anything else.

In 1955 Anaheim had seemed perfect for Disneyland because it had undergone no intensive development, yet would soon acquire its own freeway link to Los Angeles. This ideal juxtaposition of rural and urban elements could not last. Gas stations and motels replaced orchards and farms on the periphery of the theme park, changes Disney deplored. In the very year that Disneyland opened he expressed regret that he had not been able to buy more land around the park, and in a 1958 report the company emphasized that it hoped to protect its investment in the park "by assisting in the development of periphery land." But this wish went largely unfulfilled (see Figure 15). In many cases all that Disneyland could do was to react to the initiatives of others. "For example, when the Santa Ana Freeway was raised, Walt insisted on elevating the berm." [188]

Disney objected to the uses of adjacent lands on two grounds. One was aesthetic. He regarded nearby structures as tasteless in form (and sometimes in function, too) as well as uncoordinated in their layout. He would have preferred to exercise final artistic approval over his neighbors in order to eliminate contradictions between them and the park. "Our biggest mistake was not buying more of the land around Disneyland," he said again in 1964. "Then we could have had more control over the theme and nature of the construction." [189] The other concern was economic. Although Disneyland benefited from the presence of nearby businesses, its management resented the profits these businesses realized. One journalist explained Disney's side of the story:

The Disney anger flares at what has happened in Anaheim. Speculators have snatched up surrounding property and, with light regard for justice, are cashing in on Disneyland's success. Prices are astronomical, liquor is sold to minors, in spots a honky-tonk atmosphere batters the reputation of his Magic Kingdom and no one has contributed a cent to the source of prosperity. [190]

According to a member of the Anaheim planning commission, tawdry strip development outside the park was one of the factors that convinced Walt Disney to build another magic kingdom in Florida. [191] The

Figure 15. The intense commercial development stimulated by Disneyland provided essential services to guests yet detracted from the attractiveness of the theme park. Annoyed by the congestion and blight along Harbor Boulevard, shown here in 1974, Walt Disney determined to buy enough land in Florida to create a buffer zone around his new resort. Courtesy of Anaheim History Room, Anaheim Public Library (P12170).

fate of Harbor Boulevard convinced him of the need to plan on a larger scale.

Walt Disney had initially played down the idea of a second Disneyland. In 1960 he was still explaining that the Anaheim park required too much personal attention for him to consider another one, especially if it required much travel from his base in southern California, and vowing never to build a second park simply as a way to make money.[192] But while Disney professed his complete devotion to Anaheim, others in his employ began to speculate about the profits to be earned elsewhere. They pointed out that Disneyland had not made much of a dent in the market east of the Mississippi River, and they suggested building a version of the park in Florida, where the tourist trade slowed for only three months each year.[193] This argument must have proved persuasive, because in the early 1960s Walt Disney began to change his mind about a second Disneyland.

Disney's participation in the New York World's Fair of 1964–65 served in several ways as a crucial stepping-stone from California to Florida. First, the Disney organization was hired to build four major attractions for the fair: It's a Small World for Pepsi-Cola, the Magic Skyway for Ford Motor Company, the Carousel of Progress for General Electric, and Great Moments with Mr. Lincoln for the state of Illinois. Each of these creations ranked among the most popular attractions at the fair, and each was eventually integrated into the theme parks.[194] Small World, Carousel of Progress, and Great Moments helped renew Disneyland. Second, members of the organization worked more closely than before with big business. After the fair, in California as well as Florida, they rededicated themselves to providing a showcase for industrial products and ideas. Third, the company gained experience with shows on a larger scale and amid greater diversity than existed at Disneyland. Fourth, and perhaps most important, Walt Disney used the fair to increase his exposure and test his appeal to eastern audiences, whom he had expected to be "blasé about things Disney."[195]

The fair experience convinced the company that a theme park would succeed on the Atlantic seaboard. In autumn 1965 the news broke that Disney was bringing a "gold mine" to central Florida, where the company clearly intended to avoid the mistakes it had made in Anaheim. It acquired 43 square miles of largely undeveloped, swampy terrain, located in Orange and Osceola counties near the intersection of two highways, and it set out to develop the site in ways that ensured complete control over the built and natural environments. The master planning that had guided the use of 65 acres in Anaheim was now applied to a parcel twice the size of Manhattan. A Florida newspaper, familiar with Disney's feelings about Harbor Boulevard, endorsed his plans: "If he needs 27,000 acres to discourage riff-raff, so much the better."[196] Like the planners of Disneyland, the builders of the new park intended to exclude all undesirable elements, both natural and man-made.

Walt Disney originally dubbed his new venture Disneyland-East, but it soon became known as Walt Disney World. The theme park called the Magic Kingdom and modeled after Disneyland was only one element in the plan for the parcel. An industrial park, airport, and hotels were also proposed. But according to Walt Disney, "the heart of everything we'll be doing in Disney World" would be his Experimental Prototype Community of Tomorrow. EPCOT, explained John Hench, would be "an extension of the Disneyland ideas and philosophies toward people."[197] Yet it would be aimed at more than tourists. Although the company claimed that Disneyland had a positive, therapeutic effect on visitors, they saw it primarily as an escape from the outside world. Disney conceived EPCOT, on the other hand, as a means of transforming the outside world by its example. Moreover, whereas Disneyland had become a central focus of urban activity in southern California almost by default, Disney from the beginning envisioned EPCOT as a downtown for Walt Disney World.

In a brief and moving film produced shortly before his death in December 1966, Walt Disney described his plans for a model city designed, built, and equipped by the private sector. He foresaw a master-planned community of 20,000 that was perfectly zoned into three concentric rings encircling a round city center. Low-density housing characterized the outermost ring, where residents dwelled in futuristic homes that would perpetually be remodeled to incorporate the latest technology. The middle ring consisted of a green belt for churches, playgrounds, and schools. High-density apartments occupied the innermost ring, providing immediate access to the town center. Finally, the nucleus would be a business district of roughly 50 acres, entirely enclosed within a translucent dome that maintained ideal weather conditions year-round. Perhaps the most striking feature of the climate-controlled downtown was its five layers of transportation: electric People Movers on elevated tracks; surface streets given over to pedestrians; one underground level for monorails and more People Movers; a second underground level for cars; and a third underground level for trucks. EPCOT would be thoroughly rational and completely modern.[198]

In order for EPCOT to succeed, its builders required the kind of dictatorial power that conventional city planners could only covet. In footage shot especially for the Florida legislature, Walt Disney asked to be exempted from existing codes and regulations so that his company could "have the *flexibility* . . . to keep pace with *tomorrow's* world" as well as "the *freedom* to work in cooperation with American industry." The Disney organization carefully explained that it needed this authority only because it meant "to do things that are right for the people."[199] Residents of EPCOT, like customers at Disneyland, could not be trusted to know for certain what was right or what was in their own best interests. They would not be consulted or polled about matters pertaining to the city's development. In order to ensure complete control at EPCOT, the company would not permit residents to own land or to vote. And it intended to circumscribe their lives in other ways: "[T]here will be no slums because we won't let them develop. There will be no retirees. Everyone must be employed."[200] Only technological change, and not social, political, or ideological conflict, would be permitted to influence EPCOT's future.

EPCOT as envisioned by Walt Disney was never built. After he died his successors kept the name alive, but what was to have been an experimental city for 20,000 people became instead two new variations of the theme park—the high-tech Future World and the World Showcase of foreign cultures. The Disney organization considered these two creations to be more educational than its other theme parks, but still classified them as part of its "entertainment business."[201] In the mid-1960s Walt Disney had proposed to change the world, albeit strictly on his own terms; in the 1980s his successors wished primarily to amuse it. In certain respects the company had adapted quite shrewdly to changes in the larger society.

If Walt Disney's utopian city died with him, the thinking behind it survived and influenced the development of Walt Disney World. Florida granted the company the autonomy it wanted in designing, constructing, and policing its new park. It was allowed to devise its own building code, for example, thereby exempting Walt Disney World from existing regulations and reducing interference from bureaucracies and unions. The company used its autonomy to install a largely concealed, "eco-conscious" infrastructure. It also used its extra land for developing its own hotels, which were designed to conform to themes in the Walt Disney World Magic Kingdom. The Contemporary Resort provided "an architecturally compatible backdrop to Tomorrowland," and the Polynesian Village "a themed background to Adventureland."[202]

Walt Disney World grew out of the Disneyland experience, but it took selected Anaheim tendencies to new lengths, and it ultimately exceeded Disneyland both in scope and in attendance. The theme park within Walt Disney World was about 20 percent larger than Anaheim's (and as a result, according to some, was less comfortable and reassuring). It had a taller castle and wider streets, and instead of honoring one former president it featured all thirty-six.[203] The Florida park also tapped a substantially larger market. Opening in October of 1971, it surpassed Disneyland in annual volume of visitors during its first full year, to become the world's most popular tourist attraction. Its guests also differed in makeup from patrons at Disneyland. The Anaheim park depended on California residents for 60 percent of its custom. But visitors at Walt Disney World came from all across the country, although more were from the eastern states, and they vacationed longer at the resort than Disneyland guests did. Finally, accolades that had gone to Disneyland during the 1960s for its positive impact upon urban design now went to Walt Disney World.[204]

The success of Walt Disney World made it easy to overlook Disneyland. The one stood out as new and promising and uncompromised in Florida, while the other—like Coney Island two decades earlier—seemed dated and small and tainted by the surrounding metropolis. But this perception obscured the significance of the original theme park. Disneyland was no longer the biggest or the best, but it remained the first. It served as the model for much of Walt Disney World, as well as teaching many of the lessons and providing much of the capital required to build the larger park. Furthermore, southern California remained in many respects the creative center for the Florida project, for much of it was designed at the Disney studios, the WED offices, and the Anaheim site.[205] Both Disneyland and Walt Disney World were, in a sense, products of the postwar West.

Disneyland, in fact, epitomized the creativity of the rapidly urbanizing West during the mid-twentieth century. Like the remainder of the region, however, it grew increasingly vulnerable after the mid-1960s to the changes that challenged Westerners' characteristic confidence. Walt Disney World was so isolated that it could perhaps resist more effectively the changes originating outside its borders. Disneyland, by contrast, was never truly able to filter out all of the external world from which it promised an escape, and it grew steadily less immune to intrusions.

The counterculture mounted the first serious invasion. On July 31,

1970, the *Los Angeles Free Press* announced that the "First International YIPPIE! Pow Wow" would be held at Disneyland on August 6, the twenty-fifth anniversary of the atomic bombing of Hiroshima. In several ways the park made a logical target for protestors. The Disney organization was famous for its conservatism, and its park symbolized the world of big corporations and private property. In addition, although Disneyland had relaxed its grooming code in 1968, it still seemed to discriminate against those with long hair and very casual attire. "Man, that's America in there," explained one demonstrator. "That's the way it is in this country—you can play the game if you have money and look nice. But if you're different, forget about life." The hippies' concerns were serious, of course, but sympathizers described the invasion with tongue in cheek. The *Free Press* listed the day's itinerary: a "Black Panther Hot Breakfast" at Aunt Jemima's Kitchen; a "rally to liberate Minnie Mouse in front of Fantasyland"; and a plot "to infiltrate and liberate Tom Sawyer's Island. Declaring a free-state, brothers and sisters will then have a smoke-in and festival." [206]

If demonstrators regarded the proposed invasion with humor, Orange County saw nothing funny in the situation. Overreacting to the announcement by the underground paper, the *Anaheim-Fullerton Independent* warned in a morning headline of August 6 that "200,000 Hippies Plan Mass Disneyland Invasion Today." Disneyland itself took the event seriously. In preparation for the demonstrators it recruited troops from the police forces of eleven different nearby towns, the Orange County sheriff's office, and the California Highway Patrol, and stationed them behind facades along Main Street U.S.A.

Ultimately, between 180 and 300 protestors gained admission to the park. After mingling with the crowd of 29,000 customers, they gathered at a prearranged time on the steps of Disneyland's City Hall, raised their "marijuana flag" on a street lamp, and shouted obscenities and antiwar chants. As many as 700 other guests responded by singing "God Bless America." The police finally emerged from backstage, scuffled with the demonstrators, made eighteen arrests, and closed the park to all guests for the remainder of the day (see Figure 16). (The only other time the park had shut down early had been after the assassination of John F. Kennedy.) [207] The next day Disneyland turned away about 100 long-haired young men at the main gate, reverting to its old grooming policy. The company claimed that it would not be overly strict in excluding people, but security guards admitted "privately that they were drawing the line at 'just about crewcut.'" [208]

Figure 16. Youthful protestors chose the theme park as their target in 1970, on the twenty-fifth anniversary of the atomic bombing of Hiroshima. Disneyland repelled the invasion, with the help of the police, but it now seemed less immune to the turmoil of that outside world from which it offered refuge. Courtesy of Anaheim History Room, Anaheim Public Library (P6923).

Disneyland had repulsed one intrusion, but in the coming years its powers to resist them did not always keep pace with the mounting number of threats. A decade after the hippie invasion, security guards evicted two homosexual men for violating the park's long-standing ban against partners of the same sex dancing together. One guard reportedly explained, "This is a family park. There's no room for alternative lifestyles here." The evicted men, who had been seeking grounds for a test case, sued Disneyland for violating their civil rights. The courts initially denied their claim, but in 1984 reversed themselves on appeal. Technically, the ramifications of the gay victory were quite limited; the court awarded only the two plaintiffs the right to dance with each other at Disneyland. But the implications may have been broader, for Orange County itself had changed. In 1970 the local press had rallied to support Disneyland's eviction of the hippies. In 1984 it was an Orange County jury that decided for the gay men and against the theme park, much to the surprise of both sides.[209]

A wide variety of other intrusions further challenged the autonomy of Disneyland after 1970—intensifying smog, labor unrest, bomb threats, heightened competition, and slower growth. Worst of all, the parent company seemed to have lost the creativity that had characterized it before Disney's death. Its "suspended animation" was widely reported, particularly in producing motion pictures. As revenues from movies declined, the company increasingly relied on its theme parks for income. Yet the parks, too, seemed frozen in time, at least in the eyes of some observers, as if they had never really departed from the 1950s. Corporate crises finally invited a takeover bid in the early 1980s, and when that storm had passed the company's fortunes had been turned around.[210] As the firm regained something of its old form—producing better motion pictures, rereleasing earlier successes, and programming for cable television—Disneyland perhaps became even less important to the company's bottom line.

Both around the country and within southern California, Disneyland seemed less special, and its walls no longer appeared impermeable. Yet one of the reasons that Disneyland was no longer perceived as unique was that it had succeeded beyond anyone's expectations. The dilution of the theme park as a special place, and of its ability to influence the outside world, began on opening day when TV broadcast its images far and wide. Television almost allowed visits to the park without traveling. In 1971 the new, improved version of Disneyland opened in Florida, permitting people to see a theme park without going west.

During the 1980s the concept was exported further still, to Japan, and in the 1990s to France. Moreover, throughout its existence the ideas behind its design were incorporated into shopping malls, Main Streets, museums, and historic districts across the country. And Disneyland infiltrated the English language.

The parallels between region and theme park were, once again, striking. The outside world intruded upon Disneyland, just as it descended upon all of the post-1940 Far West. But the theme park in turn Disneyfied the outside world considerably, and in so doing helped to lead the growing movement of cultural forms from West to East.

CHAPTER THREE

Stanford Industrial Park: Downtown for Silicon Valley

In May 1958, an exhibit entitled Industrial Parks USA opened in the U.S. pavilion at the Brussels World's Fair. America's growing interest in this setting for manufacturing stemmed in part from its efforts to encourage industrial growth in underdeveloped countries. But Industrial Parks USA also illustrated domestic progress. The head of the Society of Industrial Realtors of America, which co-sponsored the display, viewed the rise of American industrial parks as "a vital contribution to industrial harmony," an important goal in a nation inclined to minimize class tensions. The parks also brought harmony to the landscape; they were designed for compatibility with residential neighborhoods.

Featured prominently in the exhibit was Stanford Industrial Park in Palo Alto, California. This real estate venture captured the attention of at least one fairgoer, French president Charles de Gaulle. When he visited the United States in 1960, de Gaulle set aside time for traveling to Palo Alto and touring an electronics plant in the park. There he heard from the city manager that the developer of the site, Stanford University, had intended "to create by planning, architecture, landscaping and exacting restrictions, a high quality, park-like atmosphere." The setting not only improved employee productivity, de Gaulle learned, but also blended in with the "cultural and residential" ambience of the suburban area.[1]

The president of France perhaps appreciated the careful design that made Stanford Industrial Park another magic kingdom amid the rapid urbanization of the American West, but he was most interested in its theme of advanced scientific research. By 1960 the industrial park had already made a name for itself for its contributions to the rapid growth of American high-technology industry. In an age when governments, businesses, and universities all sought to encourage science-based research and development, people from around the world recognized Stanford's industrial park as exemplary in facilitating technological innovation. Americans concerned about competing on the global stage looked to the likes of Stanford Industrial Park to give the nation an edge.

The design of the pioneering industrial park merged several midcentury trends. Industry in the postwar era wanted to locate more of its operations, especially nonmanufacturing activities, in suburban settings, and at the same time hoped to strengthen its ties to research institutions. Meanwhile Stanford, like many other American colleges, set out to capitalize upon new opportunities in science and technology in order to turn itself into a leading research center. The decisions made simultaneously by business and academic leaders produced a controlled western environment that blended elements of both suburb and campus into an unprecedented site for industry.

Between 1950 and 1980 Stanford Industrial Park evolved into a highly specialized setting. The university initially conceived the project for light manufacturing, but by the mid-1950s the district, increasingly called an "industrial park," had become devoted to the research and development activities of science-based industries, as it segregated researchers and administrators from the plants and laborers who manufactured the products. By the 1970s the development had been renamed Stanford Research Park, a phrase that hinted at the ever increasing sophistication of both the landscape and the work there.

As it evolved, Stanford Industrial Park attracted observers, from around the country and around the world, who hoped to duplicate its success. Imitation was not an easy task. Stanford Industrial Park succeeded not only because of its exemplary design and its devotion to high-tech industry but also because it was in the right place at the right time. The initial growth of the industrial park coincided with heightened expenditures on scientific research and development during the cold war. Equally important, the site was located in a section of the country that attracted millions of newcomers; in a state that received a substantial share of federal expenditures for defense industries; and in a metropolitan area where people knew how to turn the influx of migrants and money to maximum advantage.

The founders of Stanford Industrial Park specifically laid it out with the goals of attracting industry to the Pacific Coast and strengthening western economic and cultural development. In these missions the district succeeded so well that by the 1960s and 1970s it had helped to spark explosive growth between Palo Alto and San Jose by creating the nucleus of a leading center for high-technology industry. Indeed, contrary to the appearance of campus and suburb, the university and industrial park became the intellectual and technological downtown for the sprawling, urbanizing region. Moreover, Stanford Industrial Park served as a model community for white-collar workers throughout the Santa Clara Valley and as a prototype for land developers and planners. The towns surrounding Palo Alto became known as "the home of the industrial park," and the careful planning, thoughtful architecture, and extensive landscaping of the controlled working environments imposed some control on a large metropolitan area where chaotic expansion seemed to prevail.[2]

The Origins of the Park

The research-oriented industrial park marked a new phase in the layout of landscapes for manufacturing. One of the earliest planned industrial districts was Trafford Park Estates in Manchester, England, laid out in 1896 when the developer converted a twelve-hundred-acre estate along a new ship channel into a home for heavy industry. In the United States, during the first decades of the twentieth century, railroad companies and their subsidiaries laid out districts for factories and warehouses, most notably in Chicago, Kansas City, and Los Angeles. Besides offering proximity to rail service, these districts differed from previous industrial areas by providing such amenities as a common system of utilities, a coordinated plan of expansion, and landscaping of open grounds. By 1940 more than thirty such American districts had been built.[3]

Railroad domination of planned industrial districts diminished after World War II as new types of developers appeared and as industry migrated away from traditional manufacturing sites in central cities. Two sets of factors drove industry toward the outlying districts. One was the availability of inexpensive land adjacent to the suburbs to which so many workers were moving. Industry needed the extra acreage for the "land-consuming, one-story" structures required for "horizontal-line production methods," for parking and loading space, and for plant expansion.[4] The other set of factors revolved around the desire for an enhanced working environment. Municipal zoning ordinances had relegated virtually all industrial activities to the least desirable parts of central cities. Increasingly after World War II, however, manufacturers insisted that, instead of being labeled as nuisances in a body, discrete industrial activities should be judged by their specific impact upon a community.[5] For such tasks as administration, research, and product development, companies desired the same features that residents and retailers sought in suburbs: a pleasant environment, segregation from undesirable neighbors, and distance from urban problems combined with proximity to city amenities.

The planned industrial district made industry more suitable for suburbs and made suburbs more suitable for industry. It surpassed conventional zoning for manufacturing, because a single organization usually master-planned and managed the project, often providing architectural, construction, and financial services to occupants. Ideally, the developer, in conjunction with local government, restricted land uses and building types, tried to ensure compatibility among occupants, and preserved open spaces. Buyers and lessees appreciated such controls because they protected companies' investments in a working environment. Observers recognized the success of organized industrial districts as they compared them to shopping centers and planned residential subdivisions, two suburban counterparts.[6]

Planned industrial districts proliferated on the peripheries of urban areas during the 1950s and 1960s. The completion of roadways around and between major cities, culminating in the construction of the interstate highway system, facilitated their emergence by providing readier access to more lands. The state of Massachusetts, for example, completed Route 128 around Boston in the early 1950s; by 1960, sixteen planned industrial districts, containing 209 modern plants, had been located at suburban interchanges along the highway.[7] These districts housed the nucleus of the high-technology industry that was to flourish in the area in the 1960s and 1970s and would earn for Route 128 frequent comparisons to Silicon Valley.

Despite the obvious similarities, the context for high-tech manufacturing in suburban Boston differed significantly from that in Santa Clara County. Science-based industry along Route 128 was just one element in a diversified economy, and its facilities were mixed in rather haphazardly with other kinds of industry and business. In the towns around Stanford, a more malleable economy and landscape permitted high-tech industry to gain a position of dominance rather quickly. Furthermore, both the development and the siting of high-tech facilities were more carefully planned in California than in Massachusetts.[8] Industrial districts in the Santa Clara Valley attempted more consciously to bring together on the same grounds those companies or divisions of companies that had something in common. They also paid more attention to compatibility between industry and surrounding communities, and they developed stronger land-use regulations and guidelines. Nationally, this more refined version of the planned industrial district came to be known as an "industrial park."[9]

Two ideas, industry and park, that had long seemed antithetical were now joined in a single felicitous phrase. The term became popular during the 1950s and 1960s as land developers tried to make projects seem more distinguished. Few American industrial parks went as far as Silicon Valley in creating communities of industries, but developers and tenants paid greater attention to aesthetics and made the environs more parklike. At the same time, districts grew more specialized as the segregation of different industrial activities continued. The phrase "industrial park" came to seem imprecise; in the 1960s the term *research park* became common, and in the 1970s the notion of an office or business park gained acceptance.[10]

Trends toward specialization and beautification reinforced one another. A company that hired people in such white-collar occupations as research, product development, and administration found that a carefully controlled working environment helped to attract, hold, and perhaps even stimulate the highly trained labor force it needed. Employers also realized that their professional workers desired to live in a nearby community that offered ample cultural amenities, attractive residential neighborhoods, and—especially for researchers—proximity to a major university.[11] Ideally, then, the industrial park should not only imitate suburban design but be situated in a desirable suburb. Moreover, the kinds of work done inside the parks had to complement, rather than compromise, the character of surrounding neighborhoods.

Stanford Industrial Park pioneered the science-oriented version of the industrial park. Soon after its opening in 1951 as a general-purpose light manufacturing district, it acquired a high-technology theme, making it one of the first industrial parks to be devoted almost exclusively to research and development. Not coincidentally, Stanford Industrial Park was also the first to be affiliated with a university, and it became a leader in providing a suburban workplace that resembled a college campus. The district's high design standards derived not only from its association with Stanford but also from its location in the affluent residential community of Palo Alto. Stanford Industrial Park was adopted as a model nationwide. In the West, where, until the 1960s, the development of industrial parks as well as high-technology industry lagged behind the East, its influence was particularly strong.[12]

Although Stanford University possessed a unique legacy of campus design, in 1945 it had hardly seemed a likely candidate to build an innovative, research-oriented industrial park. It was "a respected but essentially regional" college, not yet a national leader in higher education. In those technical fields that would soon make a name for the school, Stanford was accustomed to seeing its graduates go east to find work. Even during the war, the university housed little in the way of war-related research and development. And after 1945, finances preoccupied the university as enrollments jumped, the demand for new facilities grew, the need for higher salaries and benefits became acute, and the endowment did not keep up with the growth of its eastern counterparts.[13]

Stanford adopted land development as a partial response to these challenges. Since academic facilities occupied only a fraction of the 8,800 acres of its lands on the peninsula south of San Francisco, the institution had plenty of room for real estate ventures. The school's founding charter specified that the lands could not be sold, so Stanford developed through leasing a shopping center, medical and professional centers, and residential subdivisions—in addition, of course, to the industrial park. Of all these projects, only the park was thematically designed with special significance for the American West.

Although the university did not participate to any significant extent in wartime research and development, after the war Stanford and the West were changed dramatically by faculty members and alumni who had gone east to work on behalf of the military effort. Frederick E. Terman, a Stanford professor of radio engineering and later dean of engineering and provost of the university, headed a research project on radar at Cambridge, Massachusetts, during the war. Drawing on lessons learned in the East, he returned to spearhead the transformation of Stanford.[14] Terman's strategy, as it evolved from the 1940s through the 1960s, required a strong grasp of the new relationship between government and universities; knowledge of how a university could strengthen itself through performing research; appreciation of the benefits universities and industry could confer on one another; and commitment to regionwide economic development. These four keys not only ushered in a new age for Stanford but also proved critical for the development of Stanford Industrial Park and the rise of Silicon Valley.

By strengthening relations between research universities and the federal government, World War II and the cold war provided the basis for a new industrial age in the American West. Terman realized that in order "to insure military security in a troubled world" after 1945, the United States had to fund university research projects. He explained that the federal monies would promote "better health, better transportation, more leisure, and a higher standard of living," but the primary thrust of the sponsored research would be defense-related, making universities important combatants in the cold war.[15] Funds for research would also provide the university with opportunities to strengthen itself academically, so Terman wasted no time in winning defense research contracts for Stanford.[16]

To maximize the benefits of research funding, Terman proposed to follow the Harvard model, about which he had learned during the war. Harvard organized programs, not on the basis of teams of researchers working on one task, but around the diverse interests of individual faculty members. Instead of focusing on projects commissioned by outsiders or assigning faculty to jobs, Terman wanted independent researchers to tackle those problems that interested them, attracted attention to the university, and contributed directly to educational activities at Stanford. He hoped to build a research university upon the prominence of individual faculty members rather than on the prominence of any specified project. Terman calculated that this method would help to recruit and retain a faculty of high quality, which would in turn attract money and attention to the university. First as dean of engineering and then as provost of the university after 1955, he helped realize his goals by furnishing such incentives as pay for summer research and by recruiting for Stanford prominent scientists and engineers from across the country—particularly those who seemed most likely to attract external funding.[17]

Other American universities also enriched themselves through defense-related research for the government. In 1952 Princeton, for instance, added the James Forrestal Research Center to its campus, where scientific and engineering research under contract to the military would be concentrated.[18] But Stanford did not want to rely solely on federally sponsored science. In building a research program, Terman stressed not only a new relationship with government but also the possibilities of stronger links with private industry. In the cold war era, manufacturers came to depend upon advances in research as heavily as universities and government did. Terman repeatedly urged industrialists and academics to get to know one another's needs and interests. Industry required the skilled personnel and new ideas that colleges produced; indeed, he argued, for many growing firms proximity to universities now counted for much more than a location near raw materials, markets, or transportation networks. Research universities, for their part, looked to private industry for jobs for students and faculty, support for scholarly projects, and practical applications for new discoveries. Terman perceived the strengthening bond between universities and industries as "the wave of the future." [19]

Terman intended Stanford's new relationship with government and industry to build up both the university and the economies of the surrounding communities. He had fought a long and difficult battle to keep his graduates in radio engineering from having to "go into 'exile in the East'" in order to find work in their fields. After World War II it became even more important, in the light of Stanford's growing ambitions and limited resources, to have first-rank industrial and academic facilities nearby as an aid in recruiting new faculty and students. Many of those associated with Stanford strongly preferred the gentle climate and social ambience of the Peninsula and wished to remain close to their mentors and the university.[20] But they required economic opportunities, and those could be provided by attracting research support and industrial jobs to the Stanford area.

Terman and Stanford assumed a still grander mission. They aimed to energize, not just one university and the adjacent towns, but an entire region. They argued that the West had depended on an agricultural and extractive economy for too long; it now needed to diversify in order to achieve parity with the East. Just as the university had founded the Stanford Research Institute in 1946 with a mandate to stimulate western economic progress, Terman now pushed for the development of industry-oriented research and research-oriented industry, insisting that business and university leaders share a regional sense of purpose.[21]

Terman's ambitious postwar agenda for Stanford was largely fulfilled, and Stanford Industrial Park epitomized its success. The high-technology orientation of the park mirrored the changes under way on campus—first in the field of microwave technology, and then in aeronautical engineering and solid-state electronics. Companies occupying the district thrived on the research advances initiated and patented by Stanford, sometimes as a result of work funded by the government.[22]

If Stanford Industrial Park embodied the university's strategy, however, its form emerged only haltingly. Terman himself did not at first grasp the park's potential. The university had had little experience with real estate development before the 1950s. Years passed before cooperation between industry and Stanford became visible on the landscape. The first lease in the park was signed in 1951, but until the mid-1950s the university viewed that part of its lands mainly as a reserve for offices and light manufacturing. Debate over uses of the Stanford lands had to be settled before the district could become a true industrial park for a community of high-tech firms.

In 1945 the university established a planning office in anticipation of land development; two years later it asked Lewis Mumford, renowned critic of urban planning and former member of the Stanford faculty, for advice on how to proceed. Mumford, impressed by the juxtaposition of urban and rural features at Stanford, encouraged the university to keep its buildings as "a concentrated urban group in a permanent rural setting" (see Figure 17). He also urged that "every tendency toward scattering and suburban isolation should be resisted as ruinous to the functions of the University, and as a serious burden upon the budget."[23]

If Mumford had had his way, Stanford would have continued to lease its surplus acres to farmers and ranchers. But the trend toward suburbia proved irresistible; without it the university would never have been able to move so quickly toward the greatness it coveted. By 1950 the rents paid by agricultural tenants hardly covered the property taxes. More important, external pressure mounted to utilize the land differently. The rapid development of surrounding tracts into suburban neighborhoods heightened the demand for Stanford lands. It also increased the university's tax bill, for state law called for assessment based not on actual use but on "highest and best use" as measured by contiguous development.[24] Stanford also feared its undeveloped lands might be condemned for public projects; it needed more income to support its educational and building activities; and it felt obligated to show potential donors that it had done all it could to raise money.[25]

The move to develop nonacademic lands for income gathered momentum in 1949 with the appointment of a new university president, J. E. Wallace Sterling. In that year and the next, officials began setting aside small parcels on the extremities of the Stanford lands for a shop-

Figure 17. In 1947 Lewis Mumford urged Stanford to keep its academic
buildings (right center) as "a concentrated urban group in a
permanent rural setting" in order to keep university lands from
following the suburban form of adjacent Palo Alto, shown here
in 1953. Following his prescription would have prevented the
building of the industrial park on the open acreage (left center)
between the town and the foothills. Photo by R. L. Copeland,
courtesy of CSS Associates, Architects.

ping center, a residential neighborhood, and a manufacturing tract.
They selected the southeast corner of the property for light industrial
development because it was serviced by a railroad and could be cor-
doned off from the main campus by a planting of trees. The decision
implied that tenants in the district would produce or distribute bulky
goods for shipment as rail freight, and it suggested that they ought to
have little contact with educational programs. A consulting engineer
recommended recruiting those businesses, such as pharmaceutical manufacturers and insurance companies, that did not require proximity to
water, raw materials, or pools of blue-collar labor.[26]

Rather undistinguished thinking typified Stanford's approach during the initial stages of land development.[27] Recognizing the shortcomings, the university in 1953 commissioned the San Francisco office of

the nationally renowned architectural firm of Skidmore, Owings, and Merrill to develop a master plan for the Stanford lands. Chosen in part because of its experience in laying out communities for Ford Motor Company in Dearborn, Michigan, and the Atomic Energy Commission in Oak Ridge, Tennessee, Skidmore, Owings, and Merrill reiterated the university's commitment to an "integrated community," adding that Stanford's "community planning and development" ought to serve as an instructive example for others.[28] The architects and planners, however, could not really suggest how to integrate the community, other than by providing a system of roads. Moreover, they did not expect that truly exemplary communities would in fact spring up around Stanford. The vision of Skidmore, Owings, and Merrill for Stanford lands grew out of the firm's perception of Palo Alto as a satellite of San Francisco. The towns of San Mateo and northern Santa Clara counties had long looked northward to "the City," and the 1953 master plan assumed that this relationship would continue to dominate the landscape around Stanford. It pointed to the highway and railroad that facilitated commuting between Palo Alto and San Francisco, and it emphasized the growing neighborhoods of high-income housing, which would increase the value of university lands. Skidmore, Owings, and Merrill primarily proposed to reinforce the "present character of the entire suburban area."[29]

In stressing preservation of a "superior environment and facilities for residential living," the master plan gave short shrift both to the potential for commercial and industrial land use and to the possibility of significant expansion of the academic campus. The architects and planners conceded that commerce and industry were increasingly welcome in suburbs, but saw few benefits to be derived from non-residential activities except that of lowering homeowners' taxes and utility rates. Consequently, the master plan allotted only 55 acres for a shopping center, 66 acres for professional and administrative offices, and 209 acres for light industry—precisely the amounts of land already set aside by the university for those purposes. It then recommended reserving 2,500 acres permanently for the campus, and buffering them with another 1,000 acres in case of academic expansion. The remaining land, more than half of Stanford's 8,800 acres, was deemed "most suitable for the development of planned residential communities."[30]

This plan for the Stanford lands was being written at about the same time that Terman began to refine his strategy for achieving academic greatness and economic growth. Terman had not paid much attention to the industrial park at its inception, but by 1953 he had begun to incorporate it into his vision of Stanford's future. Now this vision clashed with the architects' master plan. In 1954 the university's Advisory Committee on Land and Building Development issued a report—drafted largely by Terman—which criticized Skidmore, Owings, and Merrill for seeing Stanford lands solely as "a vast potential subdivision which incidentally has a university occupying some of the area." The committee regarded the university's lands as the key to "making Stanford the great intellectual and research center of the West if they are not encumbered prematurely." It insisted that the institution needed ample acreage in order to attract "a wide variety of national and regional activities which have a direct and immediate value to the University," and it pointed out that the space assigned to light industry was insufficient to meet even current demand.[31]

Whereas the Skidmore, Owings, and Merrill master plan aimed to raise money through housing development, Terman and his supporters sought to attract neighbors who could contribute directly to both academic strength and regionwide prosperity. Rejecting the suburban tracts envisioned by the architectural firm, Terman argued for what he later characterized as "a community of technical scholars," consisting of "industries utilizing highly sophisticated technologies, together with a strong university that is sensitive to the creative activities of the surrounding industry."[32]

Terman's appointment as provost in 1955 helped to ensure the triumph of his vision of Stanford. The university nominally accepted the Skidmore, Owings, and Merrill master plan but ignored its basic assumptions and recommendations. Ultimately, the acreage allocated for housing development shrank drastically. In 1954 a university representative, following the master plan, spoke of more than 40,000 people living by the year 2000 in planned residential communities on 5,000 acres of Stanford lands. Five years later only 89 acres had been leased for housing, and the likelihood that many more would be converted to housing had declined sharply. After hearing that residential rents brought only about a quarter of industrial rents and a twentieth of commercial leases, the Board of Trustees decided that virtually any nonresidential development would represent "possible higher use."[33]

The size of Stanford's academic and industrial reserves meanwhile increased. The number of acres set aside for the campus grew to 5,300 in the early 1960s and, in anticipation of future academic land requirements, the university determined that it preferred leases shorter than the ninety-nine-year agreements it had already signed, a decision that further discouraged residential use.[34] Meanwhile, the acreage reserved for limited manufacturing had doubled by 1956 and, by 1960, after the university had set aside an additional 600 acres in the foothills, industrial uses occupied more of the Stanford land than any other function except the academic campus. Of equal importance, the university increasingly insisted that its lands be occupied by tenants who would "bring prestige to the several areas of development and to the University" and enhance Stanford's academic programs.[35]

A Suburban Campus for Industry

Decisions made during the 1950s about the development of Stanford lands had several important implications for the industrial park and for urbanization in the Santa Clara Valley. Despite all the assurances about "master planning" an "integrated community," the university never truly followed a long-term blueprint for development. Instead, in the industrial park and elsewhere it tended to consider each new project on its own merits rather than as part of a unified landscape—an approach for which the institution received increasing criticism after 1960. The vision that guided land development derived primarily, not from the comprehensive designs of planners and architects, but from Terman's wish to capitalize on opportunities in government and industrial research, to improve the university, and to modernize the local and regional economies. The landscape of Stanford Industrial Park did not come from a detailed master plan. However, it had the organizing theme of high technology, keyed to rapid growth in the Far West, which lent it coherence and even distinction.

The university's decision to determine land use according to its own academic and financial needs had an even more significant implication. By rejecting the report of Skidmore, Owings, and Merrill, Stanford denied the assumption that it orbited as a satellite around the city of San Francisco; it became to some degree an urban center in its own right. The university, of course, never possessed the cultural, economic, and political resources of a real downtown, and it would never rival San Francisco, or even San Jose, as a conventional focus for urban activity. Nonetheless, its technical, intellectual, and landed capital permitted it to function as a nucleus for metropolitan expansion.

By building its own shopping center, housing subdivisions, and industrial district, Stanford became much more than a bedroom community. In 1965 Terman pointed out that Stanford land development meant that Palo Altans could work and shop in the community where they lived.[36] But Palo Alto was much more than a newly self-sufficient town. It had become an alternative to traditional central business districts in the Bay Area, a place to which people from outlying areas commuted to work or to shop. At the same time it gained, in Stanford Industrial Park, a model community for industry. The university was to become the equivalent of downtown for the high-technology economy sprouting between Palo Alto and San Jose. Silicon Valley would orbit around the research center at Stanford.

Here it is important to distinguish between form and function: although Stanford took on some of the functions of a traditional downtown, it adopted nothing of its appearance or character. On this point, the Skidmore, Owings, and Merrill plan prevailed, insisting that future developments on Stanford land remain true to the form of residential suburb and college campus. A landscape that *acted* as urban center for the Santa Clara Valley *looked* both campuslike and suburban, and projected the values associated with university and suburban populations.

Stanford Industrial Park represented a new variation on several traditions, and observers initially were unsure how to describe it. Some likened the district to a garden, others to a park, still others to a country club—all provocative comparisons for what was at bottom an industrial workplace. One booster simply listed the amenities—"broad lawns, employee patios, trees, flowers and shrubs, walls of glass, recreational clubs"—that made it such a "pleasant place" in contrast to the "smokestacks, noise, coal cars, soot, and other things" associated with industry in the East and Midwest.[37] All these features defined the park as a western hybrid of the two mid-twentieth-century strains of suburb and campus.

The suburban look of the park in part reflected the growing wish of industries to locate certain of their activities in settings resembling "an expensive residential subdivision," but it also expressed the university's effort to preserve the basic character of the well-to-do neighborhoods bordering the campus. Stanford retained its own agenda for academic greatness, which occasionally clashed with the aims of its neighbors, but many of its faculty, administrators, and alumni lived in the community and insisted on protecting it from any undesirable change. The appeal of Palo Alto, after all, had helped to make the university and

Figure 18. The university managed the development of Stanford Industrial
Park so that it would not clash unduly with the suburban
ambience of Palo Alto. Most of its buildings, including the
Hewlett-Packard corporate headquarters shown here in 1987,
blended smoothly into the landscape without cluttering views
of the foothills in the distance. Courtesy of Hewlett-Packard
Company (00753–87).

industrial park inviting environments. Moreover, the town itself annexed parcels in the district once they were leased and developed, and
it insisted that those developments conform to town guidelines for land
use and zoning. Industrial tenants were not to impinge upon Palo Alto's "fine residential neighborhoods."[38]

Stanford consequently limited buildings in the park to no more than
two stories, forbade smokestacks, and prohibited any noises, odors, or
emissions that might offend homeowners. It also insisted on deep,
grassy setbacks which, as one Stanford spokesman explained, resembled
"suburban front lawns" (see Figure 18). In 1956 a real estate magazine
paid the industrial park its highest compliment by claiming that many
nearby homeowners did not even know that a sizable employment center had been created nearby.[39]

Stanford and Palo Alto expected the industrial park to blend in socially as well as physically. From the early stages of planning in 1951,

the university intended to attract "light industry of a non-nuisance type . . . which will create a demand for technical employees of a high salary class that will be in a financial position to live in this area."[40] The well-paid, well-educated worker in the industrial park made "a very desirable kind of resident" for the community, according to the president of the Stanford Board of Trustees; employers should expect the suburban environs of the park to "attract a better class of workers," Stanford's business manager explained.[41] Like a residential suburb, the landscaped industrial park would serve to discriminate between more and less preferable kinds of neighbors and employees.

Because of its university affiliation, the park was expected to attract a well-educated, and therefore desirable, type of employee. In spatial terms, too, the idea of an industrial campus added a new ingredient to the mixture of lawns, patios, gardens, shrubs, and general affluence that implied a suburban setting. The term *campus* suggests "a balanced relationship between architecture and open space" designed to enhance creativity. By the mid-twentieth century the college campus had become an increasingly influential model not only for research-oriented industry but also for civic centers, medical complexes, corporate offices, and other environments designed for white-collar professionals.[42] Stanford's guidelines for the industrial park ensured that it came to resemble a campus as well as a suburb. Besides reserving to itself final approval over architecture, the university stipulated that buildings could cover no more than 40 percent of a leased parcel in the flat sections of the district and no more than 20 percent in the foothill sections, to ensure plenty of open space between structures. It also required a minimum front setback of fifty feet and minimum rear and side setbacks of twenty feet (one hundred feet and forty feet, respectively, in the foothills).[43]

This was not the first time Americans had sought a special workplace for creativity. Thomas Edison, typifying a desire among late-nineteenth-century inventors for some sort of retreat, located his laboratories in rural settings that removed him from urban distractions without isolating him from big-city resources.[44] By the mid-twentieth century, suburbs were similarly seen as a refuge for industrial researchers, and college campuses suggested a pattern for organizing suburban space to the best effect.

The concern for open space in Stanford Industrial Park derived in large part from the desire to replicate the "climate of creativity" associated with academic settings. Companies incorporated sports facilities, courtyards, plazas, libraries, and other campuslike features into the workplace, trying to create an environment at once stimulating and relaxed. The architecture and landscaping generally turned away from the street and from other developments, in search of the cloistered feeling identified with colleges. Low-rise buildings, casual dress, and a fairly youthful work force reinforced the campus atmosphere.[45] Only the extensive pedestrian circulation was missing; in that sense the park looked more like a suburb than a college. Employees did not have much contact with the park's well-manicured exterior.

To Stanford officials who wanted land development to remain "in cultural keeping with the University,"[46] and to Stanford graduates and professors who wished to remain associated with university programs while working in the park, it no doubt seemed natural to create a working environment that resembled a college campus. But the industrial park did not resemble the Stanford campus, with its nineteenth-century, California-mission look, but, rather, a generic, mid-twentieth-century college dominated by modern architecture. The Stanford Shopping Center was slightly more attuned to the campus. Its architect, Welton Becket, and its landscape designer, Lawrence Halprin, attempted "to relate the new architecture to the old architecture on the campus through colors, materials, textures," trees, and grass.[47] The continuity may have been difficult to see, in part because the academic campus itself had diverged from its traditional plan. Nonetheless, the shopping mall had at least tenuous stylistic links to the Stanford campus, whereas ties between the university and the industrial park were intellectual, personal, and economic.

Although Stanford did not transfer its campus architecture to the industrial park, it did transfer its architectural and landscaping standards. To obtain the desired appearance, the university used the same approval process for the park that it used for campus building programs.[48] Potential tenants presented plans to the university and could not build until they had been approved. Stanford sometimes required modification of designs to suit its preferences. The approved plans then became an official part of the lease agreement, with Stanford reserving the right to veto or modify proposed changes or additions.

In the early 1950s Stanford's development guidelines for the industrial park were lenient and sketchy.[49] By the 1960s the university had become stricter about land uses, now requiring, for example, that lessees screen parking lots from the street.[50] Finally, in the 1970s, the university codified the rules that had evolved over more than twenty-five years to make Stanford Industrial Park a model high-tech landscape. Regulations called for relatively low buildings (usually a thirty-five-foot maximum) that were appropriate to the topography; parklike expanses of lawn, seeded with "random" rather than "stylized" plantings of trees; rows of foliage to screen all pavement, blank walls, mechanical and electrical equipment, trash containers, storage areas, and loading docks; underground utility lines; "complete concealment" of storage tanks, air-conditioning equipment, duct work, generators, and transformers; and minimal use of signs ("the fewer and smaller the better").[51] In short, Stanford attempted to exclude from the park any industrial or urban look.

As Stanford's plan for the district changed from light manufacturing to industrial research, it became more selective in choosing lessees. In the early 1950s, before it had settled on a high-tech theme, the university anticipated a variety of tenants. When, in 1952, Eastman Kodak leased the second parcel in the industrial district and built a film-processing plant on it, Stanford was quite pleased. In the same way that shopping-center developers tried to recruit major department stores as anchors for malls, the university wanted to identify its industrial district with a prestigious company. Soon thereafter it leased small parcels to book publishers and a few other firms whose work involved little or no industrial research.[52]

During the mid-1950s the university resolved to give preference to those companies that would contribute directly or indirectly to Stanford's scholarly programs and fit most readily into a technological community. Research-oriented companies offered much more than rental income to Stanford. They paid doubled tuition costs so that their employees could take classes in Stanford's Honors Cooperative Program; donated substantial sums to research projects and capital improvements; sponsored scholarships and fellowships; contracted with campus laboratories for specific research tasks; offered consulting positions to faculty and employment opportunities to students and graduates; brought prestige and attention to the university by exploiting the advances of its researchers; and contributed to an economic, intellectual, and physical environment that helped to attract "outstanding scientists" whom Stanford "could not otherwise afford."[53] Not every tenant performed technical research, but almost all were evaluated primarily for their ability to contribute to a research university and for their compatibility with other lessees.[54]

Stanford Industrial Park's exclusivity did not lead to any dearth of prospective tenants. Whereas most planned industrial districts, and most towns in the Santa Clara Valley, needed to market themselves energetically, industry generally came to Stanford and Palo Alto with hat in hand.[55] The companies that leased parcels appreciated the stability and amenities of Palo Alto, especially the "supply of upper-middle income housing," as the general manager of the Lockheed Missiles and Space Division explained in 1961.[56] They also valued the park's proximity to the university, for many of the same sorts of reasons the university valued the park: it facilitated a profitable interchange of ideas, continuing education for employees, recruitment of Stanford graduates and faculty, and achievement of an element of prestige. General Electric decided to build a laboratory in the park in part because it believed that the affiliation with Stanford would increase its ability to win contracts from the U.S. Department of Defense. Lockheed's director of research explained that Palo Alto provided both "the right sort of manpower" and "the right intellectual atmosphere." Recalling his firm's former dismal record in attracting new scientists, he asserted, "It is questionable whether we could do our research elsewhere—the location is essential."[57]

The carefully controlled environment was a major attraction. The setting may have served some lessees as a form of conspicuous consumption by demonstrating that they could afford elegance and space.[58] But what university and company officials emphasized was the park's effect on employee recruitment, morale, and productivity. Although the workers themselves apparently left little testimony about their feelings toward the park, advocates of the park insisted that employees appreciated the environment. According to Stanford business manager Alf E. Brandin, workers enjoyed the industrial park in the same way that students liked the campus, and Terman contended that employees "work better and more efficiently in this atmosphere."[59] Corporate spokesmen echoed these praises and, not surprisingly, endorsed the park's relatively strict land-use regulations. In 1955 one official from Eastman Kodak, which had hoped to lower employee turnover by locating in the park, told the university, "If you're as tough on everyone as you've been with us, we'll be happy."[60]

Some companies in the park not only accepted university guidelines but carried them even further. Stanford retained the power to approve or veto tenants and their building plans and provided overall direction, but the lessees themselves chose the architects, contributed to the designs, and paid for construction. They were at bottom responsible for the appearance of buildings and grounds (which would revert to Stanford upon expiration of leases), and they generally shared the university's and the town's expectations about the look of the industrial park. They hired respected architects and landscape architects, including several firms that had designed structures and grounds for the Stanford campus. Design within the park became more elaborate and elegant, and even less "industrial," over time as standards grew more rigorous.[61]

The efforts of several leading companies contributed significantly to the evolution of design within the district. Varian Associates signed the first lease in Stanford Industrial Park and in many ways set the pace for its future development. Two brothers, Stanford graduates Russell Varian and Sigurd Varian, founded the company in 1948 in order to exploit the industrial and military opportunities inherent in new microwave technologies. Their ties to Stanford had begun with the Varians' close friendship with physics professor William G. Hansen in the 1930s, and continued as the brothers shared a patent with the university and recruited such people as Frederick Terman to sit on the firm's board of directors. Like other engineers and scientists affiliated with the university, the Varians had lamented the lack of technical employment on the West Coast before 1941. When they returned from wartime work in the East, they wanted to locate their offices close to Stanford, partly "to enjoy the benefits of interchange with the various scientific programs in progress at the University," but also to attach to themselves prospective employees in school at Stanford. Varian Associates cooperated closely with the university and, once the company began to prosper, contributed generously to Stanford's educational and research programs. The history of Varian Associates demonstrated the benefits of the industrial park for both landlord and tenant.[62]

In October of 1949 Russell Varian approached Alf Brandin about leasing a parcel of land for "an electronics manufacturing and research building." The university had not yet finalized plans for an industrial park, however. Two years elapsed before the Varians and Stanford signed a lease for ten acres. The ninety-nine-year agreement required that Varian Associates pay an annual rent, adjusted for inflation; later tenants would be required to prepay their entire leases, and by 1960 the maximum length of leases had fallen to fifty-one years. Like other lessees, the company assumed the cost of all taxes, assessments, utilities, and maintenance on its parcel.[63]

Stanford officials in 1951 still regarded the industrial park as a light manufacturing district, but the Varians demonstrated that the development could mean something more. Without much prodding from the university, Varian Associates set a high standard of design. Edward

L. Ginzton, a Stanford professor who was also a founding shareholder in the firm (and who later served on Stanford's Board of Trustees), had familiarized himself with contemporary architecture at New York's Museum of Modern Art during a stint of wartime work. He persuaded the company to commission Erich Mendelsohn, the distinguished German émigré architect, to design the first building; after Mendelsohn died, the Varians retained Mendelsohn's partner, Michael Galis, for the next three structures. The company's efforts, based on the assumption that high-quality design heightened productivity, served notice that research-oriented companies in Stanford Industrial Park could develop a style that would distinguish them from other types of industrial concerns.[64] Varian Associates also led the way for other tenants by expanding quickly. It grew from one building on ten acres in the early 1950s to several structures on seventy acres by 1962. It became common for fast-growing companies in the park to take options on adjacent parcels in order to ensure that they had room for expansion.[65]

Varian Associates set an impressive standard, and the second and third tenants, Eastman Kodak's film-processing plant and General Electric's microwave-research laboratory, brought national reputations to the grounds. But Hewlett-Packard became the flagship company in the park. Its founders, David Packard and William Hewlett, had studied with Frederick Terman. It was at his urging that in 1939 they started their electronics firm (see Figure 19). Both individually and through their company, Hewlett and Packard remained intimately associated with the university—serving on the Board of Trustees, donating funds to Stanford as well as to causes in surrounding communities, and contributing to numerous educational and research programs. The most successful local company in the park, Hewlett-Packard hosted such visitors as Charles de Gaulle and Queen Elizabeth.[66]

Hewlett-Packard completed its headquarters in Stanford Industrial Park in 1957 and kept it there while expanding into a formidable multinational corporation. By the early 1960s the company had four modern buildings in the park, housing more than 3,000 employees. Their relatively sophisticated design earned the company a reputation for having what one architect deemed "the most comfortable and human-oriented buildings" in the area.[67] Inside the structures, Hewlett-Packard had already begun to develop the relatively informal management style, appropriate for a campuslike setting, for which Silicon Valley later became famous. There were few private offices; employees dressed casually, and they called one another by their first names.

An equally distinctive feature of the complex was its landscaping (see

Figure 19. The Palo Alto garage where William R. Hewlett and David
    Packard founded their company in 1939. Courtesy of Hewlett-
    Packard Company (00001–39).

Figure 20). The grounds had been designed by Thomas Church, the
noted landscape architect who had also worked on the Stanford campus, the road medians in the industrial park, and the grounds of Varian
Associates and General Electric. Aiming to give the industrial park its
own character, Church had converted the Hewlett-Packard courtyards
into a "worker's playground" where employees could find recreation

Figure 20. In 1956 Hewlett-Packard leased acreage in Stanford Industrial
Park, and by 1959 its modern complex housed approximately 40
percent of all employees in the park. The firm continued to
expand, overflowing its parking lots, among other things, and
erecting six two-story units. The buildings were arranged around
two courtyards, such as the one shown here, where workers were
presented with such campus-like features as fountains, horseshoe
pits, and a volleyball court. Such amenities helped Hewlett-
Packard earn its reputation as a good company to work for. The
company's evolution from garage to campus exemplified not only
its own success but also the success of Stanford University, the
industrial park, and the region's high-tech economy. Undated
photo courtesy of News and Publications Service, Stanford
University (#1388–3).

and relaxation. The design exemplified the care taken to create a con-
genial place to work. Throughout its tenure in the park, Hewlett-
Packard retained its commitment to "superior working environments
which enhance their communities and improve employee morale."[68]

Hewlett-Packard's and Varian Associates' close ties with Stanford,
their sophisticated approach to architecture, landscape design, and
management within the district, and their focus on high-tech research
all made them paradigmatic of the early park. Firms doing research on
missiles and space soon built in the park as well. In 1954 the Lockheed
Aircraft Corporation shifted its missiles division from Los Angeles to
Sunnyvale, partly to be nearer to Ames Laboratory, a federal space re-

search facility, but also for its proximity to Stanford's electronics program. In 1956 Lockheed chose a site in Stanford Industrial Park for a research complex. The company so liked the area that it built a large manufacturing base nearby and soon became the largest employer in the Santa Clara Valley. In the process Lockheed helped to revitalize Stanford's aeronautical engineering program.[69]

The industrial park became home to more than electronics and engineering companies. In 1959 Carl Djerassi, one of the creators of the birth-control pill, went to teach in Stanford's chemistry department, and he soon arranged to move the American operations of his company, Syntex, to the park. One of the first major pharmaceutical firms to center its research and administration in the American West, Syntex brought a new medical focus to Stanford Industrial Park, while following other park companies' lead in building a distinctive working environment. Needing to lure employees away from the East, headquarters for chemical research, it erected "an outstandingly pleasing" complex that, by the 1980s, included an art gallery in the main entrance to one building, a sculpture display, carefully maintained gardens and groves of trees, terraced lawns, and a pond stocked with fish.[70]

The ever more elegant complexes in the industrial park offered a measure of the success of both individual companies and Stanford's standards. So did the park's growth in size, population, and prestige. The industrial district had gotten off to a slow start: by mid-1955 a mere 7 tenants had leased 53 acres. But in 1962 the number of lessees had reached 42, the number of acres leased totaled 360 (about half the reserved space), and the number of employees had topped 11,000.[71] By the early 1970s the park had about 50 tenants occupying more than 500 acres and employing more than 17,000 employees. Stanford had received $18 million in prepaid leases by 1974, a sum that generated $1 million annually in investment income—not a great deal of money, considering the university's annual budget. Twelve years later the park hosted 55 companies and 26,000 workers. With annual rentals having replaced prepaid leases in 1978, it now earned $4.3 million per year for the university and $13.5 million, in tax revenue and utility payments, for the city of Palo Alto.[72]

The success of the park provoked a change of attitude among its neighbors. Most people in Palo Alto had welcomed the new district. As its parcels were developed, the city annexed, taxed, and sold utility services to them, which reduced homeowners' cost of living. The economy of Palo Alto became more self-sufficient with the new industrial base, and yet, as *Architectural Forum* pointed out in 1961, the town had not jeopardized "its opportunity to be a garden city." City planners commented that the new industrial complexes "add prestige to the community and are attractive in building design and landscaping." So long as the industrial park did not compromise the quality of suburban life, residents approved of it.[73]

As rapid growth in the district began in the later 1950s, however, the industrial center came to be seen by some as a threat to the suburban serenity of Palo Alto. Controversy broke out in 1960 when Stanford prepared to expand the park into the largely undeveloped foothills. Even though the university agreed to significantly stronger building and land use restrictions for the more sensitive zone, it had to battle alarmed citizens before it could move ahead.[74]

Increasing traffic was another concern. In 1962, almost 80 percent of the industrial park's employees commuted to Palo Alto from outside town, most of them one to a car. The suburban orientation of the industrial park perhaps reduced its ability to respond to the urban pressures generated by growth, and Stanford's land-use regulations no doubt encouraged such reliance on automobiles. The university required that each lessee provide adequate parking for all employees and visitors, so in 1962 tenants had given over sixty acres to parking lots. Few companies encouraged alternative means of transportation. Hewlett-Packard provided no walkways between public sidewalks and plant entrances, for example, leaving pedestrians to forge their own paths.[75]

Stanford officials increasingly admitted that the industrial park had changed Palo Alto, but they argued that benefits far outweighed the drawbacks. Frederick Terman in 1965 suggested that traffic congestion and air pollution were "really a pretty small price to pay" for the economic gains of the town. Robert Augsberger, Stanford's vice president for business and finance, argued in 1971 that it would be "irresponsible" to halt growth. And all along the private university, unwavering in its mission to excel as a research institution, had insisted on autonomy in how it used its land resources.[76] But as the years passed the problems grew more acute for the citizens of Palo Alto. By the 1970s, continued expansion in an industrial park that had consumed open space and contributed to "traffic nuisance, air and noise pollution, ever-increasing capital improvements costs, and higher housing costs," in the words of local planners, seemed unacceptable. Its neighbors increasingly developed a resolve to control its growth in order to preserve the "residential character" of the community.[77]

Stanford no longer lived up to the rural image conveyed in its nickname of "The Farm." In its quest to become a first-rank research university it had taken actions that made it seem unpredictable and insensitive to Palo Altans' interests. In particular, it had seldom consulted with planners from adjacent towns, and through the 1950s and 1960s it was not guided by any master plan for land development.[78] Stanford's success in becoming a great American university was due partly to its creation of a community of technical scholars. Certain aspects of its growth as a kind of regional downtown, however, ultimately proved incompatible with the suburban character that had belonged to 1950s Palo Alto.

Stanford Industrial Park had other critics as well. Some questioned its impact on an academic environment, worrying that as industrial parks came to resemble campuses, colleges were coming to resemble factories in their efforts to serve corporate and government interests.[79] But if this seemed to be the case at Stanford, it was also true at research universities across the country. The university-affiliated industrial park was the symptom, not the cause, of a larger transformation in the American academy after World War II. Stanford simply developed its ties to industry more boldly and thoroughly than other universities, and gained more from them. Its industrial park became one of the best known and most frequently consulted examples of business's new relationship with higher education. Fifty university-affiliated research parks were established during the 1960s, and by the early 1980s one study counted eighty-one. Many failed to flourish, but MIT's Technology Square, Princeton's Forrestal Center, and North Carolina's Research Triangle Park were all regarded as successful.[80]

Although Stanford Industrial Park had its critics, many other universities and towns wanted nothing more than to copy it and reap the very success that had made some Palo Altans so nervous.[81] By the time Stanford Industrial Park was featured in the American Pavilion at the Brussels World's Fair in 1958, it had come to be recognized as a model of a new type of landscape. Officials from as nearby as Berkeley and as far away as Thailand and Japan visited Palo Alto to see for themselves "[t]he ultimate in landscaping of an industrial area." They took away for their own cities and industries and universities ideas for duplicating Stanford's success.[82] The Stanford model may have influenced the layout of whole new colleges. When the regents of the University of California moved to add branches to the state system in the early 1960s, they mentioned Stanford's land development and community planning as examples of what they hoped to achieve in laying out new campuses.[83]

From "Garden of the World" to Silicon Valley

Although the influence of Stanford Industrial Park could be detected in many places, it was most readily and successfully imitated close to home, in Santa Clara County, where it became the pattern for the siting of research-oriented industry in what came to be known as Silicon Valley. As people became aware of the technological revolution taking place along the peninsula south of San Francisco, many recognized that Stanford and its industrial park had played central roles in the rapid changes.[84] Some overemphasized the importance of the park and the university. Stanford's role in encouraging high-tech industry long antedated the founding of the industrial park, and additional ingredients—the warm climate, the proximity of other universities and colleges, the brilliant innovations of individuals—were also required.[85] Nonetheless, Stanford was a primary factor in the rise of science-based industry in the Santa Clara Valley, and its research park became a prototype for nearby development.

The reshaping of the Santa Clara Valley after 1940 entailed a shift from a largely agricultural economy, focused on the processing, market, and population center of San Jose, to a primarily industrial economy revolving around the research and technology center at Stanford. Farming and food processing had prevailed in the area since the later nineteenth century. Even during the stagnant years of the Great Depression, local chambers of commerce attempting to attract new residents and business could do little but tout the valley's rural life, which reportedly made "the children vigorous, the young men and women models of strength and beauty, and the elders sturdy and well preserved."[86]

Before 1940 Santa Clara County had little direct experience with any industry but that related to agriculture. World War II doubled the size of the county's manufacturing population, but those who planned for the postwar period worried that the economy would revert to farming and canning, with their high seasonal unemployment and limited opportunity for expansion. In planning for coming decades they had little basis for optimism about the growth of manufacturing in the region, although they saw it as crucial to their economic future.[87] San Jose emerged after the war with new leadership calling for aggressive expansion, but this elite, which offered no rationale other than that of growth for growth's sake, needed a great deal of outside support to realize its goals.[88]

The town of Palo Alto had a different tradition. An exceptional community in Santa Clara County because of its university and its stronger sense of affiliation with San Francisco, even before the war Palo Alto hinted at Stanford's industrial potential. Small, high-technology enterprises had grown up around the university, providing local residents with at least some limited preparation for the changes to come.[89] And during wartime Stanford's leaders had gained some important insights into the future of research and industry. Palo Alto was thus ready to spearhead, through the university's programs, postwar economic development in the county.

In the Santa Clara Valley, as in most of the urban West, rapid growth stemmed primarily from sustained mobilization for World War II and the cold war. California in particular received a windfall of contracts for military research, development, and production between 1940 and 1970. The infusions of federal money underwrote the expansion of high-technology industry.[90] Many Americans became aware of Silicon Valley only in the 1970s and 1980s when it began to mass-produce digital watches, handheld calculators, video games, and personal computers. But consumer goods really represented a second career for its high-tech businesses. Silicon Valley firms made their mark by developing and manufacturing products for the Department of Defense and NASA. Responding to such stimuli as the wars in Korea and Indochina and the space race, electronics and ordnance companies came to account for the majority of all industrial employment in Santa Clara County. Between 1952 and 1968 these firms made at least half of their annual sales to the federal government, mostly for its military and space programs; in 1967 as many as three-fifths of all employees in the electronics industry worked on defense-related projects.[91]

NASA and the Pentagon shaped the electronics industry profoundly. Desiring more intricate and compact systems for missile and rocket guidance, they intensified the drive for ever greater miniaturization of components. And they paid a high price for their products. During the 1960s electronic equipment accounted for between 15 and 20 percent of the cost of aircraft, and for 30 percent of the cost of missiles.[92] Although Santa Clara County had no airplane factories, it nonetheless loomed large in American aerospace.

After the late 1960s the orientation of high-technology production in the towns around Stanford shifted. The military remained a major customer, of course: in 1980 Santa Clara County, with 0.6 percent of the American population, captured 3 percent of all Department of Defense prime contracts, and 20 percent of its industrial employees (8 percent of *all* employees) worked on defense-related programs.[93] But huge new markets for electronics among civilian businesses and consumers had opened, absorbing the bulk of production after 1970. In 1965 the Pentagon had purchased 70 percent of all integrated circuits manufactured; by 1978 it bought only 7 percent.[94]

Three other events also marked this great divide in the economic history of Santa Clara County. Cutbacks in military and space programs contributed to a steep recession in 1970–71, and the Intel Corporation invented the microprocessor in 1971 at the request of a Japanese manufacturer of calculators. Both developments helped to reduce the region's dependence on production for NASA and the military. At the same time, a local journalist coined the phrase "Silicon Valley" to characterize the region between Palo Alto and San Jose. As the phrase gained currency over the next ten years it evoked images of a variety of entrepreneurs producing what appeared to be a liberating technology. By the 1980s the term connoted the development and manufacture not only of semiconductors and personal computers but also of lasers, holography, magnetic recording, medical instrumentation, and pharmaceutical products.[95]

The first burst of growth in the regional electronics industry after World War II coincided with the opening of Stanford Industrial Park. In 1951 the Western Electronics Manufacturers Association listed 20 members in the area; by 1955 it counted 53. By 1974, before the proliferation of personal computers had heightened national awareness of Silicon Valley, approximately 800 high-technology firms had located there, clustering near Stanford, at the northern end of the valley, in the towns of Sunnyvale, Mountain View, Palo Alto, and Menlo Park, and employing about 150,000 people.[96]

Four types of corporate multiplication shaped the valley's economy. Some companies that originated in the area, including Varian Associates and Hewlett-Packard, grew quickly. Large national companies, such as Lockheed, Sylvania, and Philco-Ford, built facilities in the valley in order to be nearer to the technological expertise that centered on Stanford. IBM, for example, opened a research facility in San Jose in 1952 in part because it could not recruit enough Westerners to work in New York. Another form of growth occurred when companies branched out into new research-based activities. Food Machinery and Chemicals Corporation, which had specialized in manufacturing equipment and supplies for farms and canneries, moved into ordnance production during and after World War II. General Electric set up a factory in San Jose in 1948, and in 1956 it located its Atomic Power Equipment Department in the same city. Finally, employees left existing firms, such as Varian Associates and IBM, to found their own companies, often for the purpose of exploiting some research breakthrough. Companies in the semiconductor industry became legendary for perpetually spinning off new firms. A classic example is the line founded by William Shockley. Co-inventor of the transistor, he left Bell Telephone Laboratories in the East to form Shockley Transistor in Palo Alto in 1955; two years later, key employees left Shockley to join a new division of Fairchild Camera and Instrument; and by 1979 defectors from Fairchild Semiconductor had helped to start about fifty new firms.[97]

By 1980 the dizzying growth of companies and technology had made Silicon Valley, in the minds of many, much more than a place. It was considered by some to be an important national resource, by others to be "an industry, a mind-set and a way of life."[98] Electronics dominated the economy of Santa Clara County, directly and indirectly providing employment for more than 200,000 people and winning $2 billion annually in defense contracts. The county had become the ninth leading manufacturing area in the United States, the most heavily industrialized metropolitan area, per capita, in California, and the producer of 70 percent, by value, of the durable goods in the nine-county San Francisco Bay region. Manufacturing's share of local employment—the key figure for growth-minded leaders hoping to put the agricultural era behind them—reached 36 percent in 1980. It was estimated that during the preceding decade the county had created one out of every five new jobs in American high technology.[99] Observers consequently looked to Silicon Valley's "industrial revolution" for lessons in how to ensure the nation's competitiveness in global trade.[100]

High-tech industry was largely responsible for making Silicon Valley one of the fastest-growing major metropolitan areas in the country. Between 1950 and 1980 the county's population expanded more than four times, from 290,500 to 1,250,000. Natural increase played only a small role in the growth until the 1970s; the region absorbed newcomers from all across the nation, with about half of them arriving via California's other major cities.[101] Equally important, the per capita income of the metropolitan area, which already ranked above the state average, grew even faster than the population. With a highly skilled, home-owning, white-collar work force that included one-sixth of the people with Ph.D.'s in California (a billboard kept track of this figure), Santa

Clara County ranked among the nation's leading urbanized areas in median household income.[102]

The high levels of education and income indicated that local industries did not really resemble those in most other American manufacturing centers. The number of production workers was comparatively small and getting smaller between 1950 and 1970, while non-production employees, including the well-paid professionals, technicians, managers, and salespeople, generally made up more than half of the work force producing and selling electronic components and equipment, and two-thirds or more of the work force in non-electrical machinery and ordnance.[103] Santa Clara County would have its growth and its industry, apparently without becoming another Detroit or Pittsburgh.

Changes in Palo Alto prefigured the wider trends. Between 1950 and 1960 the numbers of new residents and dwelling units doubled, the portion of the population employed in industry grew by 134 percent, the median family income in constant dollars grew by 50 percent, and the median age fell by three years. That the population of the Santa Clara Valley could become larger, richer, younger, smarter, and more industrialized suggested that the region had reached its "Era of Destiny," as one local newspaper announced in a headline accompanied, appropriately, by a photograph of Stanford Industrial Park.[104]

Success tasted even sweeter because it came in "the world's best climate." Silicon Valley industrialists had not merely built a leading space-age economy; they had done so without leaving the western amenities they valued so highly. After their years of deference to eastern centers of technology, the achievement indicated their liberation from the constraints associated with traditional manufacturing: "The creators of the Santa Clara scientific community have demonstrated that under the right circumstances Americans can first choose where they want to live and then find a way to earn an ample living."[105]

Success resulted not only from economic and demographic growth, then, but also from locating that growth in a highly desirable setting. Silicon Valley's environs thus had to be preserved because they were, in fact, a key drawing card for industry. And in the early days, the landscape did not seem threatened: one reporter wrote in 1962 that industrial expansion had occurred "without any fundamental alteration of the distinctive atmosphere of the area, which has been the major attraction to many of the firms which have started up in the area."[106]

Observers increasingly came to realize, however, that economic ex-

pansion had in fact compromised the appeal of the Santa Clara Valley. Both natives and newcomers enjoyed the area's rural-and-suburban ambience and its climate, but the rapid rise of industry and population introduced urban problems into this erstwhile "Garden of the World." As in other western cities, people began to wonder whether they did not have too much of a good thing.[107]

By 1960 Palo Altans had begun to raise doubts about the impact growth was having on the quality of life, but most residents of the valley remained eager to recruit new industries and residents throughout the 1960s. Yet regional planners and environmental activists regarded the region as a striking example of the problems of modern western cities. A succession of reports—by California Tomorrow, a group of ecologically minded advocates of regional planning; by the Stanford Environmental Law Society; by Ralph Nader's Study Group on Land Use in California—condemned the valley's urban growth. Critics highlighted the apparent irrationality of new land-use patterns and stressed the waste, confusion, speculation, and tastelessness of development (see Figures 21 and 22). Karl Belser, county planning direc-

Figures 21 and 22. These two aerial photographs of Mountain View and
vicinity, one from 1950 and the other from 1975,
illustrate the changing land uses that accompanied the
transformation of the "Garden of the World" into
industrialized Silicon Valley. New highways attracted
industrial parks (see top of Figure 22) and facilitated the
relocation of people to the housing subdivisions built
atop former farmland. The only obvious constants over
twenty-five years are Permanente Creek in the foreground
and Moffett Field, a U.S. Naval Air Station, in the
background. Photography by Pacific Aerial Surveys,
Oakland (negs. SCL-C8–3 and SCL-C8–44).

tor, termed the area "a completely irrelevant urban development."[108]
Others argued that senseless land patterns mirrored a diseased culture
that, in its city-building, had encouraged such miseries as alienation,
blight, racial segregation, and the erosion of community identity.[109]

Although critics of urban growth in the Santa Clara Valley pointed
to real problems, they probably overstated certain complaints. For one
thing, this particular kind of growth was to some extent self-correcting.
Research-oriented industry tended to attract engineers and technicians
who came to disapprove of the excesses in local towns and echoed crit-

ics' concern about the costs of unbridled growth. Such individuals contributed to the rise of a different brand of politics in the early 1970s, most in evidence in San Jose. The new leadership replaced the growth-at-any-cost mentality with a preference for more managed expansion.[110]

Some major employers joined the movement to protect the Santa Clara Valley environs. David Packard, co-founder of Hewlett-Packard, cemented high-tech industry's reputation for concern about the local quality of life. In 1961 his firm recognized the increasing urban congestion in Palo Alto and decided to locate new plants elsewhere in the county in order to protect the character of the town. In later years Packard remained committed to carefully managed growth at the regional level, for much the same reason that his firm had originally leased a parcel in Stanford Industrial Park: "Our success and progress is [sic] dependent on being located in a community that's attractive for all our employees."[111]

The people of Silicon Valley shared some of the concerns of critics, but they generally did not feel so alarmed. If they perceived drawbacks to the fluidity of their society, these were outweighed in their minds by the virtues of the region and the rewards of participating in a growth industry. Moreover, although residents disliked the extremes of rapid expansion, most of them did not object to the sprawling form it took.

Planners agonized about the absence of a strong downtown, the shortage of cultural and recreational facilities, the fate of farmland and open space, and the need for tax increases and stronger planning. But most residents had narrower interests in mind.[112] They tended to conceive their environs not as whole cities but as a collection of districts, giving greatest attention to those subdivisions, shopping centers, and highway networks where they and their families spent the most time. They typically identified not with a town or region, but with a series of small parcels connected by roads that crossed municipal boundaries. They cared less about overall design in the region than about those places where they spent their time living, shopping, driving, learning, and, not least of all, working.

Urban Order in Silicon Valley

The significance of the research-based industrial park gains clarity when it is seen in the light of the nature of urbanization in the Santa Clara Valley. Like other magic kingdoms, the park brought a semblance of community and culture to a society characterized by apparent disorder and sprawl. Critics, of course, could still perceive the industrial park as part of the problem rather than as a solution; its low-slung buildings and substantial open spaces perhaps wasted land, and its inward focus may have militated against the human circulation associated with conventional urban life.[113] Most people, however, seemed to approve of the special environment. Employees who spent every working day in the parklike setting apparently found it both safe and stimulating. It provided ample parking, well-designed architecture, and pleasing landscaping. Rather than opening outward on the problems of the metropolis, the planned industrial district, like a college campus or residential subdivision, secluded employees from the annoyances that had accompanied urbanization in the Santa Clara Valley.

Industrial parks injected an element of cohesion into what others saw as a disorganized urban scene. Moreover, in contrast to high-tech industry in the East, Silicon Valley was said to provide a comparatively relaxed and pleasant setting that lured prospective employees and facilitated the exchange of ideas and interests.[114] These advantages derived in no small part from the controlled environment of the park.

The research-oriented industrial park gradually became the spatial model for the high-technology economy of the Santa Clara Valley. A survey conducted by county planners in 1967, before the research-oriented economy had matured fully, tallied thirty-eight industrial parks in the corridor between Palo Alto and San Jose. Most lay within two miles of a major highway, and most had a diverse list of tenants, including numerous companies not involved in research, high technology, or industry. Perhaps anticipating continued rapid growth, most also had substantial vacancies—more than half of their total acreage was generally available for sale or lease. Virtually all the parks enforced regulations of some type about landscaping, setbacks, and other aesthetic features.[115]

In a dozen of the districts surveyed, a substantial portion of the lands had been leased or sold to research-based industry. These twelve sites lay primarily between Palo Alto and Sunnyvale, near either Stanford University or Moffett Field, the U.S. Naval Air Station in Mountain View that served as a center for aeronautical research.[116] Stanford Industrial Park remained the largest site and counted the most high-technology firms as occupants, but the others represented substantial concentrations of research-based industrial activity, especially of companies engaged in work for defense or space programs.

It is difficult to measure precisely the impact of Stanford Industrial Park on other districts in the valley, but the park was widely acknowledged as the regional prototype, and its success clearly encouraged emulation. Many developers visited the park and consulted with Stanford officials before launching their own projects. Moreover, as tenants in the park added facilities at other sites in the county, they borrowed freely from Stanford.[117] Varian Associates, needing more space during the early 1960s, purchased 640 acres in Cupertino and Santa Clara, along the Junipero Serra Freeway. The company, in conjunction with local landowners, developed some of the parcel into housing and a shopping center, and converted about 250 acres into Vallco Park for high-technology industry. Like its predecessor on Stanford lands, Vallco Park had stringent regulations covering architecture, signs, parking, setbacks, and storage facilities, and it required occupants' grounds to conform to a master plan drawn up by landscape architect Lawrence Halprin. In 1967 all three tenants, American Micro-Systems, Mark Systems, and Varian Associates, were engaged in research-based industry, and over the years Vallco Park acquired additional high-tech companies.[118]

The International Science Center in Sunnyvale added to the research park features that even Stanford did not have. In 1967 it had not only the normal range of high-tech tenants—Fairchild Semiconductor, Huggins Laboratory, and Signetics in electronics, General Precision, Lockheed, United Technology, and Philco-Ford in aerospace—but also special services for the surrounding industrial community. The 130-acre park included computer and data processing centers available for use by other occupants; a University of California extension facility; an Armed Services Technical Information Agency Office; and a West Coast branch of the United States Patent Library.[119]

Industrial park development kept pace with economic expansion in the Santa Clara Valley. By 1977 the San Jose Chamber of Commerce counted 57 industrial parks in Silicon Valley, and four years later it listed 107 developments occupying approximately 9,400 acres. Most sites continued to be located near major freeways. However, because most of the land available for large new projects was in the southern part of the valley, the majority of industrial parks were now situated within the city limits of San Jose and Santa Clara.[120]

By the later 1970s the occupants of Silicon Valley parks represented a substantially wider range of activities than before. Few overseers of industrial parks had ever been as strict as Stanford in adhering to a research-oriented theme, and offices and light manufacturing had co-existed with high-tech industry in many districts. A growing number of retailers acquired space in or next to industrial and business parks, in order to cater to the work forces of the parks. The new trend did not constitute a serious challenge to shopping malls, but it did offer convenience to employees who could now dine, shop, and transact some business quite near their workplace. Fast-food franchises led the way, and other services soon followed—travel agencies, banks, insurance companies, health clubs, even hotels. By 1981 the Grace Bible Church had come to San Jose's Central/Lawrence Business Park.[121]

The industrial park reached its highest stage of development when a few companies built exclusive research "campuses." IBM constructed two particularly notable complexes along these lines. In the early 1950s it erected a research center in San Jose that included classrooms, recreational facilities, an ornamental lake, a sculpture display, a pedestrian mall, and a golf course.[122] In the early 1980s, IBM opened the even more elaborate Santa Teresa research center in rural south San Jose. The architectural historian Reyner Banham viewed the complex as a perfect example of the "sharp, modern imagery" of Silicon Valley companies— "precise and elegant outwardly, almost an art gallery within, set in restrained, expensive and well-kept landscaping typified by lawns so neat they might as well be Astroturf." IBM's rationale for the Santa Teresa center illuminated how it had been guided by motives similar to those behind Stanford Industrial Park. The company explained that it needed the "isolated, rural, campus-like setting" in order "to compete with the universities for top scientists in this country—a place to which such persons will be attracted to perform basic research and to interact with other scientists."[123]

By the late 1970s the administrative headquarters of Silicon Valley companies were receiving the same treatment as their research complexes. The main offices of the Rolm Corporation, completed in 1980 in Santa Clara's Marriott Industrial Park, illustrated the suburbanization of industrial design. John Jasper, the principal architect, explained the layout in terms that echoed the rationale for research parks: "Our intention was to create a quiet, natural setting and surround it with buildings that close off the world outside—the traffic and the street noise."[124] Corporate managers apparently required the same kind of campuslike seclusion as scientists and technicians.

The elite of Silicon Valley worked amid architecture and landscaping that had earned recognition as a distinctive regional style.[125] And the influence of industrial park design spread beyond those buildings and grounds reserved for top executives and researchers. Throughout the region, well-maintained lawns and gardens, berms and setbacks, and modest signs became the rule even for undistinguished parcels developed as manufacturing and office complexes. Local officials promoted the style. City and county planners, eager to encourage any vestige of control over the rapidly changing lands, embraced the industrial park as a device to bring order to the sprawling urban pattern, and thus helped to make its suburb-and-campus image the characteristic look of the region. In 1972 Sunnyvale's planners advised new manufacturers, whether or not they were building in a planned development, to adopt industrial-park design: "Site planning should provide landscaping for buildings and parking areas. There should be ample off-street parking and loading. Nuisances, such as odors and noise, are controlled by zoning."[126]

The look of the industrial park particularly pervaded the southern Santa Clara Valley, which had more acres available for industrial development. In 1984 the city planning department of San Jose described virtually all local real estate for manufacturing as having "a low profile, landscaped industrial park character."[127] Moreover, San Jose's guidelines for developers, like Sunnyvale's, encouraged conformity to the look. The city had six different classes of industrial land use—one for heavy industry, one for light industry, and four that equaled or excelled industrial park standards. The top category of the four, for "research and development," permitted no less than fifty acres for a single user and no more than 15 percent coverage of land by buildings. The next category, "campus industrial," called for a minimum parcel of twenty-five acres, building coverage of less than 30 percent, and landscaping of at least one-quarter of the parcel. The third classification, "research, development, and administrative," required ten acres per parcel and buildings constructed on a residential scale. The fourth category, regular "industrial parks," allowed a mixture of light manufacturing, office, and retail activities.[128]

In the Santa Clara Valley, then, parks for research-based industry had become the model for a wide spectrum of land uses, helping to form the distinctive character of the region. As a special environment for workers, they had contributed to the emergence of a western center for high-technology industry. At the same time, they helped to provide a sense of order and planning, on a small scale, in a rapidly urbanizing region. The design standards that had been shaped by Stanford's unique interests and needs in the early 1950s served over ensuing decades as guidelines for districts that owed less to Stanford's direct influence.

Industrial parks succeeded in part because they represented pockets of cohesion in a seemingly chaotic cityscape. They appeared to be exempt from the problems associated with rapid, unplanned growth, and they brought together people with shared interests. However, if workers could escape urban ills inside an industrial park, that did not mean those ills had been cured or banished. While industrial parks provided coherence in people's mental maps of Silicon Valley, other problems mounted. These crises revolved not so much around the issues of culture or community as around imbalances in the local ecology, economy, and society, and the dependence on industrial parks may actually have exacerbated such imbalances.

In the Santa Clara Valley, as elsewhere on the Pacific slope, the amenities that lured newcomers to metropolitan areas came to be threatened by the very growth they had encouraged.[129] Residents' initial reaction was to attempt to manage growth in order to sustain the region's appeal to new residents and businesses; when that response proved insufficient, more stringent measures were proposed. Some towns actually considered halting growth or turning it away, reversing their long-standing commitment to expansion.

Discovery of toxic wastes from a supposedly clean industry dramatized the problems of growth. By 1987 Santa Clara led all counties in the nation in toxic waste, with nineteen different "Superfund" sites, that is, deposits of toxics so serious that the U.S. Environmental Protection Agency had given them highest priority for clean-up. One of the deposits was at Stanford Industrial Park, which had another eleven sites under investigation. Alarmed residents in Palo Alto responded by supporting new regulations so stringent that they persuaded at least one high-tech company to move its planned research and development complex from Stanford Industrial Park to the less restrictive community of Mountain View.[130]

More highly publicized was the uneven distribution of jobs and housing in Silicon Valley, which exacerbated ecological, aesthetic, and social imbalances. Every city hoped to achieve a kind of self-sufficiency by providing "employment for a number equivalent to its [resident] labor force." Approximating this ideal state supposedly would minimize the traffic that accompanied intercity commuting; attract enough industry to reduce homeowners' tax burden; and strengthen residents' sense of community identity.[131] This goal of self-sufficiency proved almost impossible to achieve, in part because of residents' high mobility and lack of attachment to towns as defined by municipal boundaries. Sunnyvale felt the imbalance acutely. After toiling between 1960 and 1975 to become a "regional industrial center," it accomplished its goal so well that in 1979 it faced a severe shortage of housing and utility services and had to declare "an emergency moratorium on industrial growth."[132]

Calling a temporary halt to industrial expansion was a small-scale attempt to solve a large-scale problem. Throughout the mid-1970s, high-tech workplaces tended to cluster near Stanford's community of technical scholars, but the majority of homes were located at the other end of the valley. Sunnyvale, Palo Alto, Mountain View, and Santa Clara had more industry than housing; together, the four towns experienced a net daily influx of 84,000 commuters in 1975. San Jose, which at the same time "lost" 45,000 commuters a day, faced the opposite situation. It housed about half the county population but provided less than one-third of the jobs. As a result its tax base was extremely weak, and its commuters generated horrendous traffic.[133]

Planners in the Santa Clara Valley seemed oblivious to the mounting problems in the mid-1970s. They had uniformly emphasized attracting to their towns more industry, with its richer revenues, without preparing to attract as well ample housing to accommodate the growing numbers of employees.[134] Furthermore, the towns differed widely in their ability to achieve or modify their goals, and they resisted cooperation. The citizens of industry-rich Palo Alto proved comparatively effective at checking growth and its attendant hazards, but their success merely heightened the pressures elsewhere. Absence of growth in Palo Alto implied greater growth in the southern end of the valley, just as tough local regulations on toxic wastes had meant more pollution for less restrictive towns. No-growth policies also drove up the price of land and housing in Palo Alto, so that even fewer commuters could afford or even find a place to live there. San Jose, meanwhile, struggled to raise revenue for the services it had to provide for the lion's share of Santa Clara Valley residents. Naturally, its calls for redistribution of county revenues from industry found little support in northern towns.[135]

By the early 1980s certain changes hinted at redress of the imbalance of jobs and housing. The initiative came in part from Silicon Valley companies, which were reputedly sensitive to workers' needs and devoted to upholding a positive corporate and regional image in order to maintain a competitive edge in recruiting new employees. In 1977 two firms headquartered at Stanford Industrial Park, Hewlett-Packard and Watkins Johnson, built manufacturing plants in a largely undeveloped section of northern San Jose, explicitly chosen as closer to the residences of workers. Other companies followed suit. By 1980, developers had carved fourteen industrial parks out of an area dominated by fields and orchards.[136] Moreover, county plans for a light-rail transit system promised relief from traffic congestion.

However, these steps amounted to too little, too late. Many companies, especially the smaller and less prosperous ones, resisted moving away from Stanford. And given a commuting population notoriously dependent on automobiles, there seemed little reason to expect a new transit system to make more than a small dent in the valley's traffic problems. Finally, as in the towns of the northern Santa Clara Valley, in San Jose the price of housing continued to climb. In 1980, among the thirty largest metropolitan areas in the country, San Jose had the highest median rent and the second highest median value of private homes.[137]

The brunt of the socioeconomic imbalances in Silicon Valley was borne, not by the employees who worked in research-oriented industrial parks, but by those in the lower half of a two-tiered work force. Engineers, scientists, and executives tended overwhelmingly to be educated, affluent, white males. Production workers in high-technology manufacturing, on the other hand, tended to be less educated and less affluent, and consisted of a high proportion of women and members of racial and ethnic minorities. These laborers gained less than white-collar professionals from the rapid growth of Silicon Valley, and they generally lacked the resources that would prepare them for participation in the upper layer of high-tech employment.[138] This segment of the Silicon Valley labor force was more vulnerable to the high price of housing, to periodic recessions in the industry, and to exposure to toxic chemicals used in manufacturing. And contrary to the traditional metropolitan pattern, in which executives and managers commuted a longer distance from suburbs to work, more semi-skilled and unskilled employees found themselves driving to and from their jobs over long distances in formidable congestion.[139]

In all likelihood, production workers found little compensation for their troubles in the high quality of the workplace, because the suburb-and-campus layout of industrial parks was not tailored for them. In devising the research-oriented industrial park as a setting that distanced professional and managerial employees from certain urban problems, Stanford and other developers had consciously increased the distance between classes. Those who created or marketed high-tech products came to have less contact than before with those who mass-produced them. Some production employees worked in settings that had been influenced by the research-oriented industrial park, but theirs was clearly a different world.

It was also a world that was shrinking. Partially in response to the urban imbalances generated in the Santa Clara Valley during the 1970s, high-technology firms began to move some of their operations away from the region. Hewlett-Packard stated that after it completed a new headquarters in Stanford Industrial Park it would no longer build facilities in Silicon Valley. Along with other companies, it looked outside the county for places where workers could find more affordable housing and less traffic congestion, and where management could find more skilled workers. Silicon Valley firms built many complexes at sites in other parts of the American West—on the northern perimeter of the San Francisco Bay Area, around Portland and Seattle and Boise, and in Colorado, Texas, and Arizona. Some of the unskilled and semi-skilled work, however, was shipped offshore to southeast Asia, which had long performed semiconductor assembly for Silicon Valley.[140] Such actions helped to disperse an industry that had become quite concentrated, and perhaps relieved some of the pressure on Santa Clara Valley towns, but they also produced dislocations felt most sharply by the lower tier of employees.

Changes in the location of certain parts of high-technology industry did not reduce the importance of the research-oriented industrial park. Indeed, they probably strengthened its influence, both far and near. When Hewlett-Packard considered expansion in the early 1980s to Roseville, California, near Sacramento, it proposed development of an industrial park there, to be styled along the lines of Stanford's. And as other companies moved to new locales in the West, they expressed a preference for sites that offered proximity to a university as well as a "campus-like environment with landscaping."[141]

The research park was to become even more prevalent in the Santa Clara Valley. Although some sectors of the industry departed the region, companies generally kept their research and development centers in the vicinity and expanded their administrative offices there. Research parks became more like business parks: between 1980 and 1988 9 percent of the new construction at Stanford Industrial Park housed manufacturing, 30 percent housed research and development, and more than half consisted of office space. High-tech firms might have exported some of their appendages to other states and countries, but they intended to keep their brains next door to Stanford.[142] The university remained the nucleus of Silicon Valley.

Stanford's efforts to transform itself and the surrounding towns into a western research center of national importance had succeeded beyond its expectations of the early 1950s. Success was accompanied by a general reshaping of the cultural landscape of the Santa Clara Valley in the campus-and-suburb image of the university and neighboring Palo Alto. The transformation of the valley had been so rapid and thorough that at times it seemed to diminish the very amenities that had made the region attractive to high-technology industry in the first place. Yet the new patterns imposed on the land had helped to insulate certain parts of the population from the problems of urbanization at the same time that it had encouraged the growth of industry. The research-oriented industrial park pervaded the Santa Clara Valley because it provided an alternative to traditional downtowns and because it brought a certain order and control to a chaotic urban scene.

CHAPTER FOUR

Sun City, Arizona:
New Town for Old Folks

Sun City, Arizona, opened for business on January 1, 1960, a new town for a new decade. On the surface the subdivision may have resembled a young Levittown—a flat, uninspiring tract offering modest, mass-produced houses. But at least three features of this community on the outskirts of Phoenix set it apart from other American suburbs. First, it promised a fairly familiar landscape, as green and well-maintained as suburbs in other parts of the country, but it did so in the middle of a desert. Second, the builder of Sun City, the Del E. Webb Corporation of Phoenix, intended to attract residents not primarily from the nearby metropolis but from cities and towns across the nation. Third, in contrast to Levittowns, Sun City had from the outset a conscious thematic orientation. The developer designed it exclusively for the elderly, a small fraction of the home-buying public, and assured prospective residents that the town would provide them with "Active Retirement" as a new "Way-of-Life." Each of these three distinguishing features—the desert location, the intended market, the thematic orientation—marked Sun City as a distinctly western development.

Sun City was not the earliest retirement community in the United States, but it was the first to capture widespread attention and the first of its kind, "a new town for retirement" that was largely self-contained and isolated from its neighbors.[1] Sun City became the largest and best-known retirement community in the country. By 1980 its population topped 45,000, its size approached 9,000 acres, and its developer had started another town for retirees called Sun City West right next door. Sun City had not only succeeded in financial terms but also seemed to address pressing concerns about the rapidly growing population of senior citizens. Observers generally agreed that its residents seemed happier and healthier than the average elderly American, in part because the community gave them a heightened sense of independence and control over their destinies. The town apparently lived up to the developer's claim that retirees in Sun City could "partake in the joy of living on *their own terms*."[2]

The effort of elderly people to protect their autonomy by retiring to Sun City paralleled very closely the attempt by Westerners as a whole in the mid-twentieth century to take life more "on their own terms" by moving to and remaining in an urban region perceived as more suitable for them than the East. Retirees, of course, were by no means average Westerners. The populace of the region, especially most newcomers, was by and large youthful. Migrants to Sun City tended to be relatively affluent, by comparison to the average person in the region. And unlike younger adults, the elderly no longer concerned themselves much with raising children, supporting local schools, or commuting to work. Above all else, they wanted amenities (see Figure 23). Their stage of life gave them a singular perspective on urban living.

Nonetheless, Sun City illustrated the pursuit by Westerners of a special spatial relationship to the metropolis that conformed to the orientations of both regional and national culture. The Arizona retirement town did for residential housing what Stanford Industrial Park did for high-tech industry and what Disneyland did for family recreation. It provided a model for a spotless, pacesetting, thematically organized cityscape that surpassed eastern conventions and fulfilled some Westerners' expectations of an enriched urban environment.

Sun City exemplified the planned-community response to the chaos of rapid urban expansion. Its careful design contrasted with the perceived inability of planning in metropolitan Phoenix to keep pace with growth. Like other planned communities in the West, urban design in Sun City evolved from the vision of a private developer and from the preferences of buyers as revealed by market research. The result was a community that held itself rather aloof, an attitude that hardly made the people of Sun City model citizens in the eyes of the rest of Phoenix. Yet comprehensive planning did make the new town itself sufficiently impressive to become a prototype both for other American retirement communities and for additional subdivisions in the Phoenix area. Although Sun City was an exceptional community, it was a highly influential one.

Sun City perhaps exerted a disproportionately strong influence on

Figure 23. Del E. Webb presented Sun City as more than another
construction project. It packaged numerous amenities into an
instant and homogeneous community for the elderly. Undated
photo courtesy of the Sun Cities Area Historical Society.

the shaping of greater Phoenix because it had few rivals as a pattern for
urban expansion. Growth in greater Phoenix took place so rapidly between 1940 and 1970, and with so few controls, that people seemed
eager to embrace any spatial pattern that appeared to offer a semblance
of order on the landscape.

The explosive growth of Phoenix during the mid-twentieth century
stemmed from the same forces that were at work throughout the western United States. Once known primarily for its cotton farms, Phoenix
lagged behind Tucson in population through 1910. Then, by steadily
shifting its economic focus from agriculture to commerce, it became
Arizona's leading urban center. Advances in technology and public relations furthered its aims. Improvements in transportation and air conditioning helped to make Phoenix more accessible and attractive to prospective residents and tourists, while boosters refashioned its image by
calling the urban basin "The Valley of the Sun." Growth consequently

proceeded at a pace that even the Great Depression hardly slowed. Between 1920 and 1940 Phoenix's population doubled, from 29,053 to 65,414, and the city emerged as the Southwest's most important oasis between El Paso and Los Angeles.[3]

The outbreak of World War II accelerated the expansion of Phoenix. By the end of 1942, three army bases and six air bases had been activated in the vicinity, and by 1945 a number of defense plants had arrived, bolstering the town's weak industrial base. Phoenix parlayed these federal investments into postwar dividends. With the onset of the cold war, Luke and Williams air force bases continued to thrive and to keep the attention of military contractors focused on the area. In 1948–49 the Motorola Corporation decided to open a new plant for defense electronics in the city, and it soon became a leading employer. The company was initially attracted by the air bases, but it also praised in Phoenix the same things that tourists applauded. Motorola regarded the town's amenities as valuable assets for attracting and keeping the well-educated employees it needed. Joined by such firms as Sperry Rand, AiResearch, and Goodyear Aircraft, Motorola spearheaded the rise of a defense-oriented, high-technology economy in the area.[4]

The development of industry in Phoenix underwrote a mid-century burst of growth. The population of Maricopa County (the Phoenix metropolitan area) ballooned from fewer than 200,000 in 1940 to almost 1,000,000 in 1970. Most accounts portrayed the arriving population as basically middle-class and paid little attention to those members of the Spanish-speaking and black minorities who dwelled in the poorer sections of the city. In 1959 more than 90 percent of the local households owned at least one car, and more than 70 percent owned their own homes. Needless to say, many of the houses had been mass-produced by developers such as the Del E. Webb Corporation.[5] The housing shortages created by rapid growth left little time for more traditional modes of construction.

Similarly, the urgency of expansion left no time for prudent planning of the city, not that much evidence exists that postwar Phoenix would have embraced careful design even if there had been time. Arizona made no substantial provisions for urban planning until the 1960s.[6] Furthermore, those officials charged with planning responsibilities devoted more attention to facilitating growth than to managing it. Rather than devise strict land-use or zoning controls, city officials in Phoenix viewed as their chief task avoiding the fate of St. Louis and other central cities back east that had been "strangled" by the growth of surrounding suburbs. Planning for Phoenix entailed a policy of aggressively annexing outlying tracts before they could throttle central city expansion. In the 1950s alone, the area of Phoenix proper multiplied eleven times, from 17.1 to 187.4 square miles, while the population increased "only" fourfold, from 106,818 to 429,170.[7]

The territorial imperative of Phoenix had a profound impact on metropolitan form. It directed attention away from the central business district and toward the fringes of the urban area, and it encouraged a generally thin and uneven pattern of settlement. As late as January 1, 1965, more than 40 percent of the land within city boundaries was classified as vacant, and agriculture occupied another 24 percent. Some of these acres were too rugged to accommodate any urban settlement, whereas others would soon be converted to "urban purposes."[8] In any case, their annexation by Phoenix had practically guaranteed a low-density cityscape.

As a consequence, the population would develop an inordinate dependence on the automobile, to the detriment of public transportation. "You can get along without a car in Phoenix," one booster allowed in 1955, "but it's a little like having only one leg."[9] The preponderance of autos, coupled with permissive zoning, led to extensive commercial strip development along major roadways, further heightening traffic congestion. The accepted antidote to this problematic pattern, of course, was not to revitalize downtown but, rather, to encourage development of outlying shopping centers that had ample off-street parking.[10]

As the preferred alternative to commercial strips and to downtown stores, the shopping center foreshadowed the impact of the planned community on the Phoenix cityscape. Both forms of land development were large-scale projects undertaken by a single builder. Both would generally be located on vacant or agricultural lands at some distance from the central business district. Both would incorporate careful internal design that was somehow to compensate for the insufficiency of external planning. Both would be encouraged by local leaders and planning policy.[11] In fact, shopping centers and packaged residential subdivisions became integral to the appearance and organization of postwar Phoenix.

Planned communities may have seemed a logical response to rapid urban expansion, but it was not initially clear that these subdivisions would be given over to the elderly. The people who migrated to Maricopa County were comparatively youthful. The median age in the metropolitan area in 1960 (26.7 years) was about three years below the national average (29.5) and about four years below the average for all American metropolitan areas (30.5).[12]

There was in 1960 little reason to expect that retirees would soon make up a considerable portion of the Arizona population, or that the elderly would have much impact on the cityscape of Phoenix. This myopia was hardly limited to the Southwest. As a nation the United States hardly counted retirement among the new frontiers it proposed to explore during the 1960s. Mid-twentieth-century Americans were just beginning to discover the phenomenon of retirement, and the elderly were just beginning to discover the Southwest as a place where they might spend their final years.

Retirement in Postwar America

There were few precedents for the emerging social pattern of retirement in the United States. Old age, of course, was hardly new, and the society had known elderly people who were generally healthy and financially independent. But there had never been so many of them before—a virtually intact generation of well and active individuals with time and money to spend—and they had never comprised such a large portion of the American people. In 1900 those aged 65 and over had accounted for about 4 percent of the population. By 1950 they amounted to 8.1 percent, or 12 million souls; by 1980 America's 25.5 million senior citizens represented 11.3 percent of the population.[13]

Improved health permitted the emergence of a generation of retirees.[14] And at the same time that the aged came to have more years of life, American society determined that their added time would not be spent on the job. It designed policies to discourage the elderly from continuing gainful employment in the economy, and it established programs to provide an increasingly adequate income that would take the place of wages, salaries, or public assistance.[15] The Social Security Act of 1935 anchored a system of growing financial support for seniors while encouraging the belief that sixty-five-year-olds had a right to retire. This piece of New Deal legislation began to have widespread influence among the elderly after 1950, and by the 1970s it had helped to eliminate the worst of the poverty that had once been associated with aging.[16] American retirees became more numerous, more prosperous, and more healthy throughout the postwar era.

From one perspective, it could be argued that national policies toward old age had succeeded in a rather negative fashion. They determined what the elderly ideally should *not* do—work, starve, or sicken—but they had little to say about how the elderly might otherwise spend their lives. Americans seemed quite prepared in 1960 to make retirees a more vital part of the society, but had little idea what role or function the elderly might serve now that they were less integral to economic production. The aging population no longer dreaded retirement as years of unremitting dependency, but they did express ambivalence, and even resistance, toward retirement, in large part because the idea seemed so ill-defined.[17]

Lest retirement come to connote social uselessness, a number of observers attempted to give shape to that phase of life. Some urged that senior citizens must hold positions of responsibility in the society. Others viewed purposeful leisure as the natural substitute for work as the central theme of elderly lives. The example of retirees might prove invaluable to a society that expected to spend more and more time away from the job, wrote one student of leisure: the elderly could show the rest of the country how to "replace work as the main source of meaning in life."[18] The implication was that the elderly could be useful by being "useless."

Most Americans, including the aged themselves, remained unprepared to make leisure "the moral equivalent of work."[19] They generally agreed that adults ought not to work after a certain age, but they hesitated to recognize leisure as a legitimate alternative. This uncertainty resulted in the peculiar tendency to see retirement as a kind of job, an activity at which people should toil. Robert K. Merton, for example, complained in 1958 that the elderly were not productive or efficient enough as consumers of leisure because they were so "highly disorganized. And without a framework for guiding their activities they waste a deplorable amount of time."[20]

Whether or not society had prepared the way, retirees now had to look upon leisure time in new ways. This reevaluation added to the number of factors that distinguished life prior to retirement from life afterward and that increasingly set elders apart from the rest of society. These accumulating distinctions may have encouraged a few older Americans to think that a change in residence ought to accompany the other changes taking place in their lives.[21]

Migration by the elderly constituted another relatively unexplored frontier. Americans have long had a reputation as a restless and mobile people, and nowhere more so than in successive Wests. However, in the later twentieth century the elderly were the segment of the population least likely to move. During the 1950s and 1960s, 7 to 8 percent of people aged sixty-five and over changed residences annually, a rate about half that of the general population. And few of those aged who did move went to another county or state; the elderly were also less likely to migrate long distances.[22] These tendencies produced a pattern that demographers termed "aging in place." Certain neighborhoods (particularly those in rural areas and central cities, and those with older housing stock) tended to acquire concentrations of the elderly as the aged remained while the younger population left.[23]

The concept of aging in place helped to explain aggregations of stationary elderly in northeastern and north central states. By the 1970s and 1980s, however, clusters of retirees had begun to appear in southern and western states; a small but growing stream of elderly had decided to age in another, warmer place.[24] These mobile retirees tended to be healthier and wealthier than those who aged in place; they had more likely moved recently before retiring, and many had vacationed in or near the area to which they chose to relocate. Unlike more youthful migrants, the elderly found lowered costs of living a strong inducement to move to the South or the West.[25]

The movement of retirees thus bore an imperfect resemblance to the general postwar migration in the same directions. Whereas California garnered the lion's share of the overall migration to the Sunbelt, Florida attracted more retirees than any other state. It and the other states along the Atlantic seaboard and Gulf Coast mostly recruited their aged newcomers from east of the Mississippi River. Elderly migrants beginning from points on the other side of the great river generally headed toward the Southwest, the Northwest, and parts of Colorado, feeding western clusters of retirees.[26]

Those who hoped to spend their final years in the West followed in the footsteps of earlier generations of health-seekers. Even more than non-elderly migrants to the region during the postwar era, they moved in pursuit of a better environment, particularly one with the pleasing climate and plentiful cultural amenities desired in a leisure-oriented lifestyle.[27] Also more than other migrants to the West, the elderly sought a manageable setting, not too distant from urban conveniences and facilities, as their place of residence. This combination of goals encouraged the rise of age-segregated communities in the United States.

Communities given over to the elderly took several forms. In certain neighborhoods "residential inertia" resulted in unplanned segregation as older households stayed behind while younger families moved away.[28] Failing health contributed to additional segregation in nursing homes and continuing-care retirement centers. Other types of age-segregated housing emerged more by design. Developers of "retirement subdivisions" marketed housing especially, but not exclusively, to the elderly. "Retirement villages" placed the elderly distinctly apart from other households, but were not laid out as self-contained communities. "Retirement new towns," pioneered by Sun City, represented the ultimate in residential segregation by age. Planned from the ground up for the retired, and marketed exclusively to people aged fifty or older, they intentionally kept their distance from "mixed" neighborhoods. They also aimed for self-sufficiency by providing business districts and cultural amenities within their borders.[29] Residents of a retirement new town never needed to leave their special community or have much contact with the "integrated" population outside. The choice of virtually complete segregation was within their grasp.

Retirement new towns did not directly touch the lives of many individuals. Rough estimates of the distribution of the elderly during the 1970s suggested that only 9 or 10 percent of people aged sixty-five and over resided in age-segregated housing, and that of that fraction perhaps only half dwelled in retirement communities designed solely for older people.[30] New towns accounted for about 1 percent of all communities built for retirees, but being substantially larger than the other kinds they housed by 1980 perhaps 30 percent of the population of all forms of retirement communities.[31]

New towns for retirees thus housed no more than 1 to 2 percent of the elderly in American society. The vast majority of senior citizens did not wish to migrate, and even for most who did they were simply too expensive. In the early 1970s it cost a couple $8,000 annually to reside in the average planned retirement community, whereas the median annual income for elderly couples stood at $5,500.[32] The planning and amenities that characterized retirement new towns generally priced them out of reach for most of the elderly.

Although new towns for retirees hardly typified housing for the aged, for two reasons they acquired a significance far out of proportion to their population. First, the earliest, largest, and best-known retirement communities were concentrated in western metropolitan areas and numbered among the many cultural exports being shipped toward the Atlantic seaboard. Sun City ranked first in size and longevity among all new towns for the retired and attracted millions of tourists, leading Arizonans to compare it to the Grand Canyon as one of the wonders of their state. But California actually had many more retirees, as well as more retirement communities, giving the region its numerical lead in special environments designed for the aged. A 1976 survey indicated that the West had both more retirement communities of all kinds (699, or 29.8 percent of the national total) and more residents of retirement communities (346,361, or 37.8 percent of the national total) than any other region.[33]

Although initially more inclined toward conventional housing for the elderly, the East eventually acquired its own retirement communities. Many were built by developers who had first tested the concept on the Pacific coast. Ross W. Cortese first opened Leisure World retirement new towns in Seal Beach, Laguna Hills, and Walnut Creek, California, during the early 1960s, and then built the next two in Maryland and New Jersey.[34] The planned development for retirees, and especially the retirement new town, was identified as a western method of providing for the elderly. As with other California creations, people interpreted it as the trend of the future, thereby assigning it more significance than its population warranted.[35]

Retirement new towns received a good deal of attention for a second reason. As a dramatic and purposeful form of voluntary segregation, they became the focus of considerable controversy over the value of isolating the elderly from the rest of the population. This debate was taken up in particular by the growing ranks of gerontologists as they developed and tested theories about the process of aging and the welfare of retirees. As a result, towns such as Sun City became one place to look for definitions of what retirement ought to mean in American society.

Opponents of segregated housing for the aged regarded retirement communities as unnatural, uncaring, and unhealthy. They agreed with the conventional wisdom, embodied in European practice during the 1950s, that the elderly ought to remain fully integrated with the rest of society, and they condemned Sun City and its ilk as destructive of the self-esteem and well-being of older people. Lewis Mumford summarized the sentiment by characterizing life in retirement communities as "progressively meaningless and empty." He suggested that segregated housing flourished because younger people found it a convenient way to dispose of the unwanted or unloved elderly.[36] Others viewed retirees' decision to relocate in a homogeneous setting as the equivalent of "withdrawal or retreatism," likely to encourage a shallow, hedonistic, and fundamentally unhappy life. Finally, critics argued that retirement communities generally did not deliver the happiness or security they promised.[37]

The objections raised by opponents of age-segregated housing, although important, tended to underestimate the benefits of segregation for the aged and to idealize the conventional retirement setting. Mere proximity to younger people did not necessarily lead to extensive contact between generations. Indeed, there was some evidence that the elderly may have felt more isolated in "integrated" settings than in segregated ones, because they felt inadequate and neglected among younger people.[38]

Criticism of age-segregated housing also overlooked some basic social trends responsible for increasing the distance between generations. Age segregation in the postwar United States did not originate with the elderly. Young adults and their children were much more likely to migrate away from parents and grandparents than vice versa, and they increasingly moved into newly completed suburbs which attracted virtually no older people.[39] Many neighborhoods across the country, such as singles communities, became more homogeneous in their generational makeup. Similarly, there were fewer "mixed" households. Whether old or young, Americans increasingly came to consider two-generation households the norm. As a result, the proportion of people aged sixty-five and over who lived in a household with a child fell constantly, from around 60 percent in 1900 to 16 percent in 1950 and 9 percent in 1970.[40]

Distance between generations did not necessarily indicate tension, although old and young doubtless found many points of disagreement. Rather, the elderly generally held that both they and their children would be happier if their lives were more separate. Senior Americans customarily voiced a desire not to interfere with or burden the lives of their children and grandchildren, and in return they expected little intervention by their children in their own lives. Owning their own houses and, for some, living in segregated communities satisfied a preference for independence from other generations.[41] Instead of contravening the fundamental values of the society, retirement communities may well have reinforced them, which would help to account for the proliferation of such communities after 1960.

Segregated housing did more than meet the desire of the elderly for independence. By the 1970s and 1980s a clear majority of studies had concluded that retirement communities constituted a more supportive and protective environment for the elderly; facilitated the transition from employment to retirement; allayed anxieties about crime, violence, and change; and gave residents a greater sense of control over their destiny than they might have had elsewhere. Those who dwelled in retirement communities reportedly tended to live longer and to be happier.[42]

Students of age-segregated housing often included two cautions in their positive assessments. First, those who moved into retirement communities tended to start out with better health and more financial security than the average senior citizen, which no doubt helped to explain their greater longevity and higher morale. Second, retirement communities did not suit everybody psychologically, but those who might have been unhappy there naturally stayed away.[43] Retirement communities succeeded, then, primarily for that rather small fraction of the aged who had the resources and the inclination to move into them.

The communities' success, however, could not be attributed entirely to the background characteristics of the residents; the towns themselves appeared to increase happiness. All caveats notwithstanding, places such as Sun City merited the praise they received. There was some truth to publicists' claim that "in Sun City you find the happiest, friendliest people you ever met."[44]

Packaging Paradise:
The Beginning of Sun City

During the late 1950s and early 1960s, the developer who created new towns for the elderly hardly perceived their benefits for the aged. The Del E. Webb Development Company (DEVCO), the subsidiary of the Del E. Webb Corporation that was responsible for building Sun City, was run primarily by men who had been builders rather than community planners, and at first it approached the retirement town as "one more construction project." Del Webb had gotten his start as a contractor around the beginning of the Great Depression, and in the 1930s and 1940s his firm grew up with the city of Phoenix. During and after World War II, Webb's company built large military installations in the West and undertook well-publicized civilian projects in Las Vegas, southern California, and New York City.[45] It also erected numerous housing tracts in and around Phoenix. But it had no special experience in housing the aged. Like most other for-profit developers of retirement homes, DEVCO's primary training came from building subdivisions for the general population.[46]

The Del E. Webb Corporation became interested in developing a retirement community when it decided in the mid-1950s that a sizable market could probably be found for age-segregated housing. The company figured that the growing financial benefits received by retirees would increase their purchasing power substantially. It also guessed that, given the increasing number of aging tourists traveling to the Southwest for its climate, some retirees might like to buy homes near Phoenix.[47] The amenities of Arizona had already begun to attract small numbers of the elderly, who settled in traditional neighborhoods as well as in trailer parks and apartment complexes set aside for retirees.[48] A handful had also begun to experiment with a retirement village.

During the later 1950s the Webb company learned from a national television show of the existence of Youngtown, Arizona, located about thirteen miles northwest of Phoenix. A realtor named Ben Schleifer had founded Youngtown in 1954 as a place where "people back east whose lives have been too much regulated can retire and do as they please." He laid out a crude grid of gravel roads and marketed inexpensive houses to "low income" retirees and others over the age of fifty. Schleifer emphasized the economical nature of his town site because, like most people, he assumed that the elderly could not afford very much. Perhaps in part because of this assumption, Youngtown never flourished. Schleifer promised features that would simulate "luxurious living" for residents, but he could not keep his word. And there were other reasons for dissatisfaction. Youngtown stood isolated on the Arizona desert, far removed from the stores and services of the larger metropolis. Moreover, the village had no deed restrictions, so those owners who decided to leave could sell their property to younger families.[49]

The example of Youngtown illustrated that, before 1960, the average American retirement community was a crude affair. Many were run on a shoestring by nonprofit organizations, and private developers tended to offer unsophisticated subdivisions and trailer parks with few real facilities for leisure, business, or health care. In most, little had been done to customize the communities for the aged. Few actually insulated the elderly effectively from younger generations, and their architects had done little to differentiate the homes from more conventional tract housing, other than to reduce the size and the price.[50] Not surprisingly, as Del Webb's associates studied retirement housing in Florida, Youngtown, and elsewhere, they concluded that the conventional approach to building for the aged had produced "drab" and "depressing" places where residents had little to do. The company did decide, against the advice of experts, that a sufficient number of the elderly would respond positively to age-segregated communities, but it also realized that, in order to succeed on a large scale, the community it built had to differ substantially from previous efforts.[51]

The key to elevating Sun City above its predecessors was the willingness of the Del E. Webb Corporation to invest more resources than had ever been devoted to a private retirement community. By spending more money on design, construction, and marketing, DEVCO distinguished Sun City markedly from other kinds of housing for the aged. The developer provided more planning, larger homes, greater publicity, and neater packaging.

DEVCO simplified the business of buying a home. It served as architect, builder, landscape designer, local government, and salesman. Purchasers dealt with one well coordinated organization to buy an entire package all at once. Moreover, it was a finished package. Learning a lesson from Youngtown and other retirement communities, DEVCO installed the amenities *before* it put Sun City on the market. Purchasers would see the golf courses, recreational facilities, and shopping centers before they decided to buy, rather than waiting for the developer to fulfill some vague promise after they had moved in. The presence of built-in amenities, which increased the price of homes, suggested another difference between Sun City and most other housing for the retired. DEVCO aimed at a slightly more affluent market than did Youngtown or any Sunbelt trailer park, raising the possibility that the elderly might not be as unprosperous as most people thought. Finally, with its greater resources DEVCO was able to provide a surer start for Sun City by launching a relentless advertising campaign.[52]

Few of Sun City's special features were entirely new, but taken together they added up to something altogether different from what had gone before. Sun City provided the elderly with an unprecedented degree of self-sufficiency and segregation by offering them a complete, predictable, and isolated landscape. This setting served as a stage for another distinctly new trait. To a much greater extent than its predecessors, Sun City was a thematically organized landscape, a place that conveyed, as well as any other magic kingdom, a bold and explicit message, in this case about the elderly. As publicists liked to say, it generated "a new Way-of-Life" for Americans by redefining the idea of retirement. In the hands of DEVCO's tireless sales force, Sun City clarified the meaning of a stage of life that had remained nebulous for most people—an accomplishment that doubtless increased Sun City's popularity. In both its implications and its size, Sun City seemed to represent an unprecedented advance.

Until 1960, the appearance of the lands on which the town was built belied the stature it would attain. The site chosen for Sun City was a cotton farm located right next to Youngtown, a dozen miles northwest of downtown Phoenix.[53] A highway called Grand Avenue bisected the subdivision and connected it to the central business district of Phoenix. In mid-1959, the Webb corporation purchased the property from the Boswell Company, which had become interested in selling its holdings because decades of irrigation by artesian wells had lowered the desert water table to an unreliable level. A housing development required less water, however, than a farm. As a crop of new homes gradually replaced the fields of cotton, the water table steadily leveled off, even though Sun City relied on the same wells.[54] The sufficiency of artesian water did not initially help matters above ground, however; there the desert prevailed. And struggling little Youngtown, adjacent to where DEVCO would erect its first houses, did not offer much hope that builders could truly create an oasis in that setting.

The Webb company paid such obstacles little heed. Setting an opening date of New Year's Day, 1960, it laid out a golf course, recreation center, motel, and shopping district to show prospective buyers (see Figure 24). It also built the model homes from which purchasers would choose the style of their own residences. The response was immediate. Thousands showed up during the first long holiday weekend, creating traffic jams two miles long on the road from Phoenix. Around 250 homes were sold in the first three days, and another 150 or so by the end of the first month. With orders in hand, DEVCO set about building the first houses, and the "pioneers" began to move in during spring and summer. By the end of 1960 the company had sold 1,300 homes. After another year the town had a population of 4,580, and by the end of 1963 there were 7,500 people dwelling in roughly 3,600 houses and apartments.[55]

Mass-production methods permitted rapid growth in the early years. The developer offered just five basic models of detached housing, which simplified and expedited the selection and construction of homes. At the same time, buyers chose from fifteen different exterior surfaces, en-

Figure 24. Planted amid cotton fields on the outskirts of metropolitan
            Phoenix in 1959, Sun City was laid out around a golf course that
            assured prospective buyers that the town, with its green grass,
            would stand apart from the surrounding desert. The fairways,
            along with the unfinished shopping center (upper left) and five
            completed model homes, helped to sell Sun City in the early
            years. Photo courtesy of the Sun Cities Area Historical Society.

suring that the residences did not look too much alike. Charles Schreiber and Arthur Schreiber, the architects of the first year's models, were
no strangers to mass-produced housing. By 1960 more than 100,000
homes had been constructed according to their plans. "We like to give
the public what it wants," one of the brothers explained, "and it seems
to like what we give."[56]

The Webb organization wanted to build Sun City quickly, but it
intended to build carefully. DEVCO permitted no land speculation in
the new town. Buyers had to purchase houses as well as lots. This policy
lent a cogency to the landscape missing in many Florida retirement
subdivisions. Similarly, the developer did not permit sprawl to get out
of hand. It laid out the streets and homesites of one relatively small

neighborhood at a time, sold most of the lots, and then moved on to the next contiguous parcel. DEVCO's strategy kept Sun City cohesive but slowed the pace at which homesites and golf courses supplanted fields of cotton and alfalfa. The agricultural pattern long continued to impinge upon the parcel; dust blew into two-foot drifts and cotton bugs swarmed the town.[57]

Despite such inconveniences, in its initial years Sun City prospered. Sales were brisk enough to encourage DEVCO to begin three more retirement new towns, in California and Florida, by 1962. In Arizona most residents expressed satisfaction with their purchases.[58] The company also had reason to be pleased with the residents, for Sun City attracted a stable and secure population. Because at least one member of a household had to be at least fifty years old, and because there could be no resident children under the age of twenty, Sun City experienced few of the annoyances associated with youth. In addition, more than half of all early buyers paid cash for their homes. Both socially and financially, the population showed every indication of being "a real asset to Arizona."[59]

The prosperity of buyers in Sun City pleased DEVCO, which was largely in the business of selling houses. However, if the developer tended to view the town as just another construction project, it recognized at the same time that it could not market the subdivision in that fashion. DEVCO understood that retirees could buy homes virtually anywhere; its task was to persuade the elderly to move to Sun City. For this reason, it regularly insisted that homes were a "secondary" consideration for those deciding to buy. More than anything else, the developer professed to sell "a Way of Life."[60] And in the early years, before many people had experienced the Sun City way of life, DEVCO unleashed its formidable marketing machinery to explain to prospective buyers exactly what living in Sun City would be like. By conveying the developer's intentions and shaping the buyer's expectations, publicists helped to invent Sun City.

Optimism about the future ranked as the central theme of the promotional campaign for Sun City. The Arizona new town, like other magic lands, projected tremendous confidence that tomorrow would be better than today. It promised the elderly that they would spend the best years of their lives in Sun City, that they would find both greater individual fulfillment and a more supportive environment that would actually prolong life. All this happiness could be purchased at a reasonable price from people who sincerely cared about the problems of retirees.[61]

In order to promote Sun City as more than another housing development, the Webb corporation had to present itself as something other than a construction company. To that end it focused a great deal of publicity on Del E. Webb himself. As co-owner of the New York Yankees baseball team, Webb had already attained celebrity status by 1960, and DEVCO advertisements embellished him further. He became an idealist with an abiding concern for the problems of old age. His publicists claimed that Webb had realized in Sun City a lifelong, "never-diminishing dream" to assist the elderly in leading fuller, happier lives. As such, the town supposedly represented Del Webb's greatest accomplishment.[62] (Late in life, Webb himself cast doubt on this claim. When asked which achievements made him proudest, he singled out the rapid completion of the Poston, Arizona, Relocation Center: "I think the greatest thing our company ever did was move the Japs out of California. We did it in 90 days back in the war.")[63]

Advertisements assured the elderly that, through the magic of market research, Del Webb's dream was theirs too. The developer had "conducted intensive research into the problems, interests and desires of America's senior citizens"; even more important, it had consulted the elderly themselves. The customer was assured that the architecture of the houses "is as perfectly matched to your wishes as if you had stood beside the architect . . . because it was your wants and desires that dictated every detail of the planning and design."

As a result of their research, Webb employees apparently concluded that, except in Sun City, retirement had imposed a terrible burden on the aged. This seemed one of the great ironies of modern life. The very generation that had created the prosperity which permitted the elderly to retire became its "victims when upon attaining the freedom of retirement they discovered that in reality it was an empty, purposeless existence of boredom, inactivity and disillusionment." Such stagnation reportedly accelerated the aging process; the implication was that conventional retirement actually hastened the arrival of death. Del Webb, of course, had a cure for this malaise, a way of life that got "retirees off the sidelines and . . . back into the game of life."[64] Instead of sleeping through old age, a DEVCO jingle exhorted the elderly, they should

Wake up and live in Sun City
For an active new way of life
Wake up and live in Sun City
Mr. Senior Citizen and Wife.
Don't let retirement get you down
Be happy in Sun City

It's a paradise town.
Wake up and live in Sun City,
Mr. Senior Citizen
The best of your life
Mr. Senior Citizen and Wife.[65]

Sun City, according to its boosters, rejuvenated the elderly by permitting them to attain a level of personal fulfillment they had never before reached. It allowed you to "Be the *real you* without a qualm." It encouraged residents "to be themselves *more completely*" (just as Disneyland ostensibly did) because it offered them the "privilege of doing what they want, when they want, and with whomever they want." Lest the satisfaction of every desire and the pursuit of self-fulfillment be perceived as hedonistic or antisocial, however, publicists hastened to identify the luxuries of Sun City as "earned pleasures" that constituted a patriotic reward for "those who have taken part in the years of America's greatest growth and development."[66]

Whereas conventional retirement was portrayed as boring and other retirement communities as offering "an incomplete way of life," "Del Webb's Active Retirement" consisted of "an unending treasure of perfect days, filled with interesting activity." Those who moved to Sun City could expect to put long-dormant abilities to use, to discover new interests and skills, to do the things they had always postponed, and to live "the greatest daily adventure, free of compulsion," that they had ever known. The natural and social environment helped to make life fuller, according to promoters. Sun City enjoyed Arizona's warm climate as well as the cultural benefits of "modern, progressive" Phoenix. Yet Sun City itself was small and carefully managed so as to avoid such big-city problems as air pollution, traffic congestion, impersonal attitudes, and industrial conditions. Retirees could visit Phoenix as often as they wished, but they would never *need* to go there, because Sun City was a "complete community," a "metropolis in miniature."

In publicizing the community's "Small Town Friendliness and Informality," DEVCO reassured the elderly that neither loneliness nor strangers existed in Sun City. All who lived there felt that they *belonged* there, in part because the population was so homogeneous. Publicists promised customers plenty of "contemporaries" who shared "their interests," "their dreams," and their memories. The advertising implied, of course, that younger neighborhoods could never have offered such social harmony.[67] By portraying Sun City as classless, the promoters suggested that Sun City had virtually no social conflict. Those who lived there were "a special kind of people." They seemed superior to the average retiree, not because they had more money, but because, as their very presence in Sun City apparently proved, they were more active, more interesting, and more outgoing. "[Y]ou cannot *buy* your way into Sun City society," the promoters explained. Rather, you will be accepted for who you are and will form enduring friendships that "*cost you nothing*."

Advertisements portrayed Sun City as paradise on a budget (see Figure 25). They listed many facilities for recreation and exercise and pictured homes that had been designed for minimum effort and maximum convenience. Yet this "country-club living" had been priced with "unbelievable modesty." Purchasers had only to pay the price for their homes and the small annual fee for use of the recreational complexes; everything else came as part of the package. Moreover, DEVCO assured buyers that Arizona had low taxes and that residents of Sun City would not have to pay for the upkeep and operation of local schools. If a couple could afford retirement at all, the message went, it could afford to retire in Sun City, where an income of $300 a month would probably suffice. In sum, those who bought into the town could expect to get "the most out of life for the least cost."

Exaggerated claims aside, the advertising provides an indication of DEVCO's thinking about Sun City. It conveys the theme that the Webb company created for this magic kingdom and the expectations the company had for the community. And, at least to a limited extent, the builder's expectations became the residents' expectations. Many buyers no doubt viewed the advertising with skepticism, yet some residents accepted at least a few of the claims as factual. For example, in part because of the way he appeared in ads, Del Webb became a hero to Sun Citizens. Many thought he had personally built their homes or that he would himself respond to complaints about the houses.[68] Similarly, in later years when Sun City's cost of living increased and the retirees felt overtaxed by a local school district, some referred back to the developer's claims about subsisting on $300 per month and paying fewer school taxes as justifications for their discontent.

Through its advertising, DEVCO helped to establish certain patterns of thought in the minds of buyers. Especially in the initial years, before settlers had formed their own sense of the town, the publicity campaign worked to create a common set of ideas about Sun City and encouraged buyer and seller to see eye to eye on many points about the community. Propagandized customers made happy customers.

Figure 25. DEVCO initially did not expect purchasers in Sun City to be very affluent. Consequently, early advertising emphasized a variety of activities and adventures for retirees in Sun City, to illustrate how much the retirees could get for their money. Photo from 1960 brochure, courtesy of the Sun Cities Area Historical Society, reprinted with permission of the Del Webb Corporation.

Residents registered their contentment by agreeing that the Webb company had generally delivered what it promised.[69]

After the first few years of Sun City's existence, however, DEVCO's publicists became less effective. They had exerted significant influence when Sun City was too new to have much independent sense of direction, but by the mid-1960s the experiences of the builder and buyers had altered expectations and rendered the original publicity campaign obsolete. It became apparent, for example, that buyers' ideas for the future of the community differed from DEVCO's. Moreover, DEVCO ads no longer worked very well among prospective customers. After the early 1960s, the rate of new purchases in Sun City fell precipitously. The decline in sales eventually produced new approaches to the building and marketing of Sun City. As a result, by the 1970s the town had become substantially different.

From Retirement Community to Resort Town

Between 1965 and 1968 a new Sun City began to emerge from the stagnation of the old. The population had grown relatively steadily in the earliest years of the decade, but between 1963 and 1967 the rate of increase diminished from about 2,000 new people annually to around 500. The near-halt to expansion of course meant shrinking profits for DEVCO. The company had sold about 1,300 homes in 1960; for 1963 that figure had been halved, and by 1965 it had fallen to about 400.[70] This drop-off coincided with similar decreases in Webb's two retirement communities in California. Something in the Sun City formula seemed to have stopped working.

In response, the Webb company considered some rather extreme possibilities. In 1964 DEVCO gave serious thought to building a conventional community on lands that had been projected as an extension of Sun City. Events had shaken the developer's faith in age-segregated housing.[71] DEVCO's doubts extended to concern about the effect of what DEVCO called cannibalism on its housing market, that is, a slow-down in the sales of new units resulting from the resale of houses it had already built and sold. In an interoffice memo, one official estimated the amount of competition DEVCO could expect as residents died and their heirs put the vacated houses on the market. Deciding that resales resulting from deaths would amount to no more than 100 homes annually, the official guessed that future sales in Sun City would level off at about 500 new houses per year.[72]

The author of this curious study seemed resigned to the idea of selling only 500 new homes annually, but others must have felt a sharp letdown from the success of previous years. After considering different methods of restoring the luster to Sun City, DEVCO ultimately determined that the best way to regain rapid growth was to make the town more expensive. The company had initially conceived of Sun City as a fancier version of the retirement village, but it still regarded the development as housing for people with relatively low incomes. It accordingly built modest homes, and it maintained this economical approach even after sales diminished.[73] In the beginning years, for example, DEVCO advertised three purchase plans. Buyers could pay cash for their homes; they could pay 10–40 percent down and get conventional mortgages; or, as the Webb company expected many would do, they could pay 3 percent down and get FHA financing. By 1962 the company was also giving serious consideration to adding a mobile home park to the development, no doubt hoping to broaden its market by appealing to an even less prosperous class of retiree.[74] Throughout the first years, DEVCO stressed that life in Sun City was a bargain.

As sales declined, it eventually became evident that the emphasis on minimal costs had hindered sales more than it had helped them. The problem with DEVCO's strategy was that Sun City tended to attract prosperous customers whose aspirations for the town called for something more sophisticated than the builder had in mind. From the first year of Sun City's existence, studies of residents counted an exceptionally large percentage of "professional and skilled people" and relatively high incomes. By and large, the purchasers ignored not only the FHA financing but also the more conventional mortgages; they paid cash for their homes. Also, many of them quickly spent substantial sums to enlarge or remodel the modest houses sold by DEVCO. And when asked how they felt about having a development for mobile homes next door, more than 90 percent of the residents polled expressed strong distaste for trailer parks and their transient style of life. About half the respondents indicated that they would never have moved to Sun City if it had included a mobile home park.[75] Clearly, the early residents had in mind a community that did not correspond in all details with the builder's plans.

DEVCO was not entirely blind to the preferences of its customers. It made a modest increase in the sizes and prices of its homes, and it abandoned the idea of building a nearby mobile home park. But the developer did not at first react quickly enough to the realities of the market. The wealth and aspirations of retirees caught the Webb corporation, like almost everyone else, by surprise. One result was a shake-up in company management in 1965.[76] Changes within DEVCO hastened the rethinking of Sun City. Over the next few years the Webb organization took a different approach to the retirement new town, an approach that dominated further construction until 1978, when virtually all the land had been developed.

DEVCO basically abandoned the lower end of the housing market, aiming increasingly to please the middle- and upper-income brackets of elderly Americans, and it changed its marketing strategy accordingly. It revised its advertising to focus less on a low-cost way of life and more on the high quality of housing and the surrounding environs, and it relied less on publicity in the conventional media and more on word-of-mouth promotion by satisfied customers. Once DEVCO fully realized that Sun City's residents were its most effective spokespersons, it paid increasing attention to pleasing those who had already bought so that they would encourage others to buy in the future. These marketing changes restored health to the real estate venture.

The most dramatic changes occurred in the housing offered by DEVCO after 1965. The developer always tended to treat Sun City homes in the same way that General Motors treated cars. It offered a variety of houses at a variety of prices, changed the models almost every year, made numerous add-on options available to purchasers, and offered the finished products in a wide array of exterior colors and surfaces in order to reassure buyers that each mass-produced unit had "a distinctive, custom built appearance."[77] After 1965, however, DEVCO built fewer Chevrolets and more Oldsmobiles and Buicks.

In the initial years DEVCO models had come in a simple box-like style with a limited number of options. Most were built out of concrete blocks painted in pastel shades, and they provided meager protection from the sun and from the eyes of inquisitive neighbors. On opening day in 1960 the cost of a Sun City home ranged from $8,000 to $11,300 for the top-of-the-line model, "The Pickford." The average price of a house purchased in 1960 was $11,120; by 1965 that figure had grown only to $15,540.[78]

Beginning in 1966 and 1967, DEVCO offered a broader variety of houses and prices, finished each model more elaborately, and provided a wider range of options. It introduced a series of fancier apartments

Figures 26 and 27. These two photos illustrate the contrast in housing styles between the early and the late 1960s. The "Montecello" model, introduced in 1960, had two bedrooms, one bath, and a carport. Publicists highlighted its "built-in range & oven" with "vent hood and exhaust fan." The "Durango," introduced in 1968 (and shown here with "optional tile roof" and landscaped yard), had three bedrooms, two baths, and a double garage with "golf cart storage." Its long list of standard features included such items as a "dressing area with walk-in closet," an "elongated water closet," and "illuminated house numbers." Courtesy of the Sun Cities Area Historical Society.

called Mediterranean Villas that highlighted southern European styling. The fronts of homes now featured gates and courtyards, which provided more privacy; double carports rather than single carports became standard; and enclosed garages were added for the first time as a built-in feature on the most expensive houses and as an option on the others. Through 1966, almost all model homes included an evaporative cooler as standard equipment, with refrigerated air conditioning optional. After 1966, the more advanced cooling system became standard on all models. Many newer houses included an extra bathroom or higher ceilings.[79]

By 1969 the gap between the typical new house and the original Sun City homes had widened further (see Figures 26 and 27). The highest-priced version, in contrast to its 1960 counterpart, had more closets and hallways, an entry space behind the front door and a pantry off the kitchen, a two-car garage that included space to park a golf cart, and such standard features as a garbage disposal, a breakfast bar, built-in shoe racks, walk-in closets, and illuminated house numbers. Whereas in 1960 the options had been limited to a larger carport and better air conditioning, in 1969 they ranged from a dishwasher to a beamed ceiling and tile roof to an automatic garage-door opener. Houses now had more seclusion from the street and the sun, and tighter security features. The range in prices was much greater—$16,000 to $32,000—and the average new house now cost about $25,000.[80]

Simple and modest new homes were no longer available in Sun City, and the developer benefited from the change. DEVCO now sold as standard many features that had been optional, permitting the company greater profits. It realized a higher return from the larger houses than it had from the smaller ones.[81] Its new houses also competed less with the older ones being resold by their residents, because they catered to a different niche within the home-buying market.

Sun City purchasers in the later 1960s and the 1970s acquired more than a house for the higher price they paid. They bought a significantly enhanced environment. As it completed construction on the acreage south of Grand Avenue, DEVCO planned a much more stylish kind of community for the neighborhoods to be built to the north of the highway (see Figure 28). The old section, known as Phase I, had been guided largely by the notion that housing for the elderly must be economy-minded. The new section, dubbed Phase II, offered fancier, more comfortable homes. It featured circular streets that evoked a sense of enclosure, and utility wires were laid underground, to reduce the

Figure 28. The retirement new town remained rather isolated from Phoenix and its suburbs as late as 1969. Phase I (located in this picture above Grand Avenue, the street running on a slight diagonal across the photograph) had been completed, and Phase II, with its circular layout, was filling in fast. Note that Youngtown (located at the lower right-hand corner of Phase I), started in the mid–1950s and now dwarfed by Sun City, offered only residential lots laid out in a rectangular grid. Courtesy of the Sun Cities Area Historical Society.

clutter of the streetscape. The recreation centers of Phase II offered more space and better equipment. One even bordered a man-made lake and a private park that contained a man-made waterfall (see Figure 29). These additions increased the developer's costs, which were passed along in the price of houses. DEVCO insisted that the new recreation centers be open to all residents. But the developer simultaneously agreed, at the urging of Phase II residents, to build private golf clubs that were not open to all, along with a private supper club overlooking the new lake.[82]

Originally, both the developer and the residents had prided them-

Figure 29. The original Sun City community center, built in 1960, was a modest building with a pool and rooms for games, crafts, exercise, and social activities. By contrast, the Lakeview Center, shown here, which opened in Phase II on January 3, 1970, provided a much wider range of activities, including boating and fishing on the adjoining man-made lake and picnicking in the private park (above and to the right of center). Courtesy of the Sun Cities Area Historical Society.

selves on the insignificance of social distinctions. One resident had explained that "the old competitive anxieties don't exist" in Sun City.[83] The elderly might have retired from competition as producers in the economy, but they had not given up their attachment to the rivalries inherent in consumption of goods and services. After 1965 the new town provided more opportunities to demonstrate gradations of status. A wider range of home styles and clubs that were exclusive served to underline differences in wealth. The changing cost of housing also evinced greater stratification. The average price of a new home in the suburb increased to $26,150 in 1970 and $42,607 in 1975. Inflation accounted for part of the rise in cost. Homes purchased for about $11,000 in 1960 sold for $30,000 or more by 1978; they had proved to be good investments. But the price of new homes in the latter year ranged from around $45,000 to around $85,000, and the median values of houses and apartments in Phase II considerably exceeded those of Phase I.[84]

As the prices of new homes climbed, so did the mean household income in Sun City. It always exceeded the average for American retirees, but each year's cohort of buyers tended to be wealthier than the previous year's. In 1969 the average family income in Sun City stood at $8,820 per year—about twice that of the average retired couple in the Phoenix area. At the same time, the average family income of new buyers for that year topped $11,000. By 1975 the average annual income for all Sun City residents, new and old, had climbed to $16,588, about $10,000 higher than it had been in 1960. Again, the disparity between earlier and later buyers took on spatial dimensions. The average household income in Phase I homes during 1975 was $14,000; in Phase II homes it was $17,900. The incomes of earlier buyers had grown with increases in Social Security benefits, but they still had fallen steadily behind the incomes of more recent buyers. Although the vast majority of residents lived comfortably, people became aware during the 1970s of some poverty in Sun City, particularly in the Phase I area. By the end of the decade about one-fifth of the town's households, primarily the single-person households, had annual incomes of less than $10,000.[85]

The new, improved Sun City had become too expensive for a few who had arrived when the community had been targeted for retirees with relatively low incomes. But on the whole the new approach met with success: the rates of home sales and population growth shot upward. In 1963 DEVCO employed seven salesmen; five years later the sales force numbered thirty-one. In 1968, for the first time, DEVCO sold more homes—1,336—than it had in 1960. In 1969 sales topped 1,900, and DEVCO completed six new houses daily during the peak building season in order to keep up with the demand. In 1971 sales exceeded 2,300 homes, and in the next year DEVCO sold eleven new homes a day during the peak buying months.[86] The population of Sun City jumped from 11,000 in 1968 to 25,000 by the end of 1972 and 44,000 by the completion of most land development in mid-1978. The rate of yearly increase, which had hovered around 500 in 1967, multiplied to roughly 5,000 newcomers annually in the early 1970s.[87] What publicists had once portrayed as a small, friendly village suddenly became a city—Arizona's eighth largest in 1980.

A new advertising strategy contributed to the spurt of growth. After 1965 DEVCO did less to publicize Sun City's "Way-of-Life" for retirees and ceased to highlight the themes of economy, "Active Retirement," and individual fulfillment. Instead, it concentrated on the various models of housing available at Sun City, presenting them as integral parts of resort living. A 1966 promotional pamphlet made the changes obvious. Slicker than any previous brochure, it stressed the beautiful built environs and country-club style of Sun City. This emphasis gained such strength in ensuing years that the development was dubbed "Arizona's Greatest Home Show" in 1967, "Exposition for Living—1969," and "Galleria '74, America's Most Timely Home Show." Advertisements for the "Heritage Collection, a Model Home Show," presented during 1976 in honor of the nation's Bicentennial, epitomized the new trend. Virtually no mention was made of life in Sun City as a bargain; the emphasis instead was on the trappings of affluence (see Figure 30).[88]

By portraying Sun City as luxurious, publicists made the place seem exclusive. Early advertising had depicted the town as a virtually classless society. Now private clubs and fancy facilities gained precedence in the publicity, and residents were described not only as friendly and active but also as "successful" and "substantial."[89] Promoters no longer billed Sun City so much as a haven for retirement as a new way of life. Rather, they now equated retirement with the much more familiar idea of a vacation, describing Sun City as a resort, with all a resort's exclusiveness and atmosphere of wealth.

Advertising that portrayed retirement as a vacation and Sun City as a resort probably proved effective because it did less to remind buyers that they were getting older.[90] Likening retirement to tourism also

HOMES, DUPLEXES, GARDEN APARTMENTS & PATIO HOUSES

DEL WEBB'S
Sun City
ARIZONA

America's Most Famous Resort-Retirement Community

Figure 30. By the time DEVCO issued this brochure in 1969, its advertising highlighted not the many features and bargain prices at Sun City but the sweet life intrinsic to an affluent resort community. Courtesy of the Sun Cities Area Historical Society, reprinted with permission of the Del Webb Corporation.

suited DEVCO's promotional strategy. The developer sold many new homes through its "Visitor Vacation Plan" which brought prospective purchasers to the new town for one or two weeks to experience Sun City directly.[91] These visits no doubt helped to make retirement synonymous with vacation in the minds of buyers.

Changes in the nature and the marketing of housing after 1965 were accompanied by a new sales strategy in which DEVCO devoted greater attention to those who had already purchased homes. It had been company policy to remain distant from residents, but now DEVCO stepped up its involvement in the daily lives of the population, for it had come to realize that satisfied residents made the most effective promoters of life in Sun City. Throughout the 1960s and 1970s, "resident referrals" accounted for somewhere between 40 and 70 percent of all new home sales.[92]

In its early planning for Sun City, DEVCO had surveyed other retirement communities to learn what the elderly wanted and could afford. After 1965 the company asked its own customers what they wanted, and tried to give it to them. The Webb organization therefore built a hospital at cost for Sun City and helped raise money for its operation; donated land for health care offices; subsidized transit and church-building; erected facilities and hired celebrities for a program of regular entertainment; and supported the various clubs and organizations started by residents.[93] Until 1978, when, all land developed, it began to withdraw from Sun City and focus attention on the even fancier Sun City West, DEVCO played a central role in the community. In return for its greater involvement, it profited from dramatically increased sales.

The Webb company's experience with a new town for retirees illustrated a trend among planned communities in the American West. Developers who attempted to have more involvement in their customers' lives adopted a new self-image. They came to see themselves as town-builders rather than mere construction companies (in 1985 DEVCO changed its name to Del E. Webb Communities, Inc.), and they likened their large-scale projects to such well-known examples of planned communities as Britain's New Towns.[94]

In fact, however, American planned communities differed substantially from the conventional New Town. In English Garden Cities, and even to some extent in Columbia, Maryland, and Reston, Virginia, designers laid out towns in accordance with certain preformed social ideals. They sought to incorporate a diversity of classes and ethnic groups, to achieve a special relationship to existing urban centers, to encourage economic self-sufficiency as well as a strong sense of community. In Sun City, Arizona, planning worked a little differently. DEVCO laid out the subdivision, sold and built the homes, and *then* asked residents what they wanted in the town. Planning was shaped less by ideals about community than by market research. In Sun City and in other planned towns in the western United States, developers based their designs upon buyers' preferences, and they changed their plans whenever they got a different reading from customers. In the eyes of the developer of Sun City, planning succeeded not because it accorded with societal ideals about the welfare of the elderly but because it produced "a city which literally sold itself." [95]

As numerous critics pointed out, this approach to urban design made something of a mockery of the comparison to Garden Cities. Planning was treated as a commodity as much for sale as the houses themselves, and it also appeared to symbolize exclusiveness and luxury. Even those developers who were sincere in their desire to build a community that was socially useful often found that the homebuyer cared little for the ideals embodied in the planning that had taken place. To the purchaser, planning often promised a safer or more profitable real estate investment. [96]

Yet it is easy to condemn too harshly the community builders' version of planning. For one thing, their local efforts at design proved commercially successful in large part precisely because urban planning on a larger scale seemed to have failed. The Webb company, for better or for worse, was one of the most effective planning agencies in greater Phoenix. Moreover, although planning according to market preferences tended to benefit only those who could afford it, in some circumstances it did give buyers a greater sense of control over the cityscape. In Sun City, DEVCO's financial dependence on market research and resident referrals gave its customers a significant voice in guiding the development of the town. By gaining a say in how the community would be defined, the elderly themselves assumed a job once reserved mainly for DEVCO publicists.

The Retirees' Community Becomes a Hometown

Retirees used their influence to make Sun City more responsive to their needs, maximizing opportunities to take life on their own terms. By helping to determine who would come to live in Sun City, retirees largely created a community in their own image. By ensuring the arrival of a fairly homogeneous population, residents encouraged a consensus about retirement and aging that made it easier to grow old in Sun City. These accomplishments made Sun City an exclusive and unmixed community, not at all typical of life for America's elderly. Yet they contributed to Sun City's success and thus encouraged people to think of the town as a model for solving the problems afflicting America's aged.

The populating of the new town illustrated the inclination of westering migrants to resettle among relatively like-minded people. Voluntarily leaving one place for another has historically permitted individuals to select as new neighbors people more similar to themselves than the old were. Retirees could perhaps do this even more freely than others, because in selecting a new residence they no longer had to worry about factors pertaining to the workplace. "Choose Your Own Neighbors . . . from Friends and Relatives 'Back Home,'" DEVCO urged its customers.[97] And Sun City residents ultimately followed the advice by promoting their community to those they had known elsewhere. This method of peopling Sun City benefited not only the developer but also the retirees themselves, who ensured that they would see familiar faces in their adopted hometown. In a sense, retirees could transplant to Sun City not just themselves but entire networks of friendship and kinship. As a result, their migration was much less rash or traumatic than students of the elderly had feared.

Studies estimated that more than half of the residents (and, by the later 1970s, perhaps as many as 72 percent) had first heard about Sun City from friends or relatives in the new town or the nearby area; fully one-quarter of the households arriving in the later 1970s had at least one sibling in the vicinity. Buyers insisted that they did not necessarily decide upon Sun City because a friend or relative lived there; they emphasized instead the climate, health and recreational facilities, and economic conditions as key reasons for purchasing. However, friends and relatives did provide a reliable source of information to prospective buyers, a way of confirming the developer's claims about the area.[98] It also seems likely that the presence of acquaintances made Sun City less strange or forbidding.

Migrants to Sun City were not content to rely solely on information from either their relatives and friends or DEVCO, however. Virtually all buyers visited the site at least once before deciding to purchase; the average newcomer visited Sun City more than twice, and had been associated with the town through visits and correspondence for up to six years.[99] Many residents initially came to know Sun City as a resort, and it was probably in this context that they first envisioned their own retirement there.

The retirees' decision to purchase a home commonly resulted from a deliberate process as the prospective buyer became acquainted with Sun City—and vice versa. The comparatively cautious method of selecting a retirement community perhaps helps to explain the sluggish rate of sales during the early years. Buyers of homes in Sun City initially came from the West; after two years of sales, Arizona and California ranked first and second among the states of origin for Sun City residents.[100] Thereafter, the upper Midwest began to supply more than its share of buyers. Retirees from Illinois, Michigan, Wisconsin, Minnesota, Ohio, Iowa, and Missouri, it seems, had taken longer to discover Sun City. Years passed before a sizable nucleus of residents from the Midwest had gathered and begun to promote Sun City to friends and relatives back home. By the 1970s, however, the Midwest accounted for more newcomers than any other part of the country. By 1980 Illinois alone had provided 19 percent of all migrants to Sun City, compared to 8 percent of all migrants to Phoenix.[101] DEVCO recognized the importance of the upper Midwest to its success by establishing a promotional office in the Chicago area during the later 1960s.[102] In some sense Sun City was as much a suburb of Chicago as it was of Phoenix.

That the bulk of newcomers hailed from the Midwest rather than the West helped to determine the settlers' attitudes toward the community. Consider for contrast California's chain of Leisure Worlds, which attracted the majority of its customers from the Golden State. Retirees who went to Leisure World were already familiar with the environment and amenities of California. They were attracted instead by the strict security measures in place at Leisure World—walls, guarded gates, police patrols, even checks on the criminal records of new applicants—which promised greater safety than could be found outside. At Sun City, on the other hand, retirees paid less attention to security and more to the climate and the concentration of recreational facilities, which must have made a deep impression on those coming from the Midwest. To people from afar, Sun City truly was more like a vacation resort. This perception, played up in DEVCO advertising after 1965, contributed to newcomers' expectations for Arizona.

Life in Sun City presented a chance to get away from colder climates and from former places of employment. It did not, however, necessarily represent an opportunity to get away from family. Migrants to Arizona, like the elderly everywhere in the United States, hoped to remain independent of their children, and living in a retirement community probably underscored that desire.[103] It generally did not, however, indicate an effort by the elderly to put more distance between themselves and their families. Migrants to Sunbelt retirement communities tended to have fewer children than the national average, in any case.[104] Furthermore, elderly couples in Sun City who did have children were not likely to have left them behind when they relocated. Most of their sons and daughters had already moved away. In fact, many of the retirees' children had already headed in the same general direction as their parents later did. In 1969 more than half of Sun City households from the Midwest had one or more children residing closer now than they had before moving; many were now closer to siblings and long-term friends from back home as well.[105] Finally, even those who did leave children behind tended to keep in steady touch with them.[106] Migration to Sun City did not tear families and friendships asunder; indeed, in many cases the retirees brought friendships with them, and most often they maintained or strengthened family contacts.

The decision to migrate was not made lightly, and it did not signify abandonment of the nuclear family. However, husbands and wives did not feel the same about the prospect of retiring to Arizona. Women apparently decided upon Sun City less quickly and moved there less willingly than men. The developer detected these attitudes in its early market research. Retirement, it concluded, affected men more than women in important ways. Retirement for males constituted a significant change in life that made it easier to uproot themselves. Women, however, did not experience retirement in the same fashion. DEVCO primarily targeted male buyers (its jingle appealed to "Mr. Senior Citizen and Wife"), but it also attempted to "convince women more pointedly that they, too, face a drastic change in their lives and that the Sun Cities offer the solution."[107]

In its calculating way, the Webb corporation identified a significant distinction in the meaning of retirement for men and women. Particularly for women in more affluent households, retirement happened primarily to their husbands, although it could disrupt their own autonomy and home life. Women who did retire from jobs outside the home could often find in housework a "highly respectable" substitute for their previous employment. Moreover, many women spent their later years developing closer bonds to families, friends, churches, and clubs, which tied them more tightly into the life of their hometowns and made them less inclined to migrate.[108] Such factors help to explain the perception that men were happier in Sun City than women, and that some marriages may have been strained by moving there. Furthermore, because wives tended to be younger and live longer than their husbands, some women doubtless feared the prospect of joining the large group of widows in Sun City, preferring instead their own hometown network of family and friends.[109]

For women especially, retiring to Sun City could be a difficult and troubling decision. Nonetheless, it was not a traumatic experience, on the whole; no study of Sun City ever reported a great deal of unhappiness there. Quite the contrary: numerous reports indicated a substantially higher than average level of morale among residents. The town seemed to make people feel at home in spite of any initial doubts they may have had. A very low rate of turnover in home ownership provided another indication of contentment with the community; and of those that did move, as many as 40 percent bought new homes in Sun City.[110]

Sun City's homogeneity helped to explain the high degree of satisfaction among the residents. Partly because residents had recruited their neighbors from among their own relatives and friends, the population must have seemed rather like-minded. But many other factors contributed to its uniform composition. The process of migration filtered out those in poor health and those with less money. Residents of Sun City tended to have had more education than the national average, to have retired from higher-paying occupations, and to have owned their homes. Age segregation, of course, confined the population to a rather narrow range of generations, and the town's emphasis on recreation and activity, as opposed to nursing homes and life-care facilities, initially attracted the "young elderly" rather than the very old.[111] Social and cultural factors reinforced the lack of diversity. Few non-whites moved to Sun City, partly because its prices were high, but also because for them it was not a homogeneous community.[112] In addition, those few young families and children who found themselves living in Sun City reportedly did not feel very comfortable there.[113]

The aged felt differently. In addition to the socioeconomic factors that set Sun City residents apart, a number of shared character traits emerged. Retirees were "highly propagandized" in favor of the town, one psychologist suggested. No doubt the developer's advertising contributed to this predisposition, but so did residents' own expectations in support of the emotional and financial investment they had made. "I told myself when I came here that this was going to be a wonderful place," one resident recalled. "I would believe that, even if it weren't true."[114] Moreover, the process of moving initiated the formation of community bonds, and the experience of living in Sun City completed the coalescing of society there and made residents acutely aware of the aging that they had in common. Purchasers who first looked upon Sun City as a vacation resort perhaps paid little attention to the prospect of getting older, because DEVCO sold the town as a kind of fountain of youth. But once within the walls of the community, it was hard to escape from the realities of old age, disease, and death. Nonetheless, residents discovered that the town's homogeneous setting made it easier to grow old; it reduced the stresses of aging and provided an environment that encouraged the evolution of mutual values appropriate for senescence.

Sun City illustrated the ability of retirement communities to offer a highly supportive setting for aging. Elderly Americans have tended to disengage from the rest of society as a matter of course. For some, retirement became a saddening or embittering experience, connoting a loss of friends and a loss of a sense of purpose. And in heterogeneous communities the elderly were constantly confronted with others who were more active and healthy, and seemingly more useful, than they were. Such contrasts between generations discouraged the full integration of the elderly into a culture that seemed to value youth above all else.[115]

Retirement communities apparently reversed the process of disengagement. They provided peers with whom the elderly could "join in a kind of communal conspiracy to continue living like human beings."[116] They widened the number of social contacts their members might have and made them feel welcome. Residents believed that their neighbors shared their own basic values. In Sun City and other retirement communities, the elderly apparently understood each other implicitly and respected one another's privacy and autonomy.[117] Simultaneously, the age-segregated community shielded the elderly from unfavorable comparisons to younger people and their standards. Retirees found it liberating not to contrast themselves continually with another generation. "You don't feel old" in Sun City, explained a physician from Detroit, "because you don't have the pressure of all those young people."[118]

Some retirees praised Sun City because it isolated them from people who were different. Given the widening generation gap after 1960, it should not be surprising that many residents felt that they had found a refuge.[119] A few of them began to think (in terms anticipated by the designers of Disneyland) that if Sun City stood for safety and sanity, the outside world might be seen as just the opposite. One man spoke of the town as a virtual fortress from which to watch the decline of civilization:

We're examples of the vanishing American. I'm convinced that . . . too much permissiveness enables our young people to dress sloppily and slovenly and it can't help but have an impact or an effect on their attitudes toward themselves and other people. Whereas most of the people you see here are of the generation where, look, you washed behind your ears and scrubbed your nails before you came to the dinner table.[120]

Retirement communities allowed the elderly to wear their age as a badge of honor: "What do I have in common with someone in their 30s. He never lived through the war or experienced the depression." Living among so many like-minded people may also have made it easy to adopt a sense of superiority. "We are a higher quality people here," explained one resident of a retirement new town near Tucson. "We are all educated and from interesting occupational backgrounds." The select retirees likened themselves to frontiersmen: "The ones of us who came [rather than stay behind] are stronger and more independent spirits than others our age, like the early pioneers."[121]

Age-segregation perhaps made the elderly less tolerant toward others but more accepting of themselves. They found that not going to work every day was acceptable in Sun City, and that they need not feel useless or guilty for devoting themselves to leisure activities there.[122] Residents of Arizona retirement communities tended to be more permissive than other retirees in their attitudes toward the amount and kind of recreation undertaken by their neighbors. To some extent, leisure now replaced work, fraternal orders, military service, and religion as a basis for social organization.[123] It became a central component of the identity of Sun City residents and, more than elsewhere, a key ingredient in the evolving meaning of retirement.

The primacy of leisure in Sun City evoked suspicion from outsiders. Some viewed its lifestyle as too driven and hedonistic, others as too passive and aloof, still others as not "intellectually strenuous" enough.[124] But it was not clear that the Sun City way of life was any less satisfactory in those respects than conventional living among the retired. Few bothered to compare the attitudes of Sun Citizens to those of the other elderly, except to suggest that those living in retirement communities seemed to accept leisure more fully as an integral part of retirement.[125] Few recalled that, for most American retirees of the 1960s and 1970s, the widespread attainment of retirement constituted a novel experience to which they had not yet fully adjusted their thinking. It was perhaps natural, then, that the elderly's approach to leisure could at times appear strained.

At play, retirees demonstrated repeatedly that, although they were no longer working, they had not abandoned the work ethic. Sun Citizens felt they had earned their leisure by their hard work, and when questioned on the subject they responded that they were no longer obligated to remain active in economic production or public service.[126] But even if they believed that they owed nothing more to society, many residents nonetheless chose to devote some of their leisure time to "worthy causes." More than the average Phoenix citizen, residents of Sun City joined civic groups, religious organizations, and other voluntary associations.[127] Of course, more than other generations, the elderly had free time to volunteer on behalf of these activities, but their participation also affirmed their desire to feel useful by working in some capacity, and reinforced their intention to shape the community as much as possible to their own tastes and needs. In addition, the high rate of voluntarism in Sun City was seen by the aged as a form of self-protection.[128] Residents took care of others in the hope that others would tend to them in their times of need.

The inhabitants of Sun City volunteered time and money to a tremendously wide range of civic, social, and medical services, especially within the new town. They organized homeowners' and taxpayers' associations which provided a multitude of services and guarded residents' political and financial interests. They staffed and funded security and maintenance organizations which protected the public safety and cleaned common grounds. They devoted enormous energy to health care, working with DEVCO to ensure the completion of a modern hospital in Sun City and providing hundreds of volunteers for the hospital auxiliary that supplemented the care provided by doctors and nurses.[129]

Voluntarism, like the homogeneity of the population and the influence of elderly buyers upon the developer, contributed to retirees' conviction that they now had "more control over their lives than in a mixed community."[130] The physical setting underscored the feeling that the retirees were masters of their own destiny. When asked why they moved to Sun City and what they liked most about it, residents uniformly emphasized features of the environment that appealed to them. The warm climate ranked first on almost every list, but the built environs also rated highly. Respondents praised the town's cleanliness and orderliness, its recreational facilities, and its numerous physical manifestations of a special way of life for the elderly.[131]

Retirees used a specific set of terms to reiterate their attachment to place. They explained that they had not moved to Sun City because of the prices of the housing or because the town offered a sense of "home," as their former communities might have. Rather, they suggested that they liked Sun City's "homes," meaning both the well-designed individual dwellings and the image of order and neatness projected by the mass-produced, planned housing. They minimized the importance of moving to be closer to their friends, and instead spoke about Sun City being "friendly." The community did not call forth the same feelings that former hometowns had; inhabitants tended to praise it in rather abstract or symbolic terms. Yet the place evoked a strong sense of identification.[132] Sun City may have been a "manufactured" and "adopted" community, rather than an "authentic" one, but residents embraced it nonetheless. Indeed they regarded it, in the words of the "Song of the Sun City Pioneers" (sung to the tune of "Home on the Range"), as "the place next to Heaven's own door."[133]

The exteriors and interiors of homes played a substantial role in distinguishing Sun City. The developer designed the houses to accommodate tastes imported from other regions of the country.[134] Moreover, residences were adapted to the preferences of the aged. Virtually all Sun City models were single-story structures, with no basement, elevated porch, or steps of any kind. They tended to be somewhat small because they were meant for one or two people rather than entire families. On the inside, light switches, electrical sockets, and bathroom fixtures were positioned at heights convenient for the aged. Outside, the residents and the builder placed a premium on minimal maintenance. In lieu of grass, DEVCO laid a cement patio behind almost every detached dwelling it sold. Instead of installing gardens and real lawns in front or leaving the desert alone (although some homeowners added cacti and palm trees), many "planted" AstroTurf or, more commonly, gravel. Often the rocks in "Leisure Lawns," as one company dubbed them, were painted green or some other shade.[135]

The Sun City yard represented an adjustment to both the arid climate and the aging of residents. Yet the fact that private yards existed at all attested the continuity of retirees' preferences for single-family, detached units. Compared to other retirement new towns, with their townhouses, apartments, and condominiums, Sun City had a disproportionately high share of both homeowners (95 percent) and single-family houses (70 percent). As a result, it was both much larger and much less "centrally managed or controlled."[136] The more private housing probably heightened residents' sense of autonomy. It did not imply, however, that inhabitants could do whatever they wished with their real estate.

Much as Sun Citizens valued property and privacy, they also felt strongly about visual order. Residents repeatedly praised the town's cleanliness as a chief virtue and as evidence of Sun City's superiority to conventional communities. By "clean" they meant not only that the town was free from dirt and litter but that it appeared neat, orderly, and well maintained. Sun City was to have "no rough edges, empty lots, junk at back doors, unpaved streets," or any other evidence of "neglect or shoddiness."[137]

To preserve the "clean" lines that the developer had designed into the community, residents policed themselves. The Sun City PRIDES (Proud Residents Independently Donating Essential Services, formed in 1980 when DEVCO turned many maintenance tasks over to understaffed county agencies) gathered every Saturday morning to pick up litter in public places, trim trees and shrubs, care for the extensive sprinkler system, and perform myriad other duties. The Homeowners Association, founded in 1963, helped to enforce the steadily growing number of deed restrictions that prevented residents from parking recreational vehicles in driveways for more than seventy-two hours, hanging laundry out to dry within sight of the public, or violating other aesthetic standards in the community. Perhaps the toughest deed restriction to enforce—and the most constitutionally questionable—was that which prohibited youths under eighteen from staying in houses for more than ninety days except in cases of hardship. Residents of the town, after having the Homeowners Association enforce this regulation ineffectively, in 1984 persuaded Maricopa County to assume the duty under its zoning authority.[138] The enforcement of deed restrictions not only preserved the "proper" appearance of Sun City but also ensured that the town lived up to buyers' expectations.

Residents of Sun City attempted to forestall undesirable changes that might make the community more similar to conventional towns.

They thrived on their isolation as well as their homogeneity. And they made few accommodations to the desert. Individual homeowners may have given up their lawns, but they hardly went without grass. DEVCO incorporated no fewer than eleven golf courses into Sun City, green acres that insulated retirees from the reality of the desert. Arizona did not closely resemble the Midwest from which many residents came, but the "country club environment" of Sun City was verdant enough to pass muster.[139]

Sun City had no public parks, but residents found in golf courses the green belts, open spaces, and exercise paths they desired. Many homes did not have their own lawns or gardens, but DEVCO tried to offer as many lots as possible bordering golf courses; people were willing to pay extra to have their backyard open onto a fairway. Golf courses gave the landscape of Sun City a distinctive cast, and DEVCO exploited its value fully. The developer named many of the early streets after nationally famous golfers and golf courses, and later made special provisions in garages, parking lots, and streets to accommodate golf carts as a widespread form of transportation around the town. More than anything else, perhaps, the golf courses offered physical proof that Sun City was truly a resort and retirement truly a vacation. Indeed, the availability of the courses enticed so many retirees to take up golf for the first time that players quickly had to form an organization to educate newcomers to the rules and etiquette of the game.[140]

Other features added to the cohesion of the place. DEVCO situated shopping centers prominently in each section of town. By 1980, when malls outnumbered golf courses, they served to tie together the blocks of tract housing. The construction of Boswell Memorial Hospital, a five-story building, gave Sun City its sole high-rise, a focal point that stood out from the otherwise flat terrain and one-story homes. And the developer erected a white brick wall around the entire subdivision, less for the sake of security and exclusiveness than as a "barrier against hot, dry winds and the dust they carry." Although the wall could not keep anyone out, it reiterated the autonomy of the inhabitants within as well as the break between town and desert.[141] Like the planned housing and golf courses, the shopping centers and central hospital, the wall heightened people's sense of place.

Automobiles loomed large as well in the landscape of Sun City. The spaciousness of the subdivision and its climate both militated against much walking, and the underdeveloped transit system of the larger metropolis further encouraged reliance on the automobile. About 95 percent of all households in Sun City owned at least one car (which was worth, on average, about twice as much as the typical car in Maricopa County), and residents relied on their cars as their primary form of transportation.[142] Many viewed the prospect of growing too old to drive as a personal tragedy in the making, and both DEVCO and senior volunteers experimented with vans, buses, and taxis in order to minimize this threat to the elderly's independence.[143] The prevalence of automobiles underlined the premium placed on autonomy by local residents. Cars ensured the retirees' rights to do "what they want, when they want, and with whomever they want."

Growing Together: Sun City and Phoenix

Autonomy by way of automobiles characterized not only the elderly's relationship to the society at large but also their relationship to the surrounding metropolis. Over the years Sun City remained self-sufficient; residents usually did not need to leave it to find health care or supplies or recreation. But if they had a car they could go to Phoenix if they wished, and most did. Thus, although Sun City was self-contained, it also developed a suburban relationship to Phoenix.

During the 1960s and 1970s, elderly Americans moved in increasing numbers to outlying areas of cities because they found central-city life threatening. Arizona boosters capitalized on this trend, slyly "warning" newcomers that the state might seem "a bit dull" (meaning safe and calm and clean) compared to the big city. Some retirees came from cities back East where their friends had already fled to the suburbs in order to escape inner-city problems, and they brought to Arizona the same impulse to distance themselves from the troubled urban core.[144]

Purchasers appreciated the security and quiet that Sun City offered, but they did not intend to become recluses who had left the city for good. Rather, they hoped to achieve the suburban ideal of taking the central city on their own terms. Because Sun City had its own services, merchants, and amenities, and because most residents did not need to commute to work daily, the town was indeed more able than most places to accomplish this goal. It seemed a part of the larger metropolis without sacrificing much autonomy to it. It was suburban without being subordinate.[145]

Indeed, the proximity of Phoenix to Sun City contributed to the town's success. DEVCO tried to build other retirement communities in Florida and California but eventually sold them because they were not profitable enough. The remoteness of each of these other Sun Cities from major metropolitan areas was largely to blame for their slow growth. Booming Sun City, Arizona, on the other hand, was situated nearer (but not too close) to a large city. Phoenix featured attractive amenities, yet did not appear very threatening. Neither too big nor too small, the metropolis generally seemed inviting to retirees.[146]

Sun Citizens found Phoenix a nice place to visit, but they preferred not to live there. One resident cited the traffic, blight, and noise of his Phoenix neighborhood as motivations for turning to Sun City's "environment of relaxation and contentment." Above all, the elderly did not wish to be burdened with central city problems. Like retirement itself, residence in Sun City implied a kind of freedom from some of the problems and obligations of urban society.[147]

Sun Citizens' peculiar sense of place put them at odds not only with other residents of greater Phoenix but also with American conventions of local self-government. That they repeatedly and overwhelmingly voted against proposals to incorporate into a municipality provided one indication of their antipathy toward traditional local politics.[148] The resistance stemmed in part from the feeling that Sun City was better off without this particular aspect of the complexities and conflicts of urban life. Like other migrants who saw the West as a blank slate where they might start their lives anew, many equated retirement in Arizona with getting "away from the hustle and bustle of a city and the wrangling that is a part of politics." Retirees spoke as if they had moved to escape those annoyances associated with municipal government back East: "We don't want city hallism as we knew it in other towns," explained the president of the Sun City Taxpayers Association in 1974.[149]

Sun Citizens doubted that they needed the kinds of politics required by other cities. They did "not have the problem of juvenile delinquency, saloons, dance halls, industry and factories," argued one retiree in 1964, and they were "not trying to build a place for the future generation or create a town for their children to live in." The more diverse and changing populations of other communities required politics as a means of reconciling differences between groups, but Sun Citizens apparently believed that they could have no real disagreements among themselves that would demand mediation by municipal government.[150]

Local politics seemed capable only of generating divisiveness. It also raised the possibility of undesirable changes among a population that professed to be basically content. Despite some evidence to the contrary, Sun City residents believed that incorporation would raise taxes and undermine the exclusiveness as well as the homogeneity of the town.[151] Of course, the presence of DEVCO helped to defeat incorporation: the developer provided many services that might otherwise have been demanded from local government. Yet DEVCO's withdrawal from the community after 1978 did not induce a great demand for incorporation. Instead, Maricopa County increased its provision of services to Sun City, and the residents themselves stepped up their voluntarism of behalf of the town.

Despite their reluctance to incorporate, retirees hardly looked upon civic affairs with indifference. They deployed their own voluntary associations to enforce deed restrictions and resolve disputes, and they found other means of redress as well. When the odors and noises from a nearby cattle feedlot became too offensive, for example, two hundred residents joined the Webb company in a lawsuit to close down the nuisance.[152] The developers of adjacent tracts became aware of the retirees' clout and gave them due consideration in planning. Proponents of a nearby theme park went out of their way to explain that they had considered the elderly at every step and would have nothing in their project "that is offensive or disharmonious to them. We've included things that will attract mature adults."[153]

The residents of Sun City were not voters or taxpayers to be trifled with. It was well known that they turned out for elections in strength and donated substantial sums to favorite candidates and causes.[154] But it was also recognized that Sun Citizens' politics did not necessarily match those of other people in the state, and this caused some animosity among other Arizonans. Residents of the new town sided overwhelmingly with the Republican Party (80 percent of them registered as Republicans, compared to about 50 percent of the state population) and acquired a reputation for selfish conservatism. Other residents of Phoenix regularly criticized the retirees as insensitive to the rest of the metropolitan area and its problems.[155] Both the residents and the developer were mindful of the constant need for Sun City to "improve its image with the rest of Arizona," but neither side seemed able to understand the other very well.[156]

Animosity toward Sun City crested in the early 1970s, when it managed to secede from the school district that served the adjacent suburb of Peoria. Since 1960 the retirees had been instrumental in defeating virtually every bond issue submitted to voters by the Peoria School

District. They complained about the costs of the proposed bonds, explained that they opposed the new taxes because many of them lived on fixed incomes, and, in some cases, went so far as to claim that retirees had no obligation to pay property taxes in support of public education. These attitudes frustrated the parents of Peoria, whose children attended classes in substandard and outdated facilities.

The issue came to a head in 1973 when Sun City attempted to set up its own district for the handful of youngsters living in the community. The Arizona Superior Court struck down the proposed district, but by the following year Sun Citizens utilized a state law that permitted them to withdraw from Peoria's jurisdiction while arranging on an individual basis to pay tuition for the children who would be attending the outside schools. The retirement suburb became "an unorganized school territory" under Arizona law, responsible for paying state but not local school taxes. Parents in Peoria expressed relief, because now they could more readily gain passage of school bond issues. But they and other residents of greater Phoenix naturally retained resentment toward Sun City.[157]

Although the actions of retirees appeared selfish and narrow-minded to outsiders, they were based in part on legitimate concerns. Because the property values and population of Sun City were comparatively high, its residents paid a larger share of school taxes than they believed to be fair. One retiree calculated that Sun City sent fewer than 1 percent of the students to Peoria classrooms but paid almost 75 percent of the property tax revenues received by the district.[158] This seemed especially burdensome in light of the retirees' expectations and fears. DEVCO had promised that taxes would be lower in Sun City, partly because there would be no schools there. A number of residents came expecting that the social overhead would be significantly lower than elsewhere. Even the more prosperous residents lived on fixed incomes, and few knew for certain that these incomes would be adequate until they died. Sun Citizens feared inflation and its consequences, so they tried to keep to a minimum all costs over which they had some control.[159]

Although attitudes toward taxes and fixed incomes helped to account for the voting records of Sun Citizens, they did not explain them entirely. Not all retirement communities responded in the same fashion to school bond issues. Residents of Leisure Worlds in California, for example, generally voted to support public education.[160] These other concentrations of the aged were not as large or powerful as Sun City, and they consisted of retirees who had not migrated very far from their former place of residence. It seems probable that some sense of attachment to the surrounding community survived the shorter move. The long-term place ties of Sun City residents, by contrast, in some ways linked the new town more with Illinois, Michigan, or California than with Arizona. Inhabitants of Sun City knew about, and had probably supported, the schools their own children had attended elsewhere, but they had less reason to feel connected to schools near their new hometown. Furthermore, if they did form strong attachments, it was as individual volunteers.[161] Voluntarism on behalf of the schools comported well not only with the retirees' sense that they had more time than money to spare but also with their notion of autonomy. As taxpayers Sun Citizens perhaps felt coerced by outsiders to spend their limited funds, but as volunteers they served by their own choice.

Sun Citizens' desire to take urban life on their own terms clashed with urban politics. Not wishing to be assessed for Peoria schools, they opted out of the district as a whole. Not wanting the headaches of municipal government, Sun Citizens opposed incorporation and depended instead upon DEVCO's paternalism as well as their voluntary organizations. Not having to commute into Phoenix to a job every day, the retirees entered and left the unwieldy city as they pleased—avoiding the rush-hour congestion, neglecting downtown in favor of outlying shopping areas, and generally enjoying the amenities of the urban area without experiencing its problems.

Such a pattern of involvement with the larger metropolis reiterated in spatial terms the independence the elderly sought in retirement. Sun Citizens hoped to preserve their autonomy not only within the society but also on the landscape. Inside Sun City, this effort resulted in a mixture of individualism and mutual self-help that made the community a remarkably successful showcase for the retired life. But retirees were not such model citizens beyond the borders of the town. Partly out of fear, partly out of self-interest, and partly out of the same suburban impulse that influenced many other Americans, they sought to keep the central city at arm's length—neither so far away as to be out of touch, nor so close as to impose upon them those obligations they hoped to leave behind.

There were limits, however, to Sun Citizens' autonomy. Senescence itself was one. Despite its image as a fountain of youth, Sun City could not halt the aging process, and the vulnerability of the elderly became steadily more apparent as segments of the population grew too old to maintain an "active way-of-life." The retirees coped with the problems of old age as well as anyone, but they could not overcome the biological limits to their independence.

The community itself also changed in ways that made the residents uneasy. In particular, it grew very quickly from a small village into a rather large town, and along the way it lost some of its charm and aura of well-being. As early as 1970, inhabitants began to lament the passing of the "good old days" of the early 1960s when people had been friendlier and life more adventurous. By the time Sun City's population exceeded 44,000 in 1978, it seemed to have too many strangers and too much crowding. A 1980 survey of inhabitants ranked "control of growth" as the "most frequently mentioned problem in the community," with "traffic congestion" right behind.[162] The most telling criticism, however, came from outside the walls of the community. When residents of a smaller retirement new town in southern Arizona began to agonize about "loss of community" and deterioration of "their 'small town' quality of life," they lamented that they had become too much like Sun City.[163]

Sun Citizens' apprehensions about growth conflicted with the developer's interests, for DEVCO naturally wished to maximize sales. By promising to add new golf courses, shopping malls, and recreation centers as the population increased, it had encouraged residents to promote Sun City to their friends and relatives back home.[164] The inhabitants, of course, had responded by extolling Sun City's virtues to their acquaintances in the hope of attracting familiar and like-minded people to the community. That such extensive favorable publicity would lead to excessive growth did not seem to occur to the residents of Sun City, at least not until it was too late.

Once it had developed virtually all the land in Sun City, DEVCO reduced its involvement with the town and directed its energies to new subdivisions for retirees. Some residents complained that the builder no longer cared about the older town. Not all inhabitants felt that way, but they did agree that Sun City had entered a new era.[165] Facing up to urban problems without the corporate paternalism of DEVCO would put Sun Citizens' cherished autonomy to the test.

At the same time that growth was making the town seem too citylike inside its borders, Phoenix steadily spread toward Sun City on the outside. In 1960 the subdivision had gotten its start in the midst of cotton fields, miles away from the urban fringe of Phoenix. A dozen years later it was evident to one retiree that his community was "going to become another part of Phoenix. It isn't a quaint little town anymore."[166] Much as the elderly might try to keep Phoenix at arm's length, the city crowded in on the town, threatening it with such urban problems as pollution, noise, crime, and congestion.

Ethnic diversity in surrounding communities was one result of the spread of Phoenix. While Sun City itself remained fairly homogeneous (only 0.2 percent of Hispanic descent, according to the 1980 census), relatively impoverished Mexican Americans dominated the nearby small towns of El Mirage (80.2 percent) and Surprise (71.7 percent). Growth also encouraged higher prices in the overall metropolitan area. During the 1950s Phoenix had ranked below the American metropolitan average for cost of living; three decades later it had become a comparatively expensive place to dwell. Retirees appreciated its highly regarded health-care facilities and cultural life, but the cost of living, shortage of housing, and growing crime rate all worried the elderly.[167] Sun City could insulate residents from some central city problems, but it could not stem the tide of urban expansion. The retirees had to become reconciled to a somewhat more urban existence than they had expected to find.

If Phoenix made its mark on Sun City, Sun City influenced Phoenix, too. As with other migrants to western areas, elderly newcomers jeopardized the very environment that had lured them. By creating pollution, taxing the water supply, consuming open space, and accelerating sprawl, retirees and their exclusive towns added to the urban problems that confronted Phoenix. At the same time, however, the elderly also contributed in more constructive ways to the growth of the metropolis. They constituted a new and clean industry that attracted enormous amounts of capital, and some degree of stability, to Arizona, and they popularized a residential pattern on the landscape that, for at least part of the population, lent a semblance of order to an otherwise chaotic urban scene.

Phoenix had only a slight reputation among the elderly before 1960, but with the rise of Sun City its appeal to the aged soared. By 1985 the number of retirees in the metropolitan area had climbed to more than 230,000, or 11.6 percent of the total population, and would soon approach 15 percent. These residents brought one type of maturity to the still young and restless city. They tended to move around less, own their homes more frequently, and contribute fresh capital to the economy. Retirees may have wished to remain somewhat aloof from the remainder of the city, but they nonetheless represented, in the words of one business editor, "a big economic asset" for the urban area. They brought with them large holdings of stocks and bonds, sizable savings accounts, and steady incomes, yet did not require in return much outlay on the part of state and local government. By spending their money locally, Sun Citizens created employment at the rate of one new job for every six retired residents.[168]

The example of Sun City perhaps encouraged as well the seasonal retirement industry in the Phoenix area, which offered its own benefits. By 1983 as many as 100,000 "snowbirds" spent each winter in mobile home parks, apartment complexes, or second homes in the vicinity, adding $200 million annually to the economy. These migrants, too, tended to have more money, better health, and a higher level of education than the average American retiree.[169]

These elderly communities on wheels resembled in fundamental ways such retirement new towns as Sun City. In fact, DEVCO's subdivision had doubtless planted the notion that central Arizona offered a better way of life for American retirees. Sun City had not been the first on the scene, but its greater investment, extensive publicity, and marked success had encouraged a good deal of imitation. Several competing new towns for retirees appeared by the early 1970s, with such names as Dreamland Village and Golden Hills–Leisure World, and by 1980 or so perhaps as many as one-third of all retirees in the Valley of the Sun resided in retirement communities.[170] At the same time, developers laid out other "new towns" for all generations, giving them such names as Carefree and Village of Paradise Valley. Planned communities were increasingly recognized as an integral part of greater Phoenix.[171]

Planned communities never housed as much of the urban population as their developers projected; indeed, many never made it off the drawing board. But they became an important component of the cityscape in Phoenix and a common feature of people's mental maps of the town. Many of these subdivisions followed the Sun City model: they consisted of large parcels of land located away from the city center along major roads or highways, and they offered an enriched built environment to a relatively affluent market. Few became as self-sufficient as Sun City, partly because their residents more regularly commuted into the city. The location of most planned communities accelerated sprawl by affirming the centrifugal forces at work in the metropolitan area. As a result, some critics saw the many new towns as a problem for greater Phoenix.[172]

But although some argued that planned communities heightened disorder in the landscape, others saw them as the foci for a new kind of urban pattern that relied less on a traditional downtown as the city center. Some new towns in suburban areas provided alternatives to the central business district of the larger metropolis. Sun City, with its stores and hospital and services, became a hub for the northwestern suburbs of Phoenix.[173] The elderly may not have generally appreciated outsiders' patronage of "their" stores, but it seems probable that others found in Sun City and its ilk a set of new centers for the larger metropolis. In the later 1970s and early 1980s, as Phoenix and Maricopa County adopted new comprehensive plans based on the idea of urban villages instead of the traditional concentric model of a city, they recognized that places such as Sun City constituted ready-made nodes for the multi-centered pattern now envisioned.[174]

The average residents living in and around Sun City probably saw the urban-village arrangement as somewhat less than perfect. Yet it seems likely that it made reasonable sense to them, if only because it corresponded roughly to their picture of Phoenix. They did not expect the desert metropolis to imitate eastern cities with their domineering downtowns, troubled inner cities, and high-density settlement. Rather, it was to be more suburban through and through. The success of Sun City contributed to the fulfillment of that western vision of the metropolis.

The influence of Sun City was not confined to the West. Developers throughout the country, and especially in the Sunbelt, took it as a model, and observers of the elderly viewed its "solutions" to the problems of aging as ones that "could be emulated elsewhere as the elderly population grows."[175] The Webb company itself attested the trend with its plans for expansion. It noted that, although the fraction of all elderly Americans willing to move more than two hundred miles upon retirement had increased from about 3 percent to about 9 percent between 1960 and 1985, most elderly citizens still preferred to age in place. If retirees would not come to Sun City, DEVCO proposed to take Sun City to them by building retirement communities near big cities across the country. The Webb company thus joined other developers building age-segregated housing—no longer just for the elderly, but also for young, single adults and for young families.[176] The retirement communities proposed by DEVCO would imitate Sun City in some ways but differ in others. They would be situated closer to existing cities and services and would aim at slightly younger buyers (forty-five years would be the new minimum age). They would demonstrate greater sensitivity to the surrounding environment. And, most important, they would be smaller.[177]

Sun City had been created in an age when people had expected limitations on development to result from the lack of income of the elderly. Two decades later, it was doubts about the availability of natural resources and an adequate supply of inexpensive land that inhibited development. In the earlier day, there had seemed no need to limit the growth of Sun City; two decades later its suburban design had been threatened by its own rapid growth into a citylike setting as well as by the expansion of Phoenix, which seemed on the verge of engulfing the retirement town. Newer planned communities could no longer be so distant from the central city. Like Sun City, they would have to find a way to flourish within the larger metropolitan setting. Striking a balance between urban and suburban was no longer as easy as it had been in the early 1960s, but neither was it impossible. Not only had such new towns as Sun City demonstrated how to keep the city at arm's length; the western metropolis itself had changed, coming to resemble more closely the planned communities on its outskirts. In the new urban pattern, the magic land of Sun City was no longer extraordinary.

CHAPTER FIVE

The Seattle World's Fair of 1962: Downtown and Suburbs in the Space Age

Americans have been holding world's fairs since the last half of the nineteenth century. From 1876, when the nation commemorated the Centennial with its first great international exposition in Philadelphia, until 1939–40, when New York and San Francisco hosted concurrent events, Americans scarcely let a decade pass without staging at least one fair to celebrate their growing sense of themselves as a distinct major civilization, and their increasing material productivity and abundance. Some of these fairs significantly reshaped their host cities, and the Chicago World's Columbian Exposition of 1893 in particular influenced numerous urban trends.

World War II, however, began a hiatus of more than twenty years without an American world's fair. The distractions of world war and cold war, the financial problems of the New York and San Francisco fairs of 1939–40, and new substitutes like television, shopping malls, and Disneyland, which kept people abreast of cultural advances better than any one-shot fair could, had made major international expositions less attractive. By the time world's fairs reappeared on the scene after 1960, they had changed substantially to suit a changed society.

The New York World's Fair of 1964–65, a disappointment for many critics as well as a money-loser, may have been the last great international exposition on American soil. Proposals for major fairs in 1976 in Philadelphia, 1981 in Los Angeles, and 1993 in Chicago were all scrapped. In their stead, smaller cities of the West and South—San Antonio, Spokane, Knoxville, New Orleans—staged lesser fairs, suited more to regional and local interests than to national and international purposes. These events occurred principally for the sake of urban re-development and local self-promotion, and they increasingly came to resemble not the prewar exposition but the postwar shopping center and theme park. They indicated that if American world's fairs were to survive the end of the twentieth century, they would do so in a much altered form.[1]

The first important American fair of the postwar era, Seattle's Century 21 Exposition of April 21 through October 21, 1962, marked the transition from a great international exposition to a more limited event. Century 21 combined the interests of world and nation with the needs of region and locality. It received sanction from the Bureau of International Expositions in Paris, featured many shows and products from other countries, and hosted sixteen foreign governments plus participants in the African Nations, European Economic Community, and United Nations exhibits. Just as significant was the fact that the United States government chose the Seattle World's Fair as a vehicle for conveying the country's achievements in science and space.

Yet the national and international messages of Century 21 were essentially superimposed on a local and regional event. The city of Seattle and the state of Washington originally proposed a fair as an economic stimulant and a key step in Seattle's rise to metropolitan big-league status. The host city had some experience with this kind of festival. In 1909 it had sponsored the Alaska-Yukon-Pacific Exposition, to celebrate its success as entrepôt for the goldfields of the Yukon and Alaska and the ports of Asia. The 1909 fair not only showed a profit but also boosted the local economy and landscaped the campus of the University of Washington on what then amounted to the outskirts of the city. The 1962 fair was designed to generate similar benefits. This time, however, downtown was supposed to gain more from the fair than the fringes of Seattle would.

The Century 21 Exposition, then, illuminated both the metropolitan evolution of Seattle and the changing nature of American world's fairs. And its major themes possessed a special meaning at both the regional and the national level. Local residents and promoters, as well as participants from across the country, shared beliefs embodied in the exposition: faith in American science and technology as sources of progress and harmony, confidence in an almost unlimited ability to master the environments of earth and outer space, and anticipation of a world of both heightened order and greater abundance. At the local level, these attitudes merged in a vision of a more prosperous, more manageable metropolis that could achieve greater recognition, while at the national level they suggested continuing affluence and technological advance, and a favorable resolution of the cold war. Such premises helped to create in Seattle an urban district that in some respects resembled Disneyland, Stanford Industrial Park, and Sun City—and in some ways did not.

Both the magic kingdom created by the fair and its urban setting differed significantly from their southwestern counterparts. Seattle was growing more slowly than other major cities of the West, in part because its isolation and topography inhibited sprawl. Postwar Seattle inherited a more intact central core from the nineteenth century and seemed less overrun by growth, although not for lack of trying. And just as mid-century Seattle appeared more contained than its counterparts, so its magic kingdom was a less influential addition to the western landscape. A fair devoted to federal and worldwide messages could not reflect so much regional shaping. More important, the fair ran for less than a year, not enough time for the lasting impact of a Disneyland or a Sun City. The size and location of the exposition also set it apart. At 74 acres, the site was small as both fairs and magic kingdoms go, and it stood adjacent to the city center, rather than on the edges of the central city (see Figure 31).

If in many respects the Seattle World's Fair did not resemble magic lands in California and Arizona, it nonetheless belonged to the same general category. Seattle displayed a more constrained version of the pattern of urbanization that was affecting the rest of the West, and the Century 21 Exposition was a related kind of response to urban conditions, for the fair represented an effort on the part of local residents to achieve metropolitan stature and bring order to a growing city. The exposition also belonged to the same cultural milieu as the other magic kingdoms. It catered particularly to the more prosperous and better-educated segments of society, as did Sun City; gave more serious attention to predicting the future than did Tomorrowland at Anaheim; rivaled Stanford Industrial Park as harbinger of the space age; and celebrated that distinctive optimism, based on growth, technology, and defense spending, that characterized all rapidly expanding cities in the region. Furthermore, the fair demonstrated how influential western cityscapes were becoming across the country: its carefully controlled environment was created with substantial help from veterans of Disneyland.

Sun City, Disneyland, and Stanford Industrial Park were all devel-

Figure 31. The Seattle World's Fair was located next to the central business district rather than in the suburbs. Its most distinctive feature was the Space Needle, which not only competed with Mount Rainier on the city's skyline but also symbolized the space-age orientation of both the fair and the town in 1962. Courtesy of the Special Collections Division, University of Washington Libraries (neg. #UW 13105).

oped on large tracts in outlying areas and helped to bring cohesion to sprawling districts located at some distance from established city centers. Century 21 was supposed to be different. Its designers intended the fair to bolster the central business district, to enable it to hold its own against the rapid growth of suburban areas. In this goal, the fair essentially failed. It did create a new cluster of cultural facilities near downtown, called the Seattle Center, but the fairgrounds never truly merged with the old central business district. Instead, they became a discrete district that lent little support to the existing downtown. Moreover, the exposition took on a decidedly suburban form, attracted an audience with a rather suburban profile, and foreshadowed an even more highly suburbanized metropolis of the future. Rather than helping to "urbanize suburbia," like other magic kingdoms, Century 21 brought the suburbs to the city center.

The world's fair did not fulfill its founders' expectations for downtown Seattle, but it did help reshape the city culturally and spatially. The fairgrounds survived the demise of the optimism that had encouraged the exposition. The Seattle World's Fair had been predicated on middle-class assumptions about continued prosperity, growing mastery of the environment, and increasing social as well as international harmony—1950s premises that encountered 1960s challenges at both the national and the local level. Consequently, predictions made about the twenty-first century seemed less and less reliable after 1962. Meanwhile, the exposition served as a model for other cities that wished to host world's fairs, and left cultural dividends that lent a sense of accomplishment to a rapidly changing Seattle.

The Downtown Origins of the Fair

In the plans of city and state leaders, the Century 21 Exposition began as a "Festival of the West." By the time the gates opened, however, the event had become "America's Space Age World's Fair."[2] The two slogans summarized the two separate sets of intentions behind the fair, one devised for local purposes and the other for national needs. Locally, Seattle's leaders hoped the festival would foster growth and support the central business district. They also intended the fair to help Seattle overcome a reputation as provincial and unsophisticated.[3]

Those who planned Century 21 did not initially conceive of the exposition as one devoted primarily to the future, but neither were they set against the idea. More than most American cities of the mid-twentieth century, Seattle, because it boldly bore the stamp of modernity, seemed a suitable host for a futuristic fair. By the 1950s such technologies as the automobile and the airplane, and such influences as the nation's involvement in global conflict, had made a strong imprint on Seattle's shape and self-image. The same forces had also begun to incorporate the relatively remote metropolis into the mainstream of American life and to establish a basis for continued expansion. Mobilization for World War II, by attracting industry, launched the new era. The population within the city limits increased from 368,302 in 1940 to 467,591 in 1950 and 557,087 in 1960, and the population of the Seattle metropolitan region (King and Snohomish counties) expanded from 844,572 in 1950 to 1,107,213 in 1960.[4]

The Boeing Airplane Company acted as mainspring in Seattle's postwar economy. The aircraft manufacturer came of age during World War II through its mass-production of bombers. Work for the military diminished in the years immediately following the conflict, but during the 1950s the company not only won once more a substantial number of defense contracts but also diversified by developing the Boeing 707 jet, the first in the world's most successful series of airliners. Production for both commercial and military buyers made aerospace dominant in the regional economy. In 1947 Boeing had employed about one out of every five manufacturing workers in King County; ten years later it employed one out of every two. In 1960, a slow year for aerospace, about 13 percent of the civilian labor force worked for Boeing. An economic forecast in 1962 stated the simple truth: "As Boeing goes, so goes this area."[5]

The Boeing Airplane Company was a primary reason local leaders felt that a "Festival of the West" was needed. Although Boeing was the leading source of the postwar growth that residents wished to celebrate with a fair, it also presented problems for the city, and especially for the downtown. Many regarded the firm as aloof from the community, "a minimal patron of the arts and civic organizations." More important, steep declines in business regularly punctuated its overall success and undercut the regional economy. Employment figures sketch the magnitude of the instability. In 1958 the company employed 72,000 workers, but two years later only 58,000 were on the payroll. In the fair year of 1962 it employed 70,000, but by 1964, with the loss of a key defense contract, the work force dropped to 50,000. Although World War II had supposedly liberated western cities from the heavy hand of eastern capital, postwar Seattle remained dependent on a single industry and, through Boeing, on the prerogatives of another eastern potentate—the federal government.[6]

From the inception of exposition planning in the mid-1950s, civic leaders justified the fair primarily on the basis of the economic benefits it promised: invigoration of local business; revitalization of Seattle's waning role as commercial gateway to Asia and Alaska; gains in state and local tax revenues; and increasing property values. The fair's theme song, "Meet me in Seattle / That's where I'll be at'll / Meet me in Seattle at the fair," underscored expectations for increased tourism. But organizers of Century 21 placed particular emphasis on the prospect of attracting additional manufacturing, to decrease dependence on Boeing. A major reason for holding an international exposition, the fair's leading officials explained during the late 1950s, was to "build a more diversified industrial economy" that would reduce the region's "heavy reliance . . . on defense spending by the Federal Government."[7]

Local supporters saw the fair as an advertisement luring new business by establishing Seattle's reputation "in financial circles across the country and even abroad." All during the planning and operation of the exposition, editorials in local newspapers reminded citizens to treat visitors well in order to foster an image of the city as an "enterprising area."[8] Officials took special pains to publicize the resources available in the region for industry, such as cheap electrical power, and they sponsored an exhibit at the fair, Headquarters City, that portrayed Seattle as an ideal location for the regional branch offices of national companies. They also stressed that the fair marked the emergence of new, more active economic leadership, particularly from within the central business district.[9]

If a world's fair promised to pull Seattle out from under Boeing's economic shadow, it also offered a chance to offset the suburbanizing influence exercised by the aerospace company. Needing plenty of room for its operations, Boeing planned and built all its major facilities in peripheral areas rather than near the downtown, and thus it accelerated the outward growth of the metropolis.[10] As these facilities expanded rapidly during the 1950s, so did the suburbs of Seattle. Between 1950 and 1960, the population of the outlying parts of the metropolitan area increased by 46 percent, while that inside the 1950 city limits grew by only 0.7 percent. Before World War II, the central city of Seattle contained 60 percent of the population of the region; in 1960, it had about half, and it retained that much only because of aggressive annexations during the 1950s.[11]

The population of suburban King County differed in character from that of the city of Seattle. Residents tended to live in larger, more valuable, owner-occupied homes, and they possessed more automobiles. Households consisted of younger people, including more children, and enjoyed higher incomes, whereas the central city tended to have more senior citizens, a smaller proportion of school-age children and married couples, and a lower percentage of single-family, detached housing. Apparently the more attractive part of the metropolis, the suburbs gained a disproportionate share of people who changed their place of residence between 1955 and 1960. And once people resided in the outlying areas, they tended to work outside rather than inside the city and more frequently took private rather than public transportation to work.[12]

Suburban expansion represented one kind of growth in the automobile age, and the central business district did stand to benefit from it, at least in part. Vitality on the urban perimeter suggested that Seattle had begun to overcome its natural barriers. An isthmus between Puget Sound and Lake Washington, surrounded by hills and mountains, the city had no wide basin into which it could easily grow. By the mid-1950s, however, a multiplying number of ferries, bridges, and roadways had begun to facilitate auto and truck transportation between the urban hub and its outlying regions. Seattle foresaw expansion both of its urban living area and of its role in regional markets. The prospect of a wider, more accessible city called for celebration. One of the original justifications for proposing a world's fair was to "commemorate the opening of the second Lake Washington bridge, the completion of the cross-Sound bridge and the Seattle freeway." [13]

Although bridges and highways were expected to benefit downtown Seattle, it soon became clear that they posed a challenge to the central business district. People could now drive more quickly into downtown, but they could also leave it just as easily. Developers, seeing this, built shopping malls and office complexes with plentiful free parking along the major transportation corridors out of downtown. The process was well underway by the time Century 21 opened. In 1946 the Bellevue Square shopping center had opened to serve communities east of Lake Washington, complete with a branch of Frederick & Nelson, a major downtown department store. In 1961 Frederick & Nelson announced its participation in Aurora Village, another mall north of the city limits. [14]

The most successful suburban development was the Northgate regional shopping center, one of the first true malls to be built in the United States, which opened for business in 1950 just north of the city limits along the proposed freeway right-of-way. The mall, which featured a branch of downtown's Bon Marché department store, prospered and expanded quickly. Even though the city of Seattle annexed Northgate in 1952 and thus captured its tax revenues, the shopping center still presented a direct challenge to the central business district. James B. Douglas, president of the Northgate Company, explained the design of the mall as an alternative to downtown:

Actually we never called Northgate a shopping center because it is more than that. It is a real city with much more than stores: There is a theater, a hospital, doctor and dental offices, bank, shoe repair, dry cleaning, beauty shops, pharmacy, post office and an insurance company. Each has drawing power to bring people just as downtown does. [15]

With the success of outlying shopping malls, the retail economy of postwar Seattle clearly thrived particularly on the fringes of the city and, at least in the eyes of downtown businessmen during the later 1950s, demanded the development of a strong central focus to act as a magnet that would hold urban society together. The civic leaders promoting Century 21 saw the fair as a tool for revitalizing Seattle's downtown, the district which, in their minds, should serve as anchor for a population that seemed to be adrift. In creating a world's fair, downtown leaders toiled to ensure that the central business district remained the undisputed focus of greater Seattle.

The international exposition was but one of many initiatives to bolster downtown Seattle. Local businessmen had already insisted on routing the proposed freeway as close to the central business district as they could.[16] Now they also paid heed to downtown's appearance, proposing improvements that would "offset the centrifugal tendencies" of suburban expansion. Learning of threatened property values, high vacancy rates, and a shortage of cultural facilities, green spaces, and parking lots, as well as of the beginnings of blight both within the district and in surrounding neighborhoods, businessmen resolved to revitalize the downtown. They hoped to compete more effectively for shoppers, so that suburban malls would not get "a disproportionate share of business," and to attract new activity, such as the regional offices of national corporations, that would keep the downtown prosperous.[17] The Central Association of Seattle, founded in 1958, helped to coordinate the efforts of downtown businessmen. "Dedicated to the development and maintenance of a strong, vigorous and attractive central Seattle," the association explored ways to improve transportation into the city center, reverse the deterioration of the central business district, and develop parking facilities that would not disrupt downtown traffic patterns.[18]

Those working to rejuvenate downtown Seattle envisioned a compact, centrally located business district that would become both more built up and more attractive to pedestrians and shoppers. Planners for downtown Seattle hoped to provide freeway access as well as plentiful parking and pedestrian landscaping. They also intended to attract new businesses and cultural activities that would help the downtown withstand the threat of suburban growth; to develop a public transit system that might forestall traffic congestion; to stimulate urban renewal in order to minimize blight; and to encourage the downtown to add new city blocks in order to increase its capacity. For all of these purposes, a world's fair located in the vicinity of the city center would serve as catalyst.

From its inception the Century 21 Exposition was associated primarily with the downtown. Legend has it that in 1955 a columnist for the *Seattle Times*, a member of the Chamber of Commerce, and a city councilman conceived of the idea over lunch in a downtown club. For the duration of planning and operation, prominent downtown merchants, executives, journalists, and politicians provided the main leadership.[19] Many fair officials played prominent roles in the Central Association of Seattle, and the association seized upon the exposition as a chance to enact its plans for the central business district. It initiated a series of efforts to spruce up the downtown in anticipation of visitors, always reminding owners of potential gains in property values, and it consulted with civic and exposition officials on transportation and parking for fairgoers.[20]

The development of a site for Century 21 promised to overcome some of the physical shortcomings of the central business district. Planners built the fairgrounds on approximately two dozen city blocks near downtown (see Figure 32). They created a pedestrian space, which the city center lacked, by closing off motor-vehicle traffic through the site but keeping the basic street grid for walkways. They kept four major structures on the grounds, remodeling them and incorporating them into the exposition, razing the remainder to make room for a new complex of cultural facilities, rides, and landscaping. In this fashion Seattle got the convention halls, arts and entertainment buildings, and green spaces that seemed in such short supply downtown.[21]

Developing the grounds for a world's fair also gave city planners a chance to improve downtown by accelerating programs of urban renewal. As early as 1957, organizers for the fair consulted with federal officials on how to coordinate the exposition with redevelopment efforts. They were determined to prevent "eastern" slum conditions from strangling central Seattle.[22] Concern about blight also justified the selection of the site for the Seattle World's Fair. Worried that deterioration would encircle the downtown and inhibit its growth, civic leaders used the exposition to revitalize the Warren neighborhood, the site of the fair, located about a mile north of the city center (see Figure 33). This district encapsulated all the traits that differentiated the central city from its suburbs. Although hardly a slum, the Warren neighborhood had a higher crime rate than the rest of Seattle, more unemployment, fewer owner-occupied homes, a higher percentage of older, less valu-

Figure 32. The Century 21 grounds were laid out at the foot of Queen Anne
Hill (background) in a district known as the Warren
neighborhood. The Armory (right center), stadium (behind
Armory), and street grid were retained as part of the fairgrounds,
but most buildings had been razed by 1961 to make room for the
exposition, which would become Seattle's new civic center.
Courtesy of the Special Collections Division, University of
Washington Libraries (photo by Hamilton, neg. #1621).

able housing, more elderly residents, lower average incomes, and fewer
families and school-age children. Offices, warehouses, factories, and
parking lots had all begun to encroach on residential streets.[23] It
seemed a prime location to build the fairgrounds as a kind of downtown renewal project (see Figure 34).

In promoting redevelopment of a neighborhood more than a mile
north of the city center, civic leaders hoped to create for downtown
more room to expand and a more supportive periphery. Between the
central business district and the exposition site lay the Denny Regrade,
an unattractive area that had resisted prosperity ever since the original
terrain, Denny Hill, had been leveled during the first three decades of

Figure 33. Downtown Seattle, located at the far right, stood about one mile
from the fairgrounds, where builders were erecting the Space
Needle in 1961. Courtesy of the Seattle Post-Intelligencer
Collection, Museum of History and Industry, Seattle.

the twentieth century in order to facilitate growth and land speculation.
Planners now hoped that the exposition would attract "close-in, multi-
story apartment and apartment-hotel development" to the regrade area,
along with more parking facilities, both of which were expected to add
vitality to the downtown.[24]

The location of the exposition at a short distance from the central
business district permitted Seattle to experiment with new forms of
urban transit. Almost all American world's fairs have featured futuristic
transportation, and the Century 21 Exposition, with its emphasis on
jet travel and space exploration, could be no exception. The high-speed
commuter train called the Monorail, however, which was built to link
the city center to the fairgrounds, amounted to more than a casual demonstration of modern technology or a prediction of some vague tomorrow. Planners' vision of a compact, busy downtown required a system
of public transportation that would replace autos in the city center and
would compete against cars for commuters from outlying areas. The
Monorail struck many local residents as a "futuristic solution" to the
prospect of downtown congestion and showed "sound, progressive city
planning" to meet the widely perceived need for rapid transit.[25] It also
served as an important bridge between the city center, with its hotels,

Figure 34. This 1957 photograph confirms fair planners' and city officials' estimation of the Warren neighborhood as a blighted district. The alley marks the approximate site of the Space Needle. Courtesy of the Museum of History and Industry, Seattle (Lengenhager Collection #8151).

offices, and stores, and the fairgrounds, with its entertainment and meeting facilities. Like urban renewal, the Monorail experiment contributed to a picture of a vital, cohesive business center for Seattle.

While organizing a world's fair in pursuit of a vision of a prosperous and well-ordered city, civic leaders added a veneer of culture designed to elevate the status of Seattle. Planning for the exposition coincided with new city initiatives to develop a civic complex that included facilities for sports, the fine arts, and the performing arts. As early as March of 1956, fair organizers coordinated their efforts with "arts activists." Anticipating little interest in the arts on the part of the growing suburbs, Allied Arts, a group concerned with the city's cultural shortcomings, pointed out the economic and aesthetic windfall that could result from a more supportive downtown environment for the arts. They envisioned the run-down Warren neighborhood, with its state-owned armory and a city-owned auditorium, ice arena, stadium, school, and parking lot, as the nucleus of a civic center that would be turned over to the city after the fair. Other sites in the Seattle area received consideration as potential fairgrounds, but the Warren district best served the interests of both cultural and business leaders, and from the initial period of planning it was the almost undisputed choice for the site of the exposition.[26]

When they selected a site near the city center and harnessed Century 21 to the needs of downtown Seattle, organizers shaped the fair profoundly by limiting its size. The greatest world's fairs, attracting between 25 million and 50 million visitors, have historically comprised hundreds of acres—in Chicago, 685 acres for the 1893 fair and 424 for the 1933–34 fair; in New York, 1,217 acres for the 1939–40 fair and 646 for the 1964–65 fair; in Brussels, 500 acres for the 1958 fair. Seattle's fair, by contrast, would occupy a central-city site of 74 acres.[27] Planners of the Century 21 Exposition never intended their event to become enormous. They decided instead upon a compact site that would contain everything except parking lots and the Monorail line to downtown.[28]

The size and scope of the Century 21 Exposition made it, in the language of the Bureau of International Expositions, a second-category rather than a first-category world's fair. While a first-rank world's fair had to have hundreds of acres so that each participating nation could erect its own pavilion, a second-rank fair grouped exhibits together in buildings provided by the host city and state. Seattle's fair would be smaller than the greatest international expositions, but organizers insisted it be just as pretty. After all, Century 21 was supposed to beautify downtown. Upon visiting the first-category Brussels fair of 1958, general manager Ewen C. Dingwall reaffirmed his commitment to building a small fairgrounds of high quality. He and others commonly spoke of the exposition as a "jewel-box" fair, just suitable for the final count of 9.6 million visitors.[29]

Neither size nor attendance gave Century 21 a position among the great world's fairs. Indeed, it seems doubtful that a much larger site, or a first-category exposition, could have attracted substantially more visitors or exhibitors to the relatively remote Pacific Northwest. Nor would an enormous spectacle, which had the potential of losing enormous sums of money, have served the aims of fair planners. Beginning with carefully defined local and regional objectives, and working with limited funding and limited space, downtown businessmen and civic

leaders planned a small, cohesive fair that suited not only their immediate purposes but also the kind of urban future they envisioned. An
overwhelming fair would have both contradicted the sense of balance
they hoped to bring to the region's economy and undermined the sense
of order and direction they wished to provide for continued growth.

An American Temple of Science

Viewed in historical perspective, the Seattle World's Fair
stands out not so much because of its limited size and local origins but,
rather, because it came to be invested with national and international
significance out of all proportion to its small scale. The fairmakers' efforts earned for the Century 21 Exposition a measure of respect from
outsiders, and the fact that it was the first American world's fair in more
than twenty years no doubt drew attention to the event. However, for-
tuitous timing played an even greater role in transforming Century 21
from a regional exposition to a fair of nationwide significance.

Planning for the Seattle fair coincided with the dawn of the space
age. The successful launch of *Sputnik I* in October 1957 seemed to
demand that the United States display its own scientific and technological prowess. American scientists and statesmen hastened to embrace
the Century 21 Exposition as one vehicle for responding to the challenge of *Sputnik*. And once the federal government had begun to invest
heavily in the fair, other participants were drawn to Seattle's exposition.[30] By heightening cold war tensions, then, *Sputnik* ensured the
transformation from a "Festival of the West" to "America's Space Age
World's Fair."

To a significant extent, the wonders of science eclipsed the local and
regional purposes of Century 21, and space-age priorities gave the exposition a substantially different look from what had been envisioned.
For one thing, the fairgrounds became a virtual advertisement of everything for which Boeing stood. The Space Needle, the U.S. Science Pavilion, the glimpses of the future, and the numerous rides into outer
space all paid homage to the aerospace manufacturer rather than to
downtown business or the tourist trade. And, 1962 being a busy year
at Boeing, the company, in an advertisement on the very first page of
the *Official Guide Book*, invited visiting engineers and scientists to stop
by its employment information center on the fairgrounds.[31]

Equally significant, the increased scale of activity required to put on a truly international exposition perhaps made planning for the following years more difficult. By 1962, promoters were so busy trying to keep up with the ballooning size and import of Century 21 that they essentially postponed most of the planning for subsequent use of the exposition site until after the fair was more than half over.[32] Thereafter, indecision and conflict became hallmarks of planning for the Seattle Center.

The needs and preferences of downtown interests became steadily less pertinent to Century 21, but the message of the international exposition was hardly incompatible with either the average resident's sense of the metropolitan area or the world view of the urban West after World War II. Space and science impinged far more closely upon the personal interests of fairgoers than did the concerns of downtown businessmen. Residents remained ever conscious of the local economic orientation toward space exploration, aviation, and high technology. Even before the federal government had seized upon the fair to promote its work in science and space, the proximity of airplane factories and naval facilities suggested to publicists that the fair might commemorate the "jet air age" and modern shipping. Regional hydroelectric plants provided another distinctive technology worthy of display, and the Hanford nuclear complex in eastern Washington recommended an exhibit on atomic energy, and perhaps even an operating reactor on the fairgrounds. If the fair succeeded in attracting industry to the region, organizers hoped that the new companies, too, would be high-tech.[33]

The themes of science and space may have compromised some of the plans of those who saw the fair as a key to revitalizing downtown, but they probably made the fair more successful. Federal involvement enriched the fairgrounds and increased both attendance and publicity, contributing to the fair's ability to build a new cultural complex and helping to advertise the Puget Sound area. Moreover, as the fair came to revolve around the themes of science and space, it increasingly highlighted the society's apparently growing ability to manage its economy and its environment successfully, through planning and technology. In emphasizing the products and the methods of science, the Century 21 Exposition held out to Americans and to the world a promise of a future of greater economic vitality, more orderly social relations, and heightened mastery of surroundings—much the same commodities Seattle itself hoped to derive from the fair.

The Seattle World's Fair of 1962 was hardly the first international exposition to forecast the future or emphasize the achievements of science, but the cold war lent special emphasis to these themes and to the exposition's focus on the new frontier of space. World's fairs have generally been arenas for rivalry, between companies and cities and nations, and the Century 21 Exposition almost automatically became enmeshed in cold war struggle.[34] At the same time, however, tension between Americans and Soviets, which had tainted the Brussels fair of 1958, seemed muted in Seattle during 1962. Planners tried to minimize hostilities, and the absence of participation by communist governments reduced the opportunity for direct confrontation. More important, fair exhibits that emphasized the peaceful dimensions of science ultimately outweighed those that implied international competition. Balance between the two attitudes became easier to achieve as the alarm caused by *Sputnik* gradually receded and attitudes toward the cold war became more ambivalent.

During the late 1950s and early 1960s, the formative years for Century 21, *Sputnik* stood as the most powerful symbol of cold war rivalry. The desire to catch up to the Soviets as quickly as possible motivated much of the federal government's interest in educational reform, military reorganization, and other new frontiers in the years after 1957. The nation's investment in the Seattle fair served as one measure of Americans' fearful response to Soviet advances in space.[35]

Leading scientists spearheaded America's reaction to *Sputnik*. They shared the nation's concern about ranking behind the Soviet Union in an important respect, and they wanted to ensure that the fame of *Sputnik* did not eclipse their own achievements. Members of the scientific community proposed some kind of national or international exposition to illustrate the vitality of American research and development. Disappointed with the scientific exhibits in the U.S. pavilion at Brussels, they eyed Seattle's exposition as a forum for their message.[36] The nation's scientists and Seattle's boosters proved to be a powerful team. Together they secured the greatest amount of federal aid given to an international exposition before 1962, and they brought to the fair a significant national theme. Century 21 featured not only a NASA display but also a federally sponsored hall of science that exceeded in size the entire American pavilion at the Brussels World's Fair.[37] The $10 million United States Science Exhibit became the brightest gem in the jewel-box fair.

The theme of science sold the federal government on Seattle's exposition, and the fair in turn sold science to the American people. The many arguments in favor of federal participation portrayed government expenditures on Century 21 as timely investments in national security. In hearings before the House Committee on Science and Astronautics and in publicity about the exposition, congressmen, scientists, and promoters explained how *Sputnik* had demonstrated that America's "very survival during the next century depends upon how well we develop our scientific resources." Youth constituted one resource that needed particular attention, as an official from the Atomic Energy Commission told local backers of the fair: "If out of this Exposition, a few thousand young people are stimulated into taking up science careers, you have provided this government with a priceless gift." Adults apparently needed an education as well. To sustain political support for the military and civilian science that would ensure "international supremacy" in coming decades, the country required "a giant showcase where the American taxpayer can see graphically and at first hand where his money is going and why it is being spent." Efforts to publicize American science programs did not stop at the country's borders. The nation also wished to illustrate for the world, especially its "undecided people," how American science contributed to peace by creating the "abundance which would make war unnecessary." [38]

That American science received attention not only for its role in national defense but also for its ability to raise standards of living across the globe illuminated the paradox inherent in holding an international exposition during the cold war. Century 21 gained support because it could serve the United States in its rivalry against the Soviet Union. Traditionally, however, international expositions have purported to improve relations between nations. Aware of the peaceable heritage of fairs, local supporters of Century 21 tried to reduce offensive displays of nationalism. When the Advertising Council proposed an exhibit called "The Present Danger" with a strong anticommunist message, fair officials asked it to replace the "negative" theme with a "positive 'free world' sales effort." Organizers wanted to avoid insulting the nations of the eastern European communist bloc, which, however, despite invitations to full participation, sent only Yugoslavian merchandise and Soviet entertainers to the fair. The exposition also played host to the second annual National Conference on the Peaceful Uses of Space. And the futuristic theme itself, as Vice President Lyndon B. Johnson noted during his visit, attested American faith "that there will be a Century 21." [39]

If Americans believed in a twenty-first century, however, they insisted upon entering it on their own terms. The legislation authorizing federal involvement in the exposition anticipated participation by "the varied cultures of the nations of the Pacific Rim," but "no Communist de facto government holding any people of the Pacific Rim in subjugation" would be invited. The act barred North Korea, North Vietnam, and the People's Republic of China from attendance.[40] The fair, then, was not completely divorced from what one industrial designer termed "the unrelenting struggle for the minds of men and markets of the world." No exposition during the cold war could function as "a good-natured display case. It is a powerful instrument for communicating our philosophy and presenting our way of life."[41]

The exposition offered ample opportunities to condemn communism. George Meany, president of the AFL-CIO, attacked the Soviets in a Labor Day speech by contrasting the fair's Space Needle, "a towering monument to the aspirations of humanity for a better life," to the Berlin Wall, which stood for "the basic cruelty of the Communist conspiracy and its utter disregard for human life and human values." Exhibits staged by West Berlin and Nationalist China provided occasions to speak out against communism in similar terms.[42] Perhaps the most poignant contrast between the Soviets and the Americans occurred in the receptions held for cosmonaut Gherman Titov and astronaut John Glenn, who visited the fair separately within the same seven days in May. When questioned pointedly about whether he saw a divine presence in outer space, the "indoctrinated" Titov, second man to orbit the earth, retorted: "I don't believe in God. I believe in man—his strength, his possibilities, his reason." Americans preferred Glenn's rejoinder: "The God I pray to is not small enough that I expected to see him in outer space."[43]

Fairgoers applauded Glenn during his visit as the hero who stood for American progress in the space race. They contrasted his successful flight, a public spectacle in an open society, with the secret work of the "closed, totalitarian" Soviet Union. The astronaut won praise for more than his contributions to cold war competition, however. A symbol of technological achievement, Glenn's flight transcended international rivalry and took on a universal meaning. The astronaut's profession of religious faith proved less important than the inspiration derived from the force of science that had made his orbits possible. Popular response to *Friendship 7*, Glenn's Mercury spaceship, demonstrated the sentiment. The capsule had toured twenty-four other countries before arriv-

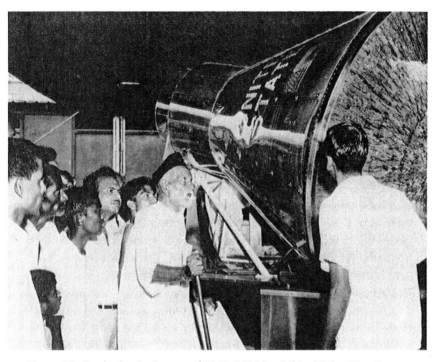

Figure 35. Beginning in August of 1962, NASA exhibited John Glenn's
Mercury spaceship, *Friendship 7*, in the halls of the U.S. Science
Exhibit. The success of *Sputnik I* had initially encouraged
Americans to consider the Seattle World's Fair as a rather blunt,
anti-Soviet tool of the cold war. The anticommunist message
remained but softened, and by 1962, especially within the federal
science pavilion, space and science had taken on a less earthly and
more religious significance. Courtesy of the Special Collections
Division, University of Washington Libraries (neg. #UW
13108).

ing at Century 21 in August for its first public display in the United
States. Many fairgoers regarded the spacecraft as a sacred object, count-
ing the opportunity to touch it as the high point of the fair (see Figure 35).[44]

Americans' worship of Glenn and *Friendship 7* sprang from their
conversion to science as a way of life. Although supporters of the exposition had argued for a science theme on the quite practical grounds
of national security, its presentation at the fair, shaped in large part by
scientists themselves, paid comparatively little attention to cold war rivalry and instead gave the federal science exhibit a broader and seem-

ingly more lasting appeal. Housing the displays in the exposition's most inspiring architecture, designers tried to present science not as an intimidating world or a potentially destructive activity but as a quite understandable and engaging process. Presented as a source of inspiration, comfort, and universal understanding, science assumed at Century 21 some of the functions once reserved for religion.

Science did not have the pulpit to itself at the fair. Concerned that an emphasis on the material world should not go unchallenged, three church-sponsored exhibits and a personal appearance by evangelist Billy Graham presented more conventional spiritual messages. One Christian theme, captured in the Sermons from Science exhibit, argued the essential compatibility of science and religion. "Science is showing that there is a Grand Designer who created the Universe," Graham explained.[45] If religion and science ultimately reinforced one another, however, the self-styled Salesmen for Christ, particularly at the Christian Witness Pavilion, worried that modern civilization had put too much faith in the benefits of science. "Our scientific advancement is progressing out of all proportion to our moral and spiritual progress," Graham warned. "As the sands of our age are falling in the hour glass, our hope and confidence should not rest alone in our mighty scientific achievement, in space exploration, but in God!"[46]

Christian concern about the tension between science and religion did not make much of an impact on fairgoers. To some extent the religious exhibits preached to the converted. About 52 percent of the visitors to the United States Science Exhibit, when polled on their religious faith, agreed that "God's word is more important" than the findings of science and that the ability of scientists to understand or modify human nature remained quite limited.[47] The other half of the visitors to the federal science pavilion, however, did not concur in ranking religious truth above scientific truth—in part, perhaps, because they did not accept the simplistic distinction between the two.

At the Seattle World's Fair, science did not so much supplant religion as people's preferred faith as supplement it by offering a new means to achieve traditional Judeo-Christian ends. Fairgoers tended to regard religious belief as a private sentiment that needed little reaffirmation at Century 21; only about a third of them visited one or more of the church-sponsored exhibits.[48] By contrast, science as presented by the national government entailed a much more extensive and public ritual. The U.S. Science Exhibit formed the centerpiece of the Century 21 Exposition. Before coming to the fair most people listed the Space

Needle as the item of greatest interest, but by the time they left they had been converted to science. More than 6.7 million guests had visited it, compared to less than 3 million each for the Space Needle and Washington state's futuristic theme show, the World of Tomorrow. The federal pavilion so impressed Robert Moses that he immediately demanded one for his own New York World's Fair of 1964.[49] The United States Science Pavilion emerged in 1962 as the temple of Century 21.

The attendance at the federal exhibits proved easier to measure than the quality of the experience. Observers noted that visitors spent only short amounts of time inside the science pavilion and departed with only a superficial grasp of what they had seen.[50] The federal hall may in fact have offered ritual communion rather than rigorous catechism. Already committed to science as a technique, Americans primarily reaffirmed their beliefs at the Seattle World's Fair and absorbed some of the finer points of the faith. Many fairgoers doubtless did not see or accept all the messages intended by the scientists and industrial designers who staged the exhibits, yet they returned to the federal pavilion repeatedly and praised it highly. They appreciated the opportunity to be exposed to the work of science, and they strongly approved of the general idea of the pavilion.[51]

The popular presentation of science required careful planning. During the first tense months after *Sputnik* was launched, in a survey conducted by Stanford Research Institute on prospective themes for a fair, a number of experts recommended exploiting the country's new interest in science. The sociologist Robert K. Merton suggested that the fair emphasize science so that the average citizen could better understand a "totally new world and a totally new way of life."[52] Before Congress had authorized a federal pavilion, an advisory committee of leading scientists from government and universities began to discuss the exhibit design. After considering a number of proposals, they determined that the United States Science Exhibit in Seattle would focus on "the history, development and nature of pure science—devoid of gadgetry, advertising and chauvinism."[53] Thus they minimized, in the federal pavilion, the cold war anxiety that had originally proved so instrumental in encouraging national participation in the fair. Much like the American manned space program, the science exhibit began as a tool of international rivalry but gradually acquired a focus and an elegance that partially removed it from the realm of earthly competition.[54]

The complex that housed the federal exhibits was ideal for presenting science as inspiring but not intimidating (see Figure 36). Project

Figure 36. The United States Science Exhibit at Century 21, designed by
architect Minoru Yamasaki, consisted of five modern buildings,
grouped intimately around several fountains, pools, and "space-
gothic" arches. The graceful design of the complex not only
helped to make it the fair's most popular attraction but also
underscored the exhibitors' effort to present science in a peaceful
and positive light. Courtesy of the Special Collections Division,
University of Washington Libraries (neg. #UW 13106).

architect Minoru Yamasaki conceived the plan partly in reaction against
the recent fair practice of erecting monumental structures that competed against one another. Influenced by the light and graceful Swedish
Pavilion at the New York World's Fair of 1939, Yamasaki designed a
low-profile structure of five exhibit rooms, each intimate and comfortable, that were linked together to enclose several pools of water and an
outdoor court. Five soaring white arches made a centerpiece for the
complex that implied "uplift" and "man's constant striving for knowledge of the universe." Several features dated the structure as belonging
to the cold war era: the style of the arches earned the label "space-
gothic"; the composition was precast, prestressed concrete panels because "it seemed important to construct the Federal building for a

World's Fair with the most modern methods possible"; and a children's science laboratory occupied a fallout shelter that had been added to the original design at the request of the Office of Civil Defense.[55] Nonetheless, Yamasaki's pavilion, like other temples, possessed an enduring appeal. Joining the flood of praise for the structure, publisher Henry Luce named it "the building of the decade"; and another critic recognized a "religious" quality in it.[56]

The inspiring design of the pavilion set the stage for the carefully sequenced exhibits inside, which urged viewers to put their faith in science.[57] A film by industrial designers Charles Eames and Ray Eames, "The House of Science," occupied the first hall and prepared visitors for the upcoming displays. By "humanizing" science and scientists, it welcomed visitors to a world not too far removed from their own. The realism of the exhibits, and the encouragement given to audience participation, also strengthened the message that "science is for everybody."[58]

The exhibit's designers wanted to present Disneyesque displays that brought out the playful, artistic, and thoughtful elements in fairgoers. They likened science to art as a framework for human creativity and a force capable of producing an enriched life and a harmonious world. Athelstan F. Spilhaus, U.S. Science Commissioner for Century 21, said he wanted the pavilion to show "that the scientific method is actually a channeling of man's innate curiosity into a disciplined search for the principles which underlie the workings of the universe. We want to point out that science is truly a high type of intellectual entertainment akin to a symphony, a painting, or a poem." Other observers, including British biologist and philosopher Sir Julian Huxley, concurred: People could express creativity through science just as well as through art.[59]

While the Eames film presented science as a familiar form of creativity, halls devoted to the Boeing Spacearium and the Horizons of Science made the activity seem practical and beneficent. The Spacearium, featuring a film that simulated a voyage to the sun and back, and the Horizons display, exploring current research and its potential benefits, reiterated the idea of man's growing mastery of both natural and man-made environments.[60] By helping to conquer space, control climates, minimize disease, and reduce overpopulation, the fair's *Official Guide Book* explained, scientific knowledge "enables man to harness nature's forces, to ease the burdens of living and lengthen the span of life. As it increases, man's ability to act, to mold and control his environment, will increase."[61]

Science offered nations opportunities not only to master their surroundings but also to establish order among themselves. The final message read by viewers as they left the United States Science Exhibit summarized the idea: "Everyone can appreciate the orderly scientific approach and the delight of knowing the common laws that govern things. . . . It is the benefits of science that men quarrel about, not science itself." In this light science appeared as a neutral, positive practice in which all could share, a "universal language" speaking truths that belonged to everyone. It represented progress "within a framework of international morality" and offered a way to achieve peace and mutual understanding by transcending rivalry. The American biologist Jonas Salk found in the fair's scientific theme evidence "that the world is one culture."[62]

As a basis for intellectual, artistic, and recreational creativity, as a source of higher standards of living, and as a foundation for a common humanity, science at Century 21 rivaled medieval Christianity as a means of unifying and enriching western civilization, at least for one observer. The federal pavilion prevailed at the fair, he said, as "an unblushingly intellectual exercise and one, as well, with an unexpectedly religious aura about it. By accident or design, the Science Pavilion dominated the fair very much as a medieval cathedral did its city."[63] This conclusion overstated the case, but it pointed in the right direction. The federal pavilion highlighted the qualities science shared with other endeavors. Fairgoers could be as inspired by scientists as by poets or painters or priests, but one should not be thought to take precedence over the others. Exhibitors carefully avoided any suggestion that science might challenge traditional cultural ideals—by producing machines that reduced individuals' autonomy, for instance, or by contradicting philosophical and religious beliefs. Rather, modern science seemed to offer an unprecedented opportunity to realize those ideals more fully.

The exhibition of science at Century 21 established a mood of confidence. As in most international expositions, the Seattle World's Fair presented an optimistic message. Observers regarded it as an effective response to the pessimistic voices of the period, such as those concerned about the arms race. Speaking on behalf of President John F. Kennedy on opening day, Secretary of Commerce Luther H. Hodges declared, "We are not interested in gloom or doom. We are interested in hope and confidence."[64] The exposition hinted that Americans had put behind them some of the fears evoked by the launching of *Sputnik*.

The optimism of Century 21 had few opponents. No major critic, except perhaps Billy Graham, regarded Seattle's fair as reason to bemoan the drift of civilization toward a dubious future, as Henry Adams had at the world's fairs of Chicago in 1893 and Paris in 1900.[65] Most Americans at the dawn of the space age, particularly in the Far West, believed society was on a definite upward course. Taking this direction for granted, the Seattle exposition made encouraging predictions about the nature of life in the year 2000. Yet the fair conveyed its rosy forecasts with the same seriousness that pervaded the science exhibits. The confidence exuded at Century 21 thus appeared as not a blind but a thoughtful optimism.

The careful conception of the exposition, which was laid out with the assistance of various technical experts, led observers to speak of it as "a thinking man's world's fair." The claim gained credence from the unenthusiastic responses to Show Street, which offered adult entertainment, and to the Gayway amusement zone, which featured rides and games. The majority of visitors, when polled about their reactions to exhibits, overwhelmingly favored, not thrills or nudity, but those features that provided information, education, or inspiration. More than previous expositions, perhaps, Century 21 had succeeded in incorporating serious ideas into the staple world's fair blend of amusement and commerce. In mixing together the simple pleasures of the carnival, the promotional messages of corporations and governments, and the ideas of artists, designers, and scientists, the Seattle World's Fair presented middlebrow culture to middle-class fairgoers.[66]

Suburbia at Century 21

From the early stages of planning until the opening of the exposition, organizers were hoping to attract a particular kind of crowd to a particular kind of show. The intended audience might well be labeled suburban in character. Fairmakers targeted the exposition especially at relatively affluent and well-educated families, who were expected to have the greatest interest in scientific and futuristic exhibits. Similarly, the layout of the fairgrounds borrowed significantly from such suburban models as the theme park and the shopping mall. Using the formulas suggested by these landscapes to support the basic themes of science and the future, the 1962 exposition appealed successfully to middle-class tastes in leisure and consumption. The fairgrounds looked familiarly suburban to the people who came, and the messages about life in the twenty-first century corresponded closely to the assumptions and expectations of the average fairgoer.

In tailoring Century 21 to suit the tastes of middle-class men and women, organizers created a fair that differed from its predecessors. American world's fairs held between 1876 and 1916 had attempted to convey an elite ideology regarding race and empire to many classes, and especially to workers. More recent fairs, held during the depressed 1930s, occurred in circumstances quite distinct from conditions during the postwar era. Lenox Lohr, director of the 1933–34 Century of Progress fair in Chicago, had concluded from his experience that fair-makers should emphasize "high entertainment value," and he saw the "low income family group" as fairs' primary audience.[67]

The planners of Century 21 took into account changes since 1940 that had generated a broader middle stratum in American society. Market research, commissioned in order to develop an understanding of potential visitors, highlighted the trends of rising incomes, additional schooling, increasing leisure time, and greater spatial mobility in the United States. Although these phenomena characterized the country as a whole, they had the largest impact among the middle-class, suburban whites of the American West who constituted the most likely audience for the fair. Planners anticipated that the theme of science would appeal most to comparatively prosperous, well-educated people—the kind of crowd Disneyland attracted. They predicted "'quality' attendance."[68]

The fair succeeded in attracting the people for whom it was designed. The director of operations pointedly assessed fairgoers during opening week as "a good crowd and a good-spending crowd."[69] In the same way that the profile of residents in the suburbs of Seattle differed from the picture of an average central-city dweller, so the typical fair visitor differed from the national mean. In 1960 about 52 percent of American households had incomes under $5,000, but only about 20 percent of fairgoers fell into that category, according to one survey; 36 percent of American families had incomes between $5,000 and $10,000, and 12 percent had incomes over $10,000, while fairgoers' averages for the same income brackets were about 52 percent and 28 percent, respectively. In the same poll of heads of households at the fair, 42 percent had a college education and 48 percent a high school education, compared to 1960 national averages of 8 and 33 percent. Attendance at the U.S. Science Exhibit, as well as at the foreign pavilions and fine arts shows, was even more skewed to the affluent and better-educated population, whereas the Space Needle, Monorail, and Gay-way held relatively greater interest for the less prosperous and for those with fewer years of schooling.[70]

In addition to attracting a disproportionate number of the better-paid and the better-educated, the fair found its largest audience among Westerners, especially those from Washington, California, Oregon, and British Columbia.[71] The price of a trip to the relatively remote Puget Sound region very likely discouraged many non-Westerners, as well as the less affluent, from attending. But it was also true that residents of the Pacific coast, perhaps more than Easterners and Midwesterners, shared Seattle's fascination with space and technology. In this sense, the world's fair did in fact become a "Festival of the West": it stressed those economic activities that had provided the basis for regional growth after World War II. It was therefore no surprise that the science pavilion, the World of Tomorrow, the Monorail, and the Space Needle were the most popular features of the fair.[72] In sum, the fair attracted exactly the kind of affluent and educated audience for which designers planned. In local terms, it was a crowd more attuned to the suburbs and Boeing than to the problems of downtown.

In order to present a quality show for a quality audience, the planners of Century 21 had to strike a proper balance among commerce, entertainment, and edification. In the attempt they found they could not satisfy all observers. The need for financial success weighed heavily on the businessmen who promoted the fair. Yet proposals to import nude showgirls from Las Vegas and Paris, as well as to repeal local blue laws for the duration of the exposition, lent credence to the charge that fairs catered to the lowest common cultural denominator.[73] Organizers recruited corporate participants by emphasizing the marketing value of entertainment and escapism, the prospective purchasing power of fair-goers, and the possibilities for tying the fair into advertising campaigns. And in the busy months prior to opening, standards intended to keep industrial exhibits from becoming too commercial gradually eroded, while peddlers took out leases on much of the scarce open space at the site.[74]

Like theme parks and shopping malls, Century 21 constituted a commercial venture designed to appeal to varied tastes and to convey many messages. It consequently irritated some critics, who wished that loftier aspirations had prevailed. Alistair Cooke, who praised the science pavilion highly, labeled the rest of the exposition "a trade fair overlaid with Coney Island."[75] But although a few complained that the fair was tawdry and commercial, most people found the mixture of business, entertainment, and culture just about right. In one poll of visitors, only 4 percent of the respondents thought the exposition was too much like a carnival, about the same proportion that viewed it as too scientific.[76]

Fairgoers bestowed upon Century 21 the same kind of favor that mid-twentieth-century Americans gave to shopping malls and theme parks, and for much the same reasons. Although such places owed their existence to the pursuit of commerce, people experienced them as much more than business propositions. Visitors to each establishment were treated more as guests than as customers. They purchased goods and services and absorbed the messages of advertisers, but they simultaneously learned new information and enjoyed themselves. The Seattle World's Fair illustrated how participation in modern consumer society meant not simply engaging in monetary transactions but also pursuing such ends as self-improvement and entertainment—tasks that helped to create and sustain essential cultural meaning.[77]

Consultants to Century 21 had anticipated fairgoers' response to the exposition. Rolf Meyersohn of the Center for the Study of Leisure at the University of Chicago, when asked how visitors might react to the world's fair, explained that the leisure practices of average people now demonstrated greater sophistication: "Americans have become remarkably adept at moving successfully through such fairlike places as department stores, shopping centers or Times Square, and they are facile in making choices when it comes to picking a program on television or a movie." Rather than dismiss department stores and shopping malls as mere commerce, and movies and television as mere entertainment, Meyersohn and others recognized that middle-class Americans had become increasingly serious and skillful as spenders of money and time. They viewed consumption as more than a business arrangement, and they valued leisure as more than an opportunity for pleasure and escape. Both activities comprised part of a new way of life that demanded the cultivation of new skills and values, and both possessed greater significance than they had ever had before as sources of personal fulfillment.[78]

Assuming that a quality audience would have somewhat sophisticated tastes, the planners of Century 21 decided to present exhibits, events, and grounds that contained a relatively high amount of educational content. They wanted to avoid going to extremes—they insisted, for example, that science have box-office appeal—but they also tried to ensure that displays geared toward advertising products or entertaining people also edified fairgoers, especially in regard to the themes of the fair. Some exhibitors from private industry followed the guidelines closely. IBM helped to increase awareness of how computers worked, while Boeing and Ford offered two of the fair's many educational simulated rides into space. Perhaps the best corporate entry did not seem like an exhibit at all. The Monorail, carrying visitors between downtown Seattle and the fairgrounds, was built by Alweg, a European company, at its own risk as a showcase for its product.[79] But riders generally regarded it as a credible portrayal of urban transportation in coming decades. It was thus enterprising and entertaining as well as educational; it blended commerce, culture, and amusement so completely that few stopped to see it from just one angle.

To assemble a middlebrow exposition, designers drew on a wide range of contemporary models. The Seattle fair differed significantly in scale from most previous fairs, but it found at least one similarly sized exposition that had proved worthy of imitation. Located on a London site of about 25 acres, the 1951 Festival of Britain had helped to restore vitality to a rundown city district by generating business and leaving behind some permanent buildings. Equally important, it focused quite closely on a single theme and followed it through thoroughly. The smaller grounds allowed organizers to have greater control over the flow of the crowd so that more visitors saw the exhibits in the sequence best designed to illuminate the theme.[80] The Festival of Britain suggested that an exposition with a dominant concept and a limited fairgrounds could be quite successful.

The Seattle World's Fair learned as well from the experiences of earlier American expositions. Administrators found useful some parts of the world's fair manual by Lenox Lohr, and the exhibits incorporated the themes of science and the future that had worked so well at American fairs during the 1930s.[81] Indeed, some of the people involved in planning the New York World's Fair of 1939–40 developed the major exhibits for Century 21. Professional industrial designers made especially significant contributions to both events. Walter Dorwin Teague played a crucial role at the New York fair, and his company helped to design the United States Science Exhibit. Raymond Loewy, one of the world's most influential industrial designers, also served at New York as well as at the science pavilion in Seattle, and the firm of Donald Deskey, who had helped to create the communications exhibits of 1939–40, held principal responsibility for designing the Washington state theme show at Century 21.[82] Experts at styling consumer goods with an eye toward changing popular tastes, new technologies, and aesthetic values, industrial designers realized the Seattle fair's aspiration to combine commerce, education, and entertainment in projecting the future from present trends.

The Century 21 Exposition also called upon designers of special landscapes for help in laying out the fair. It had become increasingly apparent during the later 1950s that shopping malls provided not just retail outlets but also entertainment, culture, and services in a novel form of public space. Not surprisingly, James B. Douglas, president of the Northgate company, helped to lay out the Century 21 Exposition with suggestions based upon shopping center practices.[83] The retail mall proved to be a useful source of ideas for fair organizers, and a means of bringing some of the flavor of the suburbs to central Seattle.

Disneyland, itself something of a shopping mall and a permanent world's fair, influenced the landscape of Century 21 more strongly than any other external force. Like the Seattle World's Fair, Disneyland provided a special suburban environment for pedestrians. It gave the middle classes an irresistible combination of entertainment, commerce, and culture; presented ideas in a carefully arranged sequence of attractions; maintained uniformly high standards of cleanliness, service, and attractiveness; regulated the movement of crowds through a limited space; and exploited moviemakers' techniques of industrial design in order to present a world that improved on reality.

From the outset, fair organizers consulted with Walt Disney and visited Disneyland to learn how it worked. By the time the exposition opened, its Monorail and Skyride had been built by the very firms that had developed the same rides in Anaheim, and the official bank at the fair operated according to Disneyland precedents.[84] The exposition also recruited veterans of the theme park, who brought Disneyland techniques of managing crowds to Seattle. Leo F. Wagman handled tickets, admissions, and advance sales; George K. Whitney, Jr., became director of concessions and amusements and helped to develop the high-volume, low-overhead Food Circus dining area; other Disney people worked in personnel, operations, wardrobe, and mechanical maintenance.[85]

Frederic V. Schumacher, one of the original members of Disneyland management, became director of operations and services for Century 21 in 1960. Before he returned to Disney's employ in mid-1962 to work on projects for the New York World's Fair of 1964, he supervised the maintenance of a sparkling fairgrounds, established a discreet but effective security force, and, with Max Burland, trained a friendly, efficient corps of college-age employees to run the rides and meet the crowds. The attractive, uniformed staff earned extensive praise for its courtesy and warmth.[86] The Disney way had prevailed at Century 21.

Popular response to the fair indicated the success of the combined influences on its design. The grounds and architecture received as much praise as the staff. Fenced off from the surrounding dull city blocks, and enriched by a degree of coherence instilled by supervising architect Paul Thiry, the fairgrounds impressed people as unimposing, sensible, and tidy. The most common criticisms of the fair—that the grounds were too crowded and the lines too long—highlighted no specific defect so much as they reflected the relatively compact size of the exposition and its overall success in attracting customers. Observers regarded the fair's small scale and careful focus as a refreshing departure from "portentous" expositions.[87]

Like other magic lands, the Seattle World's Fair seemed manageable. It did not overwhelm visitors, in part because its downtown location had limited its size. Yet, although it stood near the city center, it did not seem intensely urban. Rather, again like other magic kingdoms, it tended to attract those Westerners who fit most closely a suburban profile—well-educated and prosperous families. And it resembled suburban institutions, such as theme parks and shopping malls, with which fairgoers were already familiar. Although the fairgrounds contained novelties that evoked "awe" and "a sense of adventure," these were viewed in the context of a cultural landscape that was not too novel.[88] The built environment of Century 21 worked because it seemed familiar enough to put people at ease, but not so familiar that it inhibited people's imaginations.

The Future According to 1962

The Washington state theme of the exposition, life in the twenty-first century, like the fair's built environment, attracted attention because it envisioned tomorrow's world, yet was premised upon the continuation of those mid-twentieth-century trends—rising levels of affluence, growing mastery of the environment, soaring faith in science and technology—that evoked optimism as well as a sense of order during the postwar years. At bottom, the fair's version of the future was not very imaginative; it seldom took into account the possibility of fundamental social and cultural changes. Like many Americans during the later 1950s, fairmakers took for granted that improvement implied "more of the same," rather than seeing tomorrow as an altogether different world. In this frame of mind, even the alarm caused by *Sputnik* could be muted by defining the Soviet success "as another in the long series of man's triumphs over his environment."[89]

The theme of a rosy twenty-first century perfectly suited local backers of the fair. Instead of attempting to review all of the nation's or the world's progress, they proposed "to present man's most recent accomplishments since the start of the 'Space Age,'" particularly in science, technology, and culture, and to "project these rapid and startling developments into man's future existence."[90] Fairmakers spared no opportunity to highlight the theme. Their fine arts show featured, in addition to more conventional collections, an exhibit of abstract-expressionist works that displeased art critics and average viewers alike. At a variety of other levels, the fair linked itself to activities that reiterated the space-age idea. It issued medallions, commissioned a fountain, and adopted a logo, all of which symbolized the exploration of the universe. It became the subject of one of the first live telecasts to be beamed by Telstar satellite to Europe. And it offered a number of features—a "space-age tunnel of love," a "space wheel" in lieu of a ferris wheel, a plethora of rides into space, and a completely automated dining area—that suggested life in the future.

Not all major participants in the Century 21 Exposition embraced the organizers' theme. Some exhibits, singled out for putting "too much emphasis on showing consumer products," represented the efforts of less developed countries that had little of science, space, and the future to display for an American audience.[91] Yet fair organizers worked to ensure the participation of even the least developed countries, coaching them to present themselves in the most modern light by illustrating their determination to catch up to the most advanced western societies. Fairmakers assumed that the rising affluence of the space age would ultimately engulf everyone, and that the Third World thus represented a potentially huge market: "The folks in Puyallup, Punjab and Peru are hungry for what we produce as living standards go up everywhere."[92]

Domestic industries cleaved more closely to the space-age theme of the fair. The Standard Oil Company of California, the Carnation dairy products corporation, and the forest products industry featured re-

Figure 37. The space-age motif which guided design everywhere at Century
21 led to the suggestion that the cars of tomorrow, including the
General Motors "Firebird III," would be shaped like rockets.
What mattered most in 1962 was how fast and how stylishly one
traveled—not how much fuel was consumed or how much
pollution was produced. Courtesy of the Special Collections
Division, University of Washington Libraries (neg. #UW 1540).

search and development geared toward maximizing harvests for the
twenty-first century. The Bell System, IBM, and RCA highlighted coming improvements in communications and electronics. Railway and pe-
troleum companies, as well as Ford and General Motors, predicted
high-speed vehicles and automated roadways (see Figure 37), and three
exhibitors erected versions of tomorrow's homes. Throughout these
commercial exhibits, images of abundance, push-button convenience,
and advanced but subservient technology told "the story of man's better
tomorrow."[93]

The Space Needle became the most famous survivor of Century 21.
Almost every international exposition has included a spectacular theme
structure, but not many remain from before World War II. One that
does is the Eiffel Tower, to which Seattle publicists liked to compare

their own tower. The Space Needle came relatively late in fair planning, but emerged as the most important landmark of central Seattle. Conceived and built by private interests, it adhered to the theme of the fair in almost all details. High-speed elevators, similar to "space capsules with large vision ports," zoomed guests up to an observation deck and to a revolving restaurant that resembled a flying saucer and was lighted at night to look as if it were hovering in the sky. The Needle's dining hostesses wore "skin-tight gold coveralls," and the color scheme on the outside of the building consisted of "astronaut white, galaxy gold, re-entry red and orbital olive." [94] Hardly a trick was missed.

As a theme structure, the Space Needle gave greater visibility to the Seattle fair. More important, it became the city's best-known landmark. For non-residents of the area, the Space Needle symbolized Seattle in the same way that Disneyland represented Los Angeles. It also assumed a prominent place on local residents' mental maps. Even after the central business district began to acquire its own outsized skyscrapers, the Space Needle served as a more common reference point than any downtown edifice, and it acted as a beacon to the cultural center that had been created by the world's fair.

The Space Needle made Seattle a more legible city, but it added little more than another symbol to the theme of the exposition. Neither the Space Needle nor the United States Science Exhibit sufficed to tell the full story of Century 21. Neither edifice really provided much insight into the future, and both seemed slightly aloof from everyday concerns. The Needle had a good view of the city and a restaurant, but no explicit message. The federal pavilion tried to make science understandable, but few fairgoers could really expect in their lives to engage the subject in any greater depth than they had at the exposition. Something else was needed to project the implications contemporary scientific advances held for the daily lives of average people in the next century. The Washington state theme show, "a detailed visual forecast of an ideal community and the living conditions therein" during the year 2000, translated space-age trends into concrete predictions for common people. [95]

The World of Tomorrow featured visions of highly organized urban and rural landscapes, a fulfilling and efficient economy, increased and purposeful leisure, and a richer domestic life. It presented a future that generally had both greater productivity and greater free time, heightened autonomy and heightened social order, more individual fulfillment and more mechanization. As with other world's fairs, the ideas were basically hopeful, but the messages may have been particularly appropriate for the postwar era. World's fairs have typically constituted "idealized consumer cities" where everybody "was presumed to be able to buy, and the world was shown as becoming more 'civilized,' with the middle-class consumer dominant."[96] Perhaps no society, however, had ever come closer to approximating the ideal of a middle-class, consumer-oriented culture than the United States in 1962. The Century 21 Exposition, and the World of Tomorrow in particular, not only perpetuated the world's fair pattern but also captured much of the outlook of postwar America.

The assumptions of middle-class consumers formed one basis for the predictions of life in the year 2000 that characterized the state theme show. The exhibit consisted of a multimedia presentation set in the new Washington State Coliseum, a futuristic structure of concrete, glass, and aluminum. Several industrial displays and the French national exhibit lined the perimeter of the hall, all coordinated to present life in the next century.[97] The World of Tomorrow was suspended in midair in the center of the building, "symbolically just beyond reach and yet within modern man's range of vision." Its 3,250 aluminum cubes combined to form a "cloud," sixty feet high and two hundred feet square, to which fairgoers were transported by an elevator. The cubes served as screens for slides and films, presented photographic images of the future, concealed loudspeakers and dioramas, and formed passageways that took visitors to the five different segments of the show. Ever-changing lighting and sound effects created the appropriate mood for each sequence and helped to cue visitors briskly through the exhibit.[98]

The World of Tomorrow provided twenty-one minutes of the twenty-first century. A sphere-shaped glass lift called the Bubbleator carried groups of one hundred into the future (see Figure 38). The operator of the elevator, the only "live" person with whom the voyagers came into contact, wore a nondescript uniform and welcomed visitors in a bored voice that suggested that for him the future had become routine: "Utopia Century 21 . . . first floor, threats and thresholds, frustrations and fulfilments [sic], challenges and opportunities." As he spoke, the lighting warmed from "iridescent to glowing amber and surprise pink," and a theme song played, at first "slightly eerie" but definitely "optimistic," and then positively "celestial." Next came the rather unctuous, tape-recorded voice of the future, scripted to sound at once "masculine, intelligent, friendly and realistic, yet with a quality of poetry born of agelessness. It has both humor and compassion." These effects continued until the show concluded with a crescendo of color and music, and an excerpt from John F. Kennedy's inaugural address.[99]

The president's uplifting words summarized the idealistic message of

Figure 38. At the state of Washington's World of Tomorrow, a glass elevator
known as the Bubbleator (center) lifted fairgoers into the exhibit,
where they could see predictions of how people would live in the
year 2000. The World of Tomorrow was located in the new
Washington State Coliseum, built for the fair with state funding,
which in 1967 was to become home to Seattle's first major-league
sports franchise, the SuperSonics basketball team—also named
with the future in mind. Courtesy of the Special Collections
Division, University of Washington Libraries (neg. #UW
13111).

the presentation. Occasional reminders of the possibility of nuclear war
did punctuate the script, titled "The Threat and the Threshold." Early
in the show, images of pastel flowers and childbirth changed suddenly
into dark pictures of barbed wire and ruined buildings. As the music
grew harsh and foreboding, there appeared a "grimly well-ordered fallout shelter" containing an isolated, desperate family, caught in the days
after World War III. This portrayal recurred briefly at several points in
the production, but it generally added up to little more than a small
"question mark above a future depicted as slum-free and almost
burden-free but nonetheless challenging and exciting." Fairgoers spent
most of the show viewing images of a "richer life in a better world,"

and their last view was of a final scene that emphasized hope and peace.[100] The World of Tomorrow, like the science pavilion, left little room for pessimism.

To Americans in 1962, the future promised to be orderly, efficient, and prosperous, as well as humane and enlightened and automated. In the World of Tomorrow, many of these traits were on display in City Century 21, a prediction of how Seattle would look in the year 2000. City Century 21 anticipated Walt Disney's EPCOT. It showed a city zoned in perfectly concentric rings—industrial and residential communities located on the periphery; parks, farms, and recreation areas forming a lush greenbelt in the middle; and a climate-control-domed downtown in the exact center, "the nucleus of administration, commerce, education and culture. It is rather like an archery target." The twenty-first century, apparently, would have no doubts about where the true center of the city lay. Nobody in this vision would have to live more than ten minutes from work, cars could not enter the central district, and a high-speed monorail network, combined with "electronic" highways, ferried passengers and goods back and forth with a minimum of delay, noise, and exhaust.[101]

Work was just as well organized as the city in the World of Tomorrow, thanks to the promise of automation. By the year 2000, industrial designers predicted, the proper application of machinery to various jobs would heighten productivity, minimize drudgery, and enhance creativity. Future industrial plants would "produce more of everything for less in materials, time and money." Tomorrow's farms would reduce world tensions by maximizing the production of food through elaborate chemistry, controlled climates, reclamation of arid lands, and greater industrialization. Office workers would become more productive through the use of improved machinery and with the help of an air conditioning system that gave them a boost by adding scents, ions, and oxygen to the atmosphere. With the minor exception of nuclear war, new technology presented little threat to Century 21. Designers repeatedly insisted that mechanization would make work more, not less, fulfilling and would never replace human faculties. People would become better educated and more skilled in order to work with machines, and such devices as computers would permit more time for "creative thought."[102] Such detailed predictions elaborated upon the underlying expectations of the larger fair for greater world and urban order, scientific and technical advances, heightened material abundance, and a more intelligent and fulfilled society.

As production became more efficient it took less time. The World of

Tomorrow predicted a twenty-four-hour work week (with no reduction in pay, of course) and contended that people would make sophisticated use of their increased leisure hours. To a generation bent on automation, the future seemed to require an ability to adjust quickly to rapid cultural and technological changes, so lifelong schooling became essential. Adults might enroll routinely in continuing education courses in order to keep ahead of automation, get better jobs, and enjoy a longer and more satisfying retirement. Schoolchildren would benefit from the new educational technology, too. They would take pills to accelerate learning, occupy more mechanized classrooms, and receive more individual attention from teachers.[103]

Just as automation would not undermine the humanity of the space-age workplace and classroom, and science would not challenge received moral truths, so increased mechanization of the home would not weaken the nuclear family of Century 21. In a fair devoted to the consumer society, domestic life provided perhaps the best context for projecting an increase in consumption. The home of tomorrow in the state theme show incorporated new materials and prefabricated methods of construction, solar and atomic energy, automatic climate control, and a plethora of "undreamed of conveniences." The shape, color, and lighting of the house could all be changed quickly in order to meet shifting preferences, and the kitchen seemed "a miracle of push-button efficiency." All of this modernization would not detract from the strength of the family unit, however. Indeed, contrasted with the mass-produced tract homes, barracks-style apartments, and unsightly slum dwellings of 1962, the house of the future appeared more natural as well as more humane. It would nurture family values and become, even more than before, a "*haven*," if need be, from the "push-button age."[104]

For all the changes forecasted in the World of Tomorrow, the exhibit did not envision any significant change in the role of women. Projections of the future suggested that women would benefit most from an automated kitchen, that wives and mothers would devote increasing leisure hours "to the aesthetics of cooking" in order to make the family meal an anchor of domesticity in a quickly changing world.[105] This traditional view of women's roles pervaded Century 21. Its emphasis on science had from the outset provoked men to ask what the fair would offer "for the ladies," and the question had repeatedly been answered with references to the daily fashion shows presented as a component of "the art of living" on display at the Interiors, Fashion, and Commerce Pavilion. These displays, which took place around a pool filled with Revlon perfume, had a cold war thrust as well as a message

Figure 39. The Century 21 logo took literally the exposition's motto—"Man
in Space." The tenor of the fair's publicity and exhibits made it
clear that women were not expected to join in the exploration of
the heavens or any other scientific frontier. Courtesy of the
Special Collections Division, University of Washington Libraries
(neg. #UW 13109).

about the sexes. The Miracle of American Fashion glorified modern
capitalism by illustrating "the ability of the American mass-production
fashion industry to make clothes that are clearly fashionable at prices
within the reach of all." It seemed a matter of national security for the
American woman to remain "the best dressed . . . in the world." Century 21 offered her no more liberated role.[106]

Exhibits portraying the roles of women in Century 21 point up the
shortsightedness of the fair's vision (see Figure 39). Like most portray-

als of the future, the exposition never examined the fundamental assumptions of its day. The fair straddled the dividing point in American civilization between that period of supposed domestic calm, conventionally categorized as the 1950s, when the pace of change seemed manageable, and the turbulence often associated with the 1960s, when very little appeared to be under control. By the opening of the Seattle World's Fair, of course, much of the groundwork for the coming unrest had been laid. But the events of 1962 and immediately afterward provided a sharp counterpoint to the mentality that had produced Century 21.

Michael Harrington's *The Other America* and Rachel Carson's *Silent Spring* both appeared in 1962, too late for designers to incorporate into the fair the awareness they created regarding the limits of affluence and the environment. In the same year the deaths of American soldiers in South Vietnam and the formulation of the Port Huron Statement by the Students for a Democratic Society gave another taste of things to come. Still greater violence and uncertainty characterized the year or so after the fair. In 1963 the killings of John F. Kennedy in Dallas, Ngo Dinh Diem in Saigon, and Medgar W. Evers in Jackson left no doubt that another historical era had begun. The publication of Betty Friedan's *The Feminine Mystique* helped to ignite the women's movement, and the March on Washington signaled the increasing stridency of the struggle for civil rights. In the months after the fair, it became ever harder to believe in the orderly and satisfying world of Century 21.

At the fair itself some ominous notes sounded, but few heard them clearly. One was struck on opening day when a jet fighter, after flying a salute over the fairgrounds, lost control and crashed into a northern suburb of Seattle, killing two people and damaging several homes. The accident offered a little-remarked contradiction to the exposition's faith in technological progress. Like the glimpses of a fallout shelter in the World of Tomorrow, the fatal crash hardly dented the overall optimism.[107]

The French National Exhibit offered perhaps the most thoughtful challenge to the predominantly upbeat mood. The largest foreign exhibitor at the fair, France cast doubt on the promise of Century 21 by warning that "all our problems cannot be solved by science and techniques alone." In a brief film full of flashes of speed, rock music, sex, and violence, the display pondered "the threatened loss of individual identity and sensitivity in a shrinking world of mass information and automation." It suggested that through education, appreciation of the arts, and heightened mastery of nature, people could learn to fulfill timeless needs in a changing world. The French exhibit proved controversial, baffling, and not very popular. Yet it had predicted some of the turmoil experienced by Americans in ensuing years.[108] The exhibit seemed to incorporate lessons that the postwar French had learned but Americans had not yet encountered. By 1962 France, unlike the United States, had experienced social and political fragmentation and had lost international strength. Indochina provided the best point of contrast: France had already extricated itself from the Vietnam war, whereas Americans were just stumbling into the morass.

Events such as war in southeast Asia would soon overtake the mood of Century 21, relegating the already remote fair to a still more distant corner of American awareness. Indeed, dramatic headlines eclipsed the conclusion of the exposition and essentially undermined its entire premise. President Kennedy had intended to attend closing ceremonies on October 21. But at the last minute, on the pretext of a cold, he canceled his trip to Seattle and flew back to the White House to manage the Cuban missile crisis. On the day after the fair ended, Kennedy announced the dramatic blockade of Cuba.[109] Suddenly, after five years during which the tensions created by *Sputnik* had been defused, the fair's portrayal of a future of international harmony seemed inconsequential. The fallout shelter, merely a fleeting image in the World of Tomorrow, now became a central feature of American consciousness.

Other issues helped to push Century 21 further from the national spotlight. The fair earned compliments for its commitment to improved race relations and its equality in hiring.[110] During its closing months, however, the drama surrounding the admission of the first black student to the University of Mississippi suggested that Century 21 stood some distance from the larger quest for civil rights in the United States. Similarly, the exposition presented a perception of the environment that soon became untenable. In the vision of Century 21, people not only gained greater control over nature but also regarded natural resources as unlimited, both in their ability to respond to the manipulations of producers, scientists, engineers, and planners and in their ability to absorb the disposable goods, chemicals, and effluents of advanced technology. The years after 1962 punctured these predictions. A dozen years after Century 21, when the city of Spokane hosted a fair based in large part on the Seattle model for downtown renewal, it chose the endangered environment as the central theme.[111]

Century 21 belonged, not to the doubting, pluralistic 1960s, but to a culture that had not really overturned the assumptions of white, middle-aged, middle-class males, which had made the 1950s appear a decade of consensus. The fair embodied a mentality that took for granted that the future would be better than today and that increase equaled improvement, particularly in the realms of science and consumption. Although the exposition succeeded in predicting some future trends, such as the proliferation of computers and the automation of the kitchen, it gave little hint of many other fundamental changes beginning to unfold. The future in 1962 appeared as a richer, easier, and speedier version of the present—not as one in which cultural values and social relationships had changed, and not as one in which there existed significant limitations to America's global power and natural environment.

Century 21's Legacy to Seattle

Just as American scientists responding to *Sputnik* and industrial designers envisioning the year 2000 fell short in their predictions of the future, so the local boosters of Century 21 could not predict correctly how the fair would change the host city, and especially the central business district. The exposition by no means injured downtown Seattle, but neither did it provide the windfall that local officials had anticipated. For one thing, its planners had overestimated their ability to alter the direction of urban development. Moreover, the fair outgrew its original inspiration. In a sense, it succeeded too well: instead of creating an adjunct to downtown it developed a district that stood apart in many ways from the central business district. Despite its location near the city center, the exposition paid homage less to the old downtown than to the new, outlying areas of the city. It functioned less as a defense against suburban sprawl than as a suburban invasion of the core of the city.

This outcome did not immediately become apparent. On the contrary, as the fair wound down its local supporters began to reassert the downtown agenda that had underlain the fair's inception. Joe Gandy, a local Ford dealer who served as president of the world's fair corporation, estimated that more than 2,000 of the nation's "top executives passed through our office" during the exposition and were impressed with Seattle's "astonishing assets." Ever the salesman, he insisted that city leaders follow up on the new contacts in an attempt to attract additional trade and industry to the region. Meanwhile, city planners devised programs to ensure that, even with the expected growth around Puget Sound, downtown Seattle would grow, too, and "become an even more vital center of the metropolitan area than it is today."[112]

One major objective had been to diminish the predominance of Boeing in the local economy, and Seattle did have some success along these lines. During the years after the fair it gained more branch offices of national companies, exported more manufactured goods, attracted more residents, catered to more tourists, and capitalized more on its port facilities. Improved transportation and continued economic expansion were largely responsible for these increases, but local businessmen regarded the world's fair as a crucial catalyst for accelerating growth. Besides advertising Seattle, it had created an urban cultural sophistication that helped attract firms and personnel to the city.[113]

Such gains, however, did not produce enough diversification to stave off hard times less than a decade after the fair. When Boeing's total state employment dropped from about 101,000 in 1967 to 38,000 in 1971, it dragged down the Puget Sound economy. As the unemployment rate skyrocketed and thousands of people left town to find work elsewhere, billboards and bumper stickers "asked the last person leaving Seattle to please turn out the lights."[114] Residents of greater Seattle realized once more how much they depended upon Boeing and perhaps began to see that the diversification for which they hoped would take decades to achieve.

The fair could not weaken the supremacy of the aerospace industry, and neither could it check the outward pattern of growth in the metropolis. New ferries, highways, and bridges accelerated the growth of suburban districts, which by 1980 contained about two-thirds of the population of the metropolis. And these outlying areas developed their own centers for business and shopping and government, challenging downtown as a focus of activity. The central business district retained its primacy, particularly as an administrative and financial center, but it was no longer an essential part of urban life for the metropolitan population. Moreover, the suburban motifs that dominated the exposition lived on in the fairgrounds and kept them from becoming an integrated part of downtown.

Once the fairgrounds became the Seattle Center, after the close of the Century 21 Exposition in October 1962, they attracted a more diverse group of visitors, as befits a central city. But the site itself remained relatively aloof from nearby parts of Seattle, in large part as a result of design. Needing to control access to the site for the sake of collecting admissions fees, builders of the world's fair had fenced in the exposition. The fences were not taken down after the fair, even though the new Seattle Center charged no general admission, for those responsible for the fairgrounds wanted to keep them distinct from the unattractive blocks surrounding the site. Consequently, despite the planners' intention that the fairgrounds not only become fully integrated with downtown but also stimulate rejuvenation of the Denny Regrade, the exposition site remained cut off from the rest of Seattle.[115]

Fences, busy streets, building walls, and parking lots created a moat around the Seattle Center. The former fairgrounds, rather than becoming a subservient adjunct to downtown, were "visually isolated" from adjoining districts.[116] In its detachment the Seattle Center resembled such suburban enclaves as the shopping mall or the theme park. Perhaps in part because the fairgrounds had stood apart from surrounding blocks, rather than blending in with them, the neighborhoods outside the walls never measured up to the appealing setting within. In 1973 Victor Steinbrueck, an urban-design activist, characterized the district to the west of the center as "a zooland of modern Seattle architecture in a state of chaos" and dubbed the Denny Regrade, to the south and east, a "mixed-up no man's land."[117]

The Seattle Center never became integrated with the central business district. Its tenuous link to downtown was dramatized during the early 1980s. The fair planners had originally expected that the Century 21 Exposition would provide the meeting facilities Seattle needed to host sizable conventions, but when the Seattle Center was proposed as the site for a new convention hall, it was rejected in favor of a more expensive location atop the interstate highway that bordered the central business district. "The main attraction of the over-the-freeway site," according to officials, "was its proximity to downtown hotels and shopping."[118]

In 1962 the site for Century 21 had seemed near enough to downtown to play a vital role in the remaking of central Seattle; two decades after the world's fair, the Seattle Center seemed too remote from the central business district to be included in plans for a new convention center. Its only direct connection to downtown was the Monorail. Once a credible prototype for local rapid transit, the Monorail still retained some popularity. But Seattle's inability to extend the Monorail into a comprehensive transit system focused on downtown further weakened the district's claim on residents of peripheral neighborhoods. In 1968 and 1970, Seattle voters rejected bond issues that would have supported construction of a rapid transit network. Left on its own, the Monorail continued to operate, shuttling passengers between downtown and the former fairgrounds, but the amount of traffic between the two districts never met expectations. With the vast majority of visitors to the Seattle Center arriving by car, the Monorail remained peripheral to the city's public transit system, serving mainly as a bridge over the Denny Regrade.[119]

During the 1950s the downtown businessmen of Seattle, trying to modernize the central business district, had envisioned an international exposition that would provide the open space and cultural infrastructure missing from the downtown. After the fair had closed, however, the lament that the downtown lacked open spaces or sufficient other pleasures for pedestrians was still often heard. The city did create or renew certain public spaces, with its historic preservation of Pioneer Square and the Pike Place Market, redevelopment along the waterfront, and construction of a domed stadium and Freeway Park.[120] But, like the exposition site, these projects tended to thrive on the periphery of the core business blocks, while the city center itself accumulated tall buildings, parking garages, and intense traffic. The district continued to attract some shoppers and many office workers during the day, but it did not become the round-the-clock "downtown for people" that planners had envisioned.

People failed to flock to the city center at night or on weekends in part because it lacked a wide array of cultural facilities. The Century 21 Exposition, by contrast, had created a complex for arts and entertainment at the fairgrounds that did attract evening and weekend crowds. The people who went to the Seattle Center to attend the theater, enjoy the opera, and watch sporting events generally did not have to pass through downtown to get there, and they did not see their destination as part of the business district. People who visited the site of the former exposition spoke of going to "the center," but they meant the Seattle Center, not, as planners had hoped, the central business district.

The center belonged less to one part of the city than to the entire multi-centered metropolis. This status perhaps became a sticking point in 1975 when voters in the municipality of Seattle were asked to approve bonds that would be used to expand and upgrade the Seattle Center. Twice within three months, the bond issue failed narrowly. Observers speculated that some city dwellers had opposed the measure out of reluctance to bear the entire costs of improvements themselves, because so many users of the aging fairgrounds—almost 40 percent, according to one 1972 survey—came from outside the city limits.[121] If the Seattle Center served a regional population, why should not the entire metropolitan area pay for improvements?

Regardless of who footed the bill, the site of the Century 21 Exposition was, at bottom, just another of the many new nodes in an increasingly polycentric city. Most of the new subcenters, of course, were located closer to or in the suburbs, but all exerted the same deleterious effect on the old single, downtown focus of the city. In this sense, the former fairgrounds lived up to the suburban ethos that had permeated the Century 21 Exposition. The Seattle World's Fair had followed such suburban models as Disneyland and the shopping mall; attracted a crowd that appeared to be suburban in character; and featured a theme of science and space that honored the strongest suburbanizing force of all, the Boeing Airplane Company. That the exposition site further challenged downtown by siphoning off its cultural appeal merely confirmed the overall pattern. A fair planned to serve downtown actually came to illustrate the larger pattern of urban deconcentration at work in greater Seattle.

The assumptions and projections of fair organizers, city planners, participating scientists, and industrial designers did not realistically presage the future, but they did give form to a vital cultural center that survived the changes of the ensuing years. The fairgrounds retained the qualities that made all magic kingdoms durable. Other cities looked to Century 21 as a model for staging successful fairs across the country.[122] And, on the local scene, the exposition and its grounds contributed to the further development of a western city. The fair supported additional growth in the Puget Sound area, thus for a time fulfilling the regional ethic of expansion. It also brought cultural maturity to the city by helping to overcome the traditional western sense of cultural inferiority. That the fairgrounds contributed to both the quantity of growth and the quality of life suggested that the site of Century 21 could adapt to changing circumstances better than the world's fair exhibits had done.

In the first years after the fair closed, residents of Seattle gave special emphasis to material contributions made by Century 21 to the metropolis. During the 1950s the city had lacked the capital to build a complete cultural infrastructure. Consequently, although the majority of buildings at previous world's fairs had been demolished after closing ceremonies, Seattle had determined very early in fair planning to retain much of the exposition as a civic center. This strategy helped to create the cultural complex known as the Seattle Center, which to many people represented rapid progress. The city concluded that it had gained, in one burst of construction, as much as twenty-five years' worth of development on its civic center—and at bargain prices.[123]

The fair generated other practical benefits as well. It sparked a business boom in the metropolis as well as throughout the state. Construction and remodeling of buildings, employment before and during the exposition, and profits and revenues from fairgoers all stimulated the economy. The fair also demonstrated the potential for tourism in the Northwest, encouraging local citizens to devote more resources to that budding industry.[124] The success of the Century 21 Exposition gave local businessmen greater self-assurance and suggested that only a lack of confidence and imagination stood in the way of further progress. "Seattle is on the map in a big way," Joe Gandy explained. "The city and state will be reaping the rewards from this fair for decades."[125]

For five years after the fair closed the trend indeed was uniformly upward. The exposition helped to sustain the postwar economic boom, vindicating the efforts of the businessmen who had promoted it. The leadership of the city in the 1950s and early 1960s, facing very little opposition, had dedicated the resources of the community to heightened economic and demographic expansion. In Seattle, as in the rest of the West, the idea of growth seemed synonymous with progress, even if it were at the expense of the natural beauty that distinguished the city. In a letter written to a local newspaper just after the start of the fair, William E. Merry, editor of the *Washington Motorist*, urged residents to accept expansion as their destiny. Merry sympathized with those who wanted above all else to preserve the attractions and comforts of the pre-fair metropolis, but the future had arrived with Century 21 and the city could no longer afford hesitation: "Seattle DOES want new pathways to progress, though it may well be true that a heavy influx of people will threaten the very things that bring them here— the great untouched, undefiled, unspoiled outdoors. Seattle knows in its heart that things cannot always remain the same."[126]

By 1970 the emphasis on unchecked growth as Seattle's first priority had come into serious question. The Boeing recession of the late 1960s and early 1970s proved that expansion was not automatic in any case, but, even more important for the long term, the majority of citizens no longer found acceptable many of the consequences of unchecked growth. A movement to reconsider the direction of the city, part of a trend throughout the urban West, culminated late in the 1960s when the city elected leaders who favored a more carefully planned approach to urban expansion. New policies aimed for greater protection of natural attractions, local traditions, and cultural amenities. The downtown received some attention, but officials focused more on the city's many residential and commercial neighborhoods, which now pursued greater autonomy, power, and stability. The city's population, quite unsettled during the 1950s, increasingly came to regard Seattle as "a place to live rather than a place to make income from," in the words of local historian Murray Morgan.[127]

Controversy over the future of the former fairgrounds mirrored the shifting attitudes of local residents. Business-minded interests attempted to ensure that the Seattle Center pay for itself by maintaining a vital amusement park, whereas arts activists stressed aesthetic and cultural considerations that left little room for kids' rides and carnival games. In the end the two sides reached a compromise. The amusement park remained, because it generated revenue.[128] Over the succeeding years, however, use of the facilities by arts and entertainment groups became more central in tying the civic center to the identity of city residents.

Century 21 put Seattle on the cultural map of the United States. Between opening night, when Van Cliburn played with the Seattle Symphony Orchestra, and closing night, when Carl Sandburg recited his poetry for two hours, a wide variety of well-known performers, including the Count Basie Orchestra, the Roy Rogers and Dale Evans Western Show, the New York City Ballet, and the Ringling Brothers Barnum and Bailey Circus, passed through the area. The exposition provided the backdrop for the Elvis Presley movie "Take Me to the Fair." Numerous foreign troupes performed on the fairgrounds, and an unprecedented number of shows played at local theaters during the run of the fair. The packed houses to which these acts played ensured that Seattle would host many more such acts in the future.[129]

Fairtime performances established a precedent of profitable bookings, but it was the exposition site itself that provided the facilities. The permanent complex consisted of a new playhouse, exhibit hall, indoor sports and convention coliseum, science center, and the Space Needle with its restaurant, as well as an opera house, arena, and office-and-dining building that had been remodeled from earlier structures. An older outdoor stadium and a new amusement zone completed the center. The demolition or relocation of many temporary fair structures in the months after Century 21 closed reduced the congestion of the landscape.[130]

It took some time for local residents to collect cultural dividends from the Seattle Center.[131] The pre-fair metropolis had had few resources with which to begin to develop the classical performing arts. In April 1962, during Van Cliburn's rehearsal for opening night, the pianist's mother said of the accompanying Seattle Symphony Orchestra, "Well, it's certainly not the New York Philharmonic."[132] Yet if the symphony orchestra lacked professionalism, it nonetheless constituted the city's chief asset in the performing arts.

Century 21 changed all that. It challenged the orchestra to do more and provided a facility in which it could attract larger crowds, play more frequently, and earn more money. The fair was hardly the only reason for improvement, as citizens' groups emerged in force to support the flowering of the performing arts, but it certainly quickened the pace of development. The symphony orchestra staged an opera during the exposition, and this art flourished in succeeding years to such an extent that Seattle has become internationally renowned for its annual presentation of Wagner's *Ring* cycle. The city's Repertory Theatre also gained a building from the fair, and dance and other performing arts followed. In 1967 the city got its first major-league sports franchise, a basketball team that played at the Seattle Center Coliseum. Named after another futuristic bauble of the 1960s, the SuperSonics provided an additional sign of urban maturity. The team's financial success lured other big-league sports franchises.[133]

The Seattle Center thus became central to the identity of a city that, before the fair, had tended to be unsettled and provincial. Local residents and tourists integrated the former exposition site into urban life, attending the many events scheduled for its facilities and sampling the daily pleasures it offered. In 1981 more than 9 million people used the center for one purpose or another, almost as many as had come during the fair. Even though the city-run facility regularly lost money on operations, the former fairgrounds continued to contribute to the prosperity of the town. The site attracted as many as 3 million tourists in 1981 and, by enriching the quality of local life, made Seattle more alluring to potential newcomers. After the mid-1960s, however, most residents regarded the center not primarily as an economic asset but, in the words of a local newspaper columnist, "as a symbol of our coming of age, as a place to go to retreat, escape and enjoy."[134]

The fair added more than a new city district to the Pacific Northwest. It brought new attitudes and practices that permeated urban life and transformed local ways. The exposition attracted visitors from across the country whose expectations and preferences helped to stimulate changes in Seattle that took many forms—repeal of the prohibition on Sunday liquor sales; proliferation of restaurant chains, fast-food franchises, and high-quality dining; emergence of new entertainment and artistic companies.[135] Such changes forced local residents to reconsider their status. In the months preceding the exposition, some residents thought of Seattle as a small, remote, relatively unsophisticated community, struggling against long odds to become "a major world's fair host city." After basking in the success of the fair and the praise of the nation in 1962, the metropolis perceived itself to be maturing, not simply in terms of economic and physical growth, but also by developing the amenities that characterize cosmopolitan living and major-league status.[136]

The new cityscape the fair created and the cultural polish it brought to the region were Century 21's major legacies, but had hardly constituted its primary inspirations. The fair was conceived as a project to spur economic growth and stability and to strengthen the central business district against the inroads of suburbia. It produced some benefits for downtown and for local business interests, but hardly enough by the 1970s to slow outward development or to overthrow the primacy of Boeing. In later stages of planning, the fair became an expression of faith in science and a vision of a richer, more orderly future, but these themes soon seemed outdated, too. The space age continued, of course, but never in a fashion that justified the optimism of Century 21.

The fairgrounds themselves, however, not only survived post-fair changes but grew steadily more important as a fundamental part of metropolitan identity. They served not only the downtown but all of greater Seattle, helping to provide the trappings of urban belonging—architecture such as the Space Needle, such amenities as professional performing arts and big-league sports—and encouraging the development of a sense of place. The fair could not prolong indefinitely the growth it was meant to celebrate, and it became a part of the process of urban deconcentration in Seattle, rather than a bulwark for the downtown against the suburbs. Nonetheless, the Century 21 Exposition, like other magic lands, succeeded in bringing maturity and identity to a city in the throes of rapid expansion.

CHAPTER SIX

Western Cityscapes
and American Culture

In the space of one decade, the urban character of Phoenix changed drastically, at least in the eyes of local planning officials. In 1969 *The Comprehensive Plan, 1990* bemoaned the fact that drivers and developers seemed to have had their mindless way with the city. Unplanned land use and blind devotion to automobiles, according to this view, had destroyed urban form and produced quick profits for a few while exacting high payments from the community as a whole. By accepting chaotic expansion, citizens had assumed that they could afford sprawl because they had "unlimited resources, unlimited land, unlimited distances, and unlimited growth" at their disposal.[1] This attitude was certain to produce waste in the long run, and it neglected those poorer residents who were unable to afford a car and unlikely to benefit from land development.

Uncontrolled expansion, it was argued, had unnecessarily driven up the cost of infrastructure, encouraged the "poor or thoughtless design" of neighborhoods, and undermined the vitality of the downtown. Moreover, the character of expansion in Phoenix had defeated one of the key aims of urban living, according to many experts—the greatest possible amount of interpersonal contact within a diverse population. To approximate that urban ideal more nearly, Phoenix needed higher residential densities, stricter zoning, a stronger central district, and better public transit. Until then, the City Planning Department declared, the shape of Phoenix would continue to represent "a gross distortion of the values of urban life."[2]

Ten years later, the Phoenix Planning Commission no longer re-garded sprawl as a major problem. Perhaps making a virtue of necessity, officials now essentially accepted the pattern that had been produced with little input from planners. During the later 1970s Phoenix adopted the notion of "urban villages" as the key to its development for the remainder of the century. The *Phoenix Concept Plan 2000* di-vided the city into nine districts, each of which ideally "would become relatively self-sufficient in providing living, working and recreational opportunities for residents." Within a large metropolitan area, each ur-ban village would "help satisfy the psychological need to belong to an identifiable community with a sense of control over its environment." Instead of looking to the old downtown for an urban focus and ex-pecting public transit or roadways to radiate from there, residents would now look to the core of each village—the office complex, shop-ping mall, commercial strip, or public institution where people tended to congregate during working hours. The plan appealed to many people, in Phoenix and around the country as well, because it promised more manageable communities within a metropolitan framework.[3]

Although we should not make too much of comprehensive city plans, they can serve as evidence of how people see urban form and as assessments of a city's direction measured against an ideal. In the case of the *Phoenix Concept Plan 2000*, it could be argued that the new gen-eral plan represented a way of seeing the city that differed substantially from the perspective of *The Comprehensive Plan, 1990*. The more recent view was based on an increased respect for unplanned land-use practices that were already well developed in Maricopa County. Sprawl was no longer defined simply as a problem. In 1982 Mayor Margaret T. Hance explained that the term denoted the "compatible, low-density neigh-borhoods" that had attracted many newcomers to Phoenix.[4]

The authors of the new comprehensive plan saw order where only years before a different group of planners had perceived chaos. And instead of asking Phoenix to develop a downtown along conventional lines, planners now recognized existing subcenters within the metrop-olis that many people already regarded as integral to their daily lives. Because the city suddenly made more sense, those in charge of guiding its growth now thought less in terms of trying to reverse the direction of urban development so that Phoenix would better resemble an eastern ideal of the city, and more in terms of fine-tuning the more western patterns that already existed in the cityscape.

The turnabout in planning for Phoenix dramatized what happened throughout much of the urban West after World War II. Two distinct but closely related processes brought a new meaning and a new sense of cohesion to the regional metropolis. First, people saw the city differently than they had. In Phoenix, planners discovered order in a landscape that had once seemed chaotic. Similarly, urbanites throughout the West found logic in an unprecedented and explosive urban environment. The region's cities embodied the cultural orientations of those newcomers and residents who, regarding the West as special, attempted to ensure that its cities would not duplicate the eastern pattern.

Second, while people were changing the way they interpreted the urban scene, the form of the city itself changed to become more distinctly coherent as time passed. New subcenters or urban villages emerged as alternatives to the traditional downtown, and, with time, faceless land developments acquired character. In sum, the western metropolis and its component parts became increasingly legible. That is, they acquired their own image and identity and seemed to fit "into a coherent pattern."[5] As a result, western urbanites' sense of place was strengthened.

The appearance of magic kingdoms in western cities epitomized the two processes at work. Disneyland, Stanford Industrial Park, Sun City, and the Seattle Center were among the earliest and boldest exemplars of the new urban form in their respective metropolitan areas. They changed the look of cities, both by contributing landmarks to the urban scene and by providing models for other developments. They represented achievements in the realm of culture as well as contributions to a sense of community. Magic kingdoms were exceptional places, but they nonetheless demonstrated how people could come to perceive the explosive city as a familiar and understandable environment. Relatively homogeneous, suburban enclaves, they seemed to simplify the metropolis. At the same time, they gave physical expression to the cultural orientations that made the West and its cities so attractive to migrants and residents. Magic kingdoms appeared to uphold the promise of amenities, prosperity, spaciousness, freedom, and autonomy that loomed so large in expectations of what the West and its cities should be. They projected not only an urban identity for their respective cities but a regional one for the entire West.

Yet thematic western cityscapes were not simply creations of a region or a locality. The motivations behind urbanization in the West had much in common with the desire of many Americans to move to the suburbs, and the pattern of land use that appeared in the regional metropolis derived in no small part from the trends remaking cityscapes across the country: the rise of shopping malls, the completion of freeway systems, the migration of jobs and homes to the suburbs. The conventionally shaped city, identified with eastern traditions inherited from the nineteenth century, was being challenged not only in the West but all across the country. As a result, the entire nation proved receptive to innovations in urban form created in the West between 1950 and 1965.

The Urban West as a Chosen Land

Cities tend to change more readily than do experts' image of how they should look: "all new urban types appear in their early stages to be chaotic." For those students of urban America who continued to regard the central city with a prominent downtown as the norm, Sunbelt cities of the mid-twentieth century appeared to verge on the "pathological."[6] The planning director of Santa Clara County condemned the "confused pattern" of urbanization around San Jose because it did not correspond to what eastern experience had shown to be appropriate: "[W]e are appalled because we can see very clearly that this kind of development is not going to wind up with a *properly* integrated urban community with a nucleus core and *proper* elements of community living."[7]

To at least a few observers, however, it did not seem sensible to measure the modern urban West against a yardstick derived from nineteenth-century eastern cities. In 1957 the architect Richard Neutra, writing about southern California, contended: "No one from elsewhere will be able to teach us urban design. We shall have to evolve it, as we have evolved the California home." Three years later Catherine Bauer Wurster, the housing and urban planner, pointed out that city planning in California could not pursue the course it had taken in the East. There, she noted, planning had served largely as "a *remedial* operation." But in the West the main challenge was not to fix old mistakes but "to shape entirely new growth." Others believed the eastern experience was not only irrelevant but perhaps even destructive. As architectural historian Reyner Banham explained, "While conventional planners are almost certainly right in asserting that without planning Los Angeles *might* destroy itself, the fact remains that conventional planning wisdom certainly *would* destroy the city as we know it."[8]

Accepted planning wisdom was also challenged by average residents of the urban West who simply did not see the problems that troubled urban critics. "Designers" and "users," as Amos Rapoport has explained, tend to "perceive and evaluate environments differently so that meanings intended by designers may not be perceived [by users]; if perceived, not understood; and, if both perceived and understood, may be rejected." Designers are inclined to conceive the built environment in "perceptual" terms that measure it against an ideal; they often see it as a rather abstract whole that is largely susceptible to rational manipulation. Users, by contrast, assign meaning to portions of the built environment in "associational terms"; they come to identify certain attitudes or feelings or circumstances with an environment as they are "taking possession [of it], completing it, changing it." Users develop a sense of control over their share of the urban setting not by trying to plan or rationalize it but by occupying and modifying it. In this way they are capable of making sense out of a place that seems senseless to "the planning/design subculture," as they develop a different comprehension of "the nature of the rules embodied or encoded" in the built environment.[9]

A study of the San Jose metropolitan area illustrated the differing perspectives of designers and users in the urban West. In the early 1970s an investigator compared the attitudes of planners in the Santa Clara Valley to those of a cross-section of residents. He found that the two groups concurred on a number of general ideals for their community, including desegregation and better schools. But the planners surveyed in the study expressed more support for policies that would have created a stronger urban identity along the lines of the eastern city. They advocated measures to restore vitality to the downtown area and to reduce the predominance of autos and shopping centers. By contrast, citizens from both Anglo-American and Mexican-American districts agreed that neighborhood and family issues deserved greater priority. They wanted more police protection, better nearby homes and neighbors, lower taxes, and improved roads. They did not worry much about the consequences of sprawl.[10]

Westerners may not have known much about fine cities, but they knew what they liked. Indeed, the inhabitants of the urban West generally felt greater satisfaction with the form of their cities than the critics thought possible. Writing in *Harper's* in 1955, Bruce Bliven explained that, in contrast to the "insecurity, confusion, and . . . breakdown of standards of behavior" to be expected in southern California, people seemed remarkably content with life in Los Angeles, and even fairly skillful at developing a sense of community. On the whole, another observer explained, the populace was "quite satisfied with the drift of things."[11]

If the form of the western metropolis did not live up to planners' expectations, it did seem to please many of its residents. In crude terms, satisfaction was demonstrated by the large numbers of migrants who continued to arrive in the region, apparently unconcerned about its reputation among experts as an unhealthful urban environment. In fact, continuous migration to western cities was crucial to the form that they assumed. Unlike those planners who wanted the urban West to adhere to eastern patterns, many residents of the region had actually come in search of a city that differed from an eastern model they either were leaving behind or trying to avoid. Inhabitants of the modern West believed they could build a special type of city, and their expectations helped to create a distinct regional urban form.[12]

One key to the identity of the postwar urban West was the mentality associated with migrating and remaining there. The region stood apart because, more than other sections of the country, it was populated, as a matter of preference, by newcomers who had freely chosen to move there and by native-born residents who explicitly resisted moving away. As the destination of choice for many, the West became a mosaic of "voluntary regions," that is, places where the population consisted not so much of people required to be there by "circumstances of birth and social heredity" as of "self-selected groups of like-minded, mobile, atomistic individuals."[13] Of course, people across the country increasingly felt liberated from the traditional compulsion to stay where they had been born and raised. But of all American sections, the West was the mid-twentieth-century destination most profoundly shaped by the newfound inclination to move.

Migration contributed in several respects to a distinctive regional mindset. "The process of moving," notes George W. Pierson, "alters the stock, temperament, and culture of the movers, not only by an original selection but on the road as well and also at journey's end." Those who arrived in the Far West tended to differ from those they left behind. Choosing to leave distinguished them at the outset, and the "middle passage" across the country transformed them some more. Migrants' destinations also affected them. Recent arrivals found themselves adapting to new climates, new customs, new neighbors. Yet the influence of destinations on newcomers should not be overestimated. Those communities receiving migrants often felt overwhelmed by them, as newcomers brought attitudes and practices that modified their adopted place of residence.[14]

To a significant extent, the identity of the postwar West was created by newcomers' expectations for the region. Migrants have often viewed their movement as a chance to start afresh. They have been able to make choices that they would not have had available without leaving their place of origin. Voluntary migrants have tended to believe they had a chance to build a better society or to join one that suited their own interests and personalities.[15] Like those retiring to Sun City, other voluntary migrants expected that through resettlement they could live among others like themselves and exert more control over their own destiny. In 1959 Nathan Glazer discerned the voluntary character of the urban West in Los Angeles, where the "sense of a chosen city, a desired way of life, a realized wish, is strong."[16]

The element of choice, not birth or happenstance or necessity, was crucial to Westerners' explanations of why they lived where they did. To be sure, there remained much variation among individuals' motives and circumstances. Some had been born in the West and turned down chances to leave; others, especially within non-white groups, had immigrated in search of work; still others had come for family reasons or had been attracted by the natural setting. Moreover, destinations within the Far West varied widely in what they offered newcomers. Salt Lake City, for example, differed markedly from both Albuquerque and Portland. Yet people throughout the diverse region were united in their tendency to account for their presence in the West by saying that they preferred it over other sections of the country. Residents in the Mountain and Pacific states in particular believed that the "swarming East," as one self-styled "refugee" termed it, was simply a less desirable place to live.[17]

Of course, for many people the East was an abstraction or an invention that had no basis in personal experience or fact. Notions about what lay back east could be just as mythic and wide-ranging as people's perceptions of what existed out west. As a result, Westerners who felt either that they were starting over from scratch or that they were pioneering new cultural trends for the entire country often neglected or underestimated eastern precedents for their actions. If the East of their imaginations did not always conform to reality, however, they nonetheless created a real western identity for themselves in large part by contrasting their adopted region to what they believed they had left behind.

A negative attitude toward older, more densely settled places was hardly new among westering peoples of Euro-American descent in North America. Moreover, since at least the beginning of the twentieth century this rejection of the East had been framed in explicitly urban terms. Newcomers to the West expected to reside, not in the wide-open spaces that comprised the region's hinterland, but in its growing towns. Los Angeles provided the best early example of migrants attempting to build a city that did not repeat the mistakes of the eastern metropolis or the midwestern small town, but inhabitants of other western towns of the early twentieth century, such as Denver and Seattle, also identified their emerging urban form as a distinct departure from "that of cities of the past."[18]

The expectation that the western metropolis would not "sink to the levels so common in dense urban life elsewhere in America" gained strength after 1940. As the region steadily urbanized, the image of the eastern metropolis deteriorated, making it an even more powerful foil than before. Westerners spoke about leaving behind the "decaying, skyscraper-clogged . . . cities" of the Atlantic seaboard, along with their more severe weather and their supposedly greater levels of congestion, pollution, racial tension, and taxation.[19] They disapproved not of cities as a way of life but of that kind of city that they identified with the East. One transplanted New Yorker summarized the sentiment in 1952:

[I]n the fading, grimy cities [of the Northeast] there are mile on mile of sooty brick slums, cobwebby Victorian factories, block after block of the most unimaginative stores, apartments and office buildings. How can New York, the apartment city where the average man can never hope to own his own home, criticize when it has Harlem and the East Side. Los Angeles has nothing to compare with that, for it is the city of homes, where even many of the slums are composed of small individual houses.[20]

Pursuit of a different type of urban environment constituted a change in westward migration. During the nineteenth century, it had been primarily the prospect of gain that had lured miners to barren mountains, loggers to isolated forests, stockgrowers to distant pastures, and farmers to formidable flatlands. That extractive economy also created urban centers such as San Francisco, Portland, and Denver, which linked their far-flung hinterlands to eastern markets and eastern capital. In these nineteenth-century cities, urban form followed urban function. Their residents viewed them not as attempts to escape from the eastern pattern but as places needing to imitate eastern models as thoroughly as possible. Faithful replication of the Atlantic-coast metropolis generally proved an elusive goal, but it nonetheless guided the evolution of western cities for most of the nineteenth century.[21]

However, beginning late in the nineteenth century a second stream of westward migration emerged, composed of people more concerned than before to avoid the eastern pattern and less concerned with economic gain. Although this stream sometimes joined the original current, as it grew larger it also spilled over into other directions. Distinctions between northern and southern California exemplified the divergent movements. While San Francisco resisted the new trend, hoping to perpetuate its identity "as the legitimate continuation of the East,"[22] greater Los Angeles seized upon the image of the West as an alternative to, rather than an extension of, the East and began to attract the lion's share of migrants. Again, although most agreed on the attractions of the climate and natural setting, migrants' motives were not uniform. Some of those headed to southern California sought to improve their health; others wished to escape the ethnic and racial minorities that allegedly "infested" eastern towns; still others sought a different style of life. But overall, in significantly larger numbers than before, migrants emphasized the appeal of the physical, social, and cultural environment and downplayed the importance of economic motivations.[23]

By the mid-twentieth century, many of those residing on or heading toward the Pacific slope identified amenities as its chief allure. "The West is mild, climatically," explained the architect Richard Neutra. "This makes it an 'aspiration area' of man in general." Its diverse topography also attracted Americans in an age when access to the outdoors became increasingly important.[24] Americans now felt freer to choose where to live, and their comparison-shopping frequently led them to select the urban West. As part of this process, they fashioned an identity for themselves that depended on real and imagined contrasts with other parts of the country.

The urban West grew because people chose to move and stay there, but it was not created solely by individual decisions. Several structural trends combined to permit the inflow of this different breed of migrant, and most of these stemmed in some fashion from the increasing integration of the Far West into modern industrial capitalism during the twentieth century.[25] A rising tide of affluence—among retirees, for instance—reduced the importance of the economic risks inherent in migrating to a new region. The reorientation of American economic culture toward consumption increasingly encouraged people to identify themselves as consumers not only of material goods but also of those kinds of environmental amenities that seemed so abundant in the West.[26] Such mass-transportation technologies as autos and planes enlarged people's ability to travel westward, and the ready availability of mechanical air-conditioners made destinations in the Southwest far more attractive than before. In short, modern capitalist culture and its products made possible the choices that defined the West as a voluntary region.

Although decisions to dwell in the West revolved less than before around its economic opportunities, migration would not have been possible for most people without the chance to earn a decent living. Mobilization for world war and cold war, of course, created tens of thousands of new jobs in the West. Moreover, many businesses relocated there for the same reasons that individuals did. Corporate managers were not only attracted to western amenities but felt less tied to old economic centers than they had been. Economic success no longer depended so much on proximity to raw materials, markets, or ports. Such newer industries as electronics did not require locations in the manufacturing belt of the northeastern United States; the aerospace industry actually sought out the West for its better flying weather.

The booming service sector of the American economy similarly had few strong ties to old manufacturing centers, and the service industry of tourism thrived particularly in the West. Some companies also saw relocating in the West as an opportunity to recruit and retain especially desirable employees. High-tech firms locating in the Santa Clara Valley figured that there they could more easily hire workers with special skills. In Phoenix, geographer D. W. Meinig observed in 1971, "The fact that so many people seek the area for other than economic reasons continues to attract a wide variety of corporations which have found that just such people make unusually contented employees."[27]

The economy and cities of the West boomed because of, not in spite of, their physical environs. It has been common to view western cities as somehow in opposition to nature; they have been portrayed as oases in hostile settings.[28] But Westerners generally did not regard their towns as the antithesis of the region's environment. Rather, beginning as early as the late nineteenth century, they developed the notion that they could realize in the West a special relationship with nature, and they clung to this idea even as their society became increasingly urbanized. Indeed, the urban orientation of most Westerners, historian Earl S. Pomeroy argues, actually helps to explain their "pre-occupation with the outdoors and with the accessibility of beaches and parks."[29]

Figure 40. This 1955 aerial photograph of San Jose illustrates some of the
factors that made far western metropolitan areas so attractive to
postwar migrants to and residents of the Far West. The balmy
Santa Clara Valley contained a city that still seemed manageable
and malleable compared to eastern counterparts, and also offered
proximity to rural life, mountains, the Pacific Ocean and San
Francisco Bay, major universities, and truly cosmopolitan San
Francisco. Photo by R. L. Copeland, courtesy of CSS Associates,
Architects.

City-dwellers customarily proved quite devoted to the natural West,
whether they found it in their backyard or in national parks. Towns
served as gateways to the attractive physical environs in the region's
hinterlands. Furthermore, most big cities encompassed within their
borders some of the West's distinguishing beaches, mountains, deserts,
orchards, or other scenery (see Figure 40). This fact affected planning
and design from an early date. In the first decade of the twentieth century, landscape architect John C. Olmsted "argued that Seattle's exceptionally scenic setting negated the need for a large landscape park." Another student of urban trends on the Pacific coast noted in 1912 that

suburbs there had already incorporated distinctive types of architecture and planning in order to make the most of natural settings.[30] In short, city-dwellers attempted, not to extricate themselves from nature, but to turn it to best advantage. This trait continued to characterize the post-war urban West. In 1963 the journalist Remi Nadeau described a regional as well as a state trend when he noted that the Californian "lives not in a society but in an environment."[31]

Urbanites' attachment to the natural West did not necessarily mean that they were always prepared to protect it. The Golden State epitomized the tension between the quantity of growth and the quality of life as measured by environmental amenities. Californians soiled their nest as quickly and thoroughly as anyone, yet they also stood in the forefront of American environmental and planning movements. Southern California became synonymous for many with pollution, yet it also pioneered certain conservation and clean-up programs.[32]

Identification with the natural West, which led to both its protection and its destruction, was crucial for explaining not only migrants' presence on the Pacific slope but also their expectations that urban life there would improve on that of the East. "We Californians are by and large self-selected to care about our physical surroundings," explained Catherine Bauer Wurster in 1960. "We are the people who came West because we thought we could live better out here."[33] One transplanted New Yorker explained that the average person in Los Angeles tended "to be friendlier, healthier, and happier than a person who has to fight slush, sleet and winter colds all his life." Spending more time outdoors made life "about ten times" as enjoyable in Phoenix as in New York, another recent arrival figured. Gentle nature stimulated cultural and anatomical improvements, too, according to one reporter's depiction of the typical southern Californian: "Just a hundred-odd miles from desert, lakes, and mountains and next door to the Pacific, he gets out and around far more than the 'cosmopolitan' New Yorker. . . . The resident of Los Angeles spends more time outdoors than even Florida press agents, and raises the country's biggest and healthiest children."[34]

The combination of a favored natural setting and millions of newcomers made the West appear more open to positive change. In other parts of the country, it was said, people had "already formed most of their attitudes, customs and institutions. . . . Good or bad, they are too often prisoners of their own conventions." The West, by contrast, seemed to offer "release from the staid, old ordinary ways of living and thinking" associated with the East. It encouraged the sense that its institutions remained more malleable, and hence more perfectible.[35]

Constructing Meaning
in the Western Metropolis

Deeming it unacceptable to duplicate the eastern experience, many Westerners focused their hopes for change on the city itself. It was not the region's wide-open spaces that perpetuated the idea of the American West as a land of opportunity, but, rather, its metropolitan areas that attracted migrants with the promise of prosperity, personal liberty, and amenities. "Virgin cities" rather than "virgin land" played the central role in upholding a regional identity in the twentieth century—so long as they could be made to seem manageable.[36]

In 1961 John Anson Ford, a Los Angeles county supervisor, described the shape most appropriate for the region's metropolis: "It must not be a second congested London or New York, but a population center with many new characteristics adjusted to the outdoor life of the region and to the era of greater leisure, greater mobility, and a wider distribution of the skills and culture of modern society."[37] Ford's ideal of the western metropolis in many respects matched new urban patterns across the nation. The proliferation of Levittowns in the mid-Atlantic states, for example, suggested that many Easterners, too, wanted to distance themselves from crowded and aging central cities. The numerous changes remaking the metropolis—the elaboration of an automobile culture, including the construction of freeways; the multiplication of peripheral subdivisions; the rise of shopping malls; the emergence of large-scale housing developers—might be summarized in the term *suburbanization*, a process affecting East and West, North and South alike.[38] By the 1980s, the accumulation of these suburban changes had, as historian Robert Fishman explains, produced an altogether new urban form:

[T]he true centre of this new city is not in some downtown central business district but in each residential unit. From that central starting point, the members of the household create their own city from the multitude of destinations that are within suitable driving distance. One spouse might work at an industrial park two exits down the interstate; the other at an office complex five exits in the other direction; the children travel by bus to comprehensive schools in their district or drive themselves to the local branch of the state university; and the family shops at several different malls along several different highways.[39]

Postwar suburbanization paralleled in many respects postwar westward migration. Both processes expressed Americans' "search for a healthy environment and an informal life style," and both reshaped comparatively unpopulated but rapidly filling landscapes. Furthermore, each migration represented in the movers' minds a liberating opportunity to improve their quality of life.[40] New arrivals both in the suburbs and in the West believed that they could now reside in a locale that was better suited to their beliefs and personality. Both the West and the suburbs promised a more casual way of living, more space, and more access to the outdoors, all at a price initially lower than could be found in eastern central cities. The virtues of suburban living, Catherine Bauer Wurster noted, were those of "the 'American way of life,' particularly here in the West."[41]

As a result of the overlapping motives and expectations of those headed toward suburbs and those moving to the American West, it has been easy to attribute western cities' distinctiveness to the timing of their development. Western cities, according to some, seemed more malleable than their eastern counterparts solely because they were newer, more expansive, and less dominated by the central business districts and rail transit systems created during the previous century. If the urban West was distinctive, some have suggested, it was merely because national tendencies could operate there more freely.[42]

This view contains some truth, but it oversimplifies the story. Urban Westerners of the mid-twentieth century were not acting just as Easterners would have acted in their place. In their own minds, at least, they had rejected the East and were creating altogether new patterns. In addition, they understood suburbs and inner cities in ways that both set them apart from other American urbanites and reiterated the sense that the western metropolis was superior.

The relative importance of "white flight" illustrates the different urban patterns. Suburbanization in the East depended heavily on an exodus of whites from central-city districts to outlying neighborhoods. Historically, however, urban settlement in southern California, the San Francisco Bay Area, and other western cities had not constituted an exodus from the central city; rather, since the late nineteenth century settlers had been "infilling" between a number of dispersed towns.[43] Furthermore, many Westerners, if they were fleeing at all, were attempting to avoid the eastern central city more than the western one. John S. Shafer, a widower who moved to Sun City, explained that he wished to get away from an invasion of central Detroit "by blacks and poor whites. . . . The attitude there changed, there was no civic spirit. All the people I wanted to associate with went to the suburbs."[44] But instead of going to suburban Detroit, Shafer moved to the outskirts of

Phoenix. Even though his feelings about Detroit affected his attitudes toward Phoenix, his objection was not so much to Arizona's inner city as to Michigan's.

In addition, there was simply less to flee from in the urban West. Such municipalities as Los Angeles, San Jose, and Phoenix generally did not have strong central cores from which to depart. From the start they appeared somewhat suburban in character. Consequently, distinctions between the inner and the outer city remained more obscure. Nathan Glazer noted the difference when he compared southern California to New York. Parts of the low-density pattern of development in Los Angeles resembled that of Long Island, he explained. But in the East the sprawling pattern would ultimately coalesce around the downtown, while in the West the extensive pattern of settlement "was the thing itself" and required no central district to provide an urban focus.[45]

The primacy of Manhattan as an anchor for the surrounding metropolis was never questioned in New York. In most cities of the West, however, the best that could be hoped for the downtown was that, as it did in Seattle, it would hold its own in the competition against growing subcenters in peripheral districts. More typically, as in San Jose, Phoenix, and southern California, central-city downtowns lost a good deal of ground to their outlying rivals. In fact, in order to compete against the growth of suburban districts, planners and builders in the central city and downtown turned to such suburban models as shopping malls, business parks, and planned neighborhoods for guidance. Although urbanites were indeed moving to suburbs in the West and across the country, the more significant fact may have been that suburban forms were becoming more prevalent throughout the metropolis, in the West even more rapidly than in the East.

A different kind of metropolis was emerging, not solely on the Pacific slope but surely with more speed and clarity there than elsewhere. Observers of the "newly-evolved urban type" understood its development as both "distinctly California in character" and "a prototype for the immediate future."[46] The inhabitants of this city, with their strong preference for single-family, detached housing, understandably anticipated that their town would expand outward, not upward or inward. They associated the sprawling, low-rise landscape with middle-class virtues, and by implication cast doubt upon the propriety of eastern highrises and row housing.[47]

The changing relationship between central city and suburb helped to distinguish further between the western and the eastern metropolis. In eastern urban centers, city boundaries frequently demarcated a significant difference in land use; districts outside the border could fairly predictably be characterized as having a lower density and a more pronounced residential character. In cities of the mid-twentieth-century West the distinction seldom held so firmly. Such towns as Phoenix and San Jose expanded so rapidly and incorporated so much new residential development into their jurisdictions that many districts that looked suburban and had actually been suburban prior to annexation were now technically inside the city limits and therefore by census definition a part of the central city. The central city of Los Angeles was far less densely settled than its average eastern counterpart; however, settlement on its fringes was denser than in the average eastern suburb.[48]

In appearance the metropolis of the Pacific coast resembled portions of the cities that had been left behind, but it had been invested with its own regional significance. Nathan Glazer pointed out that much of southern California at least superficially resembled New York's Queens and Brooklyn in its devotion to residential living. There remained a key difference, however. Brooklyn and Queens were not so much chosen as "taken out of necessity," whereas the urban West was a chosen destination that promised a significantly improved way of life.[49] The pattern that the critics termed sprawl actually conformed in many ways to the preferences of Westerners.

Residents of the Far West rejected the idea of a metropolis characterized by dense downtowns and deteriorating inner cities. Thus they did not really mind a pattern dominated by suburbs or suburban enclaves. Consequently, the peripheral districts of western cities in the mid-twentieth century played an enlarged role in bringing order to the urban scene. Slowly but surely, people began to perceive in outlying parts of the metropolis a pattern that contradicted the image of the chaotic western city.[50]

Prominent in the new pattern was a pronounced deemphasis on conventional downtowns. Shopping malls, commercial strips, office complexes, public facilities, and recreation centers had once been seen as part of a suburbia that was subordinate to the traditional central business district; now these foci of suburban life came to be seen as alternatives to downtown that made outlying regions of the metropolis much more self-sufficient. Westerners could increasingly view their city as an assemblage of urban villages, each of which was anchored by one or more of the new centers of activity.[51]

The transition from an ideal of a relatively compact and single-centered metropolis to a preference for a widely dispersed and many-centered form of settlement did not take place quickly or simultaneously throughout the West. Planners in Los Angeles had anticipated the emergence of something like urban villages as early as World War II, and during the 1960s they had officially adopted the idea as a guide to development. Planners in Phoenix accepted the possibility only during the later 1970s.[52] No one city was fully cognizant of the emerging order, and by no means did the evolving pattern solve most of the ills associated with city life, West or East.

Although migrants to the West came prepared for something different from the eastern city, they did not always get precisely what they wanted, and it frequently took them some time to decipher what they had found. To understand the metropolis, residents had to overcome their sense of its newness. They needed to put down roots, familiarize themselves with their surroundings, develop a feeling for the history of the place, and acquire a sense of community. For some people of the postwar West, these kinds of attachments never formed because their lives were too transient. Perpetual in-migration and out-migration worked against the development of an enduring sense of place. Numerous households in such centers of defense manufacturing as Orange County, for example, came and went as federal contracts were won and lost or completed by employers. Many such migrants never had the time or the inclination to build ties to the area.[53] These kinds of residents heightened the West's notoriety for the politics of anomie or maladjustment and perpetuated its reputation for being uninterested in regulating growth and urban planning.

As prominent as transience was in the region, however, it was not the way of life of the majority. Most people settled down, formed attachments to a metropolitan area, and took an interest in local government. Most urbanites did not keep entirely aloof from local affairs; rather, they shared with other Westerners a desire to preserve—via the ballot box, if necessary—the special environments they inhabited. Residents of the region had a large stake in protecting the home they had chosen. Moreover, the type of voters attracted to sprawling western cities—comparatively affluent and well-educated, youthful and appreciative of amenities—were precisely those who were best prepared to engage in politics on behalf of environmental protection and other quality-of-life issues.[54]

To at least a limited extent, then, the rapid growth of regional cities was a self-correcting phenomenon. After 1965 or so, significant support emerged for preserving the distinctive physical surroundings and amenities of the urban West. Even conservative communities like Palo Alto assumed a progressive stance on local land-use issues. Throughout the region, even in right-wing Orange County, the politics of managing or limiting growth gained popularity—much to the chagrin of members of the old pro-growth elites, who now found themselves in the minority.[55] As voters in Santa Clara County began to challenge the growth ethos in the early 1970s, a member of San Jose's postwar leadership lamented the new direction in local affairs: "[S]omewhere along the road the chauvinism that seemed to be the legacy of every Westerner, the California pioneer spirit, the excitement of it all, had gone. The voices of the builders and the *doers* became lost in the many-voiced demands of the *users*."[56]

Westerners did not remain isolated from society or politics, but, rather, overcame the newness of their communities in order to protect what they perceived to be a distinctive, attractive, and sometimes exclusive setting. Similarly, they familiarized themselves with their new places of residence by "plotting" themselves within increasingly well-defined mental images of the city. This process of fixing position within a metropolis and acting politically to protect its environment never occurred very quickly or very thoroughly, but it sufficed to recreate for uprooted people a sense of attachment to place. It thus helped people to derive from the urban region some of the satisfactions for which they had come in the first place.

Geographers have pointed out that urbanites tend to identify with a city at two different levels, both of which entail the simplification of urban reality.[57] On one level, they identify with the city as an abstract whole and attach themselves to a symbol—such as its name, slogan, or chief landmark—that encapsulates the larger complexity of the city for residents. In the urban West, all or part of a magic kingdom, such as Disneyland or the Space Needle, could connote an entire metropolis. On the second level, urbanites become familiar with those specific locales within the metropolis where they spend their time. This familiarity depends on a concrete knowledge of fragments of the city and leaves out the rest of the metropolis. To utilize Rapoport's terms once more, "users" gain a sense of control over the built environment by "taking possession" of those parts of it that are most relevant to their lives.[58] In planned developments such as Stanford Industrial Park and Sun City, users found places that enabled them to feel in command of the larger urban area.

People experienced the city of the postwar West not as a single place but as a series of environments catering to different needs or tastes. The traditional focus of city life, the mixed-use city center, engaged an ever smaller percentage of the population as urbanites moved increasingly from one enclave to another within the metropolis. They dwelled in housing subdivisions, worked in industrial or business parks, shopped at shopping malls and commercial strips, and found entertainment at recreational and cultural centers.[59] These enclaves were not always functionally pure: the industrial park, for example, might contain commercial and recreational facilities; the shopping mall might include offices and amusements; and the roadside strip often offered many diverse activities. Nonetheless, such enclaves constituted the essence of people's images of the urban setting, provided that a person could travel between them with relative ease.

More than other American urbanites, Westerners tended to come to terms with their cities through constant movement in private autos. This mobility frequently followed a consistent pattern. Individuals developed a regular "orbit," specific to their "social worlds," that took them to the same districts over and over again.[60] Continuous contact with selected portions of the metropolis bred familiarity with only those parts of the city covered during their "spatial patterns of regular activity." The result was mental maps that defined urban life—and indeed a sense of community—in terms of individuals' particular orbits rather than in terms of fixed places or a single political entity. These cognitive maps made the urban world comprehensible by reducing it to human scale.[61]

Mental maps screened out many aspects of city life and deepened the gulf between the social worlds of urbanites whose orbits did not intersect. In this sense, Westerners' urban images did isolate them—often intentionally—from others in the society. In any case, the selective character of mental maps was to some extent inevitable: given the size, shape, and rapid growth of the western city, its inhabitants could not be expected to comprehend its every part. In towns that seemed especially formless and chaotic, a device that simplified the city was essential.[62] The city had to be made manageable if people were to reap the rewards they anticipated from the West.

The notion of mental maps helps to explain why average citizens did not often share planners' and tourists' anxiety about the shapelessness of western cities. By profession, the planner assumed a bird's-eye view that took in all the city and its many possible orbits and paid close attention to the political borders that marked the edges of town. Given this image, and the somewhat traditional ideal of a city that planners often brought to their task, it was no wonder the city seemed chaotic to them. Similarly, tourists found it difficult to grasp the order inherent in the western city because they lacked the time and the ability to become familiar with its urban pattern, and because they often measured it against an eastern yardstick.[63] However, to the average resident, driving from enclave to enclave, crossing city boundaries without noticing them, and following a mental map that omitted the clutter of unnecessary details, the city made sense.

To understand how Westerners came to terms with cities that appeared senseless to others, then, we must take account of the mentality they brought to the urban scene. Wishing to distance themselves from the setting associated with eastern cities, they sought from the urban West a different environment, or more properly a series of different environments, around which they would organize their lives. Through the process of cognitive mapping, these urbanites began to comprehend the city from the perspective of their particular orbits. Their selective images of the city limited their contact with diverse peoples, but their mental mapping gave a sense of order to urban chaos.

Building a Legible City

At the same time that Westerners adjusted their perceptions and expectations of the city, the urban morphology itself was changing in ways that facilitated efforts to form regional attachments. As the story of each magic land illustrates, builders increasingly succeeded in creating readily identifiable, thoughtfully planned, distinctively western environments that, like a mental map, simplified land-use patterns. As alternatives to downtowns, or as American versions of New Towns, these developments made the metropolis easier to comprehend.

New alternatives to the downtown area often separated the functions of workplace, market, and recreational center into discrete outlying districts—industrial park, shopping mall, cultural complex—that became foci of everyday urban activity. In some instances, these substitutes for the downtown gathered into a single site the activities of tourism, shopping, working, dining, and entertainment. In either case, they often grew to be better defined, more prosperous, and livelier than the central business district itself.[64] American versions of New Towns (also known as new communities), by contrast, rather than provide an assortment of centers for a large metropolitan area, attempted to bring the full range of urban activity to one relatively cohesive, mostly residential suburb. Sun City, Arizona, and Irvine, California, were examples of these new communities.

The construction of such large and carefully conceived districts was not unprecedented in American urban history. Frederick Law Olmsted and others had planned self-contained, residential suburbs during the later nineteenth century, largely for the well-to-do. Chicago's World's Columbian Exposition of 1893 presaged such later developments as Disneyland in its regular cleaning, strict controls on architecture, sophisticated techniques of policing, and elaborate transportation systems. And the City Beautiful movement at the turn of the century once more encouraged thoughtful design of urban districts.[65]

Influential as these antecedents were, they did not represent a rejection of nineteenth-century urban form as it was manifested in cities of the Atlantic seaboard, and they did not create a new regional urban pattern. But in the urban West of the mid-twentieth century, the region's inhabitants expected their cities to differ from the eastern type. They conceived of their suburbs as more than residential enclaves, and they challenged the primacy of existing downtowns in numerous ways. Moreover, whereas Olmsted's planned suburbs and the City Beautiful creations constituted exceptions in the prevailing urban scene, the new western pattern became a major source of cohesion in cities.

A rapid pace of growth helped to bring about this ordering process by generating a tremendous demand for new development. Builders could attempt bigger construction projects in the West, because a quickly expanding market reduced the risk of failure. Economies of scale also permitted more planning. Developers undertaking a large-scale effort, one California state real estate commissioner explained, could afford to bring together "planners, engineers, architects, landscape architects and other technicians to design cities from the bottom up, and do it right the first time." City planning became, more clearly than before, the province of private enterprise as well as of public agencies. A California-based builder of shopping centers explained, "The role of the developer is really that of a sort of small city builder. He's no longer just creating stores and being the landlord."[66]

City and regional planners had not entirely relinquished their role, but in the same way that Phoenix officials had had to accept the sprawling shape that now characterized their city, public-agency planners throughout the region increasingly worked with urban designers from the private sector. These latter included, besides shopping-center builders, individuals whose experience in environmental design came from building studio sets, such as the people of Walt Disney Productions; large-scale tract developers such as the Del E. Webb company, builders of Sun City; and institutions such as Stanford University, which brought academic motifs to city planning.

Large-scale developments with ample private planning were neither new to urban America nor confined to towns beyond the Mississippi River. However, their importance was heightened in the West by their size and numbers there, and by their location in relatively young, rapidly expanding, and largely unplanned cities with populations receptive to virtually any substitute for the suspect downtown. Two projects in southern California highlighted the trend. During the early 1960s the Aluminum Corporation of America built a "complete city-within-a-city" on 180 acres that had been the back lot of Twentieth Century Fox Studios (see Figure 41). The new commercial and financial center, called Century City, consisted of super-blocks arranged around an axial boulevard, the Avenue of the Stars, "patterned after the Champs Elysee [*sic*] in Paris." Located next to some of the wealthier neighborhoods in Los Angeles, Century City featured hidden parking, shopping facilities, hotel and apartment accommodations, open spaces, and "majestic" buildings designed by famous architects—all of which made it "a city of the future" in the eyes of developers.[67] The Tishman Realty and Construction Company of New York erected another "new 'downtown'" called Wilshire Center at about the same time. The president of the development firm explained how the construction process in Los Angeles differed from his company's experience in the East: "In any other city, you put a building on a logical site in the existing community and produce a good result. Here, you can find an area and develop a new business community"—provided, of course, that "adequate parking can be supplied."[68]

New land development in the urban West did not need to be located according to municipal planning guidelines or to established patterns of related land uses. In fact, if parking were an issue, as it frequently was, developers were well advised to situate new projects at some distance from densely occupied areas. Such considerations reinforced the tendency of the metropolis to spread outward and further undermined the importance of older downtowns. Century City and Wilshire Center

Figure 41. An instant substitute for downtown was created in the early
1960s when developers laid out Century City in Los Angeles on
what used to be the back lot of Twentieth Century Fox Studios.
This 1963 photograph shows some of the earliest construction:
the completed Gateway West office building; the not-yet-
completed Gateway East office building; and in the rear the first
layer of a proposed three-level regional shopping center. High-rise
hotels and apartments were also planned. Copyright, Whittington
Collection, California State University, Long Beach (neg. #37–
55–1A).

provided offices, shopping, hotels, and apartments. In Orange County,
such malls as South Coast Plaza and Fashion Island offered retail outlets, pedestrian space, theaters, restaurants, and other cultural attractions (see Figure 42). The city of Irvine, organized around a university,
and the Leisure World retirement communities in Seal Beach and Laguna Hills were complete towns in themselves, and Disneyland helped
to transform Anaheim into a focus of urban activity.[69]

With such a mixture of new alternatives to downtown and American
versions of New Towns growing up around it, downtown Los Angeles,
the traditional central business district of southern California, became

Figure 42. When developing the former Irvine Ranch in Orange County, the Irvine Company made the Fashion Island shopping mall in circular Newport Center (shown here in 1968, one year after opening) a nucleus for nearby housing subdivisions, with office buildings to be located on the perimeter of the circle. In the background is another circular development—the new Irvine campus of the University of California, the nucleus for the planned community of Irvine. Copyright, Whittington Collection, California State University, Long Beach (neg. #87-54-RI#23).

increasingly irrelevant to the daily lives of most people in the metropolitan area. Only the highways that conveyed people from one specialized center to another—and constituted a special enclave unto themselves—seemed truly indispensable. Charles Moore, dean of the Yale School of Architecture, pondered "where one would go in Los Angeles to have an effective revolution of the Latin American sort":

Presumably, that place would be in the heart of the city. If one took over some public square, some urban open space in Los Angeles, who would know? A march on City Hall would be inconclusive. The heart of the city would have to be sought elsewhere. . . . The only hope would seem to be to take over the freeways.[70]

The style of cityscape coming into existence so dramatically in greater Los Angeles was not confined to the West. Downtowns diminished in stature across the country, to the point where some of them became specialized districts for government and administration. By the 1980s, when twice as many Americans commuted between suburbs as commuted into central cities from outlying homes, the importance of a variety of "often livelier satellite centers" or "subnuclei" had become clear. Large shopping centers attracted the most comment, but other variations, such as the "suburban freeway corridor" and the commercial strip, also received attention. Together they made up a "series of relatively self-contained and self-sufficient regional units. Each approximates a modified city; all are linked together in a galaxy of interdependent relationships."[71] The pattern remained most striking in the Far West, where both the prevailing attitudes and the enormous extent of recent urban growth had allowed it to make a bolder imprint (see Figure 43). In 1972 the geographer James E. Vance, Jr., concluded that "the Bay Area, California, and the West Coast have risen in their impact on American settlement structure as New York and megalopolis have sunk."[72]

The presence of so many alternatives to downtown suggested a widespread city in which people had to drive long distances in order to accomplish their daily business. However, once the substitutes for downtown became themselves centers of activity, people began to recognize them as cores of relatively self-sufficient urban villages. Like the ideal suburb, the urban village promised the best of both urban and exurban worlds. A shopping mall, office complex, or government center might serve as the heart of a small city within a city. Ideally, people would reside, work, shop, and find amusement in one relatively confined geographic area—the village—without suffering isolation from other districts that offered amenities their own village lacked.[73] Moreover, each village ideally offered a somewhat homogeneous setting for one of the many groups in the larger metropolis, thereby promising more support for a diversity of lifestyles.[74]

Phoenix became known for adopting urban villages as a basis for planning during the 1970s, but other cities had already begun to move in the same direction. Planners for Los Angeles had expressed a similar ideal in the 1920s and 1930s, and they expounded it more fully during the decade after 1945 when imagining development in the San Fernando Valley. They insisted that shopping centers, if properly located, would become the foci for "small, compact, planned communities which will possess all the amenities of a country town and be self-sustaining in every respect. All the planned communities are separated from one another and encircled by agricultural greenbelts."[75]

Figure 43. Driving along Wilshire Boulevard toward the Pacific Ocean in
1970, travelers passed through or by a number of alternatives to
downtown and enclave communities, including the Miracle Mile
(a "prototype linear downtown" since the 1920s, in Reyner
Banham's words), Century City, Westwood Village near the
UCLA campus, and Santa Monica. Each of these nodes weakened
the primacy of the central business district of Los Angeles
(foreground). Copyright, Whittington Collection, California
State University, Long Beach (neg. #02–75–15).

The village ideal appealed to many American builders of subdivisions in the postwar years, leading to the rise of privately built planned
communities. The towns of Columbia, Maryland, and Reston, Virginia, became the best-known efforts to realize the ideal. Once again,
however, the trend was most eagerly embraced in the West, which had
a disproportionately large share of American new communities, and
particularly in California, which contained several planned retirement
villages as well as the largest planned community of all—the city of
Irvine. Like Columbia, which was developed under the direction of
shopping-center mogul James Rouse, most western new communities
were laid out by leading architects and urban designers who performed

for private companies the function of city planners. These builders found a sizable market for planned environments that duplicated neither the aging central city associated with the East nor the unstable and chaotic cityscape associated with the Pacific coast.[76]

American new communities paid homage to the British Garden City ideal that originated with Ebenezer Howard in the years before World War I.[77] Of course, the Garden City was quite different from what passed for New Towns in the United States. The Garden City movement aimed to relieve urban congestion and encourage residential deconcentration by forming physically and economically distinct communities in the countryside, overseen by the government and populated by a mixture of social classes.[78] New Towns in the postwar United States were often simply suburbs glorified by a greater degree of planning than others.

American new communities tended to emerge within a metropolitan area rather than outside it. They appealed primarily to the wealthiest third of the population, who saw them as residential havens from which to commute to work; they took not diversity but homogeneity as the norm for their population; and they were developed as private, relatively exclusive subdivisions rather than as public projects. Some Americans viewed the new community as a chance to create an environment that resembled the small town of old, a place that would restore to the urban scene some of the order assumed to have been associated with the village of legend.[79] But they located such communities on the fringes of large cities where they tended to become simply enclaves in the midst of metropolitan sprawl rather than models for other developments. One southern Californian hoped that his new community of Valencia would become "an island of reason in the path of the metropolitan sprawl" and a town that would "never need the violent therapy of rebuilding." But few home-buyers shared those hopes. Seeking peace and quiet and higher property values, they cared little for the ideal of the self-sufficient village.[80]

American new communities seldom lived up to designers' aspirations, but, along with shopping malls, industrial parks, and civic centers, they made outlying urban neighborhoods more legible by serving as focal points of settlement and activity.[81] Meanwhile, to compete with economic success on the urban periphery, some city centers gradually became more suburban in character, acquiring their own versions of the specialized shopping, housing, and working complexes once reserved for peripheral neighborhoods. In 1963, planners in Seattle tried

to adapt "the extensive U.S. postwar experience with outlying and suburban shopping centers" to the needs of downtown. They proposed
that the interior of the central business district become a pedestrian
mall surrounded by "huge parking lots," which in turn would be ringed
by a road system connecting the downtown to freeways. The downtown would try to beat outlying districts at their own game.[82]

Suburbanizing forces carried a great deal of weight in western cities.
Yet the process that created new communities, urban villages, and substitutes for downtowns was slow and highly selective. It generally
worked from the outside of cities toward the inside, beginning in the
newer and wealthier neighborhoods on the urban fringes. Large-scale,
private-sector planning was driven primarily by market considerations
and therefore responded most readily to the people who could best
afford to consume in shopping malls, commute from suburbs, and buy
in planned communities. The more and the less affluent users of cityscapes in the postwar West thus experienced urban changes in different
ways.

The process that created new communities and alternative downtowns often worked directly against the interests of blue-collar workers
and the poor, who were least able to afford to live near the new urban
villages. As a result, they increasingly had to bear the brunt of the burden of commuting long distances—either by car, which was both expensive and wasteful, or by transit systems that remained notoriously
inadequate, inconvenient, and unsuited to the widely dispersed population.[83]

And when poorer districts finally did experience the reordering of
the cityscape, their residents were generally the most vulnerable to
forced relocation, either because increases in property values and rents
would drive them away or because redevelopment plans called for their
displacement. When the city of Los Angeles determined that Chavez
Ravine would become the home for Dodger Stadium, a magic kingdom for baseball, it had to evict several Hispanic families from the site,
which had originally been acquired for public housing. When Seattle
laid out the grounds for its Century 21 Exposition, it razed housing
occupied largely by the poor. When the municipality of San Jose attempted to renew its downtown area by linking it to new freeways, and
when it annexed adjacent farmlands, it uprooted well-established Mexican-American communities.[84]

Figuratively if not literally, many disadvantaged groups remained on
the fringes of the new urban pattern. Their mental maps of the city

remained underdeveloped, because their social worlds and orbits were highly confined.[85] Whereas middle-class urbanites lived, shopped, worked, and played in relatively new, carefully designed districts, the lower classes tended to concentrate in enclaves of their own, few of which seemed magical. The oldest and poorest urban districts segregated minorities and in many cases rendered them almost invisible to the rest of the population. Discriminatory practices on the part of the majority contributed to this pattern, but both impoverishment and the inclination to live with members of the same social group also helped to create enclaves for minorities.[86]

People of Asian descent generally fared better in the postwar urban West than did Mexican and African Americans. Anglo-Americans did not immediately discard nativist sentiments against Asian Americans after the war, but they ultimately showed greater tolerance, first toward Chinese Americans and then toward Japanese Americans. Western cities retained those inner-city districts known as Chinatowns and Japantowns, but over time they became less residential and more commercial in character. Like whites, many Asian Americans migrated away from city centers and toward suburbs during the 1950s and 1960s. Some continued to cluster together in their new neighborhoods, but their continued segregation was less compulsory than before.[87]

Residential integration was furthest advanced among those groups most strongly rooted in the United States. Among people of Japanese descent, the *sansei* or third-generation members of immigrant families "were more apt to reflect the ambience of their surrounding communities, rather than a strictly ethnic one." Among Chinese Americans, those born and raised in the United States tended by the 1970s "to be college-educated, have middle-class occupations, and live outside of the inner-city Chinatowns." Recently arrived immigrants, by contrast, had less education, dwelled in old, central-city Chinatowns, and worked at ill-paid industrial or service jobs.[88]

A somewhat similar pattern obtained among generations of Mexican descent. In cities of the American Southwest, the proximity of the international border permitted many immigrants, especially more recent ones, to return quite easily to Mexico. Consequently, many perceived little need to adapt to *norteamericano* ways and demonstrated correspondingly little interest in residential integration. Moreover, during the postwar period the steady influx of both legal and illegal aliens sustained Mexican culture in selected urban enclaves. Newcomers, especially, preferred to dwell in these relatively familiar districts where life was "much simpler" than it was when coping with non-Hispanic "strangers . . . full of surprises and unexpected behavior."[89]

Students of these Spanish-speaking enclaves disagreed over their desirability. Some valued them as chosen places where Mexican culture could survive, whereas others regarded them as involuntary impediments to Hispanic "progress" in making accommodations to Anglo-American culture. All agreed, however, that voluntary or not, barrios and *colonias*—particularly those peopled by first-generation immigrants—were highly impoverished. The vast majority of Mexican Americans resided in or near these "cores of poverty" which anchored Hispanic communities in the American West. Only those families who had long been in the United States had a fair chance of escaping this poverty by literally moving away from it.[90]

African Americans in western cities had even fewer chances to move to an even smaller number of desegregated neighborhoods.[91] In southern California the barriers created by restrictive deeds continued to keep blacks out of many neighborhoods long after the U.S. Supreme Court had struck down such covenants. In the early 1960s only 3.1 percent of blacks in Los Angeles lived outside ghetto areas, largely because suburban housing remained unavailable and unaffordable for them.[92] The Watts riots of 1965 publicized this fact. Indeed, rioters who boasted, "We put ourselves on the map," had overcome the invisibility imposed upon them by segregation. Dissatisfaction with ghetto conditions, however, did not always imply a lack of attachment to the African American community, which, after all, was identified with black culture. Like many Mexican Americans, some blacks regretted that their neighborhoods were particularly vulnerable to the dislocations incurred by efforts at urban renewal and school desegregation.[93]

Like Anglo-Americans, many Asian, Mexican, and African Americans regarded the West and its cities as preferred destinations where they could have a better life than they had known elsewhere. And as much as they resented the restrictive and impoverished conditions under which they lived, they professed attachment to their particular urban enclaves, in part because cultural opportunities were offered there that were not available elsewhere. For minorities, too, then, at least to a limited extent, the urban West constituted a voluntary region. But minorities clearly had fewer choices than Anglo-Americans did, and the processes reshaping the western metropolis into a more suburban, multi-centered environment seldom worked to the direct benefit of the older and poorer districts in which they lived.

On the other side of the community, those who bought homes on the newer fringes of western cities tended overwhelmingly to be affluent and well-educated. They could better afford to live close to their workplaces, yet their greater mobility also permitted them to become familiar with far-flung places in the metropolis, if they wished.[94] Moreover, those who lived closest to the new substitutes for downtown, or within planned communities, tended to be sheltered from the problems caused by the recent development. Critics observed that a new subdivision or shopping mall would heighten the problem of sprawl, intensify nearby traffic congestion, or exacerbate deficiencies in the public transit system, but such drawbacks would perhaps seem less troublesome to those fortunate enough to find refuge within the new enclave.[95] The West may have pioneered a new urban shape, but it had hardly removed the inequities that characterized city life.

Although the new cityscape left many problems unattended, it nonetheless became the prevailing pattern in the urban West. Planned communities, urban villages, and alternative downtowns were not simply aberrations in cities; they became dominant aspects of the landscape. And because the reshaping of western cities proceeded gradually and selectively, certain new towns and new downtowns that emerged in bold and sensational fashion assumed tremendous importance for citizens throughout the city and for urban design across the country.

A Sense of Place

Disneyland, Stanford Industrial Park, Sun City, and the Seattle World's Fair exemplified the spatial patterns reshaping western metropolitan areas. Each appeared relatively early in the remaking of the urban West, and each proved particularly influential. The careful design and thematic orientation of these magic kingdoms made them highly legible. Because of their bold and clear meanings, magic lands made a strong imprint on the cityscapes of the region. Furthermore, each landmark embodied the mentality that permeated the culture and shaped the cities of the postwar West. In other words, they helped the urban region live up to the expectations people held for it. The four environments served as what one student of urban America has called "epitome districts," that is, "special places in cities [which] carry huge layers of symbols that have the capacity to pack up emotions, energy, or history into a small space."[96]

Like other new communities and new alternatives to downtown, the carefully controlled environments in Anaheim, Palo Alto, Sun City, and Seattle mitigated some of the problems of explosive growth. They countered the impression of urban chaos by turning inward, away from sprawl. Each was either landscaped or walled off so that outside distractions could not intrude on the more orderly life within. The designers of Silicon Valley industrial parks hoped to shield employees from traffic and urban confusion, just as the builders of the Century 21 Exposition fenced the fairgrounds off from surrounding city blocks. According to the designers, such exclusion helped to distinguish magic kingdoms from their eastern counterparts. Disneyland represented a rejection of Coney Island, and Sun City offered retirees a refuge from the drawbacks of urban life as they had known it in other places. Magic lands confirmed the belief that urban form in the West could improve upon eastern city types.

In western towns where rapid, horizontal growth threatened to erase all common points of reference, magic kingdoms helped to preserve a sense of mastery over the environment by providing landmarks for the cityscape of the eye and the mind. Landmarks not only play a centering role in mental maps but serve as symbols that "offer a quick, shorthand method of characterizing a place."[97] The Space Needle, created for the world's fair, became a point of reference for residents and visitors in Seattle. It was a tall landmark, befitting a city center. The other three, more suburban magic lands—each rising from a more rural setting—were no less influential. Stanford Industrial Park became the downtown center for Silicon Valley. Sun City pioneered the urban village ideal for the Phoenix metropolitan area. And Disneyland, in addition to making Anaheim the first identifiable business district for all of Orange County, became both landmark and symbol for the entire region. "Disneyland is not in Los Angeles. But to millions of people from every country in the world, . . . Disneyland is Los Angeles—or vice versa."[98]

Each magic kingdom became a fixture in an ever-changing scene for an ever-changing population, and each place attracted tourists who identified the special environment as the essence of the surrounding metropolis. As landmarks, tourist attractions, and definitive symbols, magic kingdoms assumed a prominent place on people's mental maps of the urban West. But each was itself also a kind of mental map of the western city. Mental maps, by simplifying the landscape, help individuals to understand it. Thus they strengthen "a sense of meaning and a sense of place."[99] Magic lands performed exactly this function. They eliminated the complexities normally associated with urban settings by minimizing contradictions in land use and function and by incorporating careful planning, thus enabling the mind to "read" special districts quite easily. They shut out the chaos of the larger city by distilling its visual and functional diversity to a few basic images and ideas.[100]

Magic kingdoms tended to oversimplify the social realities of the western city at the same time that they oversimplified its physical nature. Each was tailored to the tastes of a relatively homogeneous segment of the middle and upper classes. Those who visited Disneyland and the Seattle World's Fair were expected to conform to standards already implicit in the design of the setting. And such places as Sun City and Stanford Industrial Park became quite exclusive settings that distanced their occupants from other groups. Residents of the retirement community lived apart from most younger, poorer, and non-white people, just as the mostly male executives, scientists, and office personnel in the high-technology research park isolated themselves from the mostly female, blue-collar employees in Silicon Valley factories.

Whether exclusive or not, magic kingdoms were generally seen as cultural accomplishments for the urban West. They brought a measure of refinement by establishing high standards of design, by facilitating the development of the arts, and by encouraging new forms of entertainment and amusement. Disneyland, Stanford Industrial Park, Sun City, and the Seattle Center each received acclaim for its architecture, landscaping, and concern for aesthetics. The Seattle World's Fair added cultural facilities to the city, which ultimately introduced to Seattle new kinds of performing arts as well as major-league sports. Sun City nurtured education, recreation, and artistic endeavors among its retired population. Stanford Industrial Park demonstrated that industrial architecture and landscaping could be elegant, in keeping with a campus setting, and then proceeded to incorporate the fine arts into its designs. Disneyland imported to Orange County the kind of entertainment normally associated with Hollywood and enabled Anaheim to attract big-league sports and conventions.

Every magic land attracted respectful attention to its metropolitan area from across the nation and the globe. By becoming places to see, providing things to do, and offering a source of pride, they sharpened the urban identity of a rather mobile population. They helped a region accustomed to striving for cultural refinement to feel that it was not only drawing even with other American cities but also making significant contributions to the civilization. Such a sense of accomplishment was essential in places where people explained their presence by saying that they had come to fashion a style of life that improved upon the ones available back East.

Magic kingdoms upheld the promise of a better life in the urban West. Their builders and operators insisted on high-quality design, workmanship, maintenance, and service, arguing that a better environment would not only generate more business but also elicit better behavior and citizenship from people inside the district. Disneyland aimed to make its customers happier and better-adjusted; Stanford Industrial Park helped companies to recruit and retain more efficient and highly trained workers; Sun City, according to its promoters as well as its inhabitants, attracted a more desirable type of retiree than could be found elsewhere; and the futuristic and scientific displays at Century 21 Exposition offered to fairgoers not only entertainment but also edification and inspiration. In a sense, magic kingdoms replicated for middle-class Westerners the efforts of the nineteenth-century landscape architect Frederick Law Olmsted, who had argued that New York's Central Park exercised "a distinctly harmonizing and refining influence upon the most unfortunate and lawless classes of the city—an influence favorable to courtesy, self-control, and temperance."[101]

Like the nineteenth-century park, magic lands attempted to bring forth people's "better nature in their communion with nature."[102] Each belonged to a metropolitan area where the population prized the surrounding climate and physical setting, and each represented an attempt by designers and users to take maximum advantage of the opportunities afforded by the western environment. At the same time, these twentieth-century cityscapes attempted to excel nature through space-age technology. Sun City required air-conditioning and irrigation to conquer the desert; the Seattle World's Fair promised that Americans would master urban space and outer space through scientific and mechanical innovations; Disneyland used cinematic engineering to replace vegetation, animals, and people with artificial substitutes. Only Stanford Industrial Park adhered to the example of Central Park in its use of natural-looking landscaping, as was fitting for an extension of a nineteenth-century campus laid out with Olmsted's assistance. Yet, ironically, the research-oriented firms at Stanford produced the highest technology of all. The industrial park epitomized the urban West's blend of prized amenities—natural as well as cultural—with technological advances devoted to mastering the environment.

In part, magic lands succeeded in creating a stronger sense of cohesion in western cities, and in providing a feeling of cultural and social achievement, because they were designed according to an explicit theme or concept that was appropriate to the midcentury urban West. Each theme had an economic underpinning—aerospace for Seattle, retirement for Phoenix, ordnance and electronics for Silicon Valley, movies and aerospace for Southern California, and tourism throughout the region. By honoring the economic orientations of its urban area, each magic land paid homage to the sources of that rapid growth which had permitted so many people to relocate and reside in the urban West.

But the themes that guided the design and operation of magic kingdoms suggested much more than economic expansion. Disneyland and Sun City celebrated Americans' apparently increasing leisure time as well as the rising affluence that allowed them to enjoy it. Stanford Industrial Park and the Seattle World's Fair, by demonstrating the benevolent force of science in modern life, promised heightened mastery over nature and the city. The thematic messages of every magic kingdom spoke to Americans' cold war against communism, as well as to the influence of that rivalry upon the region. Each carefully controlled environment benefited in some fashion from the regional growth that had been stimulated by wartime mobilization. Moreover, with the exception of Sun City, each was strongly identified with the new technologies—computers, jets, missiles, spaceships—that federal investments in defense and space were promoting in their respective metropolitan areas.

The futuristic material culture pioneered in the West included much more than cityscapes. Magic kingdoms implied that the urban West constituted not only a frontier of continuing migration but also a frontier of the twenty-first century. They celebrated cultural orientations which permeated all of postwar American civilization, but which were exaggerated in the West. Confidence about the future had inspired many individuals' migration to the region in the first place; continued economic and demographic expansion in the West perpetuated that confidence during the postwar period.

In the years after the mid-1960s, the optimism that had underwritten the establishment of magic lands diminished. Growing doubts about the future represented another nationwide trend that took on a distinctive cast in the West. Residents of the newly expanded cities came to worry especially about the social and environmental costs of prolonged, intense growth. They discovered that, in a sense, the East was catching up with them. Events such as the Watts riots dramatized the fact that rapid expansion had directed resources and people primarily to the fringes of urban areas, draining central-city neighborhoods of their vitality and heightening the problems of minorities and the poor.[103] Awareness of social problems mounted throughout the West. In Phoenix, blacks and Chicanos rose up in protest during the late 1960s; observers of San Jose characterized the plight of Mexican Americans there as a far more serious problem than urban sprawl; and citizens of Seattle suffered economic hardship when the region's largest employer, Boeing, endured a steep business downturn.[104] The social problems typically associated with eastern cities had never lagged too far behind westering migrants, and beginning in the later 1960s they steadily became a more recognized fixture in the region.

As the urban West became reacquainted with economic and minority tensions, it also grew anxious about environmental matters. Air and water pollution were only two symptoms of the much larger problems created by too many people and too much development. Having migrated westward in pursuit of economic opportunity as well as environmental amenities, many residents came to doubt whether they could achieve the two goals in company with so many like-minded others. It became steadily clearer that two of the urban region's distinguishing traits, its rapid growth and appealing environment, were to a significant extent mutually exclusive. As more people migrated to western cities, they seemed to diminish those features that had made the region such a desirable destination. Few Westerners yet believed that their cities' problems rivaled the crisis of the urban Northeast, but some felt sure that day was coming. In 1977 Walter Doty, former editor of *Sunset, the Magazine of Western Living*, eloquently attested to the situation. He recalled toiling for years to attract tourists to the region, confident that one out of every ten visitors would return as a resident. "We didn't know then," he explained, "that man destroys what he's after by his coming."[105]

Social, economic, and environmental concerns forced Westerners to reconsider their assumptions of the inevitability and desirability of economic and demographic expansion. As the political changes after 1965 suggested, residents across the region increasingly came to agree that unbridled expansion could not go on forever. Yet, throughout the region, proposed solutions to social and environmental problems demonstrated a continuing commitment to the low-slung, multi-centered form so characteristic of the western metropolis. They also demonstrated continuing faith in some sort of magic kingdom as one key to perpetuating the good life of western cities.

Proponents of "controlled" or "managed" growth gained influence during the later 1960s and early 1970s, particularly in San Jose and Seattle. As citizens turned away from the pro-growth leadership that had dominated postwar municipal politics, demanding that further expansion must provide a net benefit for the community rather than offering simply growth for growth's sake, they did not press for a return to a more traditional urban form. Rather, they called for more attention to urban neighborhoods and outlying districts, while demonstrating less interest in the central business districts that were supposedly serving the entire city. Quality-of-life issues revolved at least as much around smaller districts as they did around the metropolitan area as a whole.[106] Throughout the West, residents were trying to create magic kingdoms of their own in order to protect whatever amenity-rich environment remained, as well as to reconceive the swollen metropolis on a more comprehensible scale. The approach focused little attention on regional or citywide problems, but it did address more directly urbanites' desire that the city remain manageable, at least in their minds.

Versions of the magic kingdom were proposed as a response to the plights of the impoverished and minorities, but such proposals proved to have little to offer to the disadvantaged. Numerous urban experts, along with the state of California and the U.S. Congress, regarded subsidized planned communities as potential solutions to urban social malaise. Between 1966 and 1975, the federal government offered financial assistance to planned communities, provided that they included specific aid for inner-city populations, but the program offered no meaningful answer to the blight of urban centers. For the most part, the new planned community remained an enclave for the haves rather than the have-nots.[107]

Similarly, the magic-kingdom model did not reduce the overall environmental problems faced by cities; in fact, carefully planned environments tended to increase traffic, consume open space, and perpetuate urban sprawl. Furthermore, the orientation of some planned communities to specific class, interest, and age groups—well-to-do homebuyers, retirees, singles, students—not only failed "to bring real cohesion" but also may have accentuated problems by reinforcing urban social divisions.[108] Westerners who had spent their lives in environments designed to insulate them from urban chaos could sometimes lose touch both with the problems of their fellow residents and with realistic solutions to those problems.

Magic lands were not designed for an era of contraction and limits. Rather, they emerged in a milieu of growth and confidence that was unique to the postwar urban West. They could not overcome the social and ecological problems of the larger city, yet they experienced remarkable success as smaller environments that seemed to reduce the complexities and uncertainties presented by the larger setting. Magic lands became pivotal fixtures on the western scene by serving to bring a sense of order, community, and refinement to a highly fluid society. They made the western city a more coherent and therefore a more livable place. Their success helps to explain why streams of migrants so willingly accepted metropolitan areas reputed to be disorganized and anomic.

Magic lands suggested new ways to organize urban space and, implicitly if not explicitly, new ways to organize people within those spaces. They also helped to legitimate the efforts of such people as moviemakers, amusement-park operators, shopping-mall builders, housing developers, and university officials to plan and to alter the cityscape. Disneyland, Sun City, Stanford Industrial Park, and the Seattle World's Fair were studied and imitated around the country and around the world, thus enlarging the influence of the twentieth-century American West.

Yet the proliferation of magic kingdoms was not universally welcomed. Some argued that they contributed to an increasing "placelessness" in the culture by supplanting distinctive and organic environments with "inauthentic" or contrived settings.[109] There was doubtless some accuracy in this charge, since magic kingdoms had been taken out of the context of the postwar western city and transplanted to other times and places. By removing magic kingdoms from the distinctive circumstances and attitudes that had helped to create regional innovations in cityscapes, developers perhaps reduced them to formulas designed more for commercial and institutional benefit than for maintaining integrity of place.

That the theme park or retirement community could heighten the phenomenon of placelessness seems paradoxical, because the creation of such environments had actually helped to strengthen the sense of place in the urban West during the mid-twentieth century. And it remains unclear whether magic lands lost all their effectiveness when they were transplanted across time and space. Like most well-designed settings, they worked in more than one context, in large part because their consistent, predictable form enhanced people's sense of mastery over their surroundings. For most users, experiencing magic kingdoms was less a matter of the authentic versus the inauthentic than one of making interaction with the built environment—and hence with the larger culture—less "difficult and demanding."[110] And the West was not so different from the American cultural mainstream that its solutions to urban chaos seemed strange or alien outside the region.

Some observers had expressed alarm at the apparent disorder in western urban sprawl, seeing both the cities and their society as in some sense fragmented. In fact, however, the order of the western metropolis resided precisely in its fragments, and it was those fragments of the city that other Americans attempted to incorporate into their own towns. Few people may have wanted their community to become another Los Angeles, but most did not seem to mind having something like another Disneyland in their midst.

List of Abbreviations

Collections

AHR-APL	Anaheim History Room, Anaheim Public Library Anaheim, California
DP-UWL	Ewen C. Dingwall Papers, Suzzallo Library University of Washington, Seattle
HEH	Henry E. Huntington Library San Marino, California
IGSL	Institute of Governmental Studies Library University of California, Berkeley
PPL-AR	Arizona Room, Phoenix Public Library Phoenix, Arizona
PPL-RCCF	Retirement Communities Clippings File
PPL-SCCF	Sun City Clippings File
PPL-YCF	Youngtown Clippings File
PSC	Pacific Studies Center Mountain View, California
SCAHS	Sun Cities Area Historical Society Sun City, Arizona
SUA	Stanford University Archives, Green Library Stanford, California
SUNP	Stanford University News and Publications Stanford, California
SWFP	Papers of the Seattle World's Fair Washington State Archives, Bellingham

TBL   The Bancroft Library
       University of California, Berkeley
WDA   Walt Disney Archives, Walt Disney Studios
       Burbank, California

Publications

AB   *Anaheim Bulletin*
AR   *Arizona Republic* (Phoenix)
LAT   *Los Angeles Times*
NS   *News-Sun* (Sun City)
NYT   *New York Times*
OCR   *Register* (Orange County)
OGB   *Official Guide Book, Seattle World's Fair 1962*
PG   *Phoenix Gazette*
P-I   *Seattle Post-Intelligencer*
SAR   *Register* (Santa Ana)
SCRC Southern California Research Council (author)
SCTA Sun City Taxpayers Association, Inc. (author)
SOM   Skidmore, Owings, and Merrill (author)
ST   *Seattle Times*
SUACLBD Stanford University Advisory Committee on Land and
         Building Development (author)
ULI   Urban Land Institute (author)
WDP   Walt Disney Productions (publisher)

Notes

Introduction

1. On cities and historians' conceptions of the West, see John M. Findlay, "Far Western Cityscapes and American Culture Since 1940," *Western Historical Quarterly* 22 (Feb. 1991): 19–23. Quotation from Henry Nash Smith, *Virgin Land: The American West as Symbol and Myth* (reprint ed. Cambridge, Mass., 1978), xi.

2. John Hench, interview by Richard Hubler, Dick Irvine, and Marty Sklar, Sept. 24, 1968, transcript, WDA, 5.

3. Frederick E. Terman, "Stanford, Palo Alto Have Created Community of Technical Scholars," *Stanford Observer* (Feb. 1967): D.

4. One reporter concluded that the Seattle Center ranked as the nation's "fourth most popular cultural and tourist attraction," after Walt Disney World, Disneyland, and San Francisco's Pier 39: *ST*, May 27, 1990.

5. John M. Findlay, "Suckers and Escapists? Interpreting Las Vegas and Post-war America," *Nevada Historical Society Quarterly* 33 (Spring 1990): 1–15. Walter McDougall, . . . *the Heavens and the Earth: A Political History of the Space Age* (New York, 1985), explores the "radical" implications of postwar technocracy by examining the cultural and ideological changes caused almost inadvertently by Americans' "conservative" reaction to *Sputnik*. On landscape changes of the 1950s, see Kenneth I. Helphand, "McUrbia: The 1950s and the Birth of the Contemporary American Landscape," *Places: A Quarterly Journal of Environmental Design* 5: 2 (1988): 40–49.

6. Kenneth T. Jackson, *Crabgrass Frontier: The Suburbanization of the United States* (New York, 1985), chs. 13–15; Murray Bookchin, "Toward a Vision of the Urban Future," in David C. Perry and Alfred J. Watkins, eds., *The Rise of Sunbelt Cities* (Beverly Hills, 1977), 259–76.

7: David C. Perry and Alfred J. Watkins, "Introduction," in Perry and Watkins, eds., *Rise of the Sunbelt Cities*, 8–9; Jack Meltzer, *Metropolis to Metroplex: The Social and Spatial Planning of Cities* (Baltimore, 1984), 1–2, 14–19.

8. Carl Abbott, "Southwestern Cityscapes: Approaches to an American Urban Environment," in Robert B. Fairbanks and Kathleen Underwood, eds., *Essays on Sunbelt Cities and Recent Urban America* (College Station, Tex., 1990), 77.

9. Peter Orleans, "Differential Cognition of Urban Residents: Effects of Social Scale on Mapping," in Roger M. Downs and David Stea, eds., *Image and Environment: Cognitive Mapping and Spatial Behavior* (Chicago, 1973), 129.

10. D. J. Walmsley, *Urban Living: The Individual in the City* (Essex, Eng., 1988), ix, 3.

11. Amos Rapoport, *The Meaning of the Built Environment: A Nonverbal Communication Approach* (Beverly Hills, 1982), especially 15–21.

12. Roger M. Downs and David Stea, *Maps in Minds: Reflections on Cognitive Mapping* (New York, 1977).

13. On Greater California, see Carl Abbott, "The Metropolitan Region: Western Cities in the New Urban Era," in Gerald D. Nash and Richard W. Etulain, eds., *The Twentieth-Century West: Historical Interpretations* (Albuquerque, 1989), 80–81. On Las Vegas, see John M. Findlay, *People of Chance: Gambling in American Society from Jamestown to Las Vegas* (New York, 1986), chs. 4–6; Eugene P. Moehring, *Resort City in the Sunbelt: Las Vegas, 1930–1970* (Reno, 1989). Neil J. Sullivan, *The Dodgers Move West* (New York, 1987), covers Dodger Stadium. One good work on southern California freeways is David Brodsly, *L.A. Freeway: An Appreciative Essay* (Berkeley, 1981). Study of the San Diego Zoo might begin with Helen Lefkowitz Horowitz, "Seeing Ourselves Through the Bars: A Historical Tour of American Zoos," *Landscape* 25: 2 (1981): 17.

Chapter One

1. Michael P. Malone and Richard W. Etulain, *The American West: A Twentieth-Century History* (Lincoln, Neb., 1989), chs. 1, 3; Robert G. Athearn, *The Mythic West in Twentieth-Century America* (Lawrence, Kans., 1986), chs. 5–6.

2. Walter Prescott Webb, *Divided We Stand: The Crisis of a Frontierless Democracy* (New York, 1937), 157–58, 12, 221.

3. On New Deal policies in the West, see Richard Lowitt, *The New Deal and the West* (Bloomington, Ind., 1984). Donald J. Bogue, *The Population of the United States* (Glencoe, Ill., 1959), 391–96, summarizes interstate migration between 1935 and 1940. In *The American West Transformed: The Impact of the Second World War* (Bloomington, Ind., 1985) and *World War II and the West: Reshaping the Economy* (Lincoln, Neb., 1990), Gerald D. Nash depicts the war's effect on the region.

4. D. W. Meinig, "American Wests: Preface to a Geographical Interpretation," *Annals of the Association of American Geographers* 62 (June 1972): 159–84.

5. Carl Abbott, *The New Urban America: Growth and Politics in Sunbelt Cities* (Chapel Hill, 1981), especially 26–32, depicts the rise of Sunbelt cities and distinguishes between Sunbelt South and Sunbelt West. On how southern urbanization differed from that elsewhere, consult David R. Goldfield, *Cotton Fields and Skyscrapers: Southern City and Region, 1607–1980* (Baton Rouge, La., 1982); Blaine A. Brownell, "The Idea of the City in the American South," in Derek Fraser and Anthony Sutcliffe, eds., *The Pursuit of Urban History* (London, 1983), 138–50.

6. Cited in Neal R. Peirce, *The Pacific States of America: People, Politics, and Power in the Five Pacific Basin States* (New York, 1972), 24.

7. Anna Louise Strong, *My Native Land* (New York, 1940), 53.

8. Abbott, *New Urban America*, 28–29, summarizes these figures. Like him, I use the Standard Metropolitan Statistical Area, or "metropolitan area," as the primary unit for measuring population growth, unless otherwise specified.

9. Security First National Bank Research Department, "Cities Showing the Largest Numerical Gains in Population Between the 1950 Census and the 1960 Census," Aug. 29, 1960, Box 5, Fletcher Bowron Collection, HEH; Phoenix, Arizona, City Planning Department, *The Comprehensive Plan, 1990, Phoenix, Arizona* (Phoenix, 1969), 41; U.S. Bureau of the Census, *County and City Data Book, 1962* (Washington, D.C., 1962), 432–48; U.S. Bureau of the Census, *County and City Data Book, 1972* (Washington, D.C., 1973), 548–72; U.S. Bureau of the Census, *Historical Statistics of the United States, Colonial Times to 1970*, Part I (Washington, D.C., 1975), 22; Eric H. Monkkonen, *America Becomes Urban: The Development of U.S. Cities & Towns 1780–1980* (Berkeley, 1988), 85–86.

10. John Frederick Keller, "The Production Worker in Electronics: Industrialization and Labor Development in California's Santa Clara Valley," Ph.D. diss., University of Michigan, 1981, 54; Ann R. Markusen and Robin Bloch, "Defensive Cities: High Technology, Military Spending and Human Settlements," in Manuel Castells, ed., *Technology, Space, and Society: Emerging Trends* (Beverly Hills, 1984), 106–20; State of California, *Aerospace Employment, California and Metropolitan Areas, 1949–1969* (Sacramento, 1970), 1–3.

11. Carey McWilliams, *Southern California: An Island on the Land* (1946; reprint, Santa Barbara, 1979), 371–73; Carey McWilliams, *California: The Great Exception* (New York, 1949), 233; Anthony Netboy, "California's Top Problem," *Frontier* 3 (July 1952): 8–9.

12. Phoenix, Arizona, City Planning Department, *Comprehensive Plan, 1990*, 12; Bradford Luckingham, "Phoenix: The Desert Metropolis," in Richard M. Bernard and Bradley R. Rice, eds., *Sunbelt Cities: Politics and Growth Since World War II* (Austin, Tex., 1983), 310; Roger Sale, *Seattle, Past to Present* (rev. ed. Seattle, 1978), ch. 6.

13. On the impact of World War II and later defense programs on California's economy and cities, see Ted K. Bradshaw, "Trying Out the Future," *Wilson*

Quarterly 4 (Summer 1980): 66–82; James L. Clayton, "Defense Spending: Key to California's Growth," *Western Political Quarterly* 15 (June 1962): 280–93; Donald L. Foley et al., *Characteristics of Metropolitan Growth in California*, vol. I, *Report* (Berkeley, 1965), 31–33; Howard F. Gregor, "Spatial Disharmonies in California Population Growth," *Geographical Review* 53 (Jan. 1963): 103, 110.

14. Ann Markusen, "Military Spending and Urban Development in California" (1984 MS, PSC), 2; Bradshaw, "Trying Out the Future"; Center for Continuing Study of the California Economy, press release, Sept. 23, 1981, SUNP; SCRC, *Migration and the Southern California Economy* (Los Angeles, 1964), 24.

15. Walton Bean, *California: An Interpretive History* (3d ed. New York, 1978), xvii (emphasis in original).

16. Cited in Walter A. McDougall, . . . *the Heavens and the Earth: A Political History of the Space Age* (New York, 1985), 401–2.

17. D. B. Luten, "The Dynamics of Repulsion," in Carey McWilliams, ed., *The California Revolution* (New York, 1968), 17; Stewart H. Holbrook, *The Wonderful West* (Garden City, N.Y., 1963), 42.

18. Cecil B. deMille quoted in John Anson Ford, "Intermittent Diary," vol. 3, Oct. 4, 1955, John Anson Ford Collection, HEH; D. W. Meinig, "The Continuous Shaping of America: A Prospectus for Geographers and Historians," *American Historical Review* 83 (Dec. 1978): 1200.

19. Neutra's remark cited by Thomas S. Hines, *Richard Neutra and the Search for Modern Architecture: A Biography and History* (New York, 1982), 78.

20. Salisbury cited in Jack Smith, "Libels and Labels on the Protean City . . . One Man's Riposte," *California History* 60 (Spring 1981): 98–107.

21. Daniel J. Alesch and Robert A. Levine, *Growth in San Jose: A Summary Policy Statement* (Santa Monica, 1973), 11–12, 26; Richard E. Preston, "Urban Development in Southern California Between 1940 and 1965," in Robert W. Durrenberger, ed., *California: Its People, Its Problems, Its Prospects* (Palo Alto, 1971), 100; Charles S. Sargent, "Arizona's Urban Frontier—Myths and Realities," in Charles S. Sargent, ed., *The Conflict Between Frontier Values and Land-Use Control in Greater Phoenix: Report of a Conference Held at Arizona State University, November 22, 1975* (Phoenix, 1976), 21; Robert Fishman, "The Post-War American Suburb: A New Form, a New City," in Daniel Schaffer, ed., *Two Centuries of American Planning* (London, 1988), 270–72.

22. James Q. Wilson, "A Guide to Reagan Country: The Political Culture of Southern California," *Commentary* 43 (May 1967): 42–43; Roger W. Lotchin, "The City and the Sword through the Ages and the Era of the Cold War," in Robert B. Fairbanks and Kathleen Underwood, eds., *Essays on Sunbelt Cities and Recent Urban America* (College Station, Tex., 1990), 87–124.

23. Abbott, *New Urban America*, ch. 5; Robert Stapp, "Denver: A City Wakes Up," *Frontier* 1 (Dec. 15, 1949): 5–7.

24. Karl Belser, "The Making of Slurban America," *Cry California* 5 (Fall 1970): 5; George Starbird, *The New Metropolis: San Jose Between 1942 and 1972* (San Jose, 1972), 1–2; Richard Reinhardt, "Joe Ridder's San Jose," *San Francisco Magazine* 7 (Nov. 1965): 70.

25. Michael F. Konig, "Toward Metropolitan Status: Charter Government and the Rise of Phoenix, Arizona, 1945–1960," Ph.D. diss., Arizona State University, 1983; John D. Wenum, *Annexation as a Technique for Metropolitan Growth: The Case of Phoenix, Arizona* (Tempe, Ariz., 1970), 64, 72.

26. Philip J. Trounstine and Terry Christensen, *Movers and Shakers: The Study of Community Power* (New York, 1982), 10–12, 87–89, 91–92; Ford, "Intermittent Diary," vol. 1, Sept. 8–24, 1950.

27. Reinhardt, "Joe Ridder's San Jose," 66–71.

28. Richard Bigger et al., *Metropolitan Coast: San Diego and Orange Counties, California* (Los Angeles, 1958), 94; McWilliams, *California: The Great Exception*, 347–52; Michael W. Straub, "Water for California," *Frontier* 1 (Jan. 1, 1950): 3–4; Vernon Kilpatrick, "Southern California's Struggle for Water," *Frontier* 7 (March 1956): 7–9.

Christopher Rand, *Los Angeles, The Ultimate City* (New York, 1967), ch. 2, illuminates Southern California's confidence in technology, and McDougall, *Heavens and the Earth*, 400–402, explains how the success of the American space program encouraged confidence that, just as it could win the race to the moon, government-sponsored technology could solve western water problems.

29. Population Reference Bureau, Inc., "California: After 19 Million, What?" *Population Bulletin* 22 (June 1966): 29, 33; Ralph Friedman, "Booming California," *Frontier* 8 (April 1957): 10–11; James A. Barnes, "Sprawl, Density and the Sensible Use of Land," paper delivered to the League of California Cities, 66th Annual Conference, Los Angeles, Oct. 14, 1964, IGSL, 2.

30. City of Los Angeles, Department of City Planning, *City Planning in Los Angeles: A History* (Los Angeles, 1964), 33, 51; John Anson Ford, *Thirty Explosive Years in Los Angeles County* (San Marino, 1961), 51.

31. McWilliams, *California: The Great Exception*, 21; Ford, "Intermittent Diary," vol. 6, April 27, 1964.

32. Catherine Bauer [Wurster], "Social Effects of Decentralization," in *Problems of Decentralization in Metropolitan Areas: Proceedings of the First Annual University of California Conference on City and Regional Planning* (Berkeley, 1954), 41; Peter A. Morrison, "The Role of Migration in California's Growth," in Kingsley Davis and Frederick G. Styles, eds., *California's Twenty Million: Research Contributions to Population Policy*, Population Monograph Series No. 10 (Berkeley, 1971), 33–34; Edward L. Ullman, "Amenities as a Factor in Regional Growth," *Geographical Review* 44 (Jan. 1954): 119–32; Robert M. Fogelson, *The Fragmented Metropolis: Los Angeles, 1850–1930* (Cambridge, Mass., 1967), 70–75.

33. On Santa Clara County, see Santa Clara County Planning Department, "Components of Yearly Population Increase, 1950–1976, Santa Clara County," *Info*, no. 576 (July 1976): 1–2; San Jose, California, City Planning Commission, *Master Plan of the City* (San Jose, 1958), 33. For state trends, consult Leo Grebler, *Metropolitan Contrasts*, Part 1 of University of California, Los Angeles, Real Estate Research Program, *Profile of the Los Angeles Metropolis: Its People and Its Homes* (Berkeley, 1963), 7; Morrison, "Role of Migration in California's Growth," 38–39, 48–49; Foley et al., *Characteristics of Metropolitan Growth in California*, 27, 43. See Daniel W. Raaf, "Characteristics of a Sample

of Adult Males of Metropolitan Phoenix," *Arizona Business and Economic Review* 8 (June 1959): 4–5, on Phoenix.

34. Warren L. Steinberg, "Opportunity for Los Angeles," *Frontier* 16 (Jan. 1965): 15.

35. Nash, *American West Transformed*, 107; Martin Hall, "Roybal's Candidacy and What It Means," *Frontier* 5 (June 1954): 5; Leo Grebler et al., *The Mexican-American People: The Nation's Second Largest Minority* (New York, 1970), 605–8. These rough estimates of people of Mexican descent were rendered even less exact because the people being counted—"Spanish-speaking," "Spanish-origin," "Hispanic," "Mexican American"—varied from one tabulation to the next. Here I rely on the various categories used by the cited sources.

36. Grebler et al., *Mexican-American People*, 8, 16, 28, 53, ch. 13.

37. Nash, *American West Transformed*, 89; Robert M. Fogelson, ed. and comp., *The Los Angeles Riots* (New York, 1969), 3.

38. Quotation from George W. Pierson, *The Moving American* (New York, 1973), 191. Bogue, *Population of the United States*, 347, 381, and Bernard L. Weinstein and Robert E. Firestine, *Regional Growth and Decline in the United States: The Rise of the Sunbelt and the Decline of the Northeast* (New York, 1978), 69–70, attest to the higher level of education for migrants in general and Westerners in particular. Julie DaVanzo, *U.S. Internal Migration: Who Moves and Why?* (Santa Monica, 1978), iii, 1–2, depicts the national trend. On African Americans, Mexican Americans, and veterans, see: Quintard Taylor, "Blacks in the American West: An Overview," *Western Journal of Black Studies* 1 (March 1977): 7–8; Grebler et al., *Mexican-American People*, 72; McWilliams, *California: The Great Exception*, 23.

39. Professor cited in McWilliams, *California: The Great Exception*, 226; Robert V. Tishman, "Los Angeles Market: A Good Bet, with Maximum Opportunities," *Markets of America* 28 (1964): unpaginated, Box 60, Bowron Collection.

40. Preston, "Urban Development in Southern California," 99; Security First National Bank, Research Department, "New Subdivisions Recorded in Los Angeles County," Jan. 22, 1962, Box 60, Bowron Collection; Bogue, *Population of the United States*, 726, 733, 735; Foley et al., *Characteristics of Metropolitan Growth in California*, 166–68, 177–87; Gregor, "Spatial Disharmonies in California Population Growth," 117; Bruce Bliven, "The California Culture," *Harper's* 210 (Jan. 1955): 36.

41. Bigger et al., *Metropolitan Coast*, 4–5, 83, 85.

42. The quotation comes from Arthur James McFadden, "Recollections," typescript of an oral history conducted in 1963 by Donald J. Shippers, Oral History Program, University of California, Los Angeles, 1965, 55. The information in the following paragraphs comes from Peter O. Muller, *Contemporary Suburban America* (Englewood Cliffs, N.J., 1981), 11–13; George F. Will, "'Slow Growth' Is the Liberalism of the Privileged," *LAT*, Aug. 30, 1987; United California Bank, Research & Planning Division, *Orange County: Past—Present—1985* (Los Angeles, 1975), 3, 9–10, 16–18, 27; Leland S. Burns and Alvin J. Harman, *The Complex Metropolis*, Part 6 of University of California, Los Angeles, Housing, Real Estate, and Urban Land Studies Program, *Profile*

of the Los Angeles Metropolis: Its People and Its Homes (Berkeley, 1968), 1; Ralph Story, script no. 131, Dec. 4, 1966, 22, in collection of scripts for the television show "Ralph Story's Los Angeles," 1964–69, KNXT-TV, Los Angeles, in Special Collections Department, University of California, Los Angeles; Sheldon Zalaznick, "The Double Life of Orange County," *Fortune* 78 (Oct. 1968): 138–41, 184–88.

43. Jan Morris, "Los Angeles: The Know-How City" (1976), reprinted in *Destinations: Essays from "Rolling Stone"* (New York, 1980), 81–100; quotations from Karl A. Lamb, *As Orange Goes: Twelve California Families and the Future of American Politics* (New York, 1974), 18–19.

44. "More Than a Suburb, Less Than a City," *Business Week* (Sept. 5, 1977): 76–77; Zalaznick, "Double Life of Orange County," 139.

45. Data for urban California, as usual, are not only most readily available but also most striking: Kingsley Davis and Eleanor Langlois, *Future Demographic Growth of the San Francisco Bay Area* (Berkeley, 1963), 9–13; Samuel E. Wood and Alfred E. Heller, *The Phantom Cities of California* (Sacramento, 1963), 14; Foley et al., *Characteristics of Metropolitan Growth in California*, 9, 11, 200; Staff of the University of Southern California, Department of Sociology and Anthropology, Population Research Laboratory, "California's Urban Population: Patterns and Trends," in Davis and Styles, eds., *California's Twenty Million*, 272–73, 276, 277.

46. Wenum, *Annexation as a Technique for Metropolitan Growth*, xi; Konig, "Toward Metropolitan Status," 83, 337; Stanford Environmental Law Society, *San Jose, Sprawling City: A Report on Land Use Policies and Practices in San Jose, California* (Stanford, 1971), 6.

47. Commonwealth Club of California, Research Advisory Council, *The Population of California* (San Francisco, 1946), 87; Arizona State Employment Service, *The Northwestern–Sun City Sector of the Phoenix Area: A Labor Market Analysis* (Phoenix, 1960), 17; U.S. Bureau of the Census, *U.S. Census of Population: 1960. Subject Reports. Mobility for Metropolitan Areas*, Final Report PC(2)–2C (Washington, D.C., 1963), 33, 35, 37, 39; David A. Bingham, "Urban Planning in Arizona," *Arizona Review of Business and Public Administration* 10 (July 1961): 3; *Inside Phoenix: Update 1980* (Phoenix, 1980), 3.

48. McWilliams, *California: The Great Exception*, 244; quotation cited in John McPhee, *The Control of Nature* (New York, 1989), 241. Richard G. Lillard, *Eden in Jeopardy: Man's Prodigal Meddling with His Environment—The Southern California Experience* (New York, 1966), also addresses the fate of rural areas.

49. Foley et al., *Characteristics of Metropolitan Growth in California*, 127–32, 134, 139–43; Grebler, *Metropolitan Contrasts*, 28–29. For a perceptive comparison of this low-slung southwestern cityscape with eastern counterparts, see Carl Abbott, "Southwestern Cityscapes: Approaches to an American Urban Environment," in Fairbanks and Underwood, eds., *Essays on Sunbelt Cities and Recent Urban America*, 68–74.

50. Daniel Boorstin, *The Americans: The Democratic Experience* (New York, 1974), 269; Philip Hamburger, "Notes for a Gazetteer: XLI—San Jose, Calif.," *New Yorker* 39 (May 4, 1963), 148–54.

51. James E. Vance, Jr., *Geography and Urban Evolution in the San Francisco Bay Area* (Berkeley, 1964), 44–47, 65–66; Remi Nadeau, *California: The New Society* (New York, 1963), 18–19.

52. U.S. Bureau of the Census, *U.S. Census of Population: 1960*. Vol. 1: *Characteristics of the Population*. Part 49: *Washington* (Washington, D.C., 1963), 10, 17.

53. Wenum, *Annexation as a Technique for Metropolitan Growth*, v; Bradford Luckingham, *Phoenix: The History of a Southwestern Metropolis* (Tucson, 1989), 161–62, 194; Bigger et al., *Metropolitan Coast*, 89.

54. *San Jose: Design for Tomorrow* (San Jose, 1960), plate 2; Stanford Environmental Law Society, *San Jose, Sprawling City*, 6.

55. *San Jose Shapes Its Future: A Program Proposed to the Citizens of San Jose by the City Manager, City Council and the Citizens 1957 Bond Improvement Committee* (San Jose, 1957), 3; San Jose, California, City Planning Commission, *Planning San Jose: Master Plan of the City of San Jose, California, January 1958* (San Jose, 1958), 17, 18 (quotation); *San Jose: Design for Tomorrow*, plate 20; Reinhardt, "Joe Ridder's San Jose," 68, 70; Connerly and Associates, Inc., "Urban Infill Development in Northern California: Case Studies and Recommendations," 1980 MS, IGSL, 15; Trounstine and Christensen, *Movers and Shakers*, 97; Francis G. Lindsay, "The Assembly Committee on Conservation, Planning, and Public Works Sets a Course Towards Local, Regional, and State Planning," typescript of oral history conducted in 1981 by Malca Chall, in "Statewide and Regional Land-Use Planning in California, 1950–1980 Project," vol. 1, Regional Oral History Office, TBL, 1983, 71–72; Karl Belser, "Urban Dispersal in Perspective," in Ernest A. Engelbert, ed., *The Nature and Control of Urban Dispersal* (Berkeley, 1960), 3–4.

56. *San Jose: Design for Tomorrow*, 2; A. P. Hamann, "[Question of annexation laws]," paper delivered to California League of Municipalities, Oct. 30, 1956, IGSL; Starbird, *New Metropolis*, 2–3, 4, 6–7 (quotation at 2).

57. Changing land uses in the San Jose area are noted by: Yvonne Jacobson, *Passing Farms, Enduring Values: California's Santa Clara Valley* (Los Altos, Calif., 1984); Ernesto Galarza, "Mexicans in the Southwest: A Culture in Process," in Edward H. Spicer and Raymond H. Thompson, eds., *Plural Society in the Southwest* (New York, 1972), 280–82; Karl Belser, "The Conservation of Agricultural Land," May 3, 1955, MS in Carton 7, Catherine Bauer Wurster Papers, TBL, 6; Paul F. Griffin and Ronald L. Chatham, "Urban Impact on Agriculture in Santa Clara County, California," *Annals of the Association of American Geographers* 48 (Sept. 1958): 195–208; Santa Clara County, California, Planning Department, *Land Use Issues in Santa Clara County* (San Jose, 1963), 8; Robert C. Fellmeth, ed., *Politics of Land: Ralph Nader's Study Group Report on Land Use in California* (New York, 1973), 28; Trounstine and Christensen, *Movers and Shakers*, 92; Reinhardt, "Joe Ridder's San Jose," 70, 71.

58. Raaf, "Characteristics of a Sample of Adult Males of Metropolitan Phoenix," 5; Peter A. Morrison, "Urban Growth and Decline: San Jose and St. Louis in the 1960s," *Science* 185 (Aug. 30, 1974): 757. On migration in the West compared to nationwide trends, see U.S. Bureau of the Census, *U.S.*

Census of Population: 1960. Volume 1: *Characteristics of the Population.* Part 1: *United States Summary* (Washington, D.C., 1964), 257–58.

59. The quotations come from: Peter A. Morrison, *San Jose and St. Louis in the 1960s: A Case Study of Changing Urban Populations* (Santa Monica, 1973), v; McWilliams, *California: The Great Exception,* 74. The statistics come from: Morrison, "Role of Migration in California's Growth," 49; Morrison, "Urban Growth and Decline: San Jose and St. Louis in the 1960s," 758.

60. Foley et al., *Characteristics of Metropolitan Growth of California,* 38; Morrison, "Role of Migration in California's Growth," 38–46.

61. Peirce, *Pacific States,* 24; Vance, *Geography and Urban Evolution in the San Francisco Bay Area,* 15; U.S. Bureau of the Census, *U.S. Census of Population: 1960, Subject Reports, Mobility for States and State Economic Areas,* Final Report PC(2)–2B (Washington, D.C., 1963), 166; "The Nomads of Los Angeles County," American Society of Planning Officials, *ASPO Newsletter* 30 (Feb. 1964): 23; San Jose Department of City Planning, *The General Plan 1975* (San Jose, 1976), 5.

62. Yi-Fu Tuan, *Topophilia: A Study of Environmental Perception, Attitudes, and Values* (Englewood Cliffs, N.J., 1974), 189; Reinhardt, "Joe Ridder's San Jose," 70–71; Charles Hall Page and Associates, Inc., *Historic Preservation Inventory & Planning Guidelines, City of Las Vegas* (San Francisco, 1978), 16.

63. Santa Clara County, California, Planning Department, "Average Annual Percent Change by Time Period, Total Population Compared to Automobiles, Santa Clara County, 1950–1973," *Info,* no. 519 (May 1974); United California Bank, Research and Planning Division, *Santa Clara County, Past—Present—1985* (Los Angeles, 1975), 18; United California Bank, *Orange County,* 22; Foley et al., *Characteristics of Metropolitan Growth in California,* 259.

64. Arvin Tarleton Henderson, Jr., "Evolution of Commercial Nucleations in San Jose, California," M.A. thesis, San Jose State College, 1970, 21; Norbert McDonald, *Distant Neighbors: A Comparative History of Seattle and Vancouver* (Lincoln, Neb., 1987), 114; G. Wesley Johnson, *Phoenix: Valley of the Sun* (Tulsa, 1982), 130; Peirce, *Pacific States,* 133. For the complicated story of Los Angeles, see: David Brodsly, *L.A. Freeway: An Appreciative Essay* (Berkeley, 1981), especially parts 3, 4; Scott L. Bottles, *Los Angeles and the Automobile: The Making of the Modern City* (Berkeley, 1987), 239, 241. Mark S. Foster, "The Western Response to Urban Transportation: A Tale of Three Cities, 1900–1945," in Gerald D. Nash, ed., *The Urban West* (Manhattan, Kans., 1979), 31–39, depicts how autos had been embraced in Los Angeles, Seattle, and Denver by World War II.

65. "Statement by Mayor Norris Poulson Before the State Senate Interim Subcommittee on Mass Rapid Transit: State Building, Los Angeles, Tuesday, January 17, 1956," Box 14, Ford Collection, 1; "Correcting San Jose's Boomtime Mistakes," *Business Week* (Sept. 19, 1970): 75; San Jose, California, City Planning Commission, *Master Plan of the City,* 53–58; Luckingham, *Phoenix,* 162–63. The second quotation is from Peter C. Papademetriou, *Transportation and Urban Development in Houston 1830–1980* (Houston, 1982), 53, 56, 60–62, a study with much relevance for far western cities.

66. Mark S. Foster, "Prosperity's Prophet: Henry J. Kaiser and the Consumer/Suburban Culture, 1930–1950," *Western Historical Quarterly* 17 (April 1986): 172–74; City of Los Angeles, Department of City Planning, "City Planning Progress," Box 57, Bowron Collection, 87–88, 95; City of Los Angeles, *City Planning in Los Angeles: A History*, 44; Ford, *Thirty Explosive Years in Los Angeles County*, 110; *Oakland Tribune*, Aug. 14, 1957, in Stanford Lands file, SUA.

67. Bernard J. Frieden, *The Environmental Protection Hustle* (Cambridge, Mass., 1979), 17 (first quotation); Brodsly, *L.A. Freeway*, 141–45; San Jose, California, City Planning Commission, *Master Plan of the City*, 51–52 (second quotation).

68. Avery M. Guest, "Ecological Succession in the Puget Sound Region," *Journal of Urban History* 3 (Feb. 1977): 205–7; Luckingham, *Phoenix*, 162–63, 196–97; D. W. Meinig, *Southwest: Three Peoples in Geographical Change, 1600–1970* (New York, 1971), 97–98, 105.

69. Henderson, "Evolution of Commercial Nucleations in San Jose," 15, 35, 45, 145–50; Santa Clara County, California, Planning Department, "Analysis of Existing Shopping Centers in Santa Clara County," Technical Supplement No. 3 to "1970 General Plan," Santa Clara County, California, Department of Planning and Development, MS, April 19, 1963, 4; San Jose, California, City Planning Commission, *Master Plan of the City*, 89 (first quotation); Santa Clara County, California, Planning Department, *Land Use Issues in Santa Clara County*, 20; Real Estate Research Corporation, *Economic Survey and Analysis, Central Business District, San Jose, California* (San Francisco, 1967), 6–11, 35, 40, 43; Dick Barrett, ed., *A Century of Service: San Jose's 100 Year Old Business Firms, Organizations and Institutions* (San Jose, 1977), 20–21; Trounstine and Christensen, *Movers and Shakers*, 98 (second quotation).

70. San Jose, California, City Planning Commission, *Master Plan for the City*, 60, 85–88; W. N. Zavlaris, "City Image and the Urban Design Implications for the Central Core District of San Jose," M.A. paper, San Jose State University, 1977, 29–37; Galarza, "Mexicans in the Southwest," 281.

71. Lynn Turgeson, "Model for the Future," *Frontier* 12 (Jan. 1961): 8–9; Roger Daniels, *Asian America: Chinese and Japanese in the United States Since 1850* (Seattle, 1988), 294–95.

72. Margaret Clark, *Health in the Mexican American Culture* (Berkeley, 1959), 35 (quotation); Grebler et al., *Mexican-American People*, 18–23.

73. On Sunbelt conservatism, see Wilson, "Guide to Reagan Country," 37–45; Peter A. Lupsha and William J. Siembieda, "The Poverty of Public Services in the Land of Plenty: An Analysis and Interpretation," in David C. Perry and Alfred J. Watkins, eds., *The Rise of the Sunbelt Cities* (Beverly Hills, 1977), 169–90; John M. Findlay, *People of Chance: Gambling in American Society from Jamestown to Las Vegas* (New York, 1986), 187–91; Robert Fisher, "The Urban Sunbelt in Comparative Perspective: Houston in Context," in Fairbanks and Underwood, eds., *Essays on Sunbelt Cities and Recent Urban America*, 33–58.

74. Reuben W. Borough, "Pattern for the Future," *Frontier* 10 (Nov. 1958): 13; Steinberg, "Opportunity for Los Angeles," 15; State of California,

Governor's Commission on the Los Angeles Riots, *Violence in the City—An End or a Beginning?* (Los Angeles, 1965), 3.

75. Nash, *American West Transformed*, 97, 107.

76. Grebler et al., *Mexican-American People*, 8–9, 27–28, 201, 579; Hall, "Roybal's Candidacy," 6–7; Ralph Friedman, "U.N. in Microcosm: Boyle Heights," *Frontier* 6 (March 1955): 13.

77. Grebler et al., *Mexican-American People*, 18–23; Clark, *Health in the Mexican American Culture*, 35; Galarza, "Mexicans in the Southwest," 280–82, 285.

78. William Katz, *The Black West* (New York, 1973), 282 (quotation); Clinton B. Jones, "A Comparative Study of Regional Differences in Black Political, Social, and Economic Status," *Western Journal of Black Studies* 2 (Summer 1978): 102–10; Taylor, "Blacks in the American West," 4–5; Ralph Friedman, "Negroes and the Ballot," *Frontier* 8 (March 1957): 13.

79. Quintard Taylor, "Migration of Blacks and Resulting Discriminatory Practices in Washington State Between 1940 and 1950," *Western Journal of Black Studies* 2 (March 1978): 65–71; Nash, *American West Transformed*, 93.

80. Fogelson, ed. and comp., *Los Angeles Riots*, 83–84, 86, 137–38, 141 (quotation); John Caughey and LaRee Caughey, "A New Force—The Blacks," in John Caughey and LaRee Caughey, eds., *Los Angeles: Biography of a City* (Berkeley, 1976), 463.

81. LaRee Caughey, "Los Angeles: No Birmingham West," *Frontier* 14 (July 1963): 3–4, 15; Elizabeth Poe, "Watts," *Frontier* 16 (Sept. 1965): 5–7; State of California, Governor's Commission on the Los Angeles Riots, *Violence in the City*, 4 (quotation).

82. Cited in Luckingham, *Phoenix*, 197.

83. Fellmeth, ed., *Politics of Land*, 33–35, 356, ch. 9; Stanford Environmental Law Society, *San Jose, Sprawling City*, 2–3, 16, 18–19, 29–34; James P. Degnan, "Santa Cruz: A Workable Utopia," in McWilliams, ed., *The California Revolution*, 126–28 (quotations). The battle over preservation of Santa Clara Valley farmland is perhaps the best documented conflict between county and city: see [Belser], "Conservation of Agricultural Land," 5–7; Mel Scott, *The San Francisco Bay Area: A Metropolis in Perspective* (Berkeley, 1959), 299; Mel Scott, *American City Planning Since 1890* (Berkeley, 1969), 511–12; Belser, "The Making of Slurban America," 5–17; Rebecca Conard, "Green Gold: 1950s Greenbelt Planning in Santa Clara County, California," *Environmental Review* 9 (Spring 1985): 5–18.

84. Samuel E. Wood and Alfred E. Heller, *California Going, Going . . . : Our State's Struggle to Remain Beautiful and Productive* (Sacramento, 1962), 5–6 (quotation), 7, 20; Wood and Heller, *Phantom Cities of California*, 6–41, 43–60; Bradshaw, "Trying Out the Future," 74; Netboy, "California's Top Problem," 9; Samuel P. Hays, *Beauty, Health, and Permanence: Environmental Politics in the United States, 1955–1985* (New York, 1987), 44.

85. Fogelson, *Fragmented Metropolis*, especially 144–45.

86. Gordon Whitnall, "Planned Unit Development," paper delivered at the Southwestern Legal Foundation Sixth Annual Institute on Planning and Zon-

ing, Albany, N.Y., 1966, Box 57, Bowron Collection, 52–58 (quotation at 52–53); Scott, *Metropolitan Los Angeles*, 86; Scott, *American City Planning Since 1890*, 206–9; Homer Earl Smutz, "The Value and Administration of a Zoning Plan," paper delivered at the American Society of Civil Engineers Convention, Houston, 1951, Box 58, Bowron Collection, 3, 4, 6–8.

87. Milton Breivogel and Edward A. Holden, "A Review of Developments in the Los Angeles Metropolitan Area to Control Urban Dispersal," in Engelbert, ed., *Nature and Control of Urban Dispersal*, 33.

88. Brodsly, *L.A. Freeway*, 96–126; Louis J. Fuller, "Statement of Louis J. Fuller, Air Polution Control Officer, Los Angeles County Air Pollution Control District, Presented to the California State Assembly Committee on Transportation and Commerce," Dec. 8, 1965, Box 59, Bowron Collection, 5; City of Los Angeles, Department of City Planning, "City Planning Progress," 87; City of Los Angeles, Department of City Planning, *City Planning in Los Angeles*, 31; John Anson Ford, "John Anson Ford and Los Angeles County Government," typescript of an oral history interview conducted in 1961 and 1967 by L. Craig Cunningham and Elizabeth I. Dixon, Oral History Program, University of California, Los Angeles, 1967, 130–31; Harold W. Kennedy, "County Viewpoints on Metropolitan Government—Is the Lakewood Plan the Answer?" paper presented to Metropolitan Government Symposium, Los Angeles Chamber of Commerce, April 8, 1958, Box 47, Bowron Collection.

89. "Population Growth and Land Use, Maricopa County and Phoenix Urban Area," *Arizona Architect* 3 (March 1960): 27; Reinhardt, "Joe Ridder's San Jose," 49.

90. Karl Belser, "Misuse of Land in Fringe Areas and Inadequate Subdivision Standards," in *Problems of Decentralization in Metropolitan Areas*, 22, 23; City of Los Angeles, Department of City Planning, *City Planning in Los Angeles*, 25–26.

91. Attorney cited in Peirce, *Pacific States*, 256; Richard Gilbert, *City of the Angels* (London, 1964), 34–35.

92. William Irwin Thompson, *At the Edge of History* (New York, 1972), 5, 9–14.

93. Hamann cited in Reinhardt, "Joe Ridder's San Jose," 70 (first quotation); Degnan, "Santa Cruz: A Workable Utopia," 243 (second quotation).

94. Peirce, *Pacific States*, 113; Wozniak cited in Peter Schille, "The Dirty Work on the Clean Chip," paper in Electronics: Equipment—General and Miscellaneous file, 1985, PSC, 21–22.

95. Cited in Roderick Nash, *Wilderness and the American Mind* (3d ed. New Haven, 1982), 291.

96. *ST*, May 2, June 4, 1961 (letters to editor), Dec. 19, 20, 1962.

97. Sale, *Seattle, Past to Present*, 189.

98. Sargent, "Arizona's Urban Frontier—Myths and Realities," 4, 23.

99. Edward Relph, *Place and Placelessness* (London, 1976).

100. Wood and Heller, *Phantom Cities of California*, 43; Belser, "Making of Slurban America," 1–19; Murray Bookchin, "Toward a Vision of the Urban Future," in Perry and Watkins, eds., *Rise of the Sunbelt Cities*, 259–76 (quotations at 262, 265).

101. Phoenix, Arizona, City Planning Department, *Comprehensive Plan, 1990*, 22; Desmond Muirhead, "The Arizona Landscape, a Critique—II. Cities, Subdivisions," *Arizona Architect* 2 (June 1959): 12, 14–16; "Population Growth and Land Use, Maricopa County and Phoenix Urban Area," 27; quotation from Jack B. Fraser, "In Santa Clara Valley: The Debris of Development," *City* 4 (Aug.–Sept. 1970): 24.

102. Robert E. G. Harris, "Have the Freeways Failed Los Angeles?" *Frontier* 8 (Jan. 1957): 10 (first quotation); Wood and Heller, *Phantom Cities of California*, 11–12 (second quotation).

103. Huxley cited by Constantine Panunzio, "Growth and Character of the Population," in George W. Robbins and L. Deming Tilton, eds., *Los Angeles: Preface to a Master Plan* (Los Angeles, 1941), 40; the New Yorker was Turgeson, "Model of the Future," 12. For skepticism about suburbanites' support for culture, see James Schevill, "The Changing California Culture," in McWilliams, ed., *California Revolution*, 52–53; Theodore Roszak, "Life in the Instant Cities," in McWilliams, ed., *California Revolution*, 77–78; Janice Peck, "Arts Activists and Seattle's Cultural Expansion, 1954–65," *Pacific Northwest Quarterly* 76 (July 1985): 82.

104. "Population Growth and Land Use, Maricopa County and Phoenix Urban Area," 27; Ved Mehta, "Personal History; At the Gates of California," *New Yorker* 63 (May 11, 1987): 84 (quotation on Los Angeles); San Jose Department of City Planning, *General Plan 1975*, 3 (quotation on San Jose).

105. Commonwealth Club of California, *Population of California*, 130–35; Nadeau, *California: The New Society*, 186, 206, 212, 216; Ford, "Intermittent Diary," vol. 7, Nov. 15, 1965; Leonard Gordon, "Social Issues in the Arid City," in Gideon Golany, ed., *Urban Planning for Arid Zones: American Experiences and Directions* (New York, 1978), 113–14 (quotation); Jeffrey Cook, "Patterns of Desert Urbanization: The Evolution of Metropolitan Phoenix," in Golany, ed., *Urban Planning for Arid Zones*, 222.

106. Starbird, *New Metropolis*, 2; Bradford Luckingham, "Urban Development in Arizona: The Rise of Phoenix," *Journal of Arizona History* 22 (Summer 1981): 224, 226.

Chapter Two

1. *The Random House Dictionary of the English Language*, 2d ed., s.v. "mickey mouse"; *A Supplement to the Oxford English Dictionary*, s.v. "Disneyesque."

2. *The Disneyland Trademark* (WDP, 1976). This brochure, like many publications issued by the Disney company, lists no place of publication and has no pagination. Some company literature also lacks any specified date of publication.

3. *Supplement to the Oxford English Dictionary*, s.v. "Disneyland"; *Random House Dictionary of the English Language*, 2d ed., s.v. "Disneyland."

4. J. Anthony Lukas, "The 'Alternative Life-Style' of Playboys and Play-mates," *NYT Magazine* (June 11, 1972): 15; Perry Bruce Kaufman, "The Best City of Them All: A History of Las Vegas, Nevada, 1930–1960," Ph.D. diss., University of California, Santa Barbara, 1974, ch. 4; Remi Nadeau, *California: The New Society* (New York, 1963), 275; *Amarillo Daily News*, Feb. 10, 1965 (clipping in publicity files of the Houston Sports Association, The Astrodome, Houston, Texas); Hugo John Hildebrandt, "Cedar Point: A Park in Progress," *Journal of Popular Culture* 15 (Summer 1981): 99–100.

5. Neal R. Peirce, *The Pacific States of America: People, Politics, and Power in the Five Pacific Basin States* (New York, 1972), 193; *ST*, Nov. 19, 1989; William Irwin Thompson, *At the Edge of History* (New York, 1972), 6.

6. N. H. Mager and S. K. Mager, comps. and eds., *The Morrow Book of New Words* (New York, 1982), 80; Robert L. Chapman, ed., *New Dictionary of American Slang* (New York, 1986), 105. Astronaut Sally Ride described the space shuttle as "a real E ticket ride," cited in Randy Bright, *Disneyland: Inside Story* (New York, 1987), 110.

7. Anthony Haden-Guest, *The Paradise Program: Travels Through Muzak, Hilton, Coca-Cola, Texaco, Walt Disney and Other World Empires* (New York, 1973), 182; Edward Relph, *Place and Placelessness* (London, 1976), 95–101; David Lowenthal, *The Past Is a Foreign Country* (Cambridge, Eng., 1985), 408.

8. *NYT*, Oct. 3, 1971; Harrison A. Price, "A Revolution in Recreation: The Impact of Walter Elias Disney," speech to the Executives Club of Chicago, May 4, 1973, WDA, 10–12; Hildebrandt, "Cedar Point," 96.

9. James W. Rouse, "The Regional Shopping Center: Its Role in the Community It Serves," speech to the Seventh Urban Design Conference, Harvard Graduate School of Design, April 26, 1963, WDA, 1–2. Helpful assessments of Disneyland's impact upon urban design include: Charles Moore, "You Have to Pay for the Public Life," *Perspecta* 9 (Oct. 1964): 64; Paul Goldberger, "Mickey Mouse Teaches the Architects," *NYT Magazine* (Oct. 22, 1972): 40–41, 92–99; *The Disney Theme Show, from Disneyland to Walt Disney World.* Volume 1: *A Pocket History of the First Twenty Years* (WDP, 1976); *The Disney Theme Show.* Volume 2: *An Introduction to the Art of Disney Outdoor Entertainment* (WDP, 1977); Margaret J. King, "The New American Muse: Notes on the Amusement/Theme Park," *Journal of Popular Culture* 15 (Summer 1981): 60; Richard V. Francaviglia, "Main Street U.S.A.: A Comparison/Contrast of Streetscapes in Disneyland and Walt Disney World," *Journal of Popular Culture* 15 (Summer 1981): 149–51; John Hench, interview by Jay Horan, Dec. 3, 1982, transcript, WDA, 69–71.

10. See, for example, Warren Susman, "Did Success Spoil the United States? Dual Representations in Postwar America," in Lary May, ed., *Recasting America: Culture and Politics in the Age of Cold War* (Chicago, 1989), 31–33.

11. "Here's Your First View of Disneyland," *Look* 18 (Nov. 2, 1954): 86.

12. *LAT*, July 12, 1970; Ivor Davis and Sally Davis, "The Disney Money-tree: Why It Keeps Blooming While Hollywood Withers," *Los Angeles* (Sept. 1971): 37; Irwin Ross, "Disney Gambles on Tomorrow," *Fortune* 106 (Oct. 4, 1982): 66.

13. Kevin Starr, *Inventing the Dream: California Through the Progressive Era*

(New York, 1985), chs. 9–10; D. W. Meinig, "Symbolic Landscapes: Some Idealizations of American Communities," in D. W. Meinig, ed., *The Interpretation of Ordinary Landscapes: Geographical Essays* (New York, 1979), 169–72; Peirce F. Lewis, "America Between the Wars: The Engineering of a New Geography," in Robert D. Mitchell and Paul A. Groves, eds., *North America: The Historical Geography of a Changing Continent* (Totowa, N.J., 1987), 433–34.

14. Richard Schickel, *The Disney Version: The Life, Times, Art and Commerce of Walt Disney* (rev. ed. New York, 1985), 282–83.

15. "Spirit of Disneyland," film viewed by author at APL, June 13, 1985; *Disneyland: The First Thirty Years* (WDP, 1985), 11; Bright, *Disneyland*, 34–41.

16. Marvin Davis, interview by Richard Hubler, May 28, 1968, transcript, WDA, 1; Dick Irvine, interview by Richard Hubler, May 14, 1968, transcript, WDA, 1–2; John Hench, interview by Richard Hubler, May 14, 1968, transcript, WDA, 13; *Spirit of Disneyland* (WDP, 1984), 15; *Burbank Review*, March 27, 1952.

17. Harrison A. Price, William M. Stewart, and Redford C. Rollins, "An Analysis of Location Factors for Disneyland," final report prepared for Walt Disney Productions, Aug. 28, 1953, by Stanford Research Institute, AHR-APL, 1–2 (quotations), 6–13; Melbourne A. Gauer, "Anaheim Area Since 1925," transcript of oral history interview conducted by Kathy Landis, California State University, Fullerton, Oral History Project, 1974, AHR-APL, 51; Harrison A. Price, "Researching the Building of a Great Attraction," Speech at Seventeenth Annual Pacific Area Travel Association Conference, Taipei, Taiwan, Feb. 8, 1968, WDA, 5–7; Bright, *Disneyland*, 67. Earnest W. Moeller, former manager of the Anaheim Chamber of Commerce, recalls details of Disney's acquiring the property (which was not precisely the parcel first recommended by SRI) in "An Historical Sketch," 1980 MS, AHR-APL.

18. Price, "Researching the Building of a Great Attraction," 7–9; Van Arsdale France, "Backstage Disneyland: A Personal History," 1980(?), MS in author's possession, 39; Ralph Story, script no. 33 of "Ralph Story's Los Angeles" television show, Oct. 6, 1964, Special Collections, University of California, Los Angeles, 6–9.

19. *Burbank Review*, March 27, 1952 (quotation); *LAT*, March 28, 1952.

20. *AB*, June 11, 1954; Anaheim Chamber of Commerce, Board of Directors, "Minutes of Meeting," June 10, 1954, Anaheim, Calif., AHR-APL, 2 (quotation); France, "Backstage Disneyland," 54; *SAR*, Dec. 13, 1954.

21. WED Enterprises, "Disneyland," 1953 information sheet, AHR-APL; Price, Stewart, and Rollins, "Analysis of Location Factors for Disneyland," 5.

22. "Companionably Yours: Disneyland," *Women's Home Companion* 81 (June 1954): 12 (first quotation); *NYT*, March 30, April 13, 1954 (second quotation).

23. Van Arsdale France, "My Thirty Years with the Magic Kingdom," public talk, AHR-APL, June 13, 1985; *LAT*, July 6, 1975.

24. Quotations from *NYT*, April 3, 1954; Leonard Maltin, *The Disney Films* (New York, 1978), 433–34; Louis F. Thomann, "For Big Advertisers: New Wonderland," *Printers' Ink* 252 (July 15, 1955): 24. On the problem of

financing Disneyland, see *LAT*, March 1, 1965, July 6, 1975; Bob Thomas, "Uncle Walt's Greatest Stand: How There Almost Was No Disneyland," *Los Angeles* (Dec. 1976): 205; Martin A. Sklar, *Walt Disney's Disneyland* (WDP, 1964).

25. *NYT*, March 30, 1954, July 3, 1955.

26. "Dateline Disneyland," 1955 film, WDA.

27. France, "Backstage Disneyland," 41–57; *NYT*, July 19, 1955; *LAT*, Dec. 5, 1971, July 6, 1975; *SAR*, July 18, 1955; Disneyland, Inc., Public Relations Division, "First Annual Report to Disneyland Lessees," April 1956, WDA. Quotation from "Dateline Disneyland."

28. *NYT*, Feb. 2, 1958.

29. The data for this and the following paragraph come from *The Disneyland Story* (WDP, 1975); Price, "Researching the Building of a Great Attraction," 3–4; Harrison A. Price, "The Theme Park Comes of Age," speech to American Land Development Association, Hollywood, Florida, Nov. 15, 1971, WDA, 2–3; *Disneyland U.S.A.* (WDP, 1957); *Disneyland U.S.A.* (WDP, 1958); Disneyland Public Relations Division, *Disneyland Report to Anaheim and Orange County* (WDP, 1958); Disneyland Public Relations Division, *Disneyland Report to Anaheim and Orange County 1959* (WDP, 1959), 7–8.

30. France, "My Thirty Years."

31. France, "Backstage Disneyland," 94; Dick Irvine, interview by Bob Thomas, April 24, 1973, transcript, WDA, 23–24; Valerie Childs, *The Magic of Disneyland and Walt Disney World* (New York, 1979), unpaginated.

32. *Oakland Tribune*, March 14, 1965, clipping from Tencennial scrapbook (Disneyland, Inc.'s tenth-anniversary collection of newspaper articles, 1964–65, AHR-APL).

33. Jack Sayer quoted in Stanford Research Institute, "Report: 4 Sections Complete," 1957–58, DP-UWL, part 4, 42–43; France, "Backstage Disneyland," 17; Neal Goff, "Disney: Gassed Up and Ready to Go," *Financial World* 148 (Sept. 1, 1979): 16 (quotation on attendance boost); Schickel, *Disney Version*, 316 (quotation on revenues).

34. "Disneyland—World's Fastest Growing Ten-Year-Old," Disneyland press release, 1965, AHR-APL, 4. Figures on acreage inside the berm come from: "Opening Day Press Kit," Newspaper Ads scrapbook, 1955–58, WDA; *Disneyland Dictionary* (WED Enterprises, 1968), 32; David R. Smith, WDA archivist, personal communication, Jan. 29, 1990.

35. *Shreveport Times*, Nov. 1, 1964, and *San Francisco Chronicle*, Feb. 21, 1965 (quotation), both in Tencennial scrapbook.

36. Herb Caen in *San Francisco Chronicle*, Dec. 22, 1970; E. L. Doctorow, *The Book of Daniel* (New York, 1971), 286–87.

37. *Birmingham News*, Nov. 8, 1965, Tencennial scrapbook.

38. Gladwin Hill in *NYT*, Feb 2., 1958, Oct. 4, 1959. See also Bright, *Disneyland*, 49, on "attendants" and "hard sell." The Disney critique of conventional amusement parks has been voiced in: Thomas, "Uncle Walt's Greatest Stand," 207; *LAT*, March 1, 1965; Aubrey Menen, "Dazzled in Disneyland," *Holiday* 34 (July 1973): 106; Price, "Revolution in Recreation," 5.

39. See John F. Kasson, *Amusing the Million: Coney Island at the Turn of the*

Century (New York, 1978), especially 112, on Coney Island's past; *Spirit of Disneyland*, 28 (first quotation); *NYT*, July 31, 1955 (second quotation).

40. Los Angeles *Herald-Examiner*, Feb 11, 1965 (first quotation); Walt Disney, interview by Stan Hellenke of CBC television, July 22, 1960, transcript, WDA, 15; Price, "Researching the Building of a Great Attraction," 11–12 (second quotation).

41. Schickel, *Disney Version*, 347.

42. WED Enterprises, "Disneyland," 6 (first quotation); *Los Angeles Examiner*, June 14, 1959; Bright, *Disneyland*, 88 (second quotation).

43. "The Wisdom of Walt Disney," *Wisdom* 32 (Dec. 1959): 77.

44. Hench, 1982 interview, 39, 41.

45. Hench, 1982 interview, 39.

46. *NYT*, Feb 2, 1958; Sklar, *Walt Disney's Disneyland*; *Miami Herald*, Oct. 26, 1965, Tencennial scrapbook; Hench, May, 1968 interview, 26; Irvine, 1968 interview, 12; Price, "Theme Park Comes of Age," 2; *OCR*, June 2, 1985.

47. Bright, *Disneyland*, 45 (first quotation), 48; *Spirit of Disneyland*, 17, 39 (second quotation).

48. Valerie Childs, *Disneyland* (New York, 1979), 3; Bright, *Disneyland*, 63–64.

49. Sklar, *Walt Disney's Disneyland* (quotation); Irvine, 1973 interview, 17–18; Bright, *Disneyland*, 63–64.

50. *Spirit of Disneyland*, 11, 40.

51. *Disney Theme Show*, vol. 1, *Pocket History*, 8–9; John Hench, cited in *LAT*, July 6, 1975, and in Bright, *Disneyland*, 48–49 (quotation); Charlie Haas, "Disneyland Is Good for You," *New West* 3 (Dec. 4, 1978): 16, 18.

52. "Wisdom of Walt Disney," 76, 80; Schickel, *Disney Version*, 354.

53. John Hench, interview by Richard Hubler, Dick Irvine, and Marty Sklar, Sept. 24, 1968, transcript, WDA, 2; John Hench, interview by Gabe Essoe, April 13, 1972, transcript, WDA, 3–4; John Hench, interview at California Institute of the Arts, 1973, transcript, WDA, 2, 15–16; Hench, 1982 interview, 67.

54. *Disney Theme Show*, vol. 1, *Pocket History*, 30–31; Hench, 1972 interview, 1.

55. Moore, "You Have to Pay for the Public Life," 65 (quotation on "much more real"). The quotation from Walt Disney conflates two accounts of his exchange with Graham in: Haden-Guest, *Paradise Program*, 221; *LAT*, July 12, 1970.

56. Hench, 1982 interview, 42 (quotation on "mankind"); "A View of the Future Is Offered at Disney's Tomorrowland," *The Refresher* 14 (Nov./Dec. 1967): 5 (quotation on "tomorrow's world"); WED Enterprises, *Information on Disneyland's New Tomorrowland . . . A World on the Move* (Glendale, Calif., 1967), 26.

57. "Disneyland U.S.A.," 1956 film, WDA; Bright, *Disneyland*, 301.

58. "Monsanto Chemical Co.: The Organization Within the Organization," *Disneylander* 2 (March 1958): 2–3; "Preview of Tomorrow: Monsanto's House of the Future," *Disneyland Holiday* 1 (Fall 1957): 3.

59. *Edison Square, Disneyland U.S.A.* (WDP, 1958); audio tape of sound-

track for G.E.'s Carousel of Progress and Progress City exhibits, n.d. (late 1950s or early 1960s), WDA; WED Enterprises, "G.E. Carousel of Progress: Narration-Tape," July 22, 1967, AHR-APL.

60. *LAT*, June 15, 1959.

61. Davis interview, 12–13, 20–21; Irvine, 1973 interview, 21.

62. *AB*, March 17, 1967; "Disneyland's New Tomorrowland," *Vacationland* 11 (Summer 1967): 2–3.

63. Garden Grove *Daily News*, June 23, 1957; "Tomorrowland," *The Westerner* 69 (Aug. 1955): 10.

64. Bright, *Disneyland*, 72 (first quotation); Haden-Guest, *Paradise Program*, 244 (second quotation).

65. Hench, 1972 interview, 1.

66. *Spirit of Disneyland*; the official was Moeller, "Historical Sketch," part 1, 7–8.

67. "That's What Disneyland's Made of," *Aqueduct* 42 (Fall 1975): 14, 17; France, "Backstage Disneyland," 115; *Disneyland Story*; "Disneylandscaping Provides Living Decorations for 'Magic Kingdom' Stage," *Vacationland* 12 (Winter–Spring 1969): 12–13.

68. "Disneyland to Celebrate 1965 'Tencennial,'" Disneyland press release, 1964, AHR-APL, 2–3; "Polaris Missile Spawned Disney's 'Audio-Animatronics,'" *Disney News* 1 (Dec. 1965–Feb. 1966): 6; WED Enterprises, *Information on Disneyland's New Tomorrowland*, 25; James H. Bierman, "The Walt Disney Robot Dramas," *Yale Review* 66 (Dec. 1976): 231 (quotation); Hench, May, 1968 interview, 20–21; France, "Backstage Disneyland," 79.

69. *Disney Theme Show*, vol. 2, *Introduction to the Art of Disney Outdoor Entertainment*, 19.

70. *The Walt Disney Traditions at Disneyland: A University of Disneyland Handbook* (WDP, 1967) (quotation); Hench, May 1968 interview, 33, 35; *Disneyland U.S.A.* (WDP, 1958).

71. Van Arsdale France, "dean" and co-founder of the University of Disneyland, recalls early training programs in his "Backstage Disneyland," 32–33, 87–88, 91. See also: "University of Disneyland," Disneyland press release, Oct. 1964, AHR-APL, 1–2.

72. "University of Disneyland" press release, 4 (quotations on preferred employees); *Spirit of Disneyland*, 46 (quotation on "previous experience"); *You're on Stage at Disneyland!* (Disneyland, 1962) (final quotations).

73. *NYT*, Oct. 4, 1959; Heidi Schulman, "The Truth Behind All That (Golly!) Disneyland Niceness," *Los Angeles* (Nov. 1979): 98–99. Quotations in this and the following eight paragraphs, unless otherwise noted, come from one or more of the following five employee handbooks: *Your Disneyland: A Guide for Hosts and Hostesses* (Disneyland, 1955); *You're on Stage*; *Walt Disney Traditions at Disneyland*; *Disneyland and You* (WDP, 1968); *Showmanship . . . Disneyland Style* (WDP, 1973).

74. Van Arsdale France, interviewed by Peggy Matthews, July, 1979, audio tapes, WDA (quotation on "create happiness"); Disneyland advertisement in *AB*, Sept. 6, 1957 (quotation on "new industry").

75. See comments of Van Arsdale France, *SAR*, July 17, 1980.

76. C. Wright Mills, *White Collar: The American Middle Classes* (New York, 1951), xvii.

77. David Riesman with Nathan Glazer and Reuel Denney, *The Lonely Crowd: A Study of the Changing American Character* (abridged ed. New Haven, 1961), 46, 127–28, 139.

78. Riesman, *Lonely Crowd*, 135; William H. Whyte, *The Organization Man* (New York, 1956), 76.

79. Whyte, *Organization Man*, 5–7; Haden-Guest, *Paradise Program*, 248.

80. Whyte, *Organization Man*, 18; "Wisdom of Walt Disney," 76.

81. *Showmanship . . . Disneyland Style*; *New York Daily News*, Oct. 2, 1964, Tencennial scrapbook.

82. Nunis quoted in "University of Disneyland" press release, 2.

83. Disney cited by Molly Maloney, "Hats Off to Disneyland," *Orange County Illustrated* 18 (July 1980): 42–43.

84. Haden-Guest, *Paradise Program*, 231, noted that the "Disney Look" had previously been called the "All-American Look."

85. France, "Backstage Disneyland," 33.

86. *Walt Disney Traditions*; Portland *Oregonian*, March 11, 1965, Tencennial scrapbook.

87. France, "Backstage Disneyland," 32.

88. Hedda Hopper in *New York Daily News*, Aug. 24, 1954; John Hench cited in *LAT*, July 6, 1975.

89. "Wisdom of Walt Disney," 76 (quotation); Schickel, *Disney Version*, 354; Disney interview with Hellenke, 19.

90. The quotation comes from Walt Disney, "EPCOT Film," October 27, 1966, film script, WDA, 1–2. John Bright, "California Revolution 6, Disney's Fantasy Empire," *Nation* 204 (March 6, 1967): 303, noted Walt's "maximal *identification*" with the public. See also Margaret J. King, "Disneyland and Walt Disney World: Traditional Values in Futuristic Form," *Journal of Popular Culture* 15 (Summer 1981): 129.

91. Hench, 1982 interview, 37, 38, 17 (emphasis added).

92. *LAT*, Dec. 5, 1971; Disneyland Research Department, "Disneyland Guest Survey, Christmas 1972," January 1973, WDA, iii.

93. Compare themes of stories in *NYT*, May 2, 1954, and *AB*, June 11, 1954, for example, with those in Portland *Oregonian*, March 11, 1965, and *Birmingham News*, Nov. 7, 1965, both in Tencennial scrapbook.

94. Newspaper Ads scrapbooks and files of *Disneyland Holiday* and *Vacationland*, WDA; Tencennial scrapbook.

95. Rochester (N.Y.) *Democrat and Chronicle*, Jan. 4, 1965, Tencennial scrapbook.

96. "Show Business: How to Make a Buck," *Time* 70 (July 29, 1957): 76.

97. Herb Caen in *San Francisco Chronicle*, Dec. 22, 1970.

98. *AB*, July 15, 1955; "A Backward Glance and a Look Ahead," *Vacationland* 4 (Winter 1960–61): 8–9. Later tabulations suggested a ratio of 4.5 adults to 1 child: *NYT*, Oct. 3, 1971. These figures either ignored teen-agers altogether or else included them in the adult and child categories. A 1958 report on the first 13 million guests claimed that 24.5 percent were under

twelve, 12.5 percent were twelve to seventeen, and 63 percent were older than seventeen: *Disneyland U.S.A.* (WDP, 1958).

99. Disney quoted by Joe Fowler, interview by Bob Thomas, March 20, 1973, transcript, WDA, 58.

100. Newspaper Ads scrapbook, Oct. 1955–1958, WDA.

101. *Boston Sunday Herald*, May 26, 1957; Jack Smith, quoted in *Vacationland* 11 (Winter–Spring 1967): 5.

102. France, "Backstage Disneyland," 20 (quotation), 54; *AB*, July 15, 1955.

103. Disneyland, Inc., Lessee Relations Division, . . . *It Is a Small World at Disneyland: A Report to Exhibiters and Lessees, June 1, 1959*, WDA, 6; *You're in Good Company: A Report to Disneyland Lessees, Summer '68* (WDP, 1968) (quotation).

104. France, "Backstage Disneyland," 59.

105. Bright, *Disneyland*, 109.

106. Bright, *Disneyland*, 109–10; *Disneyland Diary: 1955—Today* (WDP, 1982); David R. Smith, WDA archivist, personal communication, Jan. 29, 1990.

107. *Los Angeles Free Press*, Sept. 15, 1957 (quotations on "grooming codes" and "wholesome" orientation); "Conference on Disneyland and Its Impact on the Community," Jan. 20, 1966, 30, AHR-APL (quotation on restricting "undesirables"); *San Bernardino Sun*, Sept. 20, 1967 (quotation on "hippies").

108. Irvine, 1968 interview, 11; Davis interview, 5.

109. Hench, 1982 interview, 19–20; Ettinger cited in Kevin Wallace, "Onward and Upward with the Arts: The Engineering of Ease," *New Yorker* 34 (Sept. 7, 1963): 108, 110; Walt Disney cited in Bright, *Disneyland*, 56.

110. Quotations from Card Walker, "Walt Disney World: Master Planning for the Future," speech to Urban Land Institute, Palm Beach, Florida, Oct. 5, 1976, WDA. See also Bright, *Disneyland*, 62–63.

111. Irvine, 1973 interview, 3; *NYT*, Feb. 2, 1958 (quotation on "fences"); King, "Disneyland and Walt Disney World," 123 (quotation on "illusion").

112. Hench, May, 1968 interview, 23–24; *Sacramento Bee*, April 26, 1965, Tencennial scrapbook (quotations).

113. Fowler, 1973 interview, 28 (quotation on "idle" amusement); *Disney Theme Show*, vol. 2, *Introduction to the Art of Disney Outdoor Entertainment*, 1 (quotations on "vicarious" amusement and "involvement"); *AB*, June 14, 1965 (1965 ad).

114. John Hench cited in *LAT*, July 6, 1975 (first quotation); Hench, 1982 interview, 37–38 (second quotation).

115. Fowler, 1973 interview, 58.

116. Sayer cited in Stanford Research Institute, "Report: 4 Sections Complete," part 4, 42; John Hench, interview by Randy Bright and Beth Black, Dec. 19, 1974, transcript, WDA, 22. One Disney designer described the Disneyland experience as "sugarcoated education": Harper Goff, interview by Jay Horan, Sept. 21, 1982, transcript, WDA, 120–21.

117. Kasson, *Amusing the Million*, especially 106.

118. William H. Wilson, *The City Beautiful Movement* (Baltimore, 1989), 36–37.

119. On Frederick Law Olmsted's "deft direction" of visitors to Central Park and on his attempts to create the illusion of larger space and to control crowds, see: Wilson, *City Beautiful Movement*, 25–26. Lawrence Levine, *Highbrow/Lowbrow: The Emergence of Cultural Hierarchy in America* (Cambridge, Mass., 1988), 184–98, explains how audiences were "tamed" during the later nineteenth century.

120. Levine, *Highbrow/Lowbrow*, especially 189, 207–10; Frederick Law Olmsted, "Public Parks and the Enlargement of Towns" (1870), in S. B. Sutton, ed., *Civilizing American Cities: A Selection of Frederick Law Olmsted's Writings on City Landscapes* (Cambridge, Mass., 1979), 96.

121. *Disneyland U.S.A.* (1958). See also Schickel, *Disney Version*, 319–20.

122. *You're in Good Company: A Report to Disneyland Lessees* (WDP, 1968); Disneyland, Inc., Lessee Relations Division, *It Is a Small World* (WDP, 1959), 2, 6–7 (quotations). See also: *Disneyland U.S.A.* (1956); Disneyland Public Relations Division, *Disneyland Report to Anaheim and Orange County 1959*, 7–8; Foote, Cone, and Belding Research Department, "Disneyland Registrants Survey, Fall–Winter, 1963–4," WDA, 3–5.

123. Disneyland, Inc., Public Relations Division, "First Annual Report to Disneyland Lessees, April 1956"; *Disneyland U.S.A.* (1958); Disneyland, Inc., Lessee Relations Division, *It Is a Small World*, 3; Edwin D. Ettinger to Jay Rockey, Dec. 22, 1961, DP-UWL; Gene Booth, "Can It Be a Quarter Century?" *Forum Fifty* (July 1980), 8 (clipping in AHR-APL); Disneyland Research Department, "Disneyland Guest Survey, Christmas 1972," 6.

124. Disneyland, Inc., Lessee Relations Division, *It Is a Small World*, 4; Foote, Cone, and Belding, "Disneyland Registrants Survey, Fall–Winter, 1963–4," 3–5; Disneyland Research Department, "Disneyland Guest Survey, Christmas 1972," iv, 1, 6; *Here Comes the Parade! A Report to Participants in Disneyland and Walt Disney World, 1974* (WDP, 1975).

125. *Emporia Gazette*, July 15, 1965, Tencennial scrapbook; *AB*, Oct. 3, 1965, Tencennial scrapbook.

126. *El Paso Herald-Post*, April 8, 1965, Tencennial scrapbook.

127. Bright, "California Revolution 6," 299–303; Wallace, "Engineering of Ease," 104–29; Goldberger, "Mickey Mouse Teaches the Architects," 40–41, 92–99.

128. Ray Bradbury, "The Machine-Tooled Happyland," *Holiday* 38 (Oct. 1965): 104.

129. *Nashville Banner*, Aug. 18, 1965 (first quotation); *Muncie* (Ind.) *Evening Press*, Sept. 6, 1965 (second quotation); Cleveland *Plain Dealer*, April 18, 1965 (headline), all found in Tencennial scrapbook.

130. Wilmington (Del.) *Morning News*, July 15, 1965; *NYT*, Feb. 2, 1965, both found in Tencennial scrapbook; *Chicago American*, April 13, 20, 27, 1958.

131. *Nashville Banner*, Aug. 18, 1965, Tencennial scrapbook; *Milwaukee Journal*, Sept. 28, 1958.

132. On opening day, Art Linkletter told Walt Disney that he had "made a bum out of Barnum": "Dateline Disneyland." The *Orlando Sentinel*, Nov. 28,

1965, Tencennial scrapbook, headlined a story about Walt Disney "Space Age Barnum with Class."

133. *Portland* (Me.) *Sunday Telegram*, Nov. 26, 1958. See also *Memphis Press-Scimitar*, Oct. 20, 1965, and *Columbus Dispatch*, Dec. 26, 1965, both in Tencennial scrapbook.

134. Disneyland, Inc., Public Relations Division, "First Annual Report to Disneyland Lessees, April 1956"; Disneyland, Inc., Lessee Relations Division, *It Is a Small World*, 9.

135. Baltimore *Sun*, Aug. 10, 1959; Woodland, Calif., *Daily Democrat*, Sept. 3, 1958.

136. Roland Marchand, "Visions of Classlessness, Quests for Dominion: American Popular Culture, 1945–1960," in Robert H. Bremner and Gary W. Reichard, eds., *Reshaping America: Society and Institutions 1945–1960* (Columbus, Ohio, 1982), 164, 171.

137. "Dateline Disneyland."

138. "Disneyland U.S.A."; *Tucson Daily Citizen*, May 11, 1957; *Fort Worth Press*, June 29, 1958.

139. *NYT*, Sept. 20, 1959; *St. Joseph* (Mo.) *News-Press*, Jan. 5, 1960.

140. *San Francisco Examiner*, Feb. 14, 1965, Tencennial scrapbook.

141. *SAR*, July 19, 1965, and San Fernando, Calif., *Valley Times*, July 19, 1965, both in Tencennial scrapbook; University of Disneyland, *Monsanto and Walt Disney Productions Present Adventure Thru Inner Space* (WDP, 1967).

142. *NYT*, June 27, 1965.

143. "Days of Old South Relived in Aunt Jemima's Kitchen," *Disneyland News* 2 (Aug. 1956): 7.

144. Bright, "California Revolution 6," 300; *San Francisco Examiner and Chronicle*, June 9, 1968; *NYT*, July 26, 1963; *LAT*, July 12, 1970 (quotation).

145. In "Disneyland and Walt Disney World," 116–40, King explains the theme parks as "Traditional Values in Futuristic Form."

146. See the runs of *Disneyland Holiday* and *Vacationland*, WDA.

147. "Freeway Driving Can Be Pleasant," *Vacationland* 3 (Fall 1959): 20; "The Freeways: Gateway to Vacationland," *Vacationland* 8 (Winter–Spring 1964): 5, 22.

148. Price, "Theme Park Comes of Age," 6–7; Harrison A. Price, "Disney World—A Measurable Case Study of the Effectiveness and Impact of Regional Planning," speech to Seminar on Current Approaches to Regional Economic Analysis in the Private Sector, Columbia, Maryland, 1974, WDA, 14; Foote, Cone, and Belding, "Disneyland Registrants Survey," 3–5.

149. *Milwaukee Journal*, Sept. 28, 1958; *San Francisco Chronicle*, June 21, 1959, Feb. 21, 1965; *San Francisco Examiner*, Feb. 14, July 24, 1965. The citations from 1965 were found in the Tencennial scrapbook.

150. "Tinker Bell, Mary Poppins, Cold Cash," *Newsweek* (July 12, 1965): 74; and, from the Tencennial scrapbook, *Emporia Gazette*, July 15, 1965, and *Memphis Press-Scimitar*, Oct. 20, 1965.

151. Reyner Banham, *Los Angeles: The Architecture of Four Ecologies* (1971; Middlesex, Eng., 1973), 83; Ray Bradbury, "Los Angeles: Orange Without a Navel," *Frontier* 15 (Feb. 1964): 15. See also Sally Davis, "Should We Let Disney Redesign Los Angeles?" *Los Angeles* (July 1974): 45–46, 64–66.

152. *Spirit of Disneyland*, 5. See also: Bright, *Disneyland*, 21.

153. "The Grand Tour, Family Style: A *Redbook* Guide to Travel Vacations," *Redbook* (April 1965): unpaginated, in Tencennial scrapbook.

154. Moore, "You Have to Pay for the Public Life," 64.

155. Richard Bigger et al., *Metropolitan Coast: San Diego and Orange Counties* (Los Angeles, 1958), 4. Census data for Orange County have been collected conveniently in United California Bank, Research and Planning Division, *Orange County: Past—Present—1985* (Los Angeles, 1975), 5.

156. Earnest Moeller, talk to AHR-APL, June 13, 1985; *OCR*, June 2, 1985.

157. United California Bank, *Orange County*, 5; Maloney, "Hats Off to Disneyland," 42; City of Anaheim, Calif., Development Services Department, *Market Potential, Anaheim, California* (Anaheim, 1965), 4 (quotation); *LAT*, Dec. 5, 1971.

158. *LAT*, Dec. 5, 1971; Price, "Revolution in Recreation," 8–9; "Disneyland Continues Fantastic Growth," Disneyland press release, April, 1973, AHR-APL, 3. Booth, "Can It Be a Quarter Century?" 6–7, provides the figures used for the number of hotels and restaurants. Other estimates of Anaheim hotel and motel rooms in 1955 range from as low as 60 to as high as 100.

159. Richard W. Fischle, Jr., "Anaheim and the *Anaheim Bulletin*, 1929 to 1968," transcript of interview conducted by Karol Keith Richard, California State University, Fullerton, Oral History Project, 1968, AHR-APL, 2; Wilbert H. Bonney, "Experiences in Anaheim, California," transcript of interview conducted by Karen I. Speers, California State University, Fullerton, Oral History Project, 1974, AHR-APL, 24.

160. Disneyland Public Relations Division, *Disneyland Report to Anaheim and Orange County 1959*, 1–7.

161. Price, "Theme Park Comes of Age," 6–7 (quotation); *Disneyland Story*.

162. *AB*, July 8, 1955; Moeller, "Historical Sketch," part 1, 1–11; *LAT*, July 6, 1975; *OCR*, June 2, 1985.

163. *AB*, June 14, 1965; *SAR*, June 13, 1965; Price, "Disney World," 15; Charles A. Pearson, "Politics, Growth, and Development of Anaheim, California," transcript of interview conducted by Richard D. Curtiss, California State University, Fullerton, Oral History Project, 1968, AHR-APL, 75.

164. Sheldon Zalaznick, "The Double Life of Orange County," *Fortune* 78 (Oct. 1968): 188; William Leggett, "The Heavenly Home of the Anaheim Angels," *Sports Illustrated* 25 (July 4, 1966): 53–54.

165. *OCR*, June 2, 1985; *NYT*, Jan. 11, 1967; Booth, "Can It Be a Quarter Century?" 6–7.

166. *OCR*, June 2, 1985.

167. Walt Disney, interview by Bob Wright, August 24, 1966, transcript, WDA; Moeller, "Historical Sketch," appendix 2.

168. "Matterhorn Bobsleds Give Thrilling Ride," *Disney News* 1 (Mar.–May 1965): 6–7; Zalaznick, "Double Life of Orange County," 139.

169. See Kevin Lynch, *The Image of the City* (Cambridge, Mass., 1960), especially 47–48, on the concepts of edges, paths, nodes, districts, and landmarks.

170. Booth, "Can It Be a Quarter Century?" 8 (first quotation); Moeller, "Historical Sketch," part 1, 6 (second quotation).

171. Pearson, "Politics, Growth, and Development of Anaheim," 74; *LAT*, July 6, 1975.

172. Rodney Steiner, *Los Angeles: The Centrifugal City* (Dubuque, Iowa, 1981), 156, 160.

173. *AB*, July 8, 1955.

174. See John M. Findlay, *People of Chance: Gambling in American Society from Jamestown to Las Vegas* (New York, 1986), ch. 6, on tourism's impact on another hometown.

175. George F. Kohlenberger, "Life in Anaheim, California 1904–1920," transcript of interview conducted by Vivian Allen, California State University, Fullerton, Oral History Project, 1974, AHR-APL, 30–31.

176. Morris W. Martenet, Jr., "Anaheim Politics and Urban Renewal," transcript of interview conducted by Richard D. Curtiss, California State University, Fullerton, Oral History Project, 1968, AHR-APL, 25–26.

177. *LAT*, Dec. 5, 1971; *SAR*, July 5, 1982; *OCR*, June 2, 1985.

178. *LAT*, July 6, 1975.

179. "Walt Disney Presents Views on High-Rise Proposal," Disneyland press release, 1964, AHR-APL, 1–3.

180. *Anaheim Gazette*, Jan. 9, 1964.

181. *LAT*, July 10, Sept. 1, 1964; *News-Tribune* (Fullerton), Sept. 2, 1964.

182. *OCR*, June 2, 1985. See also Gauer, "Anaheim Area Since 1925," 52.

183. King, "Disneyland and Walt Disney World," 123; Schickel, *Disney Version*, 24 (quotation).

184. WED Enterprises, *Information on Disneyland's New Tomorrowland*, 24. Walt Disney's vision of EPCOT is best depicted in Disney, "EPCOT Film" script.

185. Haden-Guest, *Paradise Program*, 295–96, 308; Davis interview, 25–26 (quotations).

186. Disney, "EPCOT Film" script, part 2, 6–7. See also Walker, "Walt Disney World: Master Planning for the Future."

187. Hench cited in Davis, "Should We Let Disney Redesign Los Angeles?" 46, 65.

188. Davis interview, 7; *Disneyland U.S.A.* (1958); *Spirit of Disneyland*, 38 (quotation on "elevating the berm").

189. The quotation comes from *Tampa Tribune*, Nov. 1, 1964, Tencennial scrapbook. See also *LAT*, Dec. 5, 1971; *Spirit of Disneyland*, 37.

190. *Orlando Sentinel*, Nov. 28, 1965, Tencennial scrapbook. See also: Hench May 1968 interview, 26–27; Walker, "Walt Disney World: Master Planning for the Future."

191. Gauer, "Anaheim Area Since 1925," 52.

192. *Daily News* (Orange, Calif.), April 3, 1958; *SAR*, April 5, 1959; *Albuquerque Tribune*, June 20, 1960.

193. Jack Sayer, cited in Stanford Research Institute, "Report: 4 Sections Complete," part 4, 42; Price, "Researching the Building of a Great Attraction," 12–13.

194. Walker, "Walt Disney World: Master Planning for the Future"; WED Enterprises, *Information on Disneyland's New Tomorrowland*, 13; Hench, May 1968 interview, 17.

195. Quotation from Bright, *Disneyland*, 170–71. See also: Hench, May 1968 interview, 15–16; Hench, September 1968 interview, 3, 6–7; Hench 1982 interview, 49; Irvine, 1968 interview, 10; Irvine, 1973 interview, 16; Fowler, 1973 interview, 39–40.

196. *Orlando Sentinel*, Nov. 28, 1965, Tencennial scrapbook. See also Disney, "EPCOT Film" script, part 2, 1–2.

197. Davis interview, 23–25; Disney, "EPCOT Film" script, part 2, 3–5, and part 3, 11–12; Hench, September 1968 interview, 5.

198. Disney, "EPCOT Film" script, part 3, 1–11; Joe Fowler, interview by Richard Hubler, July 23, 1968, transcript, WDA, 11; Fowler, 1973 interview, 54–55.

199. Disney, "EPCOT Film" script, part 4, 9–11 (first quotation); Card Walker cited in Davis and Davis, "The Disney Moneytree," 66 (second quotation). See also Hench, 1972 interview, 7.

200. Quotation cited in Michael Harrington, "To the Disney Station," *Harper's* 258 (Jan. 1979): 38. See also Haden-Guest, *Paradise Program*, 309–10.

201. Donn Tatum quoted in J. Tevere MacFadyen, "The Future as a Walt Disney Production," *Next* 1 (July–Aug. 1980): 27; John Pastier, "The Incredible Shrinking Dream," *New West* 3 (Dec. 4, 1978): 28–30; *LAT*, June 27, 1982.

202. Walker, "Walt Disney World: Master Planning for the Future"; Haden-Guest, *Paradise Program*, 277–78, 298, 223 (first quotation); MacFadyen, "The Future as a Walt Disney Production," 29; *Disney Theme Show*, vol. 1, *Pocket History of the First Twenty Years*, 20 (second quotation).

203. Haden-Guest, *Paradise Program*, 222. Francaviglia, "Main Street U.S.A.," 148, 152, contrasts Disneyland with Disney World.

204. Walker, "Walt Disney World: Master Planning for the Future"; Price, "Disney World," 8.

205. Disney, "EPCOT Film" script, part 2, 1; Haden-Guest, *Paradise Program*, 226.

206. *Los Angeles Free Press*, July 31, 1970; *AB*, Aug. 7, 1970 (quotation of demonstrator). See also: *SAR*, Aug. 5, 1970.

207. *AB*, Aug. 7, 8, 10, 1970; North Orange County *Daily News Tribune*, Aug. 7, 1970; Orange County *Evening News*, Aug. 7, 1970.

208. *AB*, Aug. 8, 1970 (quotation); North Orange County *Daily News Tribune*, Aug. 7, 1970.

209. *LAT*, Sept. 15, 23, Nov. 14, 1980, Oct. 21, 1981; *SAR*, May 19, 1984 (quotation), Aug. 8, 1970.

210. Aljean Harmetz, "The Man Re-animating Disney," *NYT Magazine* (Dec. 29, 1985): 15; *LAT*, June 27, 1982; *OCR*, June 2, 1985; Michael Wallace, "Mickey Mouse History: Portraying the Past and Disney World," in Warren Leon and Roy Rosenzweig, eds., *History Museums in the United States: A Critical Assessment* (Urbana, Ill., 1989), 158–59, 162; Goff, "Disney: Gassed Up and Ready to Go," 14. John Taylor, *Storming the Magic Kingdom: Wall*

Street, the Raiders, and the Battle for Disney (New York, 1987) examines the takeover bid and its consequences.

Chapter Three

Two collections in SUA, the Frederick Emmons Terman Papers and the J. E. Wallace Sterling Papers, are quite extensive, and numbers have been added to citations from each collection in order to provide more specific references. The roman numerals used in the Terman Papers refer to the series of papers; the two arabic numerals, separated by a colon, that are used for both collections refer first to box number and then to folder number inside each box (e.g., Terman Papers, III:34:9 is series 3, box 34, folder 9; Sterling Papers, 24:34 is box 24, folder 34). Some files in the Sterling Papers are identified by a letter and number (e.g., A–29). Both sets of papers included numerous newspaper clippings, cited here as they are identified therein.

1. *NYT*, May 9, 1958 (quotation on "industrial harmony"); *Palo Alto Times*, April 16, 1958, April 29, 1960 (quotations on design of park), in Stanford Lands file, SUA; *Palo Alto Times*, April 27, 1960; clipping from *Stanford Today* (May 1960) in Terman Papers, III:35:3.

2. Frank H. Stedman, "The California Peninsula: Laboratory of the New Industrial Age," *Industrial Development* 131 (Oct. 1962): 38.

3. ULI, Executive Group of the Industrial Council, *Industrial Development Handbook*, Community Builders Handbook Series (Washington, D.C., 1975), 10–14; Victor Roterus, *Planned Industrial Parks: A Case Study* (Washington, D.C., 1960), 3–4; Robert E. Boley, *Industrial Districts: Principles in Practice*, ULI Technical Bulletin no. 44 (Washington, D.C., 1962), 29–50; Robert E. Boley, "Effects of Industrial Parks on the Community," *Urban Land* 17 (Nov. 1958): 3–4.

4. James R. Lee and Gilbert K. H. Wong, "An Analysis of Organized Industrial Districts," Stanford Research Institute Sponsored Project 52140–17, Jan. 1958, IGSL, 8–9; Roterus, *Planned Industrial Parks*, 1 (quotation); Santa Clara County, Calif., Planning Department, *A Study of the Economy of Santa Clara County, California*, Part 1 (San Jose, 1967), 9.

5. Boley, "Effects of Industrial Parks on the Community," 3; ULI, *Industrial Development Handbook*, 15–18; H. M. Conway, L. L. Liston, and R. J. Saul, *Industrial Park Growth: An Environmental Success Story* (Atlanta, 1979), 32.

6. Charles W. Hackett, Jr., *An Analysis of Planned Industrial Districts*, University of Washington, College of Business Administration, Bureau of Business Research Occasional Paper No. 4 (Seattle, 1956), 1, 2; Lee and Wong, "Analysis of Organized Industrial Districts," 24; Roterus, *Planned Industrial Parks*, v, 1, 4; Santa Clara County, Calif., Planning Department, "Directory of Indus-

trial Parks and Industrial Districts in Santa Clara County," *InfoCommentary: Industrial Districts* 1 (Jan. 1966): 1.

7. Lee and Wong, "Analysis of Organized Industrial Districts," 5; Conway, Liston, and Saul, *Industrial Park Growth*, 5–7; Roterus, *Planned Industrial Parks*, 1; ULI, *Industrial Development Handbook*, 35–40. Some of the sites along Route 128 were depicted in Boley, *Industrial Districts: Principles in Practice*, 65–70, 173–81.

8. Jane Meredith Adams, "Valley of the Dollars: An Eastern Perspective on the Silicon Valley," *New England Business* (Feb. 21, 1983): 17–18; Lenny Siegel and Herb Borock, "Background Report on Silicon Valley, Prepared for the U.S. Commission on Civil Rights," Sept. 1982, PSC, 11, 13.

9. Boley, "Effects of Industrial Parks on the Community," 4; Robert E. Boley, "Rx for Successful Industrial Park Development," *Urban Land* 26 (June 1967): 3; Richard T. Murphy, Jr., and William Lee Baldwin, "Business Moves to the Industrial Park," *Harvard Business Review* 77 (May/June 1959): 79.

10. ULI, *Industrial Development Handbook*, 3–5.

11. Frank L. Whitney, "Planners Seek Special Environment for Location of New Research Facilities" (1966), in Conway, Liston, and Saul, *Industrial Park Growth*, A–229 to A–237.

12. Lee and Wong, "Analysis of Organized Industrial Districts," 6.

13. Frederick E. Terman, "Stanford, Palo Alto Have Created Community of Technical Scholars," *Stanford Observer* (Feb. 1967): D (quotation); Frederick Emmons Terman, "Frederick Emmons Terman," typescript of oral history conducted 1971–78 by Arthur L. Norberg, Charles Susskind, and Roger Hahn, History of Science and Technology Program, TBL, and Stanford Oral History Project, Stanford University, 138 (hereafter cited as Terman Oral History); Alf E. Brandin, interview by author, Stanford, Calif., Oct. 7, 1986, summary, SUA, 1 (hereafter cited as Brandin interview); Stanford University Board of Trustees, "Report of the Land Development Committee," Jan. 1958, Sterling Papers, Trustees and Land Development 1956–1960 file, 2; Falcon O. Baker, "City on the Campus," *Saturday Evening Post* 228 (Dec. 31, 1955): 25.

14. Rebecca Sue Lowen, "'Exploiting a Wonderful Opportunity': Stanford University, Industry, and the Federal Government, 1937–1965," Ph.D. diss., Stanford University, 1990, especially chs. 1–2. See also Stuart W. Leslie, "From Backwater to Powerhouse," *Stanford* 18 (Mar. 1990): 56.

By emphasizing Terman's role, I do not mean to suggest that he was solely responsible for the profound changes that occurred on campus or throughout the Santa Clara Valley. Stanford's president, its business officer Alf E. Brandin, its Board of Trustees, and real estate advisor Colbert Coldwell, among others, also played important roles (see Brandin interview, 1–2, 3). However, Terman exemplified the impact of faculty returning from wartime work in the East, played a crucial role in universitywide changes, and articulated especially forcefully Stanford's strategy for institutional and regional growth.

15. Stanford University press release, Oct. 3, 1977, in News and Publications Collection, SUA (quotation); Terman Oral History, 108; U.S. General Accounting Office, *The Federal Role in Fostering University-Industry Cooperation*,

Report GAO/PAD-83-22 (Washington, D.C., 1983), 17. See also Walter A. McDougall, . . . *The Heavens and the Earth: A Political History of the Space Age* (New York, 1985), especially 79.

16. Lowen, "'Exploiting a Wonderful Opportunity,'" 118–19; William L. Rivers, "Terman of Stanford," *Stanford Today*, series 1, no. 14 (Autumn 1965): 5.

17. Thomas Mahon, *Charged Bodies: People, Power and Paradox in Silicon Valley* (New York, 1985), 152–53; Terman Oral History, 109–16; Frank J. Taylor, "Stanford's Man with the Midas Touch," *Saturday Evening Post* 233 (Dec. 3, 1960): 36, 55.

18. *NYT*, May 11, 16, 18, 1952. This addition later was renamed the Princeton Forrestal Center, New Jersey's belated "answer to such university-connected office and research centers as . . . the Stanford Research Park": *NYT*, July 12, 1978.

19. Terman Oral History, 118; "Industrial Research Trend toward West," undated clipping from *Daily Palo Alto Times*, and "Dean Urges College Aid," clipping from *Stanford Daily*, Jan. 13, 1949, both in Terman Papers, IX:1:2; "Industry Seeks Brain Centers," clipping from *San Francisco Chronicle*, Nov. 8, 1959, Terman Papers, IX:1:12; Denis Blunden, "Industry and Education," clipping from *San Mateo Times and Daily News Leader*, July 18, 1964, in Miscellaneous Materials, Stanford Industrial Park file, SUA; AnnaLee Saxenian, "The Genesis of Silicon Valley," in Peter Hall and Ann Markusen, eds., *Silicon Landscapes* (Boston, 1985), 23 (Terman quotation). Terman's concern for academic linkages to industry was not new; he had long admired the ties between industry and the engineering program at the Massachusetts Institute of Technology. In fact, he initially preferred to attract industrial, not federal, sponsors for research: Leslie, "Backwater to Powerhouse," 56; Lowen, "'Exploiting a Wonderful Opportunity,'" chs. 4–5.

20. Gene Bylinsky, "California's Great Breeding Ground for Industry," *Fortune* 89 (June 1974): 131–32 (quotation); Dr. Edward L. Ginzton, Varian Associates, interview by author, Palo Alto, Calif., Oct. 1, 1986, summary, SUA, 1 (hereafter cited as Ginzton interview). Henry Lowood, *From Steeples of Excellence to Silicon Valley* (n.p., n.d.; a research paper, published without pagination by Varian Associates, Inc.), emphasizes the personal contacts between companies locating nearby and campus faculty and administrators.

21. "Industrial Research Trend toward West"; "Dean Urges College Aid"; Stanford University press release, Oct. 3, 1977, Terman file, SUNP; Mahon, *Charged Bodies*, 153–54. On Stanford Research Institute, see Weldon B. Gibson, *Stanford Research Institute: A Story of Scientific Service to Business, Industry and Government* (New York, 1968), 10–11; Harold Vagtborg, *Research and American Industrial Development: A Bicentennial Look at the Contributions of Applied R & D* (New York, 1976), 204–5, 208, 238–43. Lowen, "'Exploiting a Wonderful Opportunity,'" addresses the regional dimension and focuses in chap. 2 on Stanford Research Institute.

22. Leslie, "Backwater to Powerhouse," 56–59; Lowood, *From Steeples of Excellence to Silicon Valley*.

23. Mumford cited by Stanford University, "1949 Report on Land Use . . .

[and] A Study for the Development of the Stanford Campus Area. 1950," Land Use and Development file, SUA, 1, 10.

24. Stanford University Board of Trustees, "Report of the Land Development Committee," 2; "The Stanford University Land Use Policies Adopted by the Board of Trustees on March 12, 1974," in "Stanford Research Park," Jan. 1984, Informational Memo, Land Use, Industrial Park file, SUNP (quotation). Only those acres being used for academic purposes were exempt from property taxes.

25. James F. Crafts, "A Summary of the Statement Made to the Joint Meeting of the Land Development Committee and the Special Committee Appointed to Review Certain Phases of the Land Development Program," Nov. 18, 1959, Sterling Papers, A–33, 1; "The Stanford Lands: An Endowment to Advance Our Academic Objectives," Stanford University, *Faculty-Staff Newsletter*, Mar. 28, 1960, Terman Papers, III:35:7, 1–2.

26. Terman Oral History, 127; Stanford University Board of Trustees, "Report of the Land Development Committee," 3; Stanford University Board of Trustees, "Board of Trustees' Minutes Regarding Stanford Land Planning," Feb. 1955, Sterling Papers, 30:720, 1; E. Elmore Hutchison, Consulting Engineer, "Report on Land Use Survey of Stanford University Properties, San Mateo and Santa Clara Counties, California," June 5, 1951, Land Use and Development file, 19–20; Brandin interview, 1; "Land-Poor Stanford Opens Its Acres on 99-Yr. Leases," *Business Week* (Dec. 20, 1952): 134–38.

27. See, for example, Eldridge T. Spencer, consulting architect, to Ray Nelson Faulkner, chairman, SUACLBD, Dec. 1, 1952, Sterling Papers, 30:719; Lawrence Livingston, Jr., city and regional planning consultant, to Alfred E. Brandin, March 5, 1953, Sterling Papers, 30:719.

28. Alf E. Brandin, "Developing Stanford's Lands," excerpts from a talk delivered to Stanford Alumni Conference, La Jolla, Calif., March 20, 1954, in Brandin file, SUNP, 2; SOM, *Master Plan for Stanford Lands 1953: Report to the Board of Trustees, Stanford University* (San Francisco, 1953; Land Development, General file, SUA), foreword (quotation). The report was not paginated.

29. SOM, *Master Plan for Stanford Lands 1953*.

30. SOM, *Master Plan for Stanford Lands 1953*.

31. SUACLBD, "Master Plan for the Stanford Lands: A Review of the Skidmore, Owings and Merrill Report," June 1, 1954, Land Use and Development file, SUA, 2–5, 7–9. See also Lowood, *From Steeples of Excellence to Silicon Valley*.

32. Terman, "Stanford, Palo Alto Have Created Community of Technical Scholars," D.

33. Brandin, "Developing Stanford's Lands," 1 (1954 predictions); Crafts, "Summary of Statement Made to Joint Meeting," 4; Land Development Review Committee, report to Stanford University Board of Trustees, Nov. 19, 1959, Sterling Papers, A–33, 8–10; Stanford University Board of Trustees, "Resolution on Land Development Policy," Dec. 17, 1959, Sterling Papers, A–33 (quotation).

34. Alf E. Brandin, "Stanford as Big Business," talk delivered to Stanford Alumni Conference, 1962, in Brandin file, SUNP, 1; Livingston and Blaney,

"Stanford University Land Use Policy/Plan," Land Use and Development file, SUA, 1; Stanford University Office of the President, "A Message for the People of Palo Alto," 1960, Terman Papers, III:35:8.

35. SOM, *An Analysis of Residential Development Area 6 Stanford Lands for Stanford University October 1956* (San Francisco, 1956); Crafts, "Summary of Statement Made to Joint Meeting," 4; Stanford University Board of Trustees, "Resolution on Land Development Policy," Dec. 17, 1959 (quotation).

36. Terman, "Stanford, Palo Alto Have Created Community of Technical Scholars," D. See also "Industry Can Be Neighborly," *Architectural Forum* 114 (Jan. 1961): 57-62.

37. Stanford University Office of the President, "A Message for the People of Palo Alto." See also comments of Alf E. Brandin in clipping, *Palo Alto Times*, Jan. 14, 1960, Stanford Lands file, SUA; Minutes, SUACLBD, Oct. 13, 1959, Terman Papers, III:35:2;

38. Hugh John Reay Geddes, "Industrial Parkland: Landscapes of a New Aristocracy," M.A. thesis, University of California, Berkeley, 1986, 95 (first quotation); Palo Alto Planning Commission, *Report on the Interim General Plan* (Palo Alto, April, 1955; IGSL), introduction (second quotation), 3, 42-43.

39. Stanford official quoted in Geddes, "Industrial Parkland," 94-95; *Industrial and Housing Review* (special issue of local real estate publication devoted to Stanford Industrial Park), Sept., 1956, Terman Papers, 6, 9.

40. Hutchison, "Report on Land Use Survey of Stanford University," 19, 21.

41. David Packard, president of Stanford University Board of Trustees, cited in *Daily Palo Alto Times*, Feb. 17, 1960, Stanford Lands file, SUA; Alf E. Brandin, cited in Tom Patterson, "Stanford Project Gets Cream of Crop," clipping from unidentified 1956 southern California newspaper, in Stanford Lands file, SUA.

42. Garrett Eckbo, *Public Landscape: Six Essays on Government and Environmental Design in the San Francisco Bay Area* (Berkeley, 1978), 37.

43. Boley, *Industrial Districts: Principles in Practice*, 162.

44. Thomas P. Hughes, *American Genesis: A Century of Invention and Technological Enthusiasm 1870-1970* (New York, 1989), 24-40.

45. Quotation from David Packard in *Daily Palo Alto Times*, Feb. 17, 1960, Stanford Lands file, SUA. See also: Geddes, "Industrial Parkland," 94; "Silicon Valley U.S.A.," a reprint of a series of articles from the *San Francisco Chronicle*, Sept. 22-26, 1980, 12.

46. Comments of Alf E. Brandin in *Industrial and Housing Review*, 9.

47. Ray Faulkner, "Notes on the Meeting of the Committee on Exterior Architecture and Landscaping," March 16, 1955, Sterling Papers, A-33.

48. Brandin interview, 3.

49. Ginzton interview, 2-3. For early regulations, see Hutchison, "Report on Land Use Survey," 43-44; SUACLBD subcommittee, "Outline for the Development of a Statement to Cover a University Policy with Regard to All Building Construction on Leased Land," Dec. 3, 1952, Sterling Papers, 30:719; Brandin, "Developing Stanford's Lands," 1.

50. See the agendas and minutes, SUACLBD, 1955, 1957–60, 1963–65, Terman Papers, III:35:1–4; clipping from *San Jose Mercury-News*, Oct. 6, 1963, in Stanford Lands, SUA; Blunden, "Industry and Education."

51. "Stanford Industrial Park Land Development Guidelines," July, 1979, Land Use, Industrial Park file, SUNP, 2–6.

52. Alf E. Brandin, "Proposal for Leasing to the Eastman Kodak Company," Oct. 10, 1952, Sterling Papers, 30:719; *Stanford University News* press release, Aug. 21, 1954, Stanford Industrial Park file, SUA; Hackett, *Analysis of Planned Industrial Districts*, 21, 32; *Industrial and Housing Review*, 9.

53. L. Farrell McGhie, assistant dean, School of Engineering, to Kenneth Cuthbertson, assistant to the president, March 18, 1955, enclosed in Kenneth M. Cuthbertson to Alf E. Brandin, April 4, 1955, Sterling Papers, 30:721; Stanford University Office of the President, "Message for the People of Palo Alto" (quotation).

54. Rosemary McAndrews, Memo, in "Stanford Research Park."

55. Brandin interview, 4; Hackett, *Analysis of Planned Industrial Districts*, 34; *San Jose Mercury-News*, Sept. 16, 1960, Stanford Lands file, SUA.

56. *Palo Alto Times*, Feb. 17, 1961, Stanford Lands file, SUA.

57. Peter C. Allen to R. E. Fidoten, Dec. 21, 1955, copy in Stanford University: Land—Industrial Park Companies file, PSC; *Daily Palo Alto Times*, Feb. 29, 1956, Terman Papers, IX:1:9; General Electric officials cited in Baker, "City on the Campus," 73; Lowen, "'Exploiting a Wonderful Opportunity,'" 155–56; Lockheed official cited in London *Sunday Times*, April 23, 1967.

58. Douglas Porter, "The Development of University-Affiliated Research Parks," in Rachelle L. Levitt, ed., *Research Parks and Other Ventures: The University/Real Estate Connection* (Washington, D.C., 1985), 82–83; Geddes, "Industrial Parkland," 10–14.

59. Brandin interview, 4; Terman cited in *San Francisco News*, July 30, 1953, Terman Papers, IX:1:6.

60. Ginzton interview, 4–5; Baker, "City on the Campus," 73; *Rome* (Italy) *Daily American*, Oct. 23, 1955, Sterling Papers, 30:722 (quotation).

61. Three illustrated reports convey the evolving design of the park: *Industrial and Housing Review*, 5–19; Boley, *Industrial Districts: Principles in Practice*, 161–65; Porter, "Development of University-Affiliated Industrial Parks," 71–73. The minutes of SUACLBD, 1955, 1957–60, 1963–65, mention some architects and landscape designers commissioned to work in the industrial park.

62. "History and Introduction," *Varian Associates Magazine*, Special 25 Years Commemorative Issue, April, 1973, Varian Associates Papers, TBL, 4–5; Ginzton interview, 1, 5–6; McGhie to Cuthbertson, March 18, 1955; Lowood, *From Steeples of Excellence to Silicon Valley* (quotation).

63. Alf E. Brandin, "Report on Varian Lease Negotiations," Dec. 18, 1951, Sterling Papers, 30:719, 1–9, and Exhibit D; Stanford University Board of Trustees, "Report of the Land Development Committee," 6, 7.

64. Ginzton interview, 2, 4; Boley, *Industrial Districts: Principles in Practice*, 164; Reyner Banham, "The Architecture of Silicon Valley," *New West* 5 (Sept. 22, 1980): 48.

65. *Industrial and Housing Review*, 9, 13; "Open House," Sept. 18, 1960, brochure in Promotional Materials, Varian Associates Papers; *New York Herald Tribune*, Nov. 4, 1959, in Stanford Lands; Brandin interview, 2.

66. "Making a Run for It," *Measure* (Hewlett-Packard's in-house publication) (Dec. 1979): 2–9; McGhie to Cuthbertson, March 18, 1955; Ginzton interview, 5.

67. Stanford University news release, Feb. 2, 1956, Stanford Industrial Park file, SUA; *Industrial and Housing Review*, 13; *San Francisco Examiner*, Dec. 10, 1961, Stanford Lands file, SUA; Boley, *Industrial Districts: Principles in Practice*, 164; *San Jose Mercury News*, May 29, 1986 (quotation).

68. On Church's influence, see Brandin interview, 4; Harry Sanders, "A Stanford Planner Charts the History of Campus Planning, and Church's Contribution," typescript of an oral history conducted 1977 by Suzanne B. Riess, in "Thomas D. Church, Landscape Architect," Regional Oral History Office, TBL, 1978, vol. 2, 648; Geddes, "Industrial Parkland," 45–53 (quotations at 48, 52–53).

69. Boley, *Industrial Districts: Principles in Practice*, 164; Leslie, "From Backwater to Powerhouse," 58–59; Lenny Siegel and John Markoff, *The High Cost of High Tech: The Dark Side of the Chip* (New York, 1985), 155; "Aerospace Holds No. 1 Position in Sunnyvale," 1984 clipping from San Jose *Business Journal*, in Bay Area: Santa Clara County—Sunnyvale file, PSC.

70. Brandin interview, 2; Geddes, "Industrial Parkland," 34–35 (quotation), 38–40; Porter, "Development of University-Affiliated Research Parks," 71.

71. *Palo Alto Times*, June 30, 1962; Boley, *Industrial Districts: Principles in Practice*, 164.

72. Livingston and Blaney, "Stanford University Land Use Policy/Plan," 9; Bylinsky, "California's Great Breeding Ground," 133; City of Palo Alto, Calif., *Palo Alto Comprehensive Plan, 1977–1990* (Palo Alto, 1976), 15; Stanford University Press Release, July 14, 1986, "Land Use, Industrial Park File," SUNP.

73. "Stanford Lands: Endowment to Advance Our Academic Objectives," 3–4; "Industry Can Be Neighborly," 57, 58–59 (quotation on "garden city"); Palo Alto Planning Commission, *Report on the Interim General Plan . . . 1955*, 8, 9, 45 (quotation of planners).

74. On the controversy, see: Stanford University Office of the President, "Message for the People of Palo Alto"; "Stanford Lands: Endowment to Advance Our Academic Objectives"; "Industry Can Be Neighborly," 58, 61; and clippings and correspondence in Stanford Lands file, SUA, and Sterling Papers, A–29.

75. "Residence and Commute Patterns of Stanford Industrial Park Employees," *Varian Associates Magazine*, Jan. 1963, in Stanford University: Lands—Industrial Park file, PSC, 11–14.

76. Terman, "Stanford, Palo Alto Have Created Community of Technical Scholars," D; Augsberger cited in *San Jose Mercury*, Aug. 13, 1971. Alf E. Brandin stressed Stanford's need to assert primarily its own interests in land development programs: Brandin to J. E. Wallace Sterling, Aug. 27, 1952, Sterling Papers, 30:719; Brandin interview, 4. The university gradually became more

closely attuned to what the Board of Trustees termed the "political considerations" of its policies, but it retained its primary focus on building a great research center. See Stanford University Board of Trustees, "The Stanford University Land Use Policies," Mar. 12, 1974, reprinted in "Stanford Research Park."

77. City of Palo Alto, *Palo Alto Comprehensive Plan, 1977–1990*, 14. The Land Use—Research Park file, SUNP, contains clippings on the park versus the community.

78. Criticisms of Stanford's land policies are summarized in: "Industry Can Be Neighborly," 61–62; Joseph Curley, "From the Farm to Boomtown," *Peninsula* 1 (Feb. 1987): 34–39, 48. President Sterling confessed in 1960 that the university's land development officers had seldom met with local and county planners, and Kenneth M. Cuthbertson, vice president for finance, introduced a new land-use plan for the university in 1971 as the first to be developed since the much-ignored SOM master plan of 1953: J. Wallace Sterling, "Transcription of Talk by President Sterling, Land Development Open House," April 2, 1960, 1–2, and *Stanford Daily*, Feb. 22, 1971, both in Stanford University: Lands—General and Miscellaneous file, PSC.

79. Geddes, "Industrial Parkland," 13; Leslie, "Backwater to Powerhouse," 60. Lowen, "'Exploiting a Wonderful Opportunity,'" especially 220, analyzes the muted criticism within the university of the changes at Stanford.

80. Victor J. Danilov, "How Successful Are Science Parks?" *Industrial Research* 9 (May 1967): 76; U.S. General Accounting Office, *Federal Role in Fostering University-Industry Cooperation*, 48; Porter, "Development of University-Affiliated Research Parks," 70; *NYT*, April 26, 1987.

81. U.S. General Accounting Office, *Federal Role In Fostering University-Industry Cooperation*, 16; Therese Engstrom, "Little Silicon Valleys," *High Technology* 7 (Jan. 1987): 24–32.

82. *Berkeley Gazette*, Mar. 29, 1961, *Redwood City Tribune*, June 30, 1962, and *Riverside Enterprise*, Nov. 15, 1959 (quotation), in Stanford Lands file, SUA; Brandin interview, 5.

83. On Stanford as an influence on planning for the University of California at Santa Cruz, see *Oakland Tribune*, Mar. 19, 1961, Stanford Lands file, SUA. Although I have not found specific mention of Stanford serving as a model for the University of California, Irvine, both planning documents and the campus's actual development appeared to follow the Stanford pattern. See "University Community Character and Goals: Irvine Campus Workshop Conference," Nov. 9, 1962, in Carton 5, Catherine Bauer Wurster Papers, TBL.

84. Bylinsky, "California's Great Breeding Ground," 129; Saxenian, "Genesis of Silicon Valley," 24; Levitt, ed., *Research Parks and Other Ventures*, 11–12.

Although this analysis focuses primarily on Santa Clara County, both Silicon Valley and Stanford spread from Santa Clara County into San Mateo County. On the rise of high-tech industry and industrial parks in San Mateo County, see Alan Hynding, *From Frontier to Suburb: The Story of The San Mateo Peninsula* (Belmont, Calif., 1982), 292–97.

85. Bylinsky, "California's Great Breeding Ground," 129; "Study of the

Local Impacts of Research and Research-Based Manufacturing: Santa Clara County, California," Santa Clara County, Calif., Planning Department, *Info-Commentary*, no. 3 (Mar. 1967): 1, 14 (hereafter cited as "Local Impacts").

86. Jan Otto Marius Bröek, *The Santa Clara Valley, California: A Study in Landscape Changes* (Utrecht, Netherlands, 1932), 129–30; Glenna Christine Matthews, "A California Middletown: The Social History of San Jose in the Depression," Ph.D. diss., Stanford University, 1977, 124. Quotation from Anna Louise Strong, *My Native Land* (New York, 1940), 36.

87. Industrial Survey Associates, *San Jose and Santa Clara County: An Economic Survey with Particular Reference to Industrial Development* (San Francisco, 1948), 8–11, 13, 21; George Starbird, *The New Metropolis: San Jose Between 1942 and 1972* (San Jose, 1972), 1–2; Santa Clara County, Calif., Planning Commission, *Blueprint for the Future: A Post-War Plan for Santa Clara County, California* (San Jose, 1944).

88. Philip J. Trounstine and Terry Christensen, *Movers and Shakers: The Study of Community Power* (New York, 1982), 87–89, 91–92, 97; Starbird, *New Metropolis*, 1–2.

89. Saxenian, "Genesis of Silicon Valley," 22; Arthur L. Norberg, "The Origins of the Electronics Industry on the Pacific Coast," *Proceedings of the Institute of Electrical and Electronics Engineers* 64 (Sept. 1976): 1314–22; "Local Impacts," 1, 15.

90. Albert Shapero, Richard P. Howell, and James R. Tombough, *An Exploratory Study of the Structure and Dynamics of the R&D Industry* (Menlo Park, Calif., 1964), 23–25; Saxenian, "Genesis of Silicon Valley," 27. Students of the military-industrial complex in California generally equate high-technology industry with aerospace production. In rough terms, these manufacturing categories include: aircraft and aircraft parts; electrical equipment and supplies; electrical instruments and related products; and ordnance and accessories.

91. John Frederick Keller, "The Production Worker in Electronics: Industrialization and Labor Development in California's Santa Clara Valley," Ph.D. diss., University of Michigan, 1981, 55–58; State of California, *Aerospace Employment, California and Metropolitan Areas, 1949–1969* (Sacramento, 1970), 1–3; "Local Impacts," 2; Santa Clara County, Calif., Planning Department, *Study of the Economy of Santa Clara County*, 10–11.

92. Saxenian, "Genesis of Silicon Valley," 26–27; Siegel and Markoff, *High Cost of High Tech*, 8–9.

93. SRI International, *The Role of Defense in Santa Clara County's Economy* (Washington, D.C., 1980), v–vii; *San Jose Mercury News*, Oct. 19, 1980. Siegel and Borock, "Background Report on Silicon Valley," 15, suggest that figures for prime contracts probably underestimate the county's engagement in production for defense. FMC Corporation, a builder of armored vehicles that do not generally qualify as high-tech, accounted for a substantial proportion of the county's defense industry.

94. Siegel and Borock, "Background Report on Silicon Valley," 3.

95. Economic diversification has been depicted by Bylinsky, "California's Great Breeding Ground," 129, 133, and passim; Judith K. Larsen, *U.S. Policy and the Semiconductor Industry: An Industry Perspective* (Los Altos, Calif., 1984),

1. On the recession of 1970–71, see Richard C. Carlson, "The Bay Area Success Story," in SRI International, comp., "The Mid-Peninsula in the 1980s: Issues, Options, and Tradeoffs," transcript of SRI International Community Forum, Jan. 23–24, 1980, in Bay Area: Santa Clara County—Land Use file, PSC, 3–4. On the microprocessor, see Siegel and Markoff, *High Cost of High Tech*, 9; Tim Bajarin and Jill Morganthaller, "Silicon Valley: Birthplace of the Information Industry," *Information Times* (Fall 1984): 14. First use of "Silicon Valley" is credited to Don C. Hoefler's series of articles, "Silicon Valley, U.S.A.," *Electronic News* 16 (Jan. 11, 18, 25, 1971).

96. Bylinsky, "California's Great Breeding Ground," 133, 128–29, 130.

97. "Local Impacts," 3; Bylinsky, "California's Great Breeding Ground," 133–34; Saxenian, "Genesis of Silicon Valley," 24–25; Jon C. Iwata, "Research Roots," *Almaden Views* (publication of IBM Almaden Research Center, San Jose) 1 (Spring 1986): 1.

98. "Silicon Valley U.S.A.," 5.

99. Trounstine and Christensen, *Movers and Shakers*, 90; Charles Wollenberg, *Golden Gate Metropolis: Perspectives on Bay Area History* (Berkeley, 1985), 309; Donald L. Foley et al., *Characteristics of Metropolitan Growth in California*, vol. 1, *Report* (Berkeley, 1965), 84, 90, 91, 93; Saxenian, "Genesis of Silicon Valley," 32; San Jose, Calif., Department of City Planning, *Horizon 2000 General Plan for the City of San Jose, Adopted by the San Jose City Council November 7, 1984* (San Jose, 1984), 21.

100. "Silicon Valley U.S.A.," 3; U.S. General Accounting Office, *Federal Role in Fostering University-Industry Cooperation*; Bylinsky, "California's Great Breeding Ground," 129.

101. Saxenian, "Genesis of Silicon Valley," 29; Peter A. Morrison, *San Jose and St. Louis in the 1960s: A Case Study of Changing Urban Populations* (Santa Monica, 1973), 12; *San Jose Mercury News*, Mar. 15, 1984.

102. United California Bank, Research and Planning Division, *Santa Clara County, Past—Present—1985* (Los Angeles, 1975), 12; Connerly and Associates, Inc., "Urban Infill Development in Northern California: Case Studies and Recommendations," 1980, IGSL, 11; San Jose Department of City Planning, *The General Plan 1975* (San Jose, 1976), 5. On the number of people with Ph.D.'s, see: "Silicon Valley U.S.A.," 8; *San Jose Mercury*, Aug. 24, 1967.

103. Keller, "Production Worker in Electronics," 92–95.

104. Wayne M. Swan, "Palo Alto, a City in Transition: A Research Report About Industrial Development and the Level of Services in the City of Palo Alto from 1950 to 1962," May 24, 1963, in Carton 6, Catherine Bauer Wurster Papers, TBL, 18; *San Jose Mercury-News*, Jan. 24, 1960, Stanford Lands file, SUA.

105. Bylinsky, "California's Great Breeding Ground," 130.

106. Stedman, "California Peninsula," 35.

107. For example, the headline in *San Jose Mercury News*, Sept. 25, 1977, read, "How Many People Are Too Many People to Live the Good Life in Santa Clara County?"

108. Samuel E. Wood and Alfred E. Heller, *California Going, Going . . . : Our State's Struggle to Remain Beautiful and Productive* (Sacramento, 1962), 10;

Samuel E. Wood, "Administration, Research, and Analysis in Behalf of Environmental Quality," typescript of an oral history conducted by Malca Chall in 1981, in "State and Regional Planning Initiatives, 1950–1975," vol. 1 of Statewide and Regional Land-Use Planning in California, 1950–1980 Project, Regional Oral History Office, TBL, 1983, 142–51; Stanford Environmental Law Society, *San Jose, Sprawling City: A Report on Land Use Policies and Practices in San Jose, California* (Stanford, 1971); Robert C. Fellmeth, ed., *Politics of Land: Ralph Nader's Study Group Report on Land Use in California* (New York, 1973). Quotation from Karl Belser, "The Making of Slurban America," *Cry California* 5 (Fall 1970): 1.

109. Stanford Environmental Law Society, *San Jose, Sprawling City*, 7–15; Trounstine and Christensen, *Movers and Shakers*, 94; Santa Clara County, Calif., Planning Commission, *Facts and Forecasts: A Supplement to the General Plan of Santa Clara County* (San Jose, 1960), 3–4.

110. Daniel J. Alesch and Robert A. Levine, *Growth in San Jose: A Summary Policy Statement* (Santa Monica, 1973), 6–7, 13; Connerly and Associates, "Urban Infill Development," 19–22; Trounstine and Christensen, *Movers and Shakers*, 99–108.

111. Trounstine and Christensen, *Movers and Shakers*, 119, 145, 148 (quotation).

112. My analysis of the different outlooks of planners and residents extrapolates from the findings of Francois G. Christen, *Citizen Preference for Home, Neighborhood, and City in Santa Clara County* (Santa Monica, 1973), 6, 15–16; Alesch and Levine, *Growth in San Jose*, 4, 7–9, 23.

113. Geddes, "Industrial Parkland," 8, 103, mentions wasteful land use. Strangers to the industrial parks needed up-to-date maps in order to navigate around and through them: *Peninsula Times Tribune*, June 23, Oct. 8, 1982; *San Jose Mercury News*, Sept. 6, 1982.

114. Bylinsky, "California's Great Breeding Ground," 130; Judith K. Larsen and Carol Gill, *Changing Lifestyles in Silicon Valley* (Los Altos, Calif., 1983), 24; Stanford University press release, Oct. 3, 1977, Terman file, SUNP; Saxenian, "Genesis of Silicon Valley," 29–30.

115. "Directory of Industrial Parks and Industrial Districts in Santa Clara County: 1967," Santa Clara County, Calif., Planning Department, *Info-Commentary*, no. 5 (Sept. 1967): 1–5.

116. "Directory of Industrial Parks, 1967," 7–17.

117. Wollenberg, *Golden Gate Metropolis*, 312; Brandin interview, 4, 5; Ginzton interview, 4.

118. Ginzton interview, 3–4; David W. Fuller, "Vallco Park: From Orchards to Industry," *Cupertino Chronicle*, vol. 19 in the California History Center, Local History Studies (1975): 135–38, 142–43; "Directory of Industrial Parks and Industrial Districts in Santa Clara County: 1966," Santa Clara County, Calif., Planning Department, *Info-Commentary: Industrial Districts* 2 (Jan. 1967): 3–4; "Directory of Industrial Parks, 1967," 17; San Jose Chamber of Commerce, *1981 Thru 1982 Industrial Directory* (San Jose, 1981), 308.

119. "Directory of Industrial Parks, 1967," 10; Whitney, "Planners Seek Special Environment for Location of New Research Facilities," A–237.

120. San Jose Chamber of Commerce, *1977 Industrial Directory* (San Jose, 1977), 182–200; San Jose Chamber of Commerce, *1981 Thru 1982 Industrial Directory*, 286–308.

121. *Palo Alto Times*, March 20, Nov. 9, 1978; San Jose Chamber of Commerce, *1981 Thru 1982 Industrial Directory*, 290.

122. Geddes, "Industrial Parkland," 76–81.

123. Banham, "Architecture of Silicon Valley," 47–48; IBM official quoted in *San Jose Mercury*, Sept. 10, 1979.

124. Frank Viviano, "The Architecture of Impermanence," *San Jose Mercury News West Magazine* (Feb. 5, 1984): 10.

125. Banham, "Architecture of Silicon Valley," 48; Viviano, "Architecture of Impermanence," 10–15.

126. Santa Clara County, Calif., Planning Commission, *Facts and Forecasts*, 18; "Silicon Valley U.S.A.," 17; Sunnyvale, Calif., City Planning Commission, *1972 General Plan of the City of Sunnyvale* (Sunnyvale, Calif., 1972), II–2, II–3.

127. San Jose, Calif., Department of City Planning, *General Plan 1975*, 7; San Jose, Calif., Department of City Planning, *Horizon 2000 General Plan*, 11.

128. San Jose, Calif., Department of City Planning, *Horizon 2000 General Plan*, 106–8.

129. "Silicon Valley U.S.A.," 10–11; Trounstine and Christensen, *Movers and Shakers*, 119.

130. Lenny Siegel, "High-Tech Pollution," *Sierra* 69 (Nov.–Dec. 1984): 58–64; Siegel and Markoff, *High Cost of High Tech*, ch. 8; "Toxics Update," *Global Electronics* 80 (Dec. 1987): 3; *San Jose Mercury News*, April 28, 1988.

131. The ideal was expressed by Sunnyvale, Calif., City Planning Commission, *General Plan for Sunnyvale*, vi (quotation); "Industry Can Be Neighborly," 57–62; San Jose, Calif., Department of City Planning, *General Plan 1975*, 16.

132. Sunnyvale, Calif., City Planning Commission, *General Plan for Sunnyvale* (Sunnyvale, Calif., 1957), 4, 10–11; Sunnyvale, Calif., City Planning Commission, *1972 General Plan*, I–1 (first quotation); "Silicon Valley U.S.A.," 10–11 (second quotation).

133. Alesch and Levine, *Growth in San Jose*, 25; San Jose, Calif., Department of City Planning, *General Plan 1975*, 10–11; San Jose, Calif., Department of City Planning, *Horizon 2000 General Plan*, 14–16. Commuting figures from Santa Clara County, Calif., Planning Department, "Analysis of General Plan 'Build-Out,'" Aug. 1977, in Bay Area: Santa Clara County—Land Use file, PSC.

134. Santa Clara County, Calif., Planning Department, "Analysis of General Plan 'Build-Out'"; Marianne Rowe, "City Industrial Growth Policies in Santa Clara County: Environmental Implications," 1975, in Bay Area: Santa Clara County—Land Use file, PSC.

135. Carlson, "Bay Area Success Story," 4–6; *San Jose Mercury*, April 23, 1980; Jay Thorwaldson, "Santa Clara County: A Valley in Perpetual Motion," *Cry California* 14 (Fall 1979): 19–20.

136. *San Jose Mercury News*, Jan. 28, 1979, Sept. 7, 1980.

137. Siegel and Borock, "Background Report on Silicon Valley," 29–30;

Thorwaldson, "Santa Clara County," 20. The *San Jose Mercury News*, Mar. 15, 1984, reporting census data about the nation's thirty largest metropolitan areas, indicated that in addition to its extremely costly housing, San Jose ranked next to last in the portion of its commuters using public transit—only 3.3 percent.

138. AnnaLee Saxenian, "Silicon Chips and Spatial Structure: The Industrial Basis of Urbanization in Santa Clara County, California," Working Paper 345, University of California Institute of Urban and Regional Development (Berkeley, 1981), 166–67; Larsen and Gill, *Changing Lifestyles in Silicon Valley*, 2–3. Keller, "Production Worker in Electronics," and Siegel and Markoff, *High Cost of High Tech*, ch. 6, depict the composition and experience of Silicon Valley's lower tier.

139. AnnaLee Saxenian, "Silicon Valley and Route 128: Regional Prototypes or Historic Exceptions," in Manuel Castells, ed., *High Technology, Space, and Society* (Beverly Hills, 1985), 85–91.

140. Bylinsky, "California's Great Breeding Ground," 224; "Silicon Valley U.S.A.," 10–11; "More Elbowroom for the Electronics Industry," *Business Week* (Mar. 10, 1980): 94–100; Howard Wolff, "The New West: An Industry on the Move Changes Where and How It Does Business," *Electronics* (Aug. 28, 1980): 92, 94; Saxenian, "Silicon Chips and Spatial Structure," 167.

141. Geddes, "Industrial Parkland," 51; "California Expands as Spawning Ground for High Tech," *San Diego Business Journal*, June 20, 1983, in Silicon Valley file, SUNP (quotation).

142. Association of Bay Area Governments, *Silicon Valley and Beyond: High Technology Growth for the San Francisco Bay Area*, Working Papers on the Region's Economy, No. 2 (Berkeley, 1981), 87; Bylinsky, "California's Great Breeding Ground," 224; "Silicon Valley U.S.A.," 10–11; Ann Markusen, Peter Hall, and Amy Glasmeier, *High Tech America: The What, How, Where, and Why of the Sunrise Industries* (Boston, 1986), 78. Figures on Stanford Industrial Park from *San Jose Mercury News*, April 28, 1988.

Chapter Four

1. Joseph F. Sheley, "Mutuality and Retirement Community Success," *International Journal of Aging and Human Development* 5 (Winter 1974): 72; Michael E. Hunt et al., *Retirement Communities: An American Original* (New York, 1984), 58 (quotation).

2. Del E. Webb Development Company (hereafter cited as DEVCO), "The Country Club World of . . . Del Webb's Sun City, Arizona," 1968 advertising brochure, SCAHS. Almost all of the DEVCO promotional material for Sun City is unpaginated.

3. Bradford Luckingham, *Phoenix: The History of a Southwestern Metropolis* (Tucson, 1989), chs. 4–6.

4. Bradford Luckingham, "Urban Development in Arizona: The Rise of

Phoenix," *Journal of Arizona History* 22 (Summer 1981): 216–19; Charles S. Sargent, "Arizona's Urban Frontier—Myths and Realities," in Charles S. Sargent, ed., *The Conflict Between Frontier Values and Land-Use Control in Greater Phoenix: Report of a Conference Held at Arizona State University, November 22, 1975* (Phoenix, 1976), 19; "Phoenix: The Blemishes in Boomtown," *Business Week* (Nov. 15, 1969): 144; Ann Markusen, Peter Hall, and Amy Glasmeier, *High Tech America: The What, How, Where, and Why of the Sunrise Industries* (Boston, 1986), 98–99.

5. Michael F. Konig, "Toward Metropolitan Status: Charter Government and the Rise of Phoenix, Arizona, 1945–1960," Ph.D. diss., Arizona State University, 1983, 340; Joseph Stocker, *Arizona: A Guide to Easier Living* (New York, 1955), 55; Daniel W. Raaf, "Characteristics of a Sample of Adult Males of Metropolitan Phoenix," *Arizona Business and Economic Review* 8 (June 1959): 8; G. Wesley Johnson, *Phoenix: Valley of the Sun* (Tulsa, 1982), 129.

6. City of Phoenix and Maricopa County, Arizona, Advance Planning Task Force, *Land Use of the Phoenix Urban Area: A Study Basic to Long Range Planning* (hereafter cited as CPMC, *Land Use of the Phoenix Urban Area*) (Phoenix, 1959), i, 3, 4; David A. Bingham, "Urban Planning in Arizona," *Arizona Review of Business and Public Administration* 10 (July 1961): 3.

7. Luckingham, "Urban Development in Arizona: The Rise of Phoenix," 224, 226, 227–29; John D. Wenum, *Annexation as a Technique for Metropolitan Growth: The Case of Phoenix, Arizona* (Tempe, Ariz., 1970), xi.

8. Konig, "Toward Metropolitan Status," ch. 4; Phoenix, Arizona, City Planning Department, *The Comprehensive Plan, 1990, Phoenix, Arizona* (hereafter cited as PCPD, *Comprehensive Plan, 1990*) (Phoenix, 1969), 31; Earl C. Gottschalk, Jr., "Boom Town: Phoenix Area's Sprawl Worries City Planners," *Wall Street Journal*, June 18, 1974, 1 (quotation).

9. Stocker, *Arizona: A Guide to Easier Living*, 59–60.

10. Desmond Muirhead, "The Arizona Landscape, a Critique—II. Cities, Subdivisions," *Arizona Architect* 2 (June 1959): 12–13; CPMC, *Land Use of the Phoenix Urban Area*, iii; PCPD, *Comprehensive Plan, 1990*, 81.

11. Gottschalk, "Boom Town," 1.

12. U.S. Bureau of the Census, *United States Census of Population: 1960*, vol. 1, *Characteristics of the Population*, part 4, *Arizona* (Washington, D.C., 1963), 27; U.S. Bureau of the Census, *United States Census of Population: 1960*, vol. 1, *Characteristics of the Population*, part 1, *U.S. Summary* (Washington, D.C., 1964), 358, 767; PCPD, *Comprehensive Plan, 1990*, 43.

13. Wilma Donahue, Harold L. Orbach, and Otto Pollack, "Retirement: The Emerging Social Pattern" (hereafter cited as Donahue, "Retirement"), in Clark Tibbits, ed., *Handbook of Social Gerontology: Societal Aspects of Aging* (Chicago, 1960), 331; Robert J. Havighurst, "The Nature and Values of Meaningful Free-Time Activity," in Robert W. Kleemeier, ed., *Aging and Leisure: A Research Perspective into the Meaningful Use of Time* (New York, 1961), 310–11; Michael B. Barker, *California Retirement Communities* (Berkeley, 1966), 4–5; Martha Farnsworth Riche, "Retirement's Lifestyle Pioneers," *American Demographics* 8 (June 1986): 42; Frances FitzGerald, *Cities on a Hill: A Journey Through Contemporary American Cultures* (New York, 1986), 205–6.

14. FitzGerald, *Cities on a Hill*, 206; Barker, *California Retirement Communities*, 7.

15. American retirement policies are treated as the product of consensus, but others describe them as "essentially a political device" imposed by the managers of American capitalism on acquiescent but manipulated victims: William Graebner, *A History of Retirement: The Meaning and Function of An American Institution, 1885–1978* (New Haven, Conn., 1980), especially 268.

16. Donahue, "Retirement," 344–46; W. Andrew Achenbaum, *Shades of Gray: Old Age, American Values, and Federal Policies Since 1920* (Boston, 1983), 60, 62–64, 116–17, 120, ch. 4; Arlie Russell Hochschild, *The Unexpected Community: Portrait of an Old Age Subculture* (rev. ed. Berkeley, 1978), 19; FitzGerald, *Cities on a Hill*, 207–8.

17. Donahue, "Retirement," 334–35, 343, 375–80; Achenbaum, *Shades of Gray*, 60–61.

18. Max Kaplan, "The Uses of Leisure," in Tibbitts, ed., *Handbook of Social Gerontology*, 408, 416 (quotation); Achenbaum, *Shades of Gray*, 59–60.

19. Quotation from David Riesman, "The Suburban Dislocation," *Annals of the American Academy of Political and Social Science* 314 (Nov. 1957): 143. See also: Graebner, *History of Retirement*, 228; Donahue, "Retirement," 336.

20. Hochschild, *Unexpected Community*, x–xiii; Merton quoted in Stanford Research Institute, "Report: 4 Sections Complete," 1957–1958, DP-UWL, part 4, 61.

21. Barker, *California Retirement Communities*, 4; M. Powell Lawton, *Environment and Aging* (Monterey, Calif., 1980), 139.

22. Donald J. Bogue, *The Population of the United States* (Glencoe, Ill., 1959), 381; Donald J. Bogue, *The Population of the United States: Historical Trends and Future Projections* (New York, 1985), 333; Lawton, *Environment and Aging*, 136–37; Charles F. Longino, Jr., "American Retirement Communities and Residential Relocation," in A. M. Warnes, ed., *Geographical Perspectives on the Elderly* (Chichester, Eng., 1982), 247.

23. Robert F. Wiseman, "Concentration and Migration of Older Americans," in Robert J. Newcomer, M. Powell Lawton, and Thomas O. Byerts, eds., *Housing an Aged Society: Issues, Alternatives, and Policy* (New York, 1986), 71 (quotation); Lawton, *Environment and Aging*, 23–24; Nancy R. Hooyman and H. Asuman Kiyak, *Social Gerontology; A Multidisciplinary Perspective* (Boston, 1988), 347; Riche, "Retirement's Lifestyle Pioneers," 43.

24. Michael Baker, "Arizona Retirement Communities and the Changing Needs of an Aging Population," *Arizona Review* 32 (Fall 1984): 15. Donald R. Tuffs, formerly senior vice president for Del E. Webb Communities, Inc., states that in 1960 perhaps only 3 percent of all retirees were willing to move more than two hundred miles from their hometown. By the 1980s that had increased to 8–10 percent: Donald R. Tuffs, interview with author, Oct. 20, 1986, Sun City West, Arizona, summary, SCAHS (hereafter cited as Tuffs interview).

25. Lawton, *Environment and Aging*, 139–41; James R. Bohland and Lexa Treps, "County Patterns of Elderly Migration in the United States," in Warnes, ed., *Geographical Perspectives on the Elderly*, 140–58; Walter K. Vivrett, "Housing and Community Settings for Older People," in Tibbitts, ed., *Handbook of Social Gerontology*, 556–57, 570.

26. Bohland and Treps, "County Patterns of Elderly Migration in the United States," 151–53; Cynthia B. Flynn, "General Versus Aged Interstate Migration, 1965–1970," *Research on Aging* 2 (June 1980): 165–76.

27. James E. Vance, Jr., "California and the Search for the Ideal," *Annals of the Association of American Geographers* 62 (June 1972): 196–98; Albert Chevan and Lucy Rose Fischer, "Retirement and Interstate Migration," *Social Forces* 57 (June 1979): 1365–80.

28. Stephen M. Golant, "In Defense of Age-Segregated Housing," in Judith Ann Hancock, ed., *Housing the Elderly* (New Brunswick, N.J., 1987), 49.

29. Hunt et al., *Retirement Communities: An American Original*, 12–16, 253, 255.

30. Sheila K. Johnson, "Growing Old Alone Together," *NYT Magazine* (Nov. 11, 1973): 40; Lawton, *Environment and Aging*, 22; Golant, "In Defense of Age-Segregated Housing," 49.

31. Hunt et al., *Retirement Communities: An American Original*, 13. These figures represent quite rough calculations from the estimates in the sources listed in the previous note, which are based on crude and inconsistent data from the period 1973–84.

32. Robert N. Butler, *Why Survive? Being Old in America* (New York, 1975), 17.

33. Figures from Robert W. Marans et al., "Retirement Communities: Present and Future," in ULI, *Housing for a Maturing Population* (Washington, D.C., 1983), 88.

34. Joseph C. Buckley, *The Retirement Handbook: A Complete Guide to Your Future* (4th ed. New York, 1971), 119–21. Ross Cortese made many of the same claims for his California Leisure Worlds that DEVCO made for Sun City, and in quite similar language: "Facts You Will Want to Know About Rossmoor Leisure World, Walnut Creek," n.d. [1964 or 1965], in Carton 5, Catherine Bauer Wurster Papers, TBL. Like Sun City, Leisure World in Laguna Hills formed its own historical society and produced a journal, *Leisure World History* 1–3 (1980–1982), that helps to illuminate the development of Leisure Worlds, which paralleled the growth of Sun City in many ways.

35. Remi Nadeau, *California: The New Society* (New York, 1963), 272–73; "Retirement City—Haven or Ghetto," *Business Week* (April 11, 1964): 129; *NYT*, Jan. 18, 1970; Paul O'Neil, "For the Retired, a World All Their Own," *Life* 68 (May 15, 1970): 45.

36. Wilma Donahue, "European Experience in Operation and Services," in Ernest W. Burgess, ed., *Retirement Villages* (Ann Arbor, Mich., 1961), 103–4; Lewis L. Mumford, "For Older People, Not Segregation but Integration," *Architectural Record* 119 (May 1956): 191–94 (quotation at 191).

37. For criticism of segregated housing, see Jerry Jacobs, *Fun City: An Ethnographic Study of a Retirement Community* (New York, 1974); Gordon L. Bultena and Vivian Wood, "The American Retirement Community: Bane or Blessing," *Journal of Gerontology* 24 (April 1969): 209–210; Golant, "In Defense of Age-Segregated Housing," 50–51. Quotation from Longino, "American Retirement Communities and Residential Relocation," 258.

38. Susan R. Sherman et al., "Psychological Effects of Retirement Hous-

ing," *Gerontologist* 8 (Autumn, Part 1, 1968): 170; Irving Rosow, *Social Integration of the Aged* (New York, 1967), 78, 324.

39. Hooyman and Kiyak, *Social Gerontology*, 310; Achenbaum, *Shades of Gray*, 71; Vivrett, "Housing and Community Settings for Older People," 567–69. On suburban distancing of young and old, see William H. Whyte, Jr., *The Organization Man* (New York, 1956), 342, 342n; Henry D. Sheldon, "The Changing Demographic Profile," in Tibbitts, ed., *Handbook of Social Gerontology*, 54–55; Carol A. Christensen, *The American Garden City and the New Towns Movement* (Ann Arbor, Mich., 1986), 100–101.

40. Barker, *California Retirement Communities*, 18–20; David Hackett Fischer, *Growing Old in America* (New York, 1977), 149; Patricia Gober, "The Retirement Community as a Geographical Phenomenon: The Case of Sun City, Arizona," *Journal of Geography* 84 (Sept.–Oct. 1985): 190; Donahue, "Retirement," 373; Riche, "Retirement's Lifestyle Pioneers," 44; Stephen M. Golant, "Residential Concentrations of Future Elderly," *Gerontologist* 15 (Feb. 1975): 16–17.

41. Gober, "Retirement Community as a Geographical Phenomenon," 190; Gordon F. Streib and Wayne E. Thompson, "The Older Person in a Family Context," in Tibbitts, ed., *Handbook of Social Gerontology*, 476–78, 481; Katherine McMillan Heintz, *Retirement Communities: For Adults Only* (New Brunswick, N.J., 1976), 3–4; Hochschild, *Unexpected Community*, 27–28.

42. The best summary of the research on the benefits of life in a retirement community is provided in Golant, "In Defense of Age-Segregated Housing," 51–54. See also Susan R. Sherman, "The Choice of Retirement Housing Among the Well-Elderly," *Aging and Human Development* 2 (May 1971): 122–33; Hunt et al., *Retirement Communities: An American Original*, 1–2; *NS*, Nov. 9, 1983; *AR*, Jan. 27, 1985.

43. Golant, "In Defense of Age-Segregated Housing," 54–55; Sherman, "Choice of Retirement Housing Among the Well-Elderly," 132, 137; Bultena and Wood, "American Retirement Community: Bane or Blessing," 210–11.

44. Advertisement for Sun City in *Ladies Home Journal* (March 1963), in "1959–1967 Webb National," advertising scrapbook, SCAHS.

45. Quotation from Tom Ryan, former DEVCO senior vice president, in *NS*, Sept. 19, 1984, SCAHS. On Webb, see Jane Freeman and Glenn Sanberg, *Jubilee: A History of Sun City, Arizona* (Phoenix, 1984), 6–14; "Del E. Webb, The All American Arizonan Legend," *Arizona Highways* 50 (June 1974): 35; *AR*, Sept. 8, 1965.

46. Barker, *California Retirement Communities*, 42–43.

47. "Sun City Progress Story," DEVCO press release, June 1969, SCAHS, 1; *AR*, Jan. 1, 1967, PPL-AR-SCCF.

48. Stocker, *Arizona: A Guide to Easier Living*, 123, 129; R. Alan Thornburg, "Life Begins at Retirement," *Arizona Today Economic and Business Report* 1 (Nov. 1962): 7–8; Vivien Keatley, "Retirement in the Sun," *Arizona Days and Ways Magazine*, Sunday supplement to *AR* (Feb. 11, 1962): 87–89.

49. Bob Gottlieb, "Sun City: A Gamble in the Sun by Casino Kings," *New Times Weekly* (Phoenix) 11 (Jan. 23, 1980): 6; *AR*, March 24, 1963 (first quotation), Nov. 9, 1958, PPL-AR-RCCF; *PG*, Sept. 3, 1955, Nov. 21, 1959,

PPL-AR-YCF; "Youngtown, Arizona" promotional brochure, n.p., n.d., PPL-AR-YCF (other quotations).

50. Irving L. Webber and Carter C. Osterbind, "Types of Retirement Villages," in Burgess, ed., *Retirement Villages*, 5–7. Hunt et al., *Retirement Communities: An American Original*, 139, depicts Orange Gardens, a Florida retirement subdivision started in 1955. Roger I. Yoshino and Gary L. Buck, "Satisfaction with Life for the Retired," *Arizona Review of Business and Public Administration* 13 (March 1964): 8–14, portray some of the defects of retirees' life in Arizona trailer parks.

51. "Sun City Progress Story," 1 (quotations); *AR*, Jan. 8, 1985, PPL-AR-SCCF. On the Webb company's research into housing for the elderly, see Freeman and Sanberg, *Jubilee*, ch. 2.

52. John Meeker, former DEVCO executive, interview with author, Phoenix, Arixona, Oct. 21, 1986, summary, SCAHS (hereafter cited as Meeker interview); *AR*, July 16, 1960, PPL-AR-SCCF; Nadeau, *California: The New Society*, 273; Doris Paine, "The Sun City Story," *Phoenix Magazine* 13 (July 1978): S–5, S–6.

53. Freeman and Sanberg, *Jubilee*, 15, 20–21.

54. DEVCO, "Development Master Plan for Sun City, Arizona," February 1972, in Sun City, Del. E. Webb Corp./Correspondence, 1972–1975, 1976–1977 file, Maricopa County, Arizona, Planning and Development records, Phoenix, 5, 6.

55. There is conflicting testimony on early sales figures. I have relied on Jerry Svendsen, DEVCO director of public relations, to Caren Glotfelty, July 30, 1969, in SCAHS; Freeman and Sanberg, *Jubilee*, 30; Paine, "Sun City Story," S–6. Population data from *PG*, Jan. 1, 1962, PPL-AR-SCCF; *AR*, Jan. 2, 1964, PPL-AR-SCCF.

56. "Del Webb's Sun City, a Retirement Community," special advertising section in *AR*, Jan. 1, 1960, PPL-AR-SCCF, 7, 10–11; Esther Clark, "Arizona Architecture and the 'Hawaii Influence,'" *Arizona Days and Ways*, weekly supplement to *AR* (Oct. 28, 1962): 12 (quotation).

57. *AR*, Jan. 1, 1967, PPL-AR-SCCF; *PG*, May 14, 1960, Jan. 28, 1961, June 21, 1967, PPL-AR-SCCF; Calvin Trillin, "Wake Up and Live," *New Yorker* 40 (April 4, 1964): 123; *NS*, Jan. 14, 1975.

58. *PG*, Jan. 8, 1965, PPL-AR-SCCF; Del E. Webb Corporation, Housing Division, Marketing Research Section, "Opinion Study of One Hundred Recent Buyers, Sun City, Arizona," Oct. 15, 1962, in Del E. Webb Communities, Inc., public relations files, Sun City West, Ariz. (hereafter cited as "1962 Opinion Study"), 7–8.

59. *AR*, May 5, July 16, 1960, Nov. 10, 1962 (quotation), PPL-AR-SCCF; Hunt et al., *Retirement Communities: An American Original*, 26; *Evening American* (Phoenix), March 14, 1965, PPL-AR-SCCF.

60. Trillin, "Wake Up and Live," 134 (quotations); Tuffs interview.

61. The information and quotations in this paragraph and the seven immediately following are based in part on the following publicity materials issued by DEVCO to promote Sun City between 1959 and 1965. (Unless otherwise noted, all can be found at SCAHS. Most are not paginated, and many

are not dated; I have estimated times of publication.) "Active Living For America's Senior Citizens: Del Webb's Sun City, Arizona," 1959[?], in Arizona Collection and Arizona Historical Foundation, Hayden Library, Arizona State University; "Anyone Who Can Retire Can Afford Full-time Living in Any of Del Webb's Beautiful Cities," 1963; "Del Webb's Active Retirement," 1965[?]; Del Webb Ad Proofs scrapbook, 1965–66; "Del Webb's Sun City, Arizona," 1961; "Del Webb's Sun City, Arizona," map, 1964; "Del Webb's Sun City, Arizona," 1965; "Del Webb's Sun City, Arizona: Active Living for America's Senior Citizens," 1960[?]; "Del Webb's Sun City, a Retirement Community," advertising section in *AR*, Jan. 1, 1960, PPL-AR-SCCF; "Del Webb's Sun City, Arizona, Designed Exclusively for Active Retirement," 1963[?]; "Del Webb's Sun City, Arizona: A New Look," 1965; "Del Webb's Sun City, California, Designed Exclusively for Retirement," 1962[?]; "Nobody Plans 'em, They Just Happen," *Del Webb's Active Retirement* 1 (1963[?]); "You're Just 3 Steps Away from Your Beautiful Home in Del Webb's Sun City, Arizona," 1963[?]; 1959–1967 Webb National advertising scrapbook; and Local Advertising scrapbooks.

62. In addition to the materials cited above, see: *AR*, Jan. 10, 1965, Jan. 8, 1985, PPL-AR-SCCF.

63. *AR*, Jan. 14, 1973, SCAHS.

64. DEVCO advertisement in the *Wall Street Journal*, March 15, 1962, in 1959–1968 Webb National advertising scrapbook; Jerry Svendsen to Evelyn R. Skelly, Nov. 27, 1968, SCAHS; "The Beginning," SCAHS, a promotional film produced and distributed by DEVCO beginning in 1960. By 1965 DEVCO had shown the film to more than 24 million people (*AR*, Aug. 15, 1965, PPL-AR-SCCF).

65. Freeman and Sanberg, *Jubilee*, 243–45.

66. In addition to the cited promotional materials, consult "Sun City—An Experiment In Purposeful Living," *Arizona Days and Ways*, Sunday supplement to *AR* (May 14, 1961): 55.

67. In addition to the usual publicity, see Thomas G. Austin to Glenn B. Sanberg, Oct. 3, 1984, in Sun City Archives scrapbook, SCAHS.

68. Freeman and Sanberg, *Jubilee*, 38.

69. "1962 Opinion Study," 7–8.

70. "Population Figures, Sun City, Arizona," n.d., SCAHS; "A Matter of Life and Death," Jan. 1965, DEVCO interoffice memorandum, SCAHS, 1; *AR*, Jan. 2, 1966, Jan. 8, 1985, PPL-AR-SCCF.

71. *PG*, June 15, 1964, PPL-AR-SCCF.

72. "Matter of Life and Death," 1–4.

73. Freeman and Sanberg, *Jubilee*, 22; Meeker interview.

74. "Del Webb's Sun City, Arizona," 1961; "You're Just 3 Steps Away from Your Beautiful Home," 1963[?]; "1962 Opinion Study," vi, 16–17.

75. On the incomes of early residents, see *AR*, July 16, 1960, PPL-AR-SCCF; Arizona State Employment Service, *The Northwestern-Sun City Sector of the Phoenix Area: A Labor Market Analysis* (Phoenix, 1960), 13–14; Trillin, "Wake Up and Live," 133. On buying and enlarging houses, see "1962 Opinion Study," 56; "The Family: A Place in the Sun," *Time* 80 (Aug. 3, 1962):

46–50; Gober, "Retirement Community as a Geographical Phenomenon," 192. On attitudes toward trailer parks, see "1962 Opinion Study," vi, 16–17, 50.

76. Meeker interview; Freeman and Sanberg, *Jubilee*, 231; Gottlieb, "Sun City: Gamble in the Sun," 6–8; *AR*, Jan. 8, 1985, PPL-AR-SCCF.

77. *AR*, Jan. 22, 1967, PPL-AR-SCCF (quotation); comments of DEVCO architect Wes Matthews, cited in *Sun Cities Independent*, Jan. 16, 1985.

78. See: DEVCO publicity materials, cited above, for the years 1959–1961; Hunt et al., *Retirement Communities: An American Original*, 71; Joyce Rockwood Muench, "Sun City, Arizona, U.S.A.," *Arizona Highways* 43 (Nov. 1967): 32.

79. Information in this and following paragraphs about Sun City housing after 1965 comes from the following DEVCO publications, available at SCAHS unless otherwise indicated: "The Country Club World of Del Webb's Sun City, Arizona," 1967; "The Country Club World of Del Webb's Sun City, Arizona," 1968; Del Webb Ad Proofs, 1967–1968, scrapbook; Del Webb National Advertising, 1968–1975, scrapbook; "Del Webb's Sun City, Arizona: Homes, Duplexes, Garden Apartments & Patio Houses," 1969; "Del Webb's Sun City: Arizona's Most Beautiful City," 1966; "Exposition for Living—1969," PPL-AR-SCCF; "Fact Sheet on Sun City, Arizona," July 31, 1969.

80. In addition to the 1968–1969 advertising cited above, see Hunt et al., *Retirement Communities: An American Original*, 71.

81. SCTA, "Sun City Past Present and Future," 1977, SCAHS, 2–3; Tuffs interview.

82. Besides the publicity materials cited above, consult: *AR*, Jan. 2, 1966, Dec. 19, 1967, Oct. 6, 1968, PPL-AR-SCCF; *PG*, Dec. 22, 1967, PPL-AR-SCCF; Paine, "Sun City Story," S–7, S–11; Freeman and Sanberg, *Jubilee*, 90–92; Meeker interview.

83. "The Family: A Place in the Sun," 48; Thornburg, "Life Begins at Retirement," 30; Paine, "Sun City Story," S–17 (quotation).

84. Hunt et al., *Retirement Communities: An American Original*, 71; Paine, "Sun City Story," S–6, S–16.

85. J. Bulkeley to John Meeker et al., May 5, 1971, DEVCO interoffice memorandum, SCAHS; Hunt et al., *Retirement Communities: An American Original*, 64–65; *Inside Phoenix: Update 1980* (Phoenix, 1980), 7; Michael Baker, *The 1982 Sun City Area Long Term Care Survey: A Statistical Profile of Resident Characteristics, Attitudes and Preferences* (Tucson, 1983), 83; *PG*, May 18, 1977; *AR*, Jan. 8, 1985, PPL-AR-SCCF.

86. *AR*, July 14, 1968, PPL-AR-SCCF; Svendsen to Glotfelty, July 30, 1969; Bulkeley to Meeker et al., May 5, 1971; "Fact Sheet on Sun City, Arizona," 1969; DEVCO, "Sun City Is a Story of Beauty, Planned Growth, and Success," 1972 promotional material, SCAHS, 2; *Minneapolis Tribune*, Feb. 27, 1973.

87. "Population Figures, Sun City, Arizona"; Baker, *1982 Sun City Area Long Term Care Survey*, 13.

88. In addition to the 1966–1969 publicity materials cited above, consult

Brochure Package, 1969–1977 file, SCAHS; ads in *AR* and *PG*, Feb. 1976, in Del Webb Local Advertising 1976, scrapbook, SCAHS.

89. DEVCO, "The Sun City Story," Jan. 1970 press release, SCAHS.

90. On the complexity of selling housing to the elderly, see Barker, *California Retirement Communities*, 33–34; "Retirement City—Haven or Ghetto," 130; Allan Karl Doyle, "Sun City, Arizona: A Study of Sense of Place in a Retirement Community," M.A. thesis, University of Washington, 1984, 46.

91. Ads in Del Webb National Advertising, 1968–1975, scrapbook; Hunt et al., *Retirement Communities: An American Original*, 88.

92. Freeman and Sanberg, *Jubilee*, 231, depict DEVCO policy before 1965. The figures on "resident referrals" are rough and vary over time. See: "1962 Opinion Study," 6; *AR*, July 14, 1963, July 14, 1968, PPL-AR-SCCF; Patricia Gober and Leo F. Zonn, "Kin and Elderly Amenity Migration," *Gerontologist* 23 (June 1983): 291; Meeker interview.

93. Meeker interview; Tuffs interview; *AR*, April 20, Oct. 20, 1969, PPL-AR-SCCF; Freeman and Sanberg, *Jubilee*, 231–32.

94. Edward P. Eichler and Marshall Kaplan, *The Community Builders* (Berkeley, 1967); Tuffs interview.

95. DEVCO, "New Town Development Sequence," March 29, 1971, in materials assembled for "Sun City Commercial Brochure," 1971, SCAHS, 1–3 (quotation at 3); comments of DEVCO vice-president Owen Childress in *PG*, Jan. 6, 1969, PPL-AR-SCCF; Hunt et al., *Retirement Communities: An American Original*, 251–52.

96. See, for example, Eicher and Kaplan, *Community Builders*; Theodore Roszak, "Life in the Instant Cities," in Carey McWilliams, ed., *The California Revolution* (New York, 1968), 65; Christensen, *American Garden City and New Towns Movement*, 105.

97. "Del Webb's Sun City, Arizona: Active Living for America's Senior Citizens," 1960.

98. Gober and Zonn, "Kin and Elderly Amenity Migration," 288–93. See also Steve L. Barsby and Dennis L. Cox, *Interstate Migration of the Elderly: An Economic Analysis* (Lexington, Mass., 1975), 132.

99. Patricia Barnes, "Sun City, Arizona, U.S.A.," *Arizona Highways* 50 (June 1974): 34; Gober and Zonn, "Kin and Elderly Amenity Migration," 292.

100. "1962 Opinion Study," 7; *AR*, Feb. 10, 1963, PPL-AR-SCCF; Nadeau, *California: The New Society*, 273.

101. Baker, *1982 Sun City Area Long Term Care Survey*, 15–17; Gober, "Retirement Community as a Geographical Phenomenon," 193, 194.

102. *AR*, July 14, 1968, PPL-AR-SCCF.

103. Susan R. Sherman, "Patterns of Contact for Residents of Age-Segregated and Age-Integrated Housing," *Journal of Gerontology* 30 (Jan. 1975): 103–7; Joachim Gwosdz, "Sun City, Arizona—Lebensstil und Lebenszufriedenheit in einer Rentnersiedlung," Ph.D. diss., Ludwig-Maximilians-Universität zu Munchen, 1983, 65, on file in Sun City Library Archives, Sun City, Ariz. Gwosdz's dissertation is primarily written in German, but here I refer to Gwosdz's English-language quotations from interviews with Sun City residents.

104. Baker, *The 1982 Sun City Area Long Term Care Survey*, 26–27, 82; Bultena and Wood, "American Retirement Community: Bane or Blessing," 212; Sherman et al., "Psychological Effects of Retirement Housing," 171.

105. Bultena and Wood, "American Retirement Community: Bane or Blessing," 212–13; Gordon L. Bultena and Vivian Wood, "Leisure Orientation and Recreational Activities of Retirement Community Residents," *Journal of Leisure Research* 2 (Winter 1970): 5; Gober and Zonn, "Kin and Elderly Amenity Migration," 289–90.

106. Baker, *1982 Sun City Area Long Term Care Survey*, 84; Gordon L. Bultena and Douglas G. Marshall, "Family Patterns of Migrant and Nonmigrant Retirees," *Journal of Marriage and the Family* 32 (Feb. 1970): 90–91.

107. "1962 Opinion Study," 3–4, 22.

108. Donahue, "Retirement," 371–73, 398; *NYT*, Jan. 18, 1970.

109. Gwosdz, "Sun City, Arizona," 95–96. On widows in Sun City, see Athia L. Hardt, "Single in Sun City," *Arizona Magazine*, Sunday supplement to *AR* (Nov. 14, 1982): 6, 42–44, SCAHS.

110. Baker, *1982 Sun City Area Long Term Care Survey*, 12, 86; Barnes, "Sun City, Arizona, U.S.A.," 30; DEVCO, "Sun City Progress Story"; *AR*, Feb. 10, 1963, PPL-AR-SCCF.

111. Baker, *1982 Sun City Area Long Term Care Survey*, 34, 37–40; Bultena and Wood, "American Retirement Community: Bane or Blessing," 212; Western Savings and Loan Association, *Forecast 1981* (Phoenix, 1981), 18; Hunt et al., *Retirement Communities: An American Original*, 64.

112. *Minneapolis Tribune*, Feb. 25, 1973; Hal Lancaster, "Out to Pasture; The Old but Affluent Withdraw to Sun City to Fill Empty Days," *Wall Street Journal*, Nov. 16, 1972, 35; Gwosdz, "Sun City, Arizona," 78.

113. *AR*, Jan. 21, 1970, PPL-AR-SCCF; John Meeker, quoted in Dan Lee, "The Spread at Sun City," *Arizona Magazine*, Sunday supplement to *AR* (Nov. 12, 1978): 9.

114. Gwosdz, "Sun City, Arizona," 127; Lancaster, "Out to Pasture," 35. See also Nancy J. Osgood, *Senior Settlers: Social Integration in Retirement Communities* (New York, 1982), 260–72.

115. Hooyman and Kiyak, *Social Gerontology*, ch. 3, survey of theories of aging. Many students of retirement communities, such as Rosow, *Social Integration of the Aged*, include theoretical discussions in their works. See also Mark Messer, "The Possibility of an Age-Concentrated Environment Becoming a Normative System," *Gerontologist* 7 (Dec. 1967): 247–51.

116. Jennie-Keith Ross, *Old People, New Lives: Community Creation in a Retirement Residence* (Chicago, 1977), 198. As gerontologists discovered the benefits of age-segregated housing, some students of the city explained how clustering into more homogeneous enclaves could simplify urban life: Amos Rapoport, *Human Aspects of Urban Form: Towards a Man-Environment Approach to Urban Form and Design* (Oxford, 1977), especially 249–65.

117. Irving Rosow, "Retirement Housing and Social Integration," *Gerontologist* 1 (June 1961): 89–90; Hochschild, *Unexpected Community*, 29; Sheley, "Mutuality and Retirement Community Success," 77; John Meeker cited in Lee, "Spread at Sun City," 12.

118. Quotation from Paine, "Sun City Story," S–13. See also "The Family:

A Place in the Sun," 48; Trillin, "Wake Up and Live," 170–71; Donald R. Tuffs, quoted in *AR*, Feb. 21, 1978; Gwosdz, "Sun City, Arizona," 74.

119. O'Neil, "For the Retired, a World All Their Own," 48; Johnson, "Growing Old Alone Together," 59; Hochschild, *Unexpected Community*, 24–25; Gwosdz, "Sun City, Arizona," 74.

120. Cited in *Minneapolis Tribune*, Feb. 26, 1973.

121. Cited in Osgood, *Senior Settlers*, 110–11, 106, 107.

122. Gordon L. Bultena, "Structural Effects on the Morale of the Aged: A Comparison of Age-Segregated and Age-Integrated Communities," in Jaber F. Gubrium, ed., *Late Life: Communities and Environmental Policy* (Springfield, Ill., 1974), 19–20; Bultena and Wood, "Leisure Orientation and Recreational Activities of Retirement Community Residents," 12–13.

123. Bultena and Wood, "American Retirement Community: Bane or Blessing?" 213–14; Bultena and Wood, "Leisure Orientation and Recreational Activities of Retirement Community Residents," 7–9, 11.

124. *Minneapolis Tribune*, Feb. 25, 1973; Jacobs, *Fun City*, especially 28, 31; Trillin, "Wake Up and Live," 166–67 (quotation); Lancaster, "Out to Pasture," 35.

125. Bultena and Wood, "Leisure Orientation and Recreational Activities of Retirement Community Residents," 3–5.

126. Bultena and Wood, "Leisure Orientation and Recreational Activities of Retirement Community Residents," 7; *Minneapolis Tribune*, Feb. 25, 1973.

127. Johnson, "Growing Old Alone Together," 59; Hochschild, *Unexpected Community*, 19–20; Western Savings and Loan Association, *Forecast 1981*, 18.

128. Trillin, "Wake Up and Live," 166.

129. Trillin, "Wake Up and Live," 159; Baker, *1982 Sun City Area Long Term Care Survey*, 86; Freeman and Sanberg, *Jubilee*, chs. 11–13, 15.

130. Cited in Gwosdz, "Sun City, Arizona," 96.

131. Baker, *1982 Sun City Area Long Term Care Survey*, 22; Gober and Zonn, "Kin and Elderly Amenity Migration," 292–93; Hunt et al., *Retirement Communities: An American Original*, 67.

132. Hunt et al., *Retirement Communities: An American Original*, 67; Doyle, "Sun City, Arizona," 32–36, 48. See also Yi-Fu Tuan, *Topophilia: A Study of Environmental Perception, Attitudes, and Values* (Englewood Cliffs, N.J., 1974), 210–17, 223–24.

133. Freeman and Sanberg, *Jubilee*, 243.

134. Interview with DEVCO architect Wes Matthews, in *Sun Cities Independent*, Jan. 16, 1985.

135. These remarks stem from personal observations made in October, 1986. See also Trillin, "Wake Up and Live," 123, 150.

136. Western Savings and Loan Association, *Forecast 1981*, 18; Hunt et al., *Retirement Communities: An American Original*, 69; Johnson, "Growing Old Alone Together," 54.

137. Doyle, "Sun City, Arizona," 33–36; Muench, "Sun City, Arizona, U.S.A.," 4 (quotations).

138. *AR*, June 13, 1971, Nov. 6, 1978; Freeman and Sanberg, *Jubilee*,

123–25, 164, 172–74, 227. On the enforcement of deed restrictions against young people, see: *AR*, Nov. 29, 1964, Sept. 1, 1974, July 28, Sept. 7, 1977, Jan. 8, Mar. 17, 1985, PPL-AR-SCCF.

139. Boye DeMente, *Retiring in Arizona, Senior Citizens Shangri La* (Paradise Valley, Ariz., 1980), 56–57.

140. Freeman and Sanberg, *Jubilee*, 107–9; *AR*, July 31, 1966, PPL-AR-SCCF; *Minneapolis Tribune*, Feb. 25, 1973.

141. Doyle, "Sun City, Arizona," 1, 7–8 (quotation), 20–21, 48–50.

142. "1962 Opinion Study," 44; *AR*, Nov. 10, 1962, May 28, 1967, PPL-AR-SCCF; Baker, *1982 Sun City Area Long Term Care Survey*, 82.

143. Freeman and Sanberg, *Jubilee*, 175–77.

144. Retirement Search Service, *Arizona—Retirement Frontier* (Hollywood, Calif., n.d.), 18 (quotation); Heintz, *Retirement Communities: For Adults Only*, 29, 43, 46. See the comments of John S. Shafer, who migrated to Sun City from Detroit, in Lancaster, "Out to Pasture," 35.

145. Tuffs interview; Doyle, "Sun City, Arizona," 12–13, 16.

146. John Meeker quoted in *AR*, Feb. 21, 1978, PPL-AR-SCCF; Meeker interview; Tuffs interview; Paine, "Sun City Story," S–18, S–19. Barker, *California Retirement Communities*, 33, 34, 86, confirms the lesson DEVCO learned about locating retirement communities near major cities.

147. Tuffs interview; Charles Nelson Burlingham, "Sun City Story," *Sun City Tatler* (2 July 1961), SCAHS, 4 (quotation).

148. *AR*, Dec. 2, 1964, Dec. 9, 1971, PPL-AR-SCCF; Freeman and Sanberg, *Jubilee*, 225–26. See Osgood, *Senior Settlers*, 122–25, for another instance of retirees resisting incorporation.

149. Comments of Chris Nelson in *AR*, Nov. 15, 1964, PPL-AR-SCCF; SCTA president in *AR*, April 14, 1974, PPL-AR-SCCF. And see Jack DeBolske cited in *NS*, July 3, 1973, clipping in Sun City, Del E. Webb Corp/ Correspondence, 1972–1975, 1976–1977 file, Maricopa County, Arizona, Planning and Development Records, Phoenix.

150. *AR*, Nov. 15, 1964, PPL-AR-SCCF. Experiences in other planned American communities, notably Columbia, Maryland, and Radburn, New Jersey, were similar: Christensen, *American Garden City and New Towns Movement*, 67–68, 120.

151. *AR*, Jan. 17, 1965, Nov. 7, 1971, Jan. 30, 1978, PPL-AR-SCCF; *Minneapolis Tribune*, Feb. 26, 1973; *NS*, July 3, 1973.

152. *AR*, Sept. 12, 1970, June 10, 1971, PPL-AR-SCCF; *PG*, Feb. 14, 1970, PPL-AR-SCCF; Freeman and Sanberg, *Jubilee*, 220–22.

153. Tucson *Daily Arizona Star*, March 27, 1988.

154. *AR*, March 17, 1985, PPL-AR-SCCF.

155. Hunt et al., *Retirement Communities: An American Original*, 66; *Minneapolis Tribune*, Feb. 26, 1973; Christopher Davis, "Death in Sun City," *Esquire* 66 (Oct. 1966): 136; *AR*, July 6, 1974, PPL-AR-SCCF; Robert Gottlieb, "The Phoenix Growth Machine," *The Nation* 229 (Dec. 29, 1979): 682; Lee, "The Spread at Sun City," 14.

156. *AR*, Dec. 30, 1973 (quotation); Tuffs interview.

157. Hunt et al., *Retirement Communities: An American Original*, 87, 93;

Paine, "Sun City Story," S–25 (quotation); Freeman and Sanberg, *Jubilee*, 218–19; Doug Morris, interview with author, Sun City, Arizona, Oct. 10, 1986. The tension between Peoria and Sun City was followed in *AR*, Feb. 24, March 5, April 9, 1969, June 14, 1973, Sept. 3, 9, 1974, PPL-AR-SCCF. Gober, "Retirement Community as a Geographical Phenomenon," 194, points to a similar pattern in Sun City West.

158. *AR*, Oct. 16, 1973, March 6, 1971, PPL-AR-SCCF.

159. On DEVCO advertising about low taxes and no schools, and the expectations of residents, see "You're Just 3 Steps Away from Your Beautiful Home in Del Webb's Sun City, Arizona," 1963[?]; ads in *AR* and *PG*, Oct. 16, 23, 1966, in Del Webb Ad Proofs, 1965–66, scrapbook, SCAHS; SCTA, "Sun City Past, Present and Future," 1. On fear of inflation and higher taxes, see Trillin, "Wake Up and Live," 30; *AR*, May 17, 1977, PPL-AR-SCCF; Tuffs interview.

160. Heintz, *Retirement Communities: For Adults Only*, 143; Barker, *California Retirement Communities*, 54–58; Hunt et al., *Retirement Communities: An American Original*, 29, 55–56.

161. Gober, "Retirement Community as a Geographical Phenomenon," 196; comments of Peoria District superintendent (and Sun City resident) Ira Murphy in *AR*, March 5, 1972, PPL-AR-SCCF.

162. Quotations from Hunt et al., *Retirement Communities: An American Original*, 63. Also see Lancaster, "Out to Pasture," 35; *NS*, Jan. 14, 1975; Susan Dentzer, "Has Sun City Come of Age?" *Newsweek* 105 (May 6, 1985): 69.

163. Osgood, *Senior Settlers*, 117–18.

164. Tuffs interview.

165. *AR*, Sept. 28, 1978; editorial by Doug Morris in *Sun City Citizen*, May 20, 1981.

166. Cited in Lancaster, "Out to Pasture," 35.

167. U.S. Bureau of the Census, *1980 Census of the Population*, vol. 1, *Characteristics of the Population*, chapter B, *General Population Characteristics*, part 4, *Arizona* (Washington, D.C., 1982), 7–8; Tuffs interview; Stocker, *Arizona: A Guide to Easier Living*, 104–5; Peter A. Dickinson, *Sunbelt Retirement: The Complete State-by-State Guide to Retiring in the South and West of the United States* (Boston, 1978), 255, 271–72; Richard Boyer and David Savageau, *Places Rated Retirement Guide* (Chicago, 1983).

168. Dickinson, *Sunbelt Retirement*, 271; *AR*, July 16, 1960 (quotation), Feb. 10, 1963, Oct. 19, 1969, PPL-AR-SCCF; Keatley, "Retirement in the Sun," 87; Bulkeley to Meeker et al., May 5, 1971; SCTA, "Sun City Past, Present and Future," 3, 5; Heintz, *Retirement Communities: For Adults Only*, 100; Jeanne C. Biggar, "Reassessing Elderly Sunbelt Migration," *Research on Aging* 2 (June 1980): 177–90.

169. Steven K. Happel, Timothy D. Hogan, and Deborah Sullivan, "Going Away to Roost," *American Demographics* 6 (June 1984): 33–35, 44.

170. Don Campbell, "Living Longer in America," *Arizona Highways* 62 (April 1986): 3–21; Dickinson, *Sunbelt Retirement*, 265–66, 270. Data depicting the population dwelling in retirement communities are not very reliable

because the elderly as a group (usually defined as those aged sixty-five and over) are not exactly the same as the retired (which includes people under sixty-five and excludes some people over sixty-five). Nonetheless, see figures in Gober, "Retirement Community as a Geographical Phenomenon," 189; Baker, "Arizona Retirement Communities and the Changing Needs of an Aging Population," 17.

171. Charles S. Sargent, Jr., *Planned Communities in Greater Phoenix: Origins, Functions and Control*, Arizona State University Institute of Public Administration, Papers in Public Administration No. 25 (Tempe, Ariz., 1973), 3; Sargent, ed., *Conflict Between Frontier Values and Land Use Control in Greater Phoenix*, 57; Jeffrey Cook, "Patterns of Desert Urbanization: The Evolution of Metropolitan Phoenix," in Gideon Golany, ed., *Urban Planning for Arid Zones: American Experiences and Directions* (New York, 1978), 219; Ardelle Coleman, "Arizona's Lifestyle '74," *Phoenix* 9 (March 1974): 34–37.

172. Sargent, *Planned Communities in Greater Phoenix*, 1–2, 4–5, 22–34; Gottschalk, "Boom Town," 1, 31.

173. Bulkeley to Meeker et al., May 5, 1971.

174. William R. Mee, Jr., *Planning Commission Symposium on Phoenix Concept Plan 2000, Questions and Answers* (Phoenix, 1981), 4; Christopher B. Leinberger and Charles Lockwood, "How Business Is Reshaping America," *Atlantic Monthly* 258 (Oct. 1986): 43–52.

175. Tuffs interview; 1985 remarks of DEVCO president Paul Tatz, cited in *AR*, n.d., PPL-AR-SCCF; Erwin G. Morrison, *Retirement in the West: How and Where to Enjoy the Best Years of Your Life* (San Francisco, 1976), 74. Quotation from Dentzer, "Has Sun City Come of Age?" 68.

176. On the plans of Del E. Webb Communities, Inc., in 1986, see Tuffs interview. On U.S. homogeneous comunities, consult Gober, "Retirement Community as a Geographical Phenomenon," 191; Morrison, *Retirement in the West*, 74; *NYT*, May 4, 1986.

177. Tuffs interview; *AR*, Oct. 19, 1986. Financial troubles jeopardized the Webb company's plans for new Sun Cities: John H. Taylor, "Wrong Corner," *Forbes* 141 (Feb. 22, 1988): 58–59.

Chapter Five

1. On the historic development of American world's fairs, see Anne Mosher Sheridan, "Learning from an Urban Vision: American World's Fairs as Model Cities," paper presented at CUKANZUS, the Sixth International Conference of Historical Geographers, Baton Rouge, La., July 21, 1986.

2. *State of Washington World's Fair Commission Report to the Honorable Arthur B. Langlie, Governor, and the 1957 Session of the Legislature* (Olympia, Wash., 1956), 2; Century 21 Exposition news release, July 22, 1960, DP-UWL.

3. On Seattle's provincial reputation, see *Miami News*, Aug. 19, 1962; *Chi-*

cago Sun-Times, June 3, 1962; Horace Sutton, "There's a Great Day Coming Tomorrow," *Saturday Review* 45 (Aug. 4, 1962): 17; Stanford Research Institute, "Report: 4 Sections Complete," 1957–1958, DP-UWL, part 4, 60; Alistair Cooke, "Space-age Fair with a Coney Island Touch," *Manchester Guardian*, April 23, 1962. Citations to non-local newspapers (except *NYT* and *Manchester Guardian*) in the following notes come from clippings in DP-UWL.

4. U.S. Bureau of the Census, *U.S. Census of Population: 1960*, vol. 1, *Characteristics of the Population*, part 49, *Washington* (Washington, D.C., 1963), 10, 17–18. When depicting the population of greater Seattle, I generally rely on census data for the Seattle Standard Metropolitan Statistical Area, defined as King and Snohomish counties. On the modernity of Seattle, see Earl S. Pomeroy, *The Pacific Slope: A History of California, Oregon, Washington, Idaho, Utah, and Nevada* (Seattle, 1973), 139.

5. Roger Sale, *Seattle, Past to Present* (rev. ed. Seattle, 1978), ch. 6, especially 183–84, 187–89; John M. Mecklin, "Why Boeing Is Missing the Bus," *Fortune* 78 (June 1968): 151; *ST*, Dec. 20, 1962 (quotation); U.S. Bureau of the Census, *U.S. Census of Population: 1960*, vol. 1, *Characteristics of the Population*, part 49, *Washington*, 139; Philip Herrera, "Megalopolis Comes to the Northwest," *Fortune* 76 (Dec. 1967): 120. On Boeing's impact on Seattle, see Rodney Allen Erickson, "The 'Lead Firm' Concept and Regional Economic Growth: An Analysis of Boeing Expansion, 1963–1968," Ph.D. diss., University of Washington, 1973, ch. 4. In May 1961 The Boeing Airplane Company changed its name to The Boeing Company.

6. Sale, *Seattle, Past to Present*, 184–85 (quotation); Herrera, "Megalopolis Comes to the Northwest," 120–21; *OGB* (Seattle, 1962), 1.

7. World Fair Corporation, "Fact Sheet No. 1," Jan. 17, 1958, press release, DP-UWL, 1–5; Century 21 Exposition news release, Sept. 9, 1959, DP-UWL (quotation on "diversified economy"); Ewen C. Dingwall to Warren Bishop, Sept. 26, 1957, DP-UWL (quotation on "heavy reliance"). For the theme song, see *ST*, Nov. 3, 1961. An insider's account of the origins of the exposition is Murray Morgan, *Century 21: The Story of the Seattle World's Fair, 1962* (Seattle, 1963).

8. *ST*, Nov. 30, March 25, 1962.

9. *OGB*, 50–51, 148–49; *ST*, July 28, 1958, June 2, 1961, April 18, Oct. 28, 1962.

10. Boeing Airplane Company, *Annual Reports, 1950–1964* (Seattle, 1951–65).

11. U.S. Bureau of the Census, *U.S. Census of Population: 1960, Selected Area Reports, Standard Metropolitan Statistical Areas*, Final Report PC(3)–10 (Washington, D.C., 1963), 242; U.S. Bureau of the Census, *U.S. Census of Population: 1960*, vol. 1, *Characteristics of the Population*, part 49, *Washington*, 10, 17, 18.

12. U.S. Bureau of the Census, *U.S. Censuses of Population and Housing: 1960, Census Tracts*, Final Report PHC(1)–142, *Seattle, Wash. Standard Metropolitan Statistical Area* (Washington, D.C., 1962), 15, 35, 74, 97, 117; U.S. Bureau of the Census, *U.S. Census of Population: 1960*, vol. 1, *Characteristics of the Population*, part 49, *Washington*, 23–24, 36; *ST*, July 26, 1962.

13. *ST*, Dec. 17, 1961. By the time of the fair, Seattle's cross-Sound bridge had been dropped and the other two projects remained unfinished.

14. James R. Warren, *King County and Its Queen City: Seattle* (Woodland Hills, Calif., 1981), 248; *ST*, Nov. 19, 1961.

15. *ST*, Nov. 1, 1962. Northgate has been shrewdly assessed by Meredith L. Clausen, "Northgate Regional Shopping Center—Paradigm from the Provinces," *Journal of the Society of Architectural Historians* 48 (May 1984): 144–61.

16. Sale, *Seattle, Past to Present*, 190, 201.

17. "Centrifugal tendencies" remark, by the president of the local Chamber of Commerce, cited in Janice Peck, "Arts Activists and Seattle's Cultural Expansion, 1954–65," *Pacific Northwest Quarterly* 76 (July 1985): 86; "disproportionate share" quotation from Donald Monson, cited in *ST*, Aug. 22, 1962. See also Donald Monson, "Comprehensive Plan for Central Business District, Seattle: Technical Report prepared for the City of Seattle and the Central Association of Seattle," Feb. 1963, IGSL; Proctor Mellquist, "Address," April 19, 1960, Seattle, DP-UWL, 2–7; Richard Lawrence Nelson, "A Look at the Economic Potential of Downtown Seattle: Extracts from an Address" (1961), enclosed in Central Association of Seattle, *Downtown Newsletter*, n.d., DP-UWL.

18. Central Association of Seattle, "Special Information Bulletin No. 1," July 15, 1958, DP-UWL (quotation); *ST*, Oct. 4, 1961, Oct. 28, 1962; "Parking Garage over Freeway Feasible," Central Association of Seattle, *Downtown Newsletter* 4 (Feb. 1962): 1–2, 7.

19. Sale, *Seattle, Past to Present*, 202–3; Cyrus Noe, "Innocence Revisited: 20 Years After the Fair—A Flack Remembers," *Pacific Northwest* 16 (April 1982): 25–26.

20. *ST*, Sept. 15, 1961; "Projects Top $2,000,000 Mark!" Central Association of Seattle, *Downtown Newsletter* 4 (Feb. 1962): 3–6; Central Association of Seattle, "Information Bulletin No. 2," Sept. 10, 1958, DP-UWL, 1; Minutes, Executive Committee Meeting, Century 21 Exposition, Inc., March 12, 1959, Seattle, DP-UWL.

21. *ST*, July 13, Oct. 25, 1962.

22. Central Association of Seattle, "Information Bulletin No. 5," March 27, 1959, DP-UWL, 1; L. R. Durkee to Harold Shefelman, April 15, 1957, DP-UWL; *ST*, April 9, 1961.

23. *ST*, April 20, 1982; Ewen C. Dingwall, interview by author, Aug. 19, 1985 (hereafter referred to as Dingwall interview), summary, DP-UWL. Statistical information about the Warren district has been inferred from data regarding tracts L–001 and L–002, in U.S. Bureau of the Census, *U.S. Censuses of Population and Housing: 1960, Census Tracts*, Final Report PHC(1)–142, *Seattle, Wash., Standard Metropolitan Statistical Area*, 20, 35, 44, 74, 79, 97, 102, 117, 119.

24. Victor Steinbrueck, *Seattle Cityscape* (Seattle, 1962), 28; *ST*, April 23, 1962; City of Seattle and Central Association of Seattle, *Planning the Future of Seattle's Central Area: Criteria for the Development of a Comprehensive Plan* (Seattle, 1959), 14 (quotation).

25. "Presentation Script for Fair Exhibitors' Meeting," 1962, DP-UWL,

10 (quotation on "futuristic solution"); Barry Upson to Craig Mathison, April 25, 1960, DP-UWL (quotation on "progressive city planning").

26. *ST*, March 21, 22, 1956; *State of Washington World's Fair Commission Report*, 5–8; Peck, "Arts Activists and Seattle's Cultural Expansion," 82, 84–85, 90; "Speakers Bureau Question and Answer Sheet," n.d., DP-UWL, 2; *OGB*, 2.

27. Burton Benedict, "The Anthropology of World's Fairs," Burton Benedict et al., *The Anthropology of World's Fairs: San Francisco's Panama Pacific International Exposition of 1915* (London, 1983), 31.

28. *ST*, July 7, 1958.

29. *ST*, July 18, Aug. 7, 1958; Ewen C. Dingwall, "Gold Rush Memoranda, Brussels Campaign 1958," Sept. 26–Oct. 2, 1958, DP-UWL, 7; Dingwall interview. On recognition of Seattle's fair by the Bureau of International Expositions, see Century 21 Exposition news releases, Oct. 14, 20, 1959, May 6, 1960, DP-UWL.

30. *ST*, Oct. 1, 2, 1959.

31. *OGB*, 1.

32. Dingwall interview.

33. *State of Washington World's Fair Commission Report*, 8; Seattle *Argus*, Nov. 1, 1957 (quotation); Dingwall to Bishop, Sept. 26, 1957; "Fair Aims High," *Business Week* (April 21, 1962): 92, 96.

34. John Allwood, *The Great Exhibitions* (London, 1977), 153; Benedict, "Anthropology of World's Fairs," 7, 34–36.

35. *ST*, April 18, 1982; U.S. House of Representatives, 86th Congress, 1st Session, Science and Astronautics Committee, *Century 21 Exposition: Hearings on H.R. 7982, H.R. 8203, and H.R. 8374, July 8, 9, 23, 1959* (Washington, D.C., 1959), 11–12, 51–52 (hereafter cited as House Science and Astronautics Committee, *Century 21 Exposition*). On the American reaction to *Sputnik*, see Walter A. McDougall, . . . *the Heavens and the Earth: A Political History of the Space Age* (New York, 1985), part 3.

36. Century 21 Exposition news release, April 2, 1959, DP-UWL: *ST*, May 3, June 17, 1959; U.S. Department of Commerce, *U.S. Science Exhibit, Seattle World's Fair, Final Report* (Washington, D.C., 1963), 3.

37. *1962 Seattle World's Fair Background Information* (Seattle, 1962; DP-UWL), 5; *ST*, April 19, 1987.

38. House Science and Astronautics Committee, *Century 21 Exposition*, 4 (quotation on "survival"), 13–14 (quotations on "undecided" and "abundance"), 35 (quotations on "supremacy" and "showcase"); AEC official cited in Jim Faber, "Notes on Preparation of Federal Program—Century 21 Exposition," March 1959, DP-UWL; *1962 Seattle World's Fair Background Information*, 17; Representative Thomas M. Pelly, news release, July 8, 1959, DP-UWL.

39. Jay Rockey to Frederic W. Wile, Oct. 17, 1961, and Wile to Rockey, Nov. 16, 1961, DP-UWL (quotations on Ad Council exhibit); *OGB*, 119; *ST*, Feb. 26, May 1, 7, 10 (Johnson quotation), 1962.

40. "An Act to Provide for Participation of the United States in the World Science–Pan Pacific Exposition to Be Held at Seattle, Washington, in 1961,

and for Other Purposes" (Public Law 85–880), *U.S. Statutes at Large*, 72 (1958), 1703–4 (quotations); *ST*, June 21, 1959.

41. *ST*, May 28 1961.

42. *P-I*, Sept. 4, 1962 (quotation of Meany on Space Needle); *ST*, Sept. 3, 1962 (quotation of Meany on Berlin Wall); *OGB*, 69, 77, 79.

43. *ST*, May 6, 7, 10, 1962.

44. *ST*, Feb. 20 (quotation), Aug. 6, 1962.

45. *P-I*, March 25, 1962; *ST*, April 8, July 8 (quotation), 1962.

46. *OGB*, 65; *ST*, July 8, 1962 (quotation).

47. James B. Taylor et al., *Science on Display: A Study of the United States Science Exhibit, Seattle World's Fair, 1962* (Seattle, 1963), 82. See also Paul J. Beeman, "The Gospel and Century 21," *Christian Century* 79 (Nov. 21, 1962): 1418.

48. Needham and Grohmann, Inc., *A Comprehensive Survey of the Seattle World's Fair 1962* (New York, 1963), part 2. Although imperfect in method, this unpaginated survey contains useful data on people's reactions to the fair, compiled from about 4,000 interviews conducted with heads of households visiting the fair during August, September, and October.

49. Jay Rockey, "Public Relations Division: Final Report," Oct. 21, 1962, DP-UWL, 1; Needham and Grohmann, *Comprehensive Survey of the Seattle World's Fair*, parts 1 and 2; American Automobile Association, "Special AAA Member Survey, Seattle World's Fair and Other Subjects," Oct. 1, 1962, DP-UWL, 3; *ST*, Oct. 22, 1962; *New York Herald Tribune*, April 23, 24, 1962.

50. Taylor et al., *Science on Display*, 159–60; Sutton, "There's a Great Day Coming Tomorrow," 18; Robert S. Weiss, "Pacific Science Center," *Science* 143 (Feb. 14, 1964): 639.

51. Robert S. Weiss and Serge Boutourline, Jr., "Fairs, Pavilions, Exhibits, and Their Audiences," MS, University of Washington Libraries, 1962, 7, 19; Alistair Cooke, "Memorable US Science Pavilion," *Manchester Guardian*, Oct. 18, 1962; Morgan, *Century 21*, 15.

52. Stanford Research Institute, "Report," part 4, 59, 61.

53. U.S. House, 85th Congress, 2nd Session, H.Reports vol. 5 (Serial Set 12076), "Providing for Participation of the United States in the World Science–Pan Pacific Exposition," Report No. 2561, *Miscellaneous Reports on Public Bills, V* (Washington, D.C., 1958), 3–4; U.S. Department of Commerce, *U.S. Science Exhibit*, 4–5 (quotation).

54. Michael L. Smith, "Selling the Moon: The U.S. Manned Space Program and the Triumph of Commodity Scientism," Richard Wightman Fox and T. J. Jackson Lears, eds., *The Culture of Consumption: Critical Essays in American History, 1880–1980* (New York, 1983), 178; McDougall, *Heavens and the Earth*, 358.

55. U.S. Department of Commerce, *U.S. Science Exhibit*, 51 (quotations on "uplift" and "most modern methods"), 35; Washington State Department of Commerce and Economic Development, *Seattle World's Fair Preview, April 21–October 21, 1962* (Seattle, 1961), unpaginated (quotation on "constant striving"); "Carling Brewing Company and Mission Macaroni Present World of Tomorrow Telecast No. 21 KING-TV: World's Fair Windup, Seattle Center

Preview," script for television show, Oct. 12, 15, 1962, DP-UWL, 3 (quotation on "space-gothic").

56. *ST*, April 21, 1977 (Luce quotation); U.S. Department of Commerce, *U.S. Science Exhibit*, 49 (quotation on "religious quality").

57. *OGB*, 8–22; U.S. Department of Commerce, *U.S. Science Exhibit*.

58. Quotations from Athelstan F. Spilhaus, cited in *ST*, July 2, 1962. See also U.S. Department of Commerce, *United States Science Exhibit, World's Fair in Seattle 1962: Souvenir Guide Book* (Seattle, 1962). On the Eames film, see Russell Lynes, "Seattle Will Never Be the Same," *Harper's Magazine* 225 (July 1962): 23. On the accessible nature of science, see Irene Corbally Kuhn, "Seattle's Fair Seriously Glimpses the Coming Century," King Features Syndicate story, for release May 17, 1962, in DP-UWL, 1; *New York Herald Tribune*, April 24, 1962; *ST*, Nov. 12, 1961.

59. Spilhaus cited in Century 21 Exposition, Inc., *Seattle World's Fair, U.S.A., April 21, 1962 to October 21, 1962: Fall Status Report, 1961* (Seattle, 1961), 8; cf. Athelstan F. Spilhaus, "Foreword," *Impressions: The United States Science Exhibit, Seattle World's Fair, 1962* (Seattle, 1962). Huxley cited in *ST*, April 24, 1962. See also comments by *NYT* journalist John Canady in *P-I*, April 18, 1962, and in "Science Is the Fairest," *NYT Magazine* (May 6, 1962): 18–19; Wolfgang Clasen, *Exhibitions, Exhibits, Industrial and Trade Fairs* (London, 1968), 8.

60. U.S. Department of Commerce, *United States Science Exhibit*, 19; *OGB*, 8.

61. *OGB*, 21.

62. U.S. Department of Commerce, *United States Science Exhibit*, 34 (quotation of final message); Athelstan F. Spilhaus, "The World of Science," publicity release, n.d., SWFP (quotation on "universal language"); Jim Faber, "Notes on Preparation of Federal Program—Century 21 Exposition," Mar., 1959, DP-UWL (quotation on "international morality"); Salk cited in *ST*, June 4, 1962.

63. Gilbert Millstein, "Fair Formula: Uplift with Zest," *NYT Magazine* (Nov. 18, 1962): 90. See also Cooke, "Memorable US Science Pavilion."

64. Cited in *NYT*, April 22, 1962.

65. *The Education of Henry Adams: An Autobiography* (1918; Boston, 1961), 341–43, 379–83. The closest thing to an Adams-like critique of Century 21 was an editorial, "The Seattle Fair," in *Pacific Historian* 6 (Aug. 1962): 122.

66. The "thinking man" quotation comes from *New York Herald Tribune*, April 22, 1962. See also Dingwall interview. Conclusions about fairgoers' preferences for comparatively thoughtful exhibits are derived from the popularity of such features as the United States Science Exhibit, the Monorail, and the World of Tomorrow, and from the lack of interest in Show Street and the Gayway. See Needham and Grohmann, *Comprehensive Survey of the Seattle World's Fair*, part 2.

67. Robert W. Rydell, *All the World's a Fair: Visions of Empire at American International Expositions, 1876–1916* (Chicago, 1984); Lenox R. Lohr, *Fair Management: The Story of A Century of Progress Exposition* (Chicago, 1952), 267, 271.

68. "Financial and Business Report of the Seattle World's Fair," Century 21 Exposition news release, Feb. 27, 1962, DP-UWL (quotation). See also: Economics Research Associates, "Visitor Characteristics and Expenditures," Jan. 23, 1961, Section 4 of "The Century 21 Planning Manual," SWFP, 11–17, and Economics Research Associates, "Exhibits," April 4, 1961, Section 7 of "The Century 21 Planning Manual," SWFP, 5–6.

69. *ST*, April 29, 1962.

70. Needham and Grohmann, *Comprehensive Survey of the Seattle World's Fair*, parts 1 and 2; Taylor et al., "Science on Display," 73.

71. Needham and Grohmann, *Comprehensive Survey of the Seattle World's Fair*, parts 1 and 2; Century 21 Exposition news release, June 30, 1962, DP-UWL; *ST*, July 23, 1962; Bob Lyte to Jay Rockey, Aug. 13, 1962, DP-UWL.

72. James E. Thompson to Frederic V. Schumacher, July 7, 1962, DP-UWL; *ST*, Nov. 8, 1962. The 9.6 million visitors to the fair included approximately 3 million individuals, 2 million of whom were from out of state; each entered an average of three times.

73. Century 21 Exposition news release, April 19, 1961, DP-UWL; "Presentation Script for Fair Exhibitors' Meeting," 8; *ST*, March 10, 1962.

74. "Presentation Script for Fair Exhibitors' Meeting," 1–2, 5–6, 8, 11–13, 18; advertisement in *Wall Street Journal*, Oct. 17, 1960, DP-UWL; Century 21 Exposition, Inc., "The Seattle World's Fair, April 21–Oct. 21, 1962, Seattle, Washington, U.S.A.: A Synopsis of Its Attractions, Appeal, Attendance and Mass Audience Interest," n.d., DP-UWL.

75. Cooke, "Space-Age Fair with a Coney Island Touch."

76. American Automobile Association, "Special AAA Member Survey," 1–2.

77. On consumption, see Mary Douglas and Baron Isherwood, *The World of Goods* (New York, 1979), especially 59–78.

78. Stanford Research Institute, "Report," part 4, 54–55 (quotation), 5, 9, 11–14, 58, 60–61.

79. *OGB*, 16, 45, 56; Special Monorail Negotiating Committee to Steering Committee, May 12, 1960, DP-UWL; *ST*, Aug. 15, 1962.

80. *State of Washington World's Fair Commission Report*, 4; Ewen C. Dingwall to Bob Jones, Nov. 7, 1957, DP-UWL; *ST*, Oct. 20, 1961; Allwood, *Great Exhibitions*, 151–53, 158.

81. Dingwall interview; Lohr, *Fair Management*.

82. Century 21 Exposition news release, Feb. 2, 1959, DP-UWL; Joseph P. Cusker, "The World of Tomorrow: Science, Culture, and Community at the New York World's Fair," in Helen A. Harrison et al., *Dawn of a New Day: The New York World's Fair, 1939/40* (New York, 1980), 4–6, 8, 12; Edward Lucie-Smith, *A History of Industrial Design* (New York, 1983), 114; Alfred Stern, "Exhibit Content and Procedures for State of Washington Century 21 Pavilion" [1960?], DP-UWL, 2, 6; *OGB*, 9; *1962 Seattle World's Fair Background Information*, 19.

83. Stanford Research Institute, "Report," part 4, 54, 15, 59; Barry Upson to Ewen C. Dingwall, Feb. 13, 1959, DP-UWL; Dingwall interview.

84. On early planning, see: Ewen C. Dingwall to Chapin Collins, Nov. 7, 1957, DP-UWL; Stanford Research Institute, "Report," part 2, 2, part 4, 2,

4364 NOTES TO PAGES 244–46

6, 14, 16, 20, 41–43, 46, 49, 55; *ST*, May 18, 1958. On the various visits to and negotiations with Disneyland, see the following in DP-UWL: Russell T. Mowry to L. E. Tryon, Jan. 19, 1959; Mowry to Donn Tatum, Jan. 19, 1959; Mowry, memo, Jan. 19, 1959; George K. Whitney, Jr., to Ewen C. Dingwall, May 17, 1960; Barry K. Upson, memo, May 27, 1960; William Cottrell to Whitney, Aug. 5, 1960; Ettinger to Rockey, Dec. 22, 1961. On participating companies, see: Century 21 Exposition news releases, Dec. 10, 1958, Jan. 15, July 14, 1962, DP-UWL.

85. Dingwall interview; Joseph E. Gandy to Walter E. Disney, June 16, 1960, DP-UWL; Century 21 Exposition news releases, June 19, 1959, May 2, Sept. 4, Dec. 2, 1960, DP-UWL; *ST*, Oct. 17, 1961.

86. Century 21 Exposition news releases, Sept. 12, 1960, July 12, 1962, DP-UWL; *ST*, Feb. 9, April 12, 22, 28, June 20, 1962; Frederic V. Schumacher to Ewen C. Dingwall, Feb. 10, 1962, DP-UWL; *Cincinnati Enquirer*, July 23, 1962; Stanley Harold Brewer, "Visitors' Reactions to the Seattle World's Fair: A Report Based on a Personal Interview Program Conducted for the Washington State Department of Commerce and Economic Development," Oct. 1962, MS, University of Washington Libraries, 14.

87. General praise for design was recorded by Needham and Grohmann, *Comprehensive Survey of the Seattle World's Fair*, part 2; Ben Hall, "Fairs: Go West, Everybody," *Time* 79 (April 27, 1962): 60, 65; "Seattle Votes for Architecture," *Architectural Record* 132 (Aug. 1961): 96, 100; *ST*, April 26, 1962. On congestion and long lines, see Walt Disney's remarks in *ST*, Sept. 23, 1962; *ST*, April 18, 1982; Century 21 Exposition Guest Relations Section, "Seattle World's Fair Opinion Poll," June 28, 1962, DP-UWL; Weiss and Boutourline, "Fairs, Pavilions, Exhibits, and Their Audiences," 13. For depictions of the Seattle World's Fair as refreshing and not portentous, see *New York Herald Tribune*, April 22, 1962; Lynes, "Seattle Will Never Be the Same," 20 (quotation).

88. Weiss and Boutourline, "Fairs, Pavilions, Exhibits, and Their Audiences," 9, 10.

89. The assumptions of 1950s society were probed by William H. Whyte, Jr., *The Organization Man* (New York, 1956), 67 (quotation), 320; David Riesman, "The Suburban Dislocation," *Annals of the American Academy of Political and Social Science* 314 (Nov. 1957): 127. For the comment on *Sputnik*, see "Sputnick's [*sic*] Challenge," *Frontier* 9 (Nov. 1957): 4.

90. Century 21 Exposition, "Informational Prospectus," 6 (quotations); *Century 21 Exposition, Seattle U.S.A. 1961–1962* (Seattle, [1959?]; on file, uncatalogued Northwest materials, Seattle Public Library).

91. Charles Poletti cited in *ST*, Aug. 7, 1962. On exhibits by Third World nations, see *State of Washington World's Fair Commission Report*, 8–9; Alexander Baird to Ferando G. Lerena, Feb. 27, 1961, DP-UWL; *OGB*, 72, 76, 79.

92. See, for instance, Addy Svendsen to Bill Phillips, Aug. 31, 1960, DP-UWL, and Alexander Baird to Raymond N. Thepe, Dec. 14, 1960, DP-UWL, on African exhibits. For quotation on Puyallup (a suburb of Tacoma), Punjab, and Peru, see Alfred Stern, Doris Frankel, and Gilbert Seldes, "Final Script, Washington State Coliseum Theme Exhibit Show, *The Threat and the Threshold*" (hereafter cited as Stern, "Threat and Threshold"), 1962, DP-UWL, 17.

93. *OGB*; Century 21 Exposition news release, Feb. 16, 1960, DP-UWL; Washington State Department of Commerce and Economic Development, *Seattle World's Fair Preview* (quotation).

94. Benedict, "Anthropology of World's Fairs," 13–14; "Presentation Script for Fair Exhibitors' Meeting," 4; *ST*, Oct. 25, 1961, April 21, 1982; Noe, "Innocence Revisited," 26; "Principal Projects," *Architecture/West* 68 (April 1962): 32 (quotation on "space capsules"); Lynes, "Seattle Will Never Be the Same," 23 (quotation on "gold coveralls"); *1962 Seattle World's Fair Background Information*, 70 (quotation on Space Needle colors).

95. Stern, "Exhibit Content and Procedures," 2.

96. Benedict, "Anthropology of World's Fairs," 5. See also Warren I. Susman, "The People's Fair: Cultural Contradictions of a Consumer Society," in Harrison et al., *Dawn of a New Day*, 17–27.

97. "Seattle Votes for Architecture," 99; Washington State Department of Commerce and Economic Development, *Seattle World's Fair Preview*; *OGB*, 28, 35–40.

98. *OGB*, 26 (quotation); *ST*, Nov. 1, 5, 1961; Stern, "Threat and Threshold," 1–3.

99. Stern, "Threat and Threshold," 1–3 (quotations), 28–29.

100. Century 21 Exposition news release, Dec. 17, 1961, DP-UWL (quotations on "fall-out shelter" and "future"); Stern, "Threat and Threshold," 2 (quotation on "richer life"), 4–5, 30–31.

101. Stern, "Threat and Threshold," 9 (quotation); "What Will the Century 21 Theme Building Have to Say About Our Future? How Will Man's Environment in Century 21 Be Depicted?" DP-UWL, part 1, 4, part 8 (cited hereafter as "What Will Theme Building Say").

102. *OGB*, 30 (quotation on "more of everything"); Stern, "Threat and Threshold," 17 (quotation on "creative thought"); "What Will Theme Building Say," part 2, 1–3, part 5, 1–4; Washington State Department of Commerce and Economic Development, *Seattle World's Fair Preview*.

103. Stern, "Threat and Threshold," 16, 21–22, 24–25; *OGB*, 32; "What Will Theme Building Say," part 2, 4, part 4, 1–6.

104. On other homes of the future, see: *OGB*, 47, 52, 62; Century 21 Exposition news release, Aug. 7, 1962, DP-UWL. On tomorrow's house in the state theme show, see Stern, "Threat and Threshold," 13–14 (quotations on "convenience" and "efficiency"); "What Will Theme Building Say," part 1, 2 (quotation on "haven").

105. "What Will Theme Building Say," part 1, 1.

106. House Science and Astronautics Committee, *Century 21 Exposition*, 31–32 (quotation on "for the ladies"); *New York Herald Tribune*, April 22, 1962; *OGB*, 46 (quotation on "art of living"); Century 21 Exposition news releases, Dec. 17, 1961, Jan. 5, 1962, DP-UWL (quotations on "fashion industry" and "best dressed").

107. *P-I*, April 22, 1962.

108. Century 21 news release, Oct. 9, 1962, DP-UWL (first quotation); *OGB*, 40 (second quotation); Dingwall interview.

109. *ST*, Oct. 9, 20, 22, 23, 1962.

110. *ST*, June 25, Sept. 26, 1962, April 25, 1963.

111. *ST*, April 19, 1982. On Century 21's influence on Spokane's Expo '74, see Noe, "Innocence Revisited," 32.

112. Joseph E. Gandy, "What's the Encore?" MS of speech delivered to Rotary Club, Seattle, Jan. 16, 1963, DP-UWL, 5–6; Monson, "Comprehensive Plan for Central Business District, Seattle," 11.

113. Dingwall interview; Herrera, "Megalopolis Comes to the Northwest," 122; *P-I*, Oct. 24, 1975, April 18, 1982; Murray Morgan, *Skid Road: An Informal Portrait of Seattle* (rev. ed. Seattle, 1982), 274–75.

114. Gerald B. Nelson, *Seattle: The Life and Times of an American City* (New York, 1977), 39; Sale, *Seattle, Past to Present*, 233 (quotation).

115. See comments of Paul Thiry, principal architect of the fairgrounds, in *ST*, July 2, 1962; Steinbrueck, *Seattle Cityscape*, 178; Hall, "Fairs: Go West, Everybody," 60, 65.

116. Municipality of Metropolitan Seattle (hereafter cited as Metro), "Downtown Seattle Transit Alternatives," Draft Report, Seattle, March 20, 1979, University of Washington Libraries, 48.

117. Victor Steinbrueck, *Seattle Cityscape #2* (Seattle, 1973), 38, 43.

118. *ST*, Dec. 11, 1981. On site-selection for the new convention center, see Rebecca Boren, "Why the Convention Center Should Not Be Built Downtown," Seattle *Weekly* (March 9, 1983): 24, 26–27; David Brewster, "Why the Convention Center Should Be Built at the Seattle Center," Seattle *Weekly* (March 9, 1983): 25, 27; Rebecca Boren, "Downtown Boosters Get Their Convention Center," Seattle *Weekly* (April 16, 1983): 10; *P-I*, March 27, 1984.

119. Metro, "Downtown Seattle Transit Alternatives," 48; Karen Milburn, "Local Commotion: Is It Time to Scrap the Monorail?" *Pacific Northwest* 20 (May 1986): 24. On the failure of rapid transit, see Sale, *Seattle, Past to Present*, 227–30.

120. Seattle City Planning Commission, *Designing a Great City: Report of the Urban Design Advisory Board to the Seattle City Planning Commission* (Seattle, 1965), among other items, expresses the same concerns about downtown that fair planners had tried to address; moreover, it hardly considers the new Seattle Center a part of the central business district. For summaries of other downtown projects, see: Sale, *Seattle, Past to Present*, ch. 7; *ST*, April 19, 1987.

121. Alfred J. Schweppe to John DeDakis, Oct. 26, 1976 (copy), in Alfred J. Schweppe Papers, University of Washington Library; *P-I*, Aug. 1, 20, Sept. 10, 17, Nov. 6, 16, 1975.

122. Dingwall interview.

123. Dingwall interview; *P-I*, April 18, 1962; *ST*, Oct. 10, 1961, Sept. 6, Oct. 21, 1962; "Carling and Mission Present World's Fair Windup," 8, 18.

124. Louis C. Wagner, "Impact of the Seattle World's Fair on Retail Sales and Services in the State of Washington," *University of Washington Business Review* 23 (Feb. 1964): 7–8, 10–13; *ST*, March 3, 1963; Century 21 Exposition news release, July 20, 1962, DP-UWL.

125. Gandy cited in *ST*, July 22, 1962.

126. *ST*, April 29, 1962.

127. Morgan, *Skid Road*, 277. On changing politics, see Herrera, "Mega-

lopolis Comes to the Northwest," 118–23; Sale, *Seattle, Past to Present*, 223–27. Carl Abbott, *The New Urban America: Growth and Politics in Sunbelt Cities* (Chapel Hill, N.C., 1981), ch. 9, especially 215–17, locates Seattle within a regional framework.

128. On debates over the Seattle Center, and the changes it underwent, see Dingwall interview; Seattle Civic Center Advisory Commission, "Recommendations of the Civic Center Advisory Commission for the Use, Development and Management of Seattle Center," Sept. 1, 1962, on file in uncatalogued Northwest materials, Seattle Public Library; *ST*, May 23, June 10, 14, 19, July 2, Aug. 19, Sept. 21, 23, Nov. 6, 25, Dec. 9, 1962, April 19, 21, 1982; Russell Lynes, "Aftermath in Seattle," *Harper's Magazine* 232 (Feb. 1966): 22–28; Peck, "Arts Activists and Seattle's Cultural Expansion," 92–93.

129. *OGB*, 98–99; *ST*, Aug. 16, Oct. 1, 1961, Aug. 5, Sept. 5, 6, Oct. 22, 1962.

130. *OGB*, 4–5; *Official Guide to the Seattle Center* (Seattle, 1963), 4–5; *ST*, Nov. 25, 1962, April 19, 1982.

131. Several visitors praised the new cultural complex and urged Seattle residents to a full appreciation: *New York Herald Tribune*, April 22, 1962; *Chicago Sun-Times*, June 3, 1962; Harold Shaw, director of performing arts at the fair, in *ST*, July 4, 1962. Lincoln Kirstein, director of the New York City Ballet, compared the fair complex favorably to Gotham's new Lincoln Center: "Letter from Seattle," *Nation* 194 (April 7, 1962): 315–19.

132. Cited in *ST*, April 20, 1982. See also Peck, "Arts Activists and Seattle's Cultural Expansion," 82.

133. Dingwall interview; *P-I*, April 18, 1982; *ST*, April 20, 1982; Noe, "Innocence Revisited," 32; Peck, "Arts Activists and Seattle's Cultural Expansion," 90–91.

134. *P-I*, April 21, 1977, April 18, 1982; *ST*, April 19, 1982; Dingwall interview. Quotation from Paul Andrews in *ST*, April 18, 1982.

135. See Jack Gordon's comments in *ST*, April 20, 1982.

136. *1962 Seattle World's Fair Background Information*, 7. Both sets of attitudes are conveyed vividly throughout Morgan, *Century 21*; and by columnist Emmett Watson in *ST*, April 19, 1987.

Chapter Six

1. American Institute of Architects, Metro Phoenix Regional/Urban Design Assistance Team, *What Are the Options That Appear to Exist with Respect to Mobility, Life-Style and Urban Form in the Further Development of Metropolitan Phoenix?* (Phoenix, 1974), 30–31.

2. Phoenix, Arizona, City Planning Department, *The Comprehensive Plan, 1990, Phoenix, Arizona* (Phoenix, 1969), 15–16.

3. Christopher B. Leinberger and Charles Lockwood, "How Business Is Reshaping America," *Atlantic Monthly* 258 (Oct. 1986): 52 (quotation on

"self-sufficiency"); Phoenix, Arizona, City Planning Commission and Urban Form Directions Steering Committee, *Phoenix Concept Plan 2000: A Program for Planning* ([Phoenix, 1980?]) (quotation on "identifiable community" at 1).

4. Bradford Luckingham, *Phoenix: The History of a Southwestern Metropolis* (Tucson, 1989), 233.

5. Kevin Lynch, *The Image of the City* (Cambridge, Mass., 1960), 2–3.

6. Robert Fishman, "The Post-War American Suburb: A New Form, a New City," in Daniel Schaffer, ed., *Two Centuries of American Planning* (London, 1988), 276 (quotation on "new urban types"); Scott Greer, "Decentralization: The End of Cities?" in *California and the Challenge of Growth*, part 5, *The Metropolitan Future* (Berkeley, 1965), 47–48 (quotation on "pathological"). See also: Jack Meltzer, *Metropolis to Metroplex: The Social and Spatial Planning of Cities* (Baltimore, 1984), 15–16; David C. Perry and Alfred J. Watkins, "Introduction," in David C. Perry and Alfred J. Watkins, eds., *The Rise of the Sunbelt Cities* (Beverly Hills, 1977), 8–9.

7. Karl Belser, "Misuse of Land in Fringe Areas and Inadequate Subdivision Standards," in *Problems of Decentralization in Metropolitan Areas: Proceedings of the First Annual University of California Conference on City and Regional Planning* (Berkeley, 1954), 22–23 (emphasis added).

8. Richard J. Neutra, "Life's Human Defenses," *Frontier* 8 (Feb. 1957): 15; Catherine Bauer Wurster, "The California Environment: Must It Be Ruined by Growth and Prosperity?" in California State Department of Public Works, *Papers from the Governor's Conference on California's Urban Areas and the State Highway System* (Sacramento, 1960), 47; Reyner Banham, *Los Angeles: The Architecture of Four Ecologies* (1971; Middlesex, Eng., 1973), 137–39. See also Bernard Marchand, *The Emergence of Los Angeles: Population and Housing in the City of Dreams 1940–1970* (London, 1986), 38.

9. Amos Rapoport, *The Meaning of the Built Environment: A Nonverbal Communication Approach* (Beverly Hills, 1982), 76 (quotation on designers and users), 19–22 (quotations on "perceptual" and "associational"); Amos Rapoport, *Human Aspects of Urban Form: Towards a Man-Environment Approach to Urban Form and Design* (Oxford, 1977), 14–15 (quotations on "subculture" and "rules").

10. Francois G. Christen, *Citizen Preference for Home, Neighborhood, and City in Santa Clara County* (Santa Monica, 1973), 6, 14–16, 17–18; Daniel J. Alesch and Robert A. Levine, *Growth in San Jose: A Summary Policy Statement* (Santa Monica, 1973), 3–4.

11. Bruce Bliven, "The California Culture," *Harper's* 210 (Jan. 1955): 35 (quotation), 36–37; Greer, "Decentralization: The End of Cities?" 52 (quotation on "drift of things").

12. Amos Rapoport explains that the "values embodied in the different images one holds of what a city should be will lead to different cities": Rapoport, *Human Aspects of Urban Form*, 25.

13. Wilbur Zelinsky, *The Cultural Geography of the United States* (Englewood Cliffs, N.J., 1973), 135, discusses the concept of the voluntary region.

Decisions to move were much more complex than can be discussed here. If the twentieth-century westward movement was anything like its nineteenth-century counterpart (and evidence from Sun City suggests some similarity), men would have had more input into a family's decision than women. It should not be assumed that all who moved to the region came with the same degree of voluntarism.

14. George W. Pierson, *The Moving American* (New York, 1973), 168, 186.

15. Pierson, *Moving American*, 207–8; Earl S. Pomeroy, "What Remains of the West," *Utah Historical Quarterly* 35 (Winter 1967): 54; Carey McWilliams, *California: The Great Exception* (New York, 1949), 86.

16. Nathan Glazer, "Notes on Southern California: 'A Reasonable Suggestion as to How Things Can Be'?" *Commentary* 28 (Aug. 1959): 104.

17. Edward Abbey, *The Journey Home: Some Words in Defense of the American West* (New York, 1977), 46.

18. Quotation from Edmond S. Meany, "The Coming City of Puget Sound," 1929 MS, Edmond S. Meany Papers, University of Washington Libraries, 8. See also Robert M. Fogelson, *The Fragmented Metropolis: Los Angeles 1850–1930* (Cambridge, Mass., 1967); David Brodsly, *L.A. Freeway: An Appreciative Essay* (Berkeley, 1981); Mark S. Foster, "The Western Response to Urban Transportation: A Tale of Three Cities, 1900–1945," in Gerald D. Nash, ed., *The Urban West* (Manhattan, Kans., 1979), 31–32, 38.

19. Clifford E. Clinton, *The Clock Strikes Twelve: A Little Journey into Los Angeles as It Was, as It Is and as It Can Be—Glimpses of the Physical, Cultural and Spiritual Promise of the City of the Angels* (Los Angeles, 1945), i; Earl C. Gottschalk, Jr., "Boom Town: Phoenix Area's Sprawl Worries City Planners," *Wall Street Journal*, June 18, 1974, 31. See also: Howard N. Rabinowitz, "Reps on the Range: An Anti-Turnerian Framework for the Urban West," *Journal of Urban History* 8 (Nov. 1981): 95–96; Peter A. Lupsha and William J. Siembieda, "The Poverty of Public Services in the Land of Plenty: An Analysis and Interpretation," in Perry and Watkins, eds., *Rise of the Sunbelt Cities*, 176.

20. David K. Webster, "Los Angeles," *Frontier* 3 (June 1952): 13.

21. On the West's imitative tendencies during the nineteenth century, see Earl S. Pomeroy, "Toward a Reorientation of Western History: Continuity and Environment," *Mississippi Valley Historical Review* 41 (Mar. 1955): 597; Richard Wade, *The Urban Frontier: The Rise of Western Cities, 1790–1830* (Cambridge, Mass., 1959). Gunther Barth, *Instant Cities: Urbanization and the Rise of San Francisco and Denver* (New York, 1975), analyzes efforts to imitate the East in the nineteenth-century urban West.

22. James E. Vance, Jr., "California and the Search for the Ideal," *Annals of the Association of American Geographers* 62 (June 1972): 196.

23. Vance, "California and the Search for the Ideal," 194–97; Peirce F. Lewis, "America Between the Wars: The Engineering of a New Geography," in Robert D. Mitchell and Paul A. Groves, eds., *North America: The Historical Geography of a Changing Continent* (Totowa, N.J., 1987), 433; Marion Clawson, "What It Means to Be a Californian," *California Historical Society Quarterly* 24 (June 1945): 143; Carey McWilliams, *Southern California: An Island on the Land* (1946; reprint, Santa Barbara, 1979), 150–51 n. 39; Earl S. Pomeroy, "Has the Pacific Coast an Identifiable Culture? A Memorandum on Backgrounds," 1958 (MS in author's possession), 15–16; Kevin Starr, *Inventing the Dream: California Through the Progressive Era* (New York, 1985), 89.

24. Richard J. Neutra, "Mild-Climate Housing: California's 'Revolution-

ary' Contribution," *Frontier* 5 (April 1954): 11. See also Edward L. Ullman, "Amenities as a Factor in Regional Growth," *Geographical Review* 44 (Jan. 1954): 119, 121–22; D. W. Meinig, *Southwest: Three Peoples in Geographical Change, 1600–1970* (New York, 1971), 86, 107.

25. On the changing western economy, see Michael P. Malone and Richard W. Etulain, *The American West: A Twentieth-Century History* (Lincoln, Neb., 1989), chs. 1, 3, 6. On the region's integration into the world capitalist system, see William G. Robbins, "Western History: A Dialectic on the Modern Condition," *Western Historical Quarterly* 20 (Nov. 1989): 429–49.

26. Samuel P. Hays, *Beauty, Health, and Permanence: Environmental Politics in the United States, 1955–1985* (New York, 1987), 13.

27. McWilliams, *California: The Great Exception*, 238; Meinig, *Southwest*, 107.

28. Walter Prescott Webb, "The American West: Perpetual Mirage," *Harper's Magazine* 214 (May 1957): 28; Donald Worster, "New West, True West: Interpreting the Region's History," *Western Historical Quarterly* 18 (April 1987): 154.

29. Writing about Californians, Kevin Starr explores the special place of nature in *Americans and the California Dream 1850–1915* (New York, 1973), and *Inventing the Dream*. Remarks attributed to Earl Pomeroy by Otis Pease, "Has the Pacific Coast an Identifiable Culture?" Sept. 1959 (MS summary of 1958 conference sponsored by Pacific Coast Committee for the Humanities, in author's possession), 7.

30. Olmsted cited in William H. Wilson, *The City Beautiful Movement* (Baltimore, 1989), 167; Elmer Grey, "The New Suburb of the Pacific Coast," *Scribner's Magazine* 52 (July 1912): 36–51.

31. Remi Nadeau, *California: The New Society* (New York, 1963), 214.

32. Neal R. Peirce, *The Pacific States of America: People, Politics, and Power in the Five Pacific Basin States* (New York, 1972), 71, 134–35; Hays, *Beauty, Health, and Permanence*, 44; Ted K. Bradshaw, "Trying Out the Future," *Wilson Quarterly* 4 (Summer 1980): 74; Rodney Steiner, *Los Angeles, the Centrifugal City* (Dubuque, Iowa, 1981), 196–201.

33. Wurster, "California Environment," 45.

34. Webster, "Los Angeles," 13 (first and third quotations); Luckingham, *Phoenix*, 168 (quotation on Phoenix as "ten times" better).

35. Gifford Phillips, "Today's Frontier," *Frontier* 1 (Nov. 15, 1949): 2; Luckingham, *Phoenix*, 161.

36. The reference is to Henry Nash Smith, *Virgin Land: The American West as Symbol and Myth* (reprint ed., Cambridge, Mass., 1978).

37. John Anson Ford, *Thirty Explosive Years in Los Angeles County* (San Marino, Calif., 1961), 58.

38. Kenneth T. Jackson, *Crabgrass Frontier: The Suburbanization of the United States* (New York, 1985); Kenneth I. Helphand, "McUrbia: The 1950s and the Birth of the Contemporary American Landscape," *Places: A Quarterly Journal of Environmental Design* 5: 2 (1988): 40–49.

39. Fishman, "Post-War American Suburb," 268.

40. Yi-Fu Tuan, *Topophilia: A Study of Environmental Perception, Attitudes,*

and Values (Englewood Cliffs, N.J., 1974), 236 (quotation); Herbert J. Gans, *People and Plans: Essays on Urban Problems and Solutions* (New York, 1968), 139–40.

41. Catherine Bauer [Wurster], "Social Effects of Decentralization," in *Problems of Decentralization in Metropolitan Areas,* 44–45.

42. Kenneth Fox, *Metropolitan America: Urban Life and Urban Policy in the United States 1940–1980* (London, 1985).

43. Donald J. Bogue, *The Population of the United States* (Glencoe, Ill., 1959), 405–9; Richard E. Preston, "Urban Development in Southern California Between 1940 and 1965" (1967), in Robert W. Durrenberger, ed., *California: Its People, Its Problems, Its Prospects* (Palo Alto, 1971), 97; James E. Vance, Jr., *Geography and Urban Evolution in the San Francisco Bay Area* (Berkeley, 1964), 34–35; Peter O. Muller, *Contemporary Suburban America* (Englewood Cliffs, N.J., 1981), 55–56.

44. Cited in Hal Lancaster, "Out to Pasture: The Old but Affluent Withdraw to Sun City to Fill Empty Days," *Wall Street Journal,* Nov. 16, 1972, 35.

45. Glazer, "Notes on Southern California," 100–101, 104–5.

46. San Jose, Calif., Department of City Planning, *The General Plan 1975* (San Jose, 1976), 5 (first quotation); Ernest A. Engelbert, ed., *The Nature and Control of Urban Dispersal* (Berkeley, 1960), vii.

47. Leo Grebler, *Metropolitan Contrasts,* Part 1 of University of California, Los Angeles, Real Estate Research Program, *Profile of the Los Angeles Metropolis: Its People and Its Homes* (Berkeley, 1963), 27; San Jose, Calif., Department of City Planning, *General Plan 1975,* 6; Leonard Gordon, "Social Issues in the Arid City," in Gideon Golany, ed., *Urban Planning for Arid Zones: American Experiences and Directions* (New York, 1978), 115; Joseph Stocker, *Arizona: A Guide to Easier Living* (New York, 1955), 58, 59.

48. Donald L. Foley et al., *Characteristics of Metropolitan Growth in California,* vol. 1, *Report* (Berkeley, 1965), xv; Preston, "Urban Development in Southern California," 98.

49. Glazer, "Notes on Southern California," 104.

50. Carl Abbott, *The New Urban America: Growth and Politics in Sunbelt Cities* (Chapel Hill, N.C., 1981), 95–96; Marchand, *Emergence of Los Angeles,* 58. One guide to discerning the new pattern on the land is Robert Venturi, Denise Scott Brown, and Steven Izenour, *Learning from Las Vegas: The Forgotten Symbolism of Architectural Form* (rev. ed. Cambridge, Mass., 1977).

51. Leinberger and Lockwood, "How Business Is Reshaping America," 43; Fishman, "Post-War American Suburb," 266, 268–69.

52. Harvey S. Perloff, *Planning the Post-Industrial City* (Washington, D.C., 1980), 25, 83.

53. Sheldon Zalaznick, "The Double Life of Orange County," *Fortune* 78 (Oct. 1968): 138–41, 184–88.

54. Alesch and Levine, *Growth in San Jose,* 6–7, 13; Hays, *Beauty, Health, and Permanence,* 3–4, 33–35, 44, 46.

55. Abbott, *New Urban America,* ch. 9; San Jose Goals Committee, *Goals for San Jose* (San Jose, 1969); "Industry Can Be Neighborly," *Architectural Forum* 114 (Jan. 1961): 57–62; "Correcting San Jose's Boomtime Mistakes,"

Business Week (Sept. 19, 1970): 74–76; Zalaznick, "Double Life of Orange County," 140–41, 186; George F. Will, "'Slow Growth' Is the Liberalism of the Privileged," *LAT*, Aug. 30, 1987; Frederick Rose, "California Towns Vote to Restrict Expansion as Services Lag Behind," *Wall Street Journal*, Nov. 27, 1987, 1, 5.

56. George Starbird, *The New Metropolis: San Jose Between 1942 and 1972* (San Jose, 1972), 8.

57. Tuan, *Topophilia*, 197, 207–8.

58. Rapoport, *Meaning of the Built Environment*, 15–22.

59. Fishman, "Post-War American Suburb," 268.

60. Peter Orleans, "Differential Cognition of Urban Residents: Effects of Social Scale on Mapping," in Roger M. Downs and David Stea, eds., *Image and Environment: Cognitive Mapping and Spatial Behavior* (Chicago, 1973), 127–28. See also: Anselm L. Strauss, *Images of the American City* (Glencoe, Ill., 1961), 65–67; Grady Clay, *Close-Up: How to Read the American City* (New York, 1973), 110–15; Rapoport, *Human Aspects of Urban Form*, 136–41.

61. Roger M. Downs and David Stea, *Maps in Minds: Reflections on Cognitive Mapping* (New York, 1977), especially 78–79 (quotation), 137–38; Rapoport, *Human Aspects of Urban Form*, 114.

62. Rapoport, *Human Aspects of Urban Form*, 249–65.

63. Steiner, *Los Angeles, the Centrifugal City*, 151, contrasts residents' understanding of San Fernando Valley towns to that of "casual onlookers."

64. Paul Goldberger, "When Suburban Sprawl Meets Upward Mobility," *NYT*, July 26, 1987; Meltzer, *Metropolis to Metroplex*, 17; Gurney Breckenfeld, "'Downtown' Has Fled to the Suburbs," *Fortune* 86 (Oct. 1972): 80.

65. Wilson, *City Beautiful Movement*, 57, 304–5.

66. "California's 'Cities of Tomorrow' Will Be Attractive, Savage Says," The Ranney Company press release for El Dorado Hills planned community, n.d. [early 1960s], in Carton 5, Wurster Papers; developer Ernest Hahn, cited in William Severini Kowinski, *The Malling of America* (New York, 1985), 227.

67. *Century City Story: Facts on the City-Within-a-City Urban Complex* (n.p., n.d.; Department of Special Collections, UCLA Library), 1–2, 8.

68. *LAT*, April 19, 1967.

69. Leinberger and Lockwood, "How Business Is Reshaping America," 44; Karl Lamb, *As Orange Goes: Twelve California Families and the Future of American Politics* (New York, 1974), 2.

70. Brodsly, *L.A. Freeway*, 37, 7 (quotation); Banham, *Los Angeles*, 213. Steiner, *Los Angeles, the Centrifugal City*, chs. 8–10, surveys southern California's many "outlying urban centers."

71. Thomas J. Baerwald, "The Emergence of a New 'Downtown,'" *Geographical Review* 68 (July 1978): 308–18 (quotation on "suburban freeway corridor"); Gurney Breckenfeld, "Refilling the Metropolitan Doughnut," in Perry and Watkins, eds., *Rise of the Sunbelt Cities*, 240–41 (quotation on "satellite centers"); Greer, "Decentralization: The End of Cities?" 48 (quotation on "subnuclei"); Meltzer, *Metropolis to Metroplex*, 17 (final quotation). See also: Jon C. Teaford, *The Twentieth-Century American City: Problem, Promise, and Reality* (Baltimore, 1986), 153; Edward Relph, *The Modern Urban Landscape* (London, 1987), 160–61, 165.

72. Vance, "California and the Search for the Ideal," 205.

73. *AR*, Dec. 11, 1975, in City Planning Clippings file, PPL-AR; Leinberger and Lockwood, "How Business Is Reshaping America," 52; Peter C. Papademetriou, *Transportation and Urban Development in Houston 1830–1980* (Houston, 1982), 67.

74. Brian J. L. Berry, "The Decline of the Aging Metropolis: Cultural Bases and Social Processes," in George Sternlieb and James W. Hughes, eds., *Post-Industrial America: Metropolitan Decline and Inter-Regional Job Shifts* (New Brunswick, N.J., 1975), 183–84; Meltzer, *Metropolis to Metroplex*, 14; Muller, *Contemporary Suburban America*, 66–67.

75. Charles B. Bennett and Milton Breivogel, *Planning for the San Fernando Valley* (Los Angeles, 1945), 8 (quotation); City of Los Angeles, Department of City Planning, *City Planning in Los Angeles: A History* (Los Angeles, 1964), 31.

76. Tabulations of America's "new communities" can be found in Edward P. Eichler and Marshall Kaplan, *The Community Builders* (Berkeley, 1967), 185–86; Raymond J. Burby III and Shirley F. Weiss, *New Communities U.S.A.* (Lexington, Mass., 1976), 81–82; Gideon Golany, *New-Town Planning: Principles and Practice* (New York, 1976), 14. On the western new community experience, see William Alonso, "Urban Growth in California: New Towns and Other Policy Alternatives," in Kingsley Davis and Frederick G. Styles, eds., *California's Twenty Million: Research Contributions to Population Policy*, Population Monograph Series No. 10 (Berkeley, 1971), 319–20; Theodore Roszak, "Life in the Instant Cities," in Carey McWilliams, ed., *The California Revolution* (New York, 1968), 63, 66; Charles S. Sargent, Jr., *Planned Communities in Greater Phoenix: Origins, Functions, and Controls* (Tempe, 1973). On Irvine, see Albert F. Trevino, Jr., "The New University and Community Development on the Irvine Ranch, California," *Urban Land* 25 (Sept. 1966): 1, 3–7; Gladwin Hill, "Big But Not Bold: Irvine Today," *Planning* 52 (Feb. 1986): 16–20.

77. Karl J. Belser, "Orderly Development of the Suburbs," talk presented to National Association of County Officials, County Finance Congress, San Diego, Feb. 15, 1960, in Carton 7, Wurster Papers; William R. Mee, Jr., *Planning Commission Symposium on Phoenix Concept Plan 2000, Questions and Answers* (Phoenix, 1981), 2.

78. Peter Self, "New Towns, Greenbelts, and the Urban Region," in *California and the Challenge of Growth*, part 5, *The Metropolitan Future* (Berkeley, 1965), 32–33, 34–35.

79. Golany, *New-Town Planning*, 28–31; Relph, *Modern Urban Landscape*, 154–55; Catherine Bauer Wurster, "'New Towns' in a New Context: Can We Catch Up with the Federal Lead?" March 9, 1964, Carton 2, Wurster Papers; Eichler and Kaplan, *Community Builders*, 24, 49–51, 55–56; Carol A. Christensen, *The American Garden City and the New Towns Movement* (Ann Arbor, Mich., 1986), 6–8.

80. Roszak, "Life in the Instant Cities," 68 (quotations); Carl Werthman, Jerry S. Mandel, and Ted Dienstfrey, *Planning and the Purchase Decision: Why People Buy in Planned Communities* (Berkeley, 1965), especially ch. 8; Eichler and Kaplan, *Community Builders*, 112–19; William Alonso, "What Are New Towns For?" *Urban Studies* 7 (Feb. 1970): 37–55.

81. Wurster, "'New Towns' in a New Context," 1; Louis H. Masotti, "Prologue: Suburbia Reconsidered—Myth and Counter-Myth," in Louis H. Masotti and Jeffrey K. Hadden, eds., *The Urbanization of the Suburbs* (Beverly Hills, 1973), 16–17.

82. Donald Monson, "Comprehensive Plan for Central Business District, Seattle: Technical Report Prepared for the City of Seattle and the Central Association of Seattle," 1963, IGSL, 3, 4 (quotations). The suburbanization of downtown is discussed by Leinberger and Lockwood, "How Business Is Reshaping America," 46; Kowinski, *Malling of America*, 120, 128–29, 272–73; Howard Gillette, Jr., "The Evolution of the Planned Shopping Center in Suburb and City," *Journal of the American Planning Association* 51 (Autumn 1985): 449–60; Muller, *Contemporary Suburban America*, 128.

83. Leinberger and Lockwood, "How Business Is Reshaping America," 49–51; AnnaLee Saxenian, "Silicon Valley and Route 128: Regional Prototypes or Historic Exceptions," in Manuel Castells, ed., *High Technology, Space, and Society* (Beverly Hills, 1985), 85–87.

84. Neil J. Sullivan, *The Dodgers Move West* (New York, 1987), ch. 8; Ernesto Galarza, "Mexicans in the Southwest: A Culture in Process," in Edward H. Spicer and Raymond H. Thompson, eds., *Plural Society in the Southwest* (New York, 1972), 285.

85. Orleans, "Differential Cognition of Urban Residents," 115–30.

86. Vance, "California and the Search for the Ideal," 208.

87. Luckingham, *Phoenix*, 170; Harry H. L. Kitano, *Japanese Americans: The Evolution of a Subculture* (2d ed. Englewood Cliffs, N.J., 1976), 112; Roger Daniels, *Asian America: Chinese and Japanese in the United States Since 1850* (Seattle, 1988), 286; Harry H. L. Kitano and Roger Daniels, *Asian Americans: Emerging Minorities* (Englewood Cliffs, N.J., 1988), 75.

88. Kitano and Daniels, *Asian Americans*, 73, 49–50.

89. Margaret Clark, *Health in the Mexican American Culture* (Berkeley, 1959), 33.

90. Meinig, *Southwest*, 98; Leo Grebler et al., *The Mexican-American People: The Nation's Second Largest Minority* (New York, 1970), 83–84; Galarza, "Mexicans in the Southwest," 277–79, 268–69 (quotation on "cores of poverty").

91. Grebler et al., *Mexican-American People*, 275, 278, 286; Robert M. Fogelson, ed. and comp., *The Los Angeles Riots* (New York, 1969), 141–42.

92. Loren Miller, "Housing and Racial Covenants," *Frontier* 1 (Feb. 1, 1950): 11–13; Elizabeth Poe, "Segregation in Los Angeles Schools," *Frontier* 13 (Oct. 1962): 12–13.

93. Frederick J. Hacker with Aljean Harmetz, "What the McCone Commission Didn't See," *Frontier* 17 (March 1966): 11–12 (quotation); Constance Rice, "School Desegregation in Seattle: A Historical and Contemporary Synopsis," *Western Journal of Black Studies* 1 (Sept. 1977): 203; "The Los Angeles Negro," *Frontier* 6 (June 1955): 9–10.

94. Tuan, *Topophilia*, 214; Leinberger and Lockwood, "How Business Is Reshaping America," 49–51.

95. Charles S. Sargent, quoted in *Minneapolis Tribune*, Feb. 27, 1973; Roszak, "Life in the Instant Cities," 63–83.

96. Clay, *Close-Up*, 38–39.

97. Downs and Stea, *Maps in Minds*, 78–79, 91–92 (quotation).

98. June Rose Gader, *L.A. Live: Profiles of a City* (New York, 1980), 24.

99. Downs and Stea, *Maps in Minds*, 252.

100. Rapoport, *Meaning of the Built Environment*, 137, assesses the significance of homogeneity to a city district.

101. Frederick Law Olmsted, "Public Parks and the Enlargement of Towns" (1870), in S. B. Sutton, ed., *Civilizing American Cities: A Selection of Frederick Law Olmsted's Writings on City Landscapes* (Cambridge, Mass., 1979), 96.

102. Gunther Barth, *City People: The Rise of Modern City Culture in Nineteenth-Century America* (New York, 1980), 38.

103. SCRC, *Arresting Slums: A Regional Plan for Southern California* (Los Angeles, 1968), 7.

104. Luckingham, *Phoenix*, 174–76, 178, 214–17; Alesch and Levine, *Growth in San Jose*; Roger Sale, *Seattle, Past to Present* (rev. ed. Seattle, 1978), 232–33.

105. Jeffrey Cook, "Patterns of Desert Urbanization: The Evolution of Metropolitan Phoenix," in Golany, ed., *Urban Planning for Arid Zones*, 219; Bliven, "California Culture," 33, 34; Lamb, *As Orange Goes*, 30; *NYT*, Feb. 24, 1970 (article on the Santa Clara Valley); Luckingham, *Phoenix*, 187, 219. Quotation in Walter Doty, "A *Sunset* Editor Assesses the Development of Landscape Design Since 1939," typescript of an oral history conducted in 1977 by Suzanne B. Reiss, in "Thomas D. Church, Landscape Architect," 1978, Regional Oral History Office, TBL, vol. 1, 242.

106. San Jose Goals Committee, *Goals for San Jose*, 7–8; Philip J. Trounstine and Terry Christensen, *Movers and Shakers: The Study of Community Power* (New York, 1982), 169; Abbott, *New Urban America*, 165–66, 215–17, 256; Sale, *Seattle, Past to Present*, 223–27.

107. On new towns as solutions to inner-city concerns, see Wurster, "'New Towns' in a New Context," 2; Harvey S. Perloff, "New Towns Intown," *Journal of the American Institute of Planners* 32 (May 1966): 155; Bernard Weissbourd, "The Satellite Community as Suburb," in Masotti and Hadden, eds., *Urbanization of the Suburbs*, 495–532. On federal efforts, see Christensen, *American Garden City and the New Towns Movement*, 106–7. Eichler and Kaplan, *Community Builders*, 160, 181–82, and Alonso, "What Are New Towns For?" 37–55, account for New Towns' lack of success in the United States.

108. Peirce, *Pacific States of America*, 24.

109. Edward Relph, *Place and Placelessness* (London, 1976).

110. Rapoport, *Meaning of the Built Environment*, 65.

Bibliographical Essay

The endnotes to the chapters constitute a comprehensive list of the materials consulted for this study. Readers interested in probing the subject further may, however, wish to use the remarks below as a guide.

This exploration of western cityscapes since 1940 has made use of a wide range of materials. In turning to works in cultural geography and urban studies, it has barely scratched the surface of an extensive and diverse literature. By contrast, pertinent historical scholarship on the American West since 1890 proved far less abundant. After relying too long on such helpful syntheses as Earl S. Pomeroy's *The Pacific Slope: A History of California, Oregon, Washington, Idaho, Utah, and Nevada* (New York, 1965) and Gerald D. Nash's *American West in the Twentieth Century: A Short History of an Urban Oasis* (Englewood Cliffs, N.J., 1973), historians have recently begun to accelerate their examination of the twentieth-century region. The bibliographies in Michael P. Malone and Richard W. Etulain, *The American West: A Twentieth-Century History* (Lincoln, 1989), and Gerald D. Nash and Richard W. Etulain, eds., *The Twentieth-Century West: Historical Interpretations* (Albuquerque, 1989), indicate much recent progress in the field; yet gaps persist.

One remaining gap is in western urban history, and another is in western cultural history. To date, the history of the modern urban West has been told primarily in profiles of individual cities such as Bradford Luckingham's *Phoenix: The History of a Southwestern Metropolis* (Tucson, 1989). Among the few works that have pondered urbanization as a regional phenomenon, those by Carl Abbott stand out: *The New Urban*

America: Growth and Politics in Sunbelt Cities (Chapel Hill, 1981); "The Metropolitan Region: Western Cities in the New Urban Era," in Nash and Etulain, eds., *Twentieth-Century West*, 71–98; and "Southwestern Cityscapes: Approaches to an American Urban Environment," in Robert B. Fairbanks and Kathleen Underwood, eds., *Essays on Sunbelt Cities and Recent Urban America* (College Station, Tex., 1990), 59–86.

In addition to secondary works, students of the modern urban West have many other accessible sources to consult. The reports of the U.S. Bureau of the Census provide fundamental data on urbanization, and they have been supplemented by Donald J. Bogue's two compendiums, *The Population of the United States* (Glencoe, Ill., 1959) and *The Population of the United States: Historical Trends and Future Projections* (New York, 1985).

Journalists have filed some exceptional reports on the region. Carey McWilliams's *Southern California: An Island on the Land* (1946; reprint, Santa Barbara, 1979) and *California: The Great Exception* (New York, 1949) remain landmark studies, and Neal R. Peirce, *The Pacific States of America: People, Politics, and Power in the Five Pacific Basin States* (New York, 1972) continues to be informative. The liberal, Los Angeles-based *Frontier*, first a semi-monthly and then a monthly magazine, devoted itself to western political, social, and economic issues from 1948 through its merger with *The Nation* in 1967. It gave regular attention to the urban experience of western minorities, another topic historians have neglected. Social scientists' contemporary accounts of western minorities—Margaret Clark, *Health in the Mexican American Culture* (Berkeley, 1959), and Leo Grebler et al., *The Mexican-American People: The Nation's Second Largest Minority* (New York, 1970)—remain quite valuable.

City and county planners were another key source of information about the transformation of the western city, although the quality and quantity of their reports varied greatly from place to place. The Planning Department of Santa Clara County issued a series of periodicals called *Info* and *Info-Commentary*, which covered many dimensions of urbanization. These highly informative publications are on file, along with documents from many other western city planning offices, in the Institute of Governmental Studies Library, University of California, Berkeley. Two particularly perceptive planners were Catherine Bauer Wurster of the University of California, Berkeley, and Karl J. Belser, director of the Santa Clara County Planning Department. Wurster's papers, in The Bancroft Library, are a treasure trove of information about western and other American cities and suburbs. Many of Belser's published and unpublished papers can be found among Catherine Bauer Wurster's papers and in the historical files of the Santa Clara County Department of Planning and Development, San Jose.

Karl J. Belser was prominent among those who characterized the western metropolis as chaotic. He summarized his critique in an account of the postwar Santa Clara Valley—"The Making of Slurban America," *Cry California* 5 (Fall 1970): 1–21. The journal *Cry California*, published between 1965 and 1982 by the environmental and regional-planning organization California Tomorrow, contained numerous articles on the problems of urbanization and planning in the Golden State. Two others associated with California Tomorrow were Samuel E. Wood and Alfred E. Heller, co-authors of *California Going, Going . . . : Our State's Struggle to Remain Beautiful and Productive* (Sacramento, 1962) and *The Phantom Cities of California* (Sacramento, 1963).

Critics of urban form in the postwar West found much to condemn in San Jose and Los Angeles. On the former city, see, besides Belser's article, Robert C. Fellmeth, ed., *Politics of Land: Ralph Nader's Study Group Report on Land Use in California* (New York, 1973); Stanford Environmental Law Society, *San Jose, Sprawling City: A Report on Land Use Policies and Practices in San Jose, California* (Stanford, 1971); and Philip J. Trounstine and Terry Christensen, *Movers and Shakers: The Study of Community Power* (New York, 1982). On southern California, see Robert M. Fogelson, *The Fragmented Metropolis: Los Angeles, 1850–1930* (Cambridge, Mass., 1967); Richard G. Lillard, *Eden in Jeopardy: Man's Prodigal Meddling with His Environment—The Southern California Experience* (New York, 1966); and William Irwin Thompson, *At the Edge of History* (New York, 1972), ch. 1. For a critique of Phoenix, consult Charles S. Sargent, "Arizona's Urban Frontier—Myths and Realities," in Charles S. Sargent, ed., *The Conflict Between Frontier Values and Land-Use Control in Greater Phoenix: Report of a Conference Held at Arizona State University, November 22, 1975* (Phoenix, 1976), 4–23.

Apart from the writings of planners and other urban critics, the collections and reminiscences of several prominent individuals who were concerned in one way or another with western urbanization will reward researchers. Besides writing *Thirty Explosive Years in Los Angeles County* (San Marino, Calif., 1961), John Anson Ford, the longtime county supervisor, left a rich collection of papers to The Henry E. Huntington Library. The Huntington also houses some of the personal papers of

Fletcher Bowron, mayor of Los Angeles between 1938 and 1953, who collected materials toward an unfinished history of Los Angeles. Oral history programs associated with The Bancroft Library, the Stanford University Archives, and the Special Collections Department at UCLA have produced transcripts of interviews with such individuals as *Sunset* editor Walter Doty, architect Dione Neutra, John Anson Ford, Stanford provost Frederick E. Terman, and Stanford professor Edward L. Ginzton. Transcripts of interviews with prominent citizens of Anaheim, produced by the Oral History Program at California State University, Fullerton, can be consulted in the Anaheim History Room, Anaheim Public Library. And the Walt Disney Archives contains transcripts, audio tapes, and film footage of numerous in-house interviews of individuals associated with Disneyland and Walt Disney World.

The documentary record on Disneyland is extensive. Two veteran theme-park employees have produced valuable accounts: Randy Bright's *Disneyland: Inside Story* (New York, 1987) and Van Arsdale France's unpublished manuscript, "Backstage Disneyland: A Personal History" (1980?; in author's possession). Disney theme parks have been examined helpfully by several journalists: Anthony Haden-Guest, *The Paradise Program: Travels Through Muzak, Hilton, Coca-Cola, Texaco, Walt Disney and Other World Empires* (New York, 1973); Richard Schickel, *The Disney Version: The Life, Times, Art and Commerce of Walt Disney* (rev. ed. New York, 1985); and Kevin Wallace, "The Engineering of Ease," *New Yorker* 34 (Sept. 7, 1963): 104–29. Although historians have paid virtually no attention to Disneyland (or Stanford Industrial Park, Sun City, and the Seattle World's Fair), scholars in other fields have forged ahead. A sampling of their approaches can be found in the *Journal of Popular Culture* 15 (Summer 1981).

The Walt Disney Company has endowed two repositories with large amounts of primary source materials on Disneyland. At its Burbank studios, the company maintains the Walt Disney Archives for the primary purpose of preserving and protecting corporate records and assets, including Disney's reputation. It accommodates many scholars doing research on Disney, although, understandably, it will not make all of its records available to outsiders. The Walt Disney Archives is rich in holdings, produced or collected by the company, which put its Anaheim theme park in the best possible light. These include scrapbooks of advertisements for Disneyland and of newspaper clippings about the theme park from around the world; film footage and photographs of Disneyland; manuals and other publications for park employees; runs of magazines issued to publicize the park; and copies of speeches and papers by various people associated with the parks, including some especially informative ones by consultant Harrison A. Price.

Besides maintaining its own archives, the Walt Disney Company has deposited many publications and photographs pertaining to Disneyland in the Anaheim History Room at the Anaheim Public Library, where they are readily available to researchers. Curators for the Anaheim History Room have acquired additional materials pertaining to the theme park and its influence on Anaheim, including photos, clippings from southern California newspapers, and "An Historical Sketch" (1980) by Earnest W. Moeller, Anaheim city manager at the time the site for Disneyland was selected, bought, and developed.

The institution that created Stanford Industrial Park, like that which created Disneyland, has been both the main source of and the primary repository for information about its history. Stanford University News and Publications, a public relations office, makes available to researchers its numerous press releases, clippings, articles, photographs, and other materials pertinent to the industrial park. The Stanford University Archives houses similarly accessible and relevant collections, in particular the Frederick E. Terman Papers, J. E. Wallace Sterling Papers, News and Publications Collection, Stanford Industrial Park files, Land Use and Development files, and Stanford Lands files.

Many of these holdings contain newspaper and magazine clippings (mostly favorable to Stanford) which, having been removed from the original publications, needed (and in most cases got) their original dates of publication stamped on them. It seems likely, however, that at least a few errors were made in the process. Consequently, when clippings that may have erroneous dates are cited in the notes above, the name of the collection in which they are found has also been given.

For a scholarly introduction to the development of Stanford Industrial Park and Silicon Valley, consult Rebecca Sue Lowen, "'Exploiting a Wonderful Opportunity': Stanford University, Industry, and the Federal Government, 1937–1965," Ph.D. diss., Stanford University, 1990; Henry Lowood, *From Steeples of Excellence to Silicon Valley* (n.p., n.d.; a research paper, published without pagination by Varian Associates, Inc.); and AnnaLee Saxenian, "The Genesis of Silicon Valley," in Peter Hall and Ann Markusen, eds., *Silicon Landscapes* (Boston, 1985), 20–34. Like Disneyland, Stanford Industrial Park and Silicon Valley have been neglected by most historians but have attracted a great deal of attention from journalists writing for newspapers, magazines, and trade publications and other specialized periodicals. The Pacific Studies Center of Mountain View, California, has collected and made available to researchers a tremendous amount of this information, especially from after 1970. Besides clippings, the center's files include unpublished manuscripts, scholarly papers, planners' reports, business publications, and many other materials, including its own newsletter, *Global Electronics*.

In all the literature on Silicon Valley, it is much easier to find the predictably favorable opinions of designers and employers toward industrial parks than it is to get firsthand information about employees' and residential neighbors' perceptions of the work environment. Designers and employers were probably correct in concluding that most employees responded positively to industrial parks, but a few studies have taken a more critical view, including Hugh John Reay Geddes, "Industrial Parkland: Landscapes of a New Aristocracy," M.A. thesis, University of California, Berkeley, 1986; John Frederick Keller, "The Production Worker in Electronics: Industrialization and Labor Development in California's Santa Clara Valley," Ph.D. diss., University of Michigan, 1981; and Lenny Siegel and John Markoff, *The High Cost of High Tech: The Dark Side of the Chip* (New York, 1985). The controversy over expanding Stanford Industrial Park into the Palo Alto foothills suggests that nearby residents did not always approve of industrial parks, yet most planners in the Santa Clara Valley tended to assume that the parks were desirable additions to the landscape.

The retirement community experience has been the subject of more thorough investigation, particularly by gerontologists and other social scientists. Many observers wrote quite skeptically about age-segregated towns at first, following the lead of Lewis Mumford, "For Older People, Not Segregation but Integration," *Architectural Record* 119 (May 1956): 191–94. However, studies by later researchers came to much more favorable conclusions about retirement communities. Their praise has been summarized by Stephen M. Golant, "In Defense of Age-Segregated Housing," in Judith Ann Hancock, ed., *Housing the Elderly* (New Brunswick, N.J., 1987), 49–56. Sociological and historical contexts for retirement communities have been developed perceptively by Frances FitzGerald, "Sun City [Center, Florida]," *Cities on a Hill: A Journey Through Contemporary American Cultures* (New York, 1986); Michael E. Hunt et al., *Retirement Communities: An American Original* (New York, 1984); and Nancy J. Osgood, *Senior Settlers: Social Integration in Retirement Communities* (New York, 1982).

Arizona's Sun City has attracted its share of both scholarly and journalistic attention. Michael Baker has profiled its population in *The 1982 Sun City Area Long Term Care Survey: A Statistical Profile of Resident Characteristics, Attitudes and Preferences* (Tucson, 1983); Allan Karl Doyle, "Sun City, Arizona: A Study of Sense of Place in a Retirement Community," M.A. thesis, University of Washington, 1984, has analyzed residents' perceptions of their adopted hometown; and Patricia Gober has studied "The Retirement Community as a Geographical Phenomenon: The Case of Sun City, Arizona," *Journal of Geography* 84 (Sept.–Oct. 1985): 189–98. Calvin Trillin captured the spirit of early Sun City in "Wake Up and Live," *New Yorker* 40 (April 4, 1964): 120–77. Two Sun Citizens, Jane Freeman and Glenn Sanberg in *Jubilee: A History of Sun City, Arizona* (Sun City, 1984), provide a fond and detailed historical account from the insider's perspective.

Local newspapers covered many aspects of the retirement community's development, and numerous clippings pertaining to Sun City have been helpfully collected in the Arizona Room of the Phoenix Public Library. The Sun City Library also has a small archival and historical collection consisting of materials on the community's growth. The Del E. Webb Corporation created the bulk of the primary sources consulted in this study. Some of them remain with Del E. Webb Communities, Inc., but the majority of the developer's clippings, documents, photographs, promotional publications, and other materials pertaining to Sun City have been donated to the fledgling Sun Cities Area Historical Society of Sun City. At the time this book was being researched, the society had not fully organized its holdings.

The Seattle World's Fair of 1962 generated much primary source material at both the local and the national level. This study has relied primarily on the Ewen C. Dingwall Papers in the Suzzallo Library of the University of Washington, Seattle. This rich collection reflects the fact that, as general manager of the Century 21 Exposition, Dingwall and his staff were in constant contact with federal, state, city, and foreign officials, private exhibitors and consultants, journalists and promoters, arts activists, and downtown business organizations. Of special note in Box 9 of the Dingwall Papers is the four-part "Report" by Stanford Research Institute (1957–58). In the course of studying the prospects for Seattle's proposed fair, SRI polled numerous experts on American culture and society to develop a fascinating picture of postwar American civilization. Another helpful collection is the Papers of the Seattle World's Fair of 1962, Record Group 138 at the Washington

State Archives Regional Center, Western Washington University, Bellingham. Additional brochures, reports, photographs, and customer surveys are on file with the Pacific Northwest Collection, University of Washington Libraries.

Two important contemporary publications on the exposition are the *Official Guide Book, Seattle World's Fair 1962* (Seattle, 1962) and Murray Morgan's *Century 21: The Story of the Seattle World's Fair, 1962* (Seattle, 1963), a commissioned history. Chapter 5 has relied on complete runs of the *Seattle Times* and *Seattle Post-Intelligencer* daily newspapers between 1955 and 1963 for coverage of the fair, supplemented by additional articles and publications identified in the Pacific Northwest Regional Newspaper and Periodical Index, University of Washington Libraries. Burton Benedict et al., *The Anthropology of World's Fairs: San Francisco's Panama Pacific International Exposition of 1915* (London, 1983); Helen A. Harrison et al., *Dawn of a New Day: The New York World's Fair, 1939/40* (New York, 1980); Lenox R. Lohr, *Fair Management: The Story of a Century of Progress Exposition* (Chicago, 1952); and Robert W. Rydell, *All the World's a Fair: Visions of Empire at American International Expositions, 1876–1916* (Chicago, 1984), help put the American world's fair experience into perspective.

Chapter 6 makes especially apparent this study's reliance on a variety of scholars. Its argument has benefited significantly from works by a handful of cultural geographers with a special sensitivity to history, region, and metropolis: Peirce F. Lewis, "America Between the Wars: The Engineering of a New Geography," in Robert D. Mitchell and Paul A. Groves, eds., *North America: The Historical Geography of a Changing Continent* (Totowa, N.J., 1987), 410–37; D. W. Meinig, "American Wests: Preface to a Geographical Introduction," *Annals of the Association of American Geographers* 62 (June 1972): 159–84; D. W. Meinig, "The Continuous Shaping of America: A Prospectus for Geographers and Historians," *American Historical Review* 83 (Dec. 1978): 1186–1205; D. W. Meinig, ed., *The Interpretation of Ordinary Landscapes: Geographical Essays* (New York, 1979); D. W. Meinig, *Southwest: Three Peoples in Geographical Change, 1600–1970* (New York, 1971); Peter O. Muller, *Contemporary Suburban America* (Englewood Cliffs, N.J., 1981); Edward Relph, *The Modern Urban Landscape* (London, 1987); Edward Relph, *Place and Placelessness* (London, 1976); Edward L. Ullman, "Amenities as a Factor in Regional Growth," *Geographical Review* 44 (Jan. 1954): 119–32; James E. Vance, Jr., "California and the Search for the Ideal," *Annals of the Association of American Geographers* 62 (June

1972): 185–210; James E. Vance, Jr., *Geography and Urban Evolution in the San Francisco Bay Area* (Berkeley, 1964); and Wilbur Zelinsky, *The Cultural Geography of the United States* (Englewood Cliffs, N.J., 1973).

Several geographers and others have provided important clues to the meanings of urban and suburban forms: Grady Clay, *Close-Up: How to Read the American City* (New York, 1973); Roger M. Downs and David Stea, *Maps in Minds: Reflections on Cognitive Mapping* (New York, 1977); Kevin Lynch, *The Image of the City* (Cambridge, Mass., 1960); Amos Rapoport, *Human Aspects of Urban Form: Towards a Man-Environment Approach to Urban Form and Design* (Oxford, 1977); Amos Rapoport, *The Meaning of the Built Environment: A Nonverbal Communication Approach* (Beverly Hills, 1982); Yi-Fu Tuan, *Topophilia: A Study of Environmental Perception, Attitudes, and Values* (Englewood Cliffs, N.J., 1974); and Robert Venturi, Denise Scott Brown, and Steven Izenour, *Learning from Las Vegas: The Forgotten Symbolism of Architectural Form* (rev. ed. Cambridge, Mass., 1977).

Historians and others writing about the urban experience in southern California blazed trails the present study has followed. Especially helpful works include: Reyner Banham, *Los Angeles: The Architecture of Four Ecologies* (1971; Middlesex, Eng., 1973); David Brodsly, *L.A. Freeway: An Appreciative Essay* (Berkeley, 1981); Nathan Glazer, "Notes on Southern California: 'A Reasonable Suggestion as to How Things Can Be'?" *Commentary* 28 (Aug. 1959): 100–107; and James Q. Wilson, "A Guide to Reagan Country: The Political Culture of Southern California," *Commentary* 43 (May 1967): 37–45. As a student of greater California, Kevin Starr has written perceptively on antecedent matters relating to magic lands: *Americans and the California Dream 1850–1915* (New York, 1973), and *Inventing the Dream: California Through the Progressive Era* (New York, 1985). Finally, works on modern urban America provide useful perspective: Robert Fishman, "The Post-War American Suburb: A New Form, a New City," in Daniel Schaffer, ed., *Two Centuries of American Planning* (London, 1988); Kenneth I. Helphand, "McUrbia: The 1950s and the Birth of the Contemporary American Landscape," *Places: A Quarterly Journal of Environmental Design* 5: 2 (1988): 40–49; and Kenneth T. Jackson, *Crabgrass Frontier: The Suburbanization of the United States* (New York, 1985).

Index

African Americans: at Disneyland, 94; in urban West, 24–25, 39, 40–41, 278, 294, 300. *See also* Watts

Air-conditioners, 22, 162, 186

Alaska-Yukon-Pacific Exposition of 1909 (Seattle), 215

Amenities, 124, 273–74, 298. *See also* Cultural sophistication; Nature; Phoenix; Santa Clara County; Sun City

American Broadcasting Company (ABC), 60–61

Anaheim: Convention Center, 100–101; growth of, 97–99; as Disneyland site, 58, 61–62, 73; role of, in Orange County, 27–28, 97–98, 100–102; problems of growth in, 102–103; Stadium, 100–101. *See also* Annexation; Disneyland; Growth; Harbor Boulevard; Orange County

Annexation: in Anaheim, 98; in Phoenix, 31, 164; in San Jose, 31–33, 42; in Seattle, 31, 220; and urban form, 280; and western urban growth, 30–33

Automobiles, 22, 30; attitudes toward, 37–38; and Disneyland, 89; effects of, on cities, 36–39, 48, 265; effect of, on perceptions of cities, 283, 284; of the future, 247; increasing numbers of, 36; and Orange County, 36; and Phoenix, 164, 265; and Santa Clara County, 36; and Stanford Industrial Park, 141;

and Sun City, 202–3. *See also* Transit systems

Banham, Reyner, 153, 268

Bay Area Rapid Transit system (BART). *See* Transit systems

Bellevue (Wash.), 46, 221

Belser, Karl, 42, 46, 268

Boeing Airplane Company, 19, 228, 237, 243, 257, 300; influence of, on Seattle, 218–20; postwar expansion of, 218–19

Boorstin, Daniel, 30

Bradbury, Ray, 90, 96

Brandin, Alf E., 135

Brussels World's Fair (1958), 117

Buses. *See* Transit systems

California: effect of growth on, 23, 276; "greater", 9–10; impact of World War II and cold war on, 19–20, 144; influence of, on U.S., 16, 19, 42; Mexican Americans in, 24; planned communities in, 290; planning in, 42–43, 268; population of, 35; retirement communities in, 169; urbanization in, 278. *See also* Anaheim; Leisure World retirement communities; Los Angeles; Orange County; Palo Alto; San Francisco; San Francisco Bay Area; San Jose; Santa Clara County; Silicon Valley

Central Association of Seattle, 222, 223